Teacher's Resource Guide for the Advanced Placement Program*

The American Pageant

FIFTEENTH EDITION

David M. Kennedy
Stanford University

Lizabeth Cohen
Harvard University

Prepared by

Warren Hierl

WADSWORTH
CENGAGE Learning·

Australia • Brazil • Japan • Korea • Mexico • Singapore • Spain • United Kingdom • United States

*AP and the Advanced Placement Program are registered trademarks of the College Entrance Examination Board, which was not involved in the production of, and does not endorse, this product.

WADSWORTH
CENGAGE Learning·

Holt McDougal is pleased to distribute Cengage Learning college-level materials to high schools for Advanced Placement*, honors, and college-prep courses. Our Advanced & Elective Programs department is dedicated to serving teachers and students in these courses.

To contact your Advanced & Elective Programs representative, please call us toll-free at **1-800-479-9799** or visit us at **www.HoltMcDougal.com.**

ISBN-13: 978-0-8400-2903-4
ISBN-10: 0-8400-2903-9

Wadsworth
20 Channel Center Street
Boston, MA 02210
USA

Cengage Learning is a leading provider of customized learning solutions with office locations around the globe, including Singapore, the United Kingdom, Australia, Mexico, Brazil, and Japan. Locate your local office at: **www.cengage.com/global**

Cengage Learning products are represented in Canada by Nelson Education, Ltd.

To learn more about Wadsworth, visit **www.cengage.com/wadsworth**

Purchase any of our products at your local college store or at our preferred online store **www.cengagebrain.com**

READ IMPORTANT LICENSE INFORMATION

*AP and the Advanced Placement Program are registered trademarks of the College Entrance Examination Board, which was not involved in the production of, and does not endorse, this product.

Printed in the United States of America
1 2 3 4 5   16 15 14 13 12

FD233

Contents

PART I: Introduction

PART I: INTRODUCTION TO THE AP* U.S. HISTORY COURSE

Advanced Placement U.S. History is challenging yet stimulating. Those new to teaching the course will soon find that the stage is set for a great intellectual experience. As the school year progresses and you burrow deeper and deeper into the course work, you will, over time, identify and organize the broad concepts, movements, conflicts, resolutions, and personalities that have shaped the history of the United States. Fleshing out these forces is exciting for both you and your students. More exciting still is recognizing references and connections to those forces in today's events.

What makes AP U.S. History so rewarding for both students and teachers? How is it different from a non-AP course, even one that is taught at the honors level? Much of the excitement comes from the intensity and sophistication of your investigation into how this nation's history was shaped. Further, it is enormously satisfying to help students stretch to new levels of thinking. For students, Advanced Placement represents a foray into college-level work, and those who do well on the examination often get college credit for the course. But Advanced Placement can seem overwhelming, given the huge scope and extent of the information that you must cover to prepare your students to score well. If you are intimidated by the course load and the limited amount of time you have to teach so much material, you are not alone. Even seasoned AP teachers must constantly revise and rework their lesson plans.

The best way to prepare your students for an AP examination is to have them master the material, not let it master them. That is easier said than done. If you manage your time effectively, however, you will eliminate one major problem—teaching a considerable amount of material in a relatively short amount of time. In addition, if you can convince your students that an AP examination is not an insurmountable obstacle but, instead, an opportunity to show off how their minds work, how they've prepared themselves, and how developed their skills are, then they will have a leg up: attitude *does* help, for the student as well as the teacher. If you have overanxious students—and every teacher does—there is a great deal you can do to help them sideline their anxiety and make them confident that they can walk in to the test and perform well. This guide is designed to assist teachers new to AP in making their students masters of the AP U.S. History exam.

Advanced Placement U.S. History is currently undergoing a course redesign. The first exam reflecting the course redesign will likely take place in 2015. Details of the redesigned course and exam have not been released but there are indications that it may well include

- a shift from a focus on factual knowledge to a focus on broader themes and concepts
- additional coverage of pre-Columbian and post-1980s periods
- a significant understanding of periodization
- increased emphasis on historical thinking skills

AP U.S. History teachers will in all likelihood have to take a more conceptual approach to the presentation of units. Historical skills such as student understanding of cause/effect relationships, chronological sequencing, making inferences, their ability to analyze visual sources, and their ability to compare and contrast concepts from various time periods will need to be emphasized. It also

---

seems clear that reading comprehension skills and the ability to extract a main idea from a variety of different primary sources will take on additional importance. In all probability, multiple choice questions will be more stimulus-based then has previously been the case. That means that students will have to demonstrate increased skill in reading primary source selections, analyzing more complex pieces of visual data (maps, charts, graphs, photographs, etc.), and making inferences about periodization. Teachers of AP U.S. History should consistently check apcentral.collegeboard.com for College Board updates and releases on the course redesign.

We have included in this Teachers Resource Guide a specific Focus on Historical Thinking activity for each chapter which teachers may wish to use. All skills should be taught and reinforced throughout the year. These activities are simply some suggestions that might be incorporated as either mandatory, optional, or enrichment activities in your course. They are designed to supplement rather than replace normal AP activities.

PREPARING YOUR COURSE

As you think about the structure of your AP course, you need to start at the College Board's website: www.apcentral.collegeboard.com. The College Board website is easy to navigate, and it is chock full of information that will help you tailor your course and understand the AP exam and how it is scored. The College Board makes frequent refinements to AP, so even very experienced AP teachers are regulars at the website. On the website, the section "AP COURSES AND EXAMS" provides information on the nature and purpose of the Advanced Placement program. In its dropdown menu you will find detailed information about AP U.S. History and information on exams, such as fees, dates of the exams, and the like. "PRE-AP" offers tips on teaching the various AP courses; "INSTITUTIONS AND WORKSHOPS" gives information on Advanced Placement workshops and programs, which are especially valuable for first-time AP teachers.

Most important for your planning is the section in the Course Description where you will find the topic outline—what used to be called the Acorn Book. This lays out what you will need to cover. In addition, you will find twelve themes, from American Diversity to War and Diplomacy. The themes are the newest feature in AP U.S. History.

With the topic outline and the themes in hand, you next need to look at the textbook and decide how you are going to allocate your time. *The American Pageant*, Fifteenth Edition, by David M. Kennedy and Lizabeth Cohen, is well written and filled with a profusion of photographs, art, charts, graphs, tables, appendices, fifteen document-based questions (DBQs), and thirteen Thinking Globally essays highlighting how developments seemingly unique to the United States relate to developments elsewhere in the world. It is an excellent and engaging textbook. In about eleven hundred pages, it ranges over many topics, all of which you will have to cover within a time frame that is substantially shorter than other full-year courses in your school. In addition, you will find a variety of pedagogical aids at its accompanying website.

Pacing

What other professional says, "I have to be up to Jackson by early November at the latest"? AP U.S. history teachers make comments like this all the time. Every teacher must determine how much time to spend on each topic, but the crunch is acute for a history teacher. Faced with an onslaught of names, events, personalities, movements, wars and conflicts, treaties and agreements—not to mention the organization and dimensions of the U.S. government, as well as the social, economic, political, and intellectual forces and changes that have shaped the nation—a teacher who is new to AP U.S. History is challenged by the daunting task of getting it all in. Some teachers can organize their lesson plans down to very precise units of time; others require greater flexibility. But in the end, all AP U.S. History teachers must cover over three hundred years by early May.

In deciding how much time to spend on each topic, first think broadly. The College Board's period breakdown of the multiple-choice section of the exam is as follows:

- Pre-Columbian to 1789—20 percent of the questions

- 1790 to 1914—45 percent of the questions

- 1915 to the present—35 percent of the questions

Teacher Insight

Only a few multiple-choice questions pertain to the period from the 1990s to the present. Keep in mind that the free-response/DBQ questions will *not* specifically test the post-1990s period, but information from the period may be helpful in writing a more developed response.

The breakdown of the topics and themes as they are covered in the multiple-choice section of the exam, according to the College Board, is as follows:

- Political institutions, behavior, and public policy—35 percent of the questions

- Social, cultural, and intellectual developments—40 percent of the questions

- Diplomacy and foreign affairs—15 percent of the questions

- Economic developments—10 percent of the questions

Suppose that your school year begins on September 1 and ends June 15. A non-AP U.S. History teacher has until the end of the school year to cover the course content. But an AP U.S. History teacher has only until the first week in May, when the AP exam is given, to cover the same material. With planning and pacing, it can be done. But you cannot do it by passing off Populism as a footnote in history to save time or by reducing the progressive movement to a two-day lecture and discussion because it's April and you've got to get to World War II by the third week of the month.

A suggested unit and pacing guide follows. It is for you to decide how you want to group topics into units. For example, the struggle between Britain and France over the New World can be synthesized with the next two units because all three relate to the American Revolution. You will also need to determine whether you want to combine foreign and domestic affairs or cover them separately. Legitimate arguments can be made for both approaches. On the one hand, covering the material chronologically and not separating domestic and foreign affairs may be easier for your students to comprehend as a cohesive narrative. On the other hand, separating domestic and foreign affairs may allow you to cover longer historical periods. For example, when you discuss the antebellum period, you can cover a variety of topics chronologically, though not necessarily with thematic continuity: the age of reform, Manifest Destiny, the Mexican-American War, sectionalism and the causes of the American Civil War, and so forth. One suggestion is to cover Manifest Destiny and the Mexican-American War as part of a separate foreign-policy unit that includes other foreign-affairs events from, say, the end of the American Revolution to the eve of the Civil War. Of course, this approach will have as many detractors as supporters. The point is for you to identify an approach you are comfortable with and plan your schedule accordingly.

After you organize the units, you need to develop a time frame. While one teacher may spend more time on the Gilded Age and less on Reconstruction, all must make certain to maintain a steady pace. If it is the middle of April and you are just finishing World War II, you have only two or three weeks to cover the post–World War II period, both domestic and foreign affairs, before the AP exam date arrives. The extra days you spent on earlier units because time seemed plentiful in November and December leave fewer days to spend on twentieth-century issues and developments. On the next page is one suggestion for arranging units and assigning how much time—here, a total of 144 days—to spend on each:

Suggested Units and Pacing Keyed to *The American Pageant,* Fourteenth and Fifteenth Editions

Three days for Chapters 1–5: The age of discovery and the development of the American colonies (early sixteenth century–1700)

Six days for Chapters 6 and 7: The struggle between Britain and France over the New World and the causes of the American Revolution (early seventeenth century–1775)

Three days for Chapter 8: The American Revolution (1775–1783)

Seven days for Chapter 9: The Articles of Confederation and the framing of the U.S. Constitution (1776–1790)

Five days for Chapters 10 and 11: Jeffersonians, Hamiltonians, and the Marshall Supreme Court (1789–1812)

Four days for Chapter 12: The War of 1812 and the Era of Good Feelings (1812–1824)

Three days for Chapter 14: The development of national and sectional economies (1790–1860)

Seven days for Chapters 13 and 15: The age of reform: Jacksonian democracy (post–War of 1812–1860)

Seven days for Chapters 12 and 17: The Monroe Doctrine, territorial expansion, and Manifest Destiny (1812–1860)

Seven days for Chapters 16, 18, and 19: Slavery, sectionalism, and the road to war (1793–1860)

Three days for Chapters 20 and 21: The American Civil War (1861–1865)

Eight days for Chapter 22: Reconstruction (1865–1877)

Eight days for Chapters 22–25: Post–Civil War economic and social developments (1870s–1890s)

Six days for Chapter 26: The agricultural revolution, the Granger movement, and the rise and decline of the Populists (1865–1896)

Four days for Chapter 26: Territorial expansion (1865–1890s)

Six days for Chapter 27: Creating a global empire (1890s–early twentieth century)

Seven days for Chapters 28 and 29: The progressives in power (1900–early 1920s)

Six days for Chapter 30: The road to World War I and U.S. involvement (1914–1918)

Six days for Chapters 31 and 32: Political conservatism ascendant, the first red scare, the Harlem renaissance, and other cultural developments during the roaring twenties (1920s)

Nine days for Chapters 32–34: The Great Depression and the New Deal (1920s–1941)

Seven days for Chapters 34 and 35: World War II and the end of U.S. neutrality (1941–1945)

Six days for Chapters 36 and 37: The origins of the Cold War, the intensification of Cold War hostilities, the containment policy in Europe and Asia, and the second red scare and McCarthyism (1940s–late 1950s)

Five days for Chapter 38: The Cold War becomes hotter (early 1960s–1975)

Six days for Chapters 38 and 39: The transformation of American culture, the civil rights movement, and the Great Society (1960–1980)

Five days for Chapters 40–42: The resurgence of conservatism, the end of the Cold War, and the challenges of the contemporary world (1980–2011)

You now have a map of the school year. You next need to think about what happens in class each day. How much homework should you assign? How many papers? How much time will you devote to discussion? How often will you give quizzes and tests? You no doubt have strong views about how to use class time most effectively, views that are based on your own strengths and style and on those of your students. A hundred AP teachers will have a hundred different course designs. Every AP U.S. History course is *sui generis*.

You can take some solace in knowing that students are as much responsible for their learning (regardless of their level) as you are. But at the AP level, the demands and expectations associated with a college-level course are indeed considerable; students are expected to demonstrate higher levels of thinking by engaging in analysis, synthesis, and evaluation of information that they wouldn't generally encounter *until* they are college students. In taking AP U.S. History, your students must be willing to accept the demands of a college course and therefore shoulder the load of lengthy nightly readings and homework assignments.

Historiography

Some teachers have found that a key to stimulating and challenging class discussions is for their students to supplement their textbook readings with historiographic essays and other analytical and evaluative sources. These greatly enlarge class discussions and help you shift your approach from one of always lecturing to one in which your students, guided by your questions and comments, elaborate and explain. In order for students to describe, elaborate, and analyze, they must have a solid understanding of the factual content and relevant vocabulary. For this, the textbook reading should be assigned early in the unit to give the students a chronological and thematic overview of the topic, as well as an introduction to the relevant terms, events, and personalities. Then assign historiographic essays, which put meat on the bones.

The study of history is very much based on interpretation. In fact, the times in which we live, our own socioeconomic class, gender, race, ethnicity, political persuasion, and other factors have an impact, whether we care to admit it or not, on how we interpret events. This is true of historians as well. One of the historian's functions is to examine change—the socioeconomic, political, and ideological forces that transformed a society, nation, movement, and so forth. By and large, two schools of thought, called traditional and revisionist, have dominated the teaching of U.S. history for decades.

The Traditional, or Consensus, Perspective

The traditional school maintains that consensus is the driving force behind change (those that advocate this view are therefore referred to as either traditional or consensus historians). Although social, economic, ideological, and political differences have existed throughout U.S. history, traditional historians do not consider these distinctions fundamental. They contend that the development of the nation has relied on consensus between, say, groups and classes. As an example, they point to the compromises and agreements made at the Constitutional Convention by delegates from different states and backgrounds. Despite their differences—and there were indeed quite a few—the Framers were able to create what is today the world's oldest written constitution. Hence, their differences were not fundamental or significant enough to prevent them from reaching a consensus about the nature of the new government under the U.S. Constitution.

The Revisionist, or Conflict, Perspective

For revisionist historians, differences of race, class, ethnicity, and gender are significant in the development of the United States. These historians contend that such distinctions can lead to conflict, which in turn leads to change. Again, take the example of the Framers of the U.S. Constitution. A revisionist perspective holds that wealthy southern planter-slaveholders and northern merchants and investors joined in supporting the Constitution because they feared challenges from or conflict with the lower classes—consider Shays's Rebellion. A strong central government would promote their own socioeconomic interests and suppress internal dissent. This perspective is beautifully illustrated by Daniel Shays and Alexander Hamilton, who are quoted in *The American Pageant*, Fourteenth Edition, pp. 185 and 186 and Fifteenth Edition, pp. 168 and 169. Good examples of the opposing views of the Hamiltonians and Jeffersonians, one by John Fiske and the other by Charles Beard, are to be found in this guide, Chapter 10, in the section "Expanding the 'Varying Viewpoints.'"

To be sure, these are simplifications of the traditional and revisionist perspectives, but they do ask the teacher and the student to approach U.S. history not only as a story—albeit a compelling one—but as an opportunity to see interpretations of historical events as part of a larger school of thought. In fact, one can develop one's own view within the broader historiographic school. In developing your lesson plans, consider essays that represent different views of the same movement, period, or personality. For instance, for a unit on Reconstruction, consider having students read an essay by William Archibald Dunning, an early twentieth-century historian, and one by a contemporary revisionist historian such as Eric Foner. Dunning views Reconstruction as a dark and shameful period in U.S. history that was dominated by scalawags and carpetbaggers. Foner views Reconstruction as an "unfinished revolution" that, while it failed to significantly alter the social, economic, and political condition of African Americans in the decades following the Civil War and Reconstruction, laid the foundation for future civil rights movements. To supplement the assignment, consider having students compare and contrast the revisionist interpretations put forth by historian Kenneth Stampp in his influential book *The Era of Reconstruction* (1965) and by Foner in *Reconstruction: America's Unfinished Revolution* (1989). Historians are constantly revising one another's perspectives.

Teacher Insight

For a more complete elaboration of historiography, read the introduction to *Taking Sides: Clashing Views on Controversial Issues* (vols. I and II) by Larry Madaras and James M. SoRelle, Dushkin McGraw-Hill, 1997 and the historiographic essays for each major U.S. historical period. These essays lay out the views of both traditional and revisionist historians. With these, you can present more than a chronological overview of "what happened when." You can infuse your lectures and class activities and discussions with skills-building lessons that ask students to analyze and evaluate not only historical events themselves but also how those events have been interpreted by historians. As for the AP exam, while an understanding of historiography is not required and probably not expected, interpreting events through the lens of historiography allows for a more sophisticated and thorough understanding. To be sure, a teacher new to AP U.S. History might be overwhelmed by the enormous amount of information that needs to be covered before early May, when the AP U.S. History exam is given. But if you decide to immerse yourself in historiography, one approach is to focus on one period in particular. For example, survey the perspectives of historians of the colonial era and the American Revolution, among them Gordon Wood, Bernard Bailyn, Gary Nash, Joyce Appleby, and Edward Countryman. Then move on to another historical period. This way you can slowly build historiography into your course. Historical interpretations are always changing, so keeping up with the literature on one period or topic is a daunting task, but it is well worth the time and effort for you and the students you teach.

History from the Top Down and from the Bottom Up

Another distinction between the traditional and revisionist schools of thought has much to do with which people are the focus of research and investigations. For most of America's past, historians focused on the role played by famous political, economic, military, and ideological leaders. Revisionist historians have since come to challenge this top-down approach by offering another perspective—namely, history from the bottom up.

Historical and historiographic perceptions are expressed in the individuals, groups, ethnicities, classes, and movements seen as the focus for change. Traditionally historians focus on the ideas and actions of the nation's elites, those individuals who, historians maintain, articulated the specific sentiments and attitudes of those they represented or led. This top-down approach utilizes the diaries, memoirs, journals, public and official records, and so forth of the nation's economic, political, and ideological elites (more often than not, the upper classes) who have historically been recognized as responsible for "making" American history.

To be sure, the contributions and attitudes of, say, President George Washington, Secretary of the Treasury Alexander Hamilton, industrialist Andrew Carnegie, and General Douglas MacArthur are essential if one is to understand the course of the United States' development. However, over the past four or five decades, historians, many of them revisionists, have claimed that the top-down approach has serious limitations. They ask, What about the inarticulate, or the subsistence farmer, or the slave, or the nineteenth-century rural female settler, or the industrial laborer? Did they not play a role in the development of the nation? Or, as the twentieth-century German playwright and poet Bertolt Brecht asks in his poem "Questions from a Worker Who Reads," did Caesar conquer the Gauls alone, or were there other, less-famous individuals who took part in the conflict? Brecht's point is clear: great individuals have made history, but not without the contributions and sacrifices of less-famous participants, who have for many years been lost to history.

Suggested Classroom Activity

To make this point to your students, try the following activity:

Give your students ten seconds to quickly write down the names of five famous Americans. Ask the students for their responses and write the lists on the board. For example, a sample list might include the following:

> George Washington
>
> Abraham Lincoln
>
> Henry Ford
>
> Ronald Reagan
>
> Martin Luther King, Jr.

Can they explain their lists? Ask students to analyze the class list. What observations can be made about this list? It is composed of men, all but one of whom are white. They tend to be political leaders (three are presidents). They are all Christians who represent, by and large, a particular class of people—in short, the nation's elites. Does the list represent a top-down (famous-person) perspective? Can students put together a more diverse list that incorporates a wide variety of classes, ethnicities, races, and genders?

Of course, any discussion of American history that omits these important figures is providing a seriously flawed view. Still, the lists generated by the class may reveal to your students the limitations of their own historical perspective. The point is not to overcompensate by reducing the importance of a famous and influential leader, such as Henry Ford, but to incorporate the contributions, actions, and efforts of the industrial worker; like Ford, they too built America's automobiles—and the nation itself.

The Summer Assignment

One way to ease the time constraints that are posed by the mass of material you need to cover is to give your students an assignment over the summer before they take the course. This practice is common for AP courses. To be sure, some parents and teachers will have reservations about assigning schoolwork over the summer vacation. This is why considerable thought and preparation must go into creating a feasible and beneficial summer assignment.

Before the end of the current school year, organize a meeting of students who will be taking AP U.S. History with you the following school year. This gives you an opportunity to discuss the course—what is expected of the student on a daily basis, how to prepare for the AP exam the following May (it's never too early to prepare for the AP exam), your grading rationale, and so forth. This information can be covered when the new school year begins; however, it is in your students' best interests that they understand as early as possible, even before their first class, the rigorous demands of the AP U.S. History course. Give examples of, for instance, a typical evening's homework assignment or a long-term research paper. You can also discuss the distinction between an honors course and an AP course at this meeting. Even in schools that track students based on intellectual ability and skill level, making the transition from, say, an honors history course to an AP course is significant. There is, however, an equally important reason for meeting with students at the end of the preceding school year—namely, to assign and discuss a summer assignment.

There are numerous advantages to assigning summer work, not least of which is to reduce the amount of information that needs to be covered during the school year. If, for example, you would like to spend only a few days on the age of discovery and the development of North American colonies, you can give students a detailed assignment aimed at their gaining, on their own, a thorough understanding of these topics; when the school year begins, you can cover this material in a shorter amount of time.

Another possibility is a historiographic assignment that introduces students to the traditional and revisionist schools of thought. This can ultimately become the cornerstone of every unit in the course. You can develop a wide variety of assignments for the purpose of reducing content during the school year or simply getting a jump-start on the course when the new school year begins. (Again, some teachers and parents may be opposed to assigning work over the summer; as with all suggestions and recommendations offered in this guide, you should adopt only those ideas you believe are necessary or significant to the development of your curriculum given the time limitations associated with teaching an AP course.)

Study Groups

Obviously, preparing for the AP U.S. History exam is a lengthy process, one that can begin almost a year before the test date. But, students do not have to prepare alone. Working collectively, they can develop organizational skills and strengthen their knowledge of—or identify their weaknesses in—the course material. Further, working collectively, students can save time. This is where study groups can help.

Any activity or practice that encourages students to develop their abilities independent of the classroom experience makes the AP teacher's job easier and reduces wasted time. For your students, the benefits, both academic and personal, are considerable. Daily independent study is necessary to keep up with the day-to-day demands of the AP U.S. History course and to make the long-term preparations that are one key to doing well on the AP exam.

I suggest to my students that they consider forming study groups, to meet before school or after—or even on weekends. Study groups, common in college, are an excellent way to step into intensive independent study and to learn how to allocate time efficiently. More often than not, students devote the same amount of time to each subtopic or theme when they study for a history test on their own. But why apply the same amount of time to a topic that does not require as much as another? Students can benefit from participating in study groups, first because a group can help its members determine areas of content that require more focus.

There are a number of ways to set up a study group, but when students ask for advice, I recommend a group of four students who meet for two-hour sessions. The first hour can be a round robin of short-term and long-term content quizzing—questions that relate to a specific topic that will soon be tested in class and questions that relate to the AP exam at the end of the school year. Students can take turns adding information to the responses. As the study session progresses, students should take note of particular groupings of questions that they can or cannot discuss with ease. For example, a student who has a hard time answering questions on the causes of World War I should jot that down, then concentrate on this topic during independent study. Conversely, the student who can answer questions relating to World War I with ease may choose to spend less time on this topic and more on others. After the first hour, a break is in order. The second half of the review session can take up analytical questions that each member of the group prepares beforehand. Students can take turns organizing potential theses, supporting arguments, and supporting information such as facts and statistics. I encourage students to let me critique their questions before the study group meets. And I tell students to be pragmatic; if their study group is not working because of conflict or too much socializing, then the group needs to be dissolved and a new one organized.

HELPING STUDENTS REVIEW

Preparing for the AP exam is a collective effort that entails a strong and sustained commitment on the part of both you and your students. From the very beginning of the course, it is imperative that students not only establish a solid work ethic but also organize their time so that they can address the demands of the course in an efficient manner. Review is important; it can fairly be said that it should begin on the second day of the course.

It goes without saying that if students consistently do their homework and keep up with the course work, they will find the process of reviewing easier. One key to preparing for the examination is to begin reviewing as early as possible; students should not wait until the exam is just a week or two away to begin studying. It is important that you caution students about adopting a lazy or procrastinating approach to the course.

AP Review Books

Months before the exam date, encourage your students to purchase at least one AP U.S. History review book—it is never too early to purchase a review book. They will soon come to see this tool as an invaluable resource in attaining an excellent score. A good review book, of which there are many, summarizes major historical periods and themes, as well as provides samples of AP exam–type questions, such as multiple-choice questions and free-response essay questions, including document-based questions. Cengage Learning's *Fast Track to a 5* series includes a review book based on *The American Pageant*.

Encourage your students to set up a review schedule. If they begin review early in the school year, they can methodically nail down the facts and relate the various parts of the course's considerable content to one another. They'll be surprised—and pleased—by how much material can be covered with weekly study sessions using a good AP review book. Naturally, study sessions should increase in frequency and duration as the AP examination draws closer.

Encourage students to use their review books to take as many practice exams as possible. The benefits are significant. First, students become increasingly familiar with the types of questions that are asked on the AP exam; second, students are exposed to new information. A good review book provides lots of multiple-choice questions, along with the correct answer to each and an explanation of why a particular answer is correct. It also provides many free-response questions and sample essays.

Review Sessions

Many teachers set aside time a month or so before the AP exam for review sessions outside of class time. In addition to reviewing information and topics covered during the school year, you can use some of this time to provide students with information about the exam, as well as tips and tactics for taking the test and approaching the free-response questions.

Review sessions can vary in number and length. If you organize two-hour sessions twice a week for four weeks, the review can start in early April and be completed in time for the exam in May. Of course, review sessions held outside of school hours are optional for the students, but you should stress that review is one important route to success on the AP examination that should not be missed. Stress, too, that one objective of the review sessions is to highlight major themes, events, movements, and personalities that shaped each period. You are not reteaching an entire unit.

Below is a suggested schedule for a series of seven two-hour review sessions. Corresponding chapters in *The American Pageant* follow each review topic and are in parentheses.

First Review Session

I.   Features and composition of the AP exam
II.   Review
    A.   The age of discovery (Chapter 1)
    B.   Colonial development (Chapters 2–5)
    C.   The French and Indian War, causes of the American Revolution, and the American Revolution (Chapters 6–8)
III. Assign a practice AP U.S. History multiple-choice examination, due by the next review session. Students should complete the test in one 55-minute sitting. Answering ten questions, taking a break, then answering twenty more does not simulate the experience students will have when they take the actual exam.

Second Review Session

I.   Distribute the answer key for the practice multiple-choice exam and have students grade their own tests. Give students time to ask questions, and then encourage them to identify the historical periods in which they have clusters of incorrect answers. The practice test indicates where a student is weak and should spend extra time reviewing.
II.   Review
    A.   The post-American Revolution period, the Articles of Confederation, and the U.S. Constitution (Chapter 9)
    B.   The first administration, Jeffersonians and Hamiltonians, the "Revolution of 1800," and the Marshall Supreme Court (Chapters 10 and 11)
    C.   The development of national and sectional economies (Chapter 14)

Third Review Session

I.   Write on the board a free-response question from any historical period or topic. Allow students five minutes to create an outline. Hand out a sample outline that shows how you would approach the question and discuss with your students the information and organization appropriate for their essay
II.   Review
    A.   The age of reform, Jacksonian democracy (Chapters 13 and 15)
    B.   U.S. foreign affairs in the antebellum period: The War of 1812, the Monroe Doctrine, Manifest Destiny, and territorial expansion (Chapters 12 and 17)
    C.   Sectionalism, slavery and the causes of the American Civil War, and the American Civil War. (Chapters 16, 18–21)

Fourth Review Session

I.   Review
    A.   Reconstruction (Chapter 22)
    B.   Industrialization and the Gilded Age (Chapters 23–25)
    C.   Agrarian discontent and Populism (Chapter 26)

Fifth Review Session

I.   Review
    A.   U.S. foreign affairs from the end of the Civil War to World War I; the new imperialism, territorial expansion, and the causes of World War I; U.S. involvement in World War I (Chapters 27 and 30)
    B.   The progressive era and the post–World War I era: political conservatism, the first red scare, the Harlem renaissance, and the roaring twenties (Chapters 28, 29, and 31)
II. Discuss the multiple-choice section of the AP exam—types of multiple-choice questions, guessing, and scoring.

Sixth Review Session

I.   Review
    A.   The Great Depression and the New Deal (Chapters 32 and 33)
    B.   Foreign affairs from the end of World War I to the end of World War II (Chapters 34 and 35)
II. Briefly discuss the document-based question (DBQ) in general, then analyze the documents for a DBQ on a released AP exam.

Seventh Review Session

I.   Review
    A.   Post–World War II foreign affairs: The Cold War and the collapse of communism (Chapters 36, 37, 40, and 41)
    B.   Post–World War II domestic affairs and developments (Chapters 37–40, 42)
II. Allow time for final comments and suggestions and for answering students' questions about the exam or content.

BEFORE THE EXAM

By February, long before the exam, remind your students that they must register to take the test. Many schools take care of the paperwork and handle the fees for their AP students, but check with your administrator or the AP coordinator to verify your school's policy. Take note of any student who has a documented disability and needs test accommodations. For more information, contact AP Services at the College Board for the name of the local AP coordinator who can assist in the registration process.

Needless to say, you shouldn't have to tell your students that the evening before the exam is not the best time for revelry. But at the same time you may also want to warn them against cramming. What should your students be doing on the evening before the examination? One suggestion would be to look over class notes or to drift through their textbook, concentrating on the broad outlines, not the small details, of the course. Or they might skim through their AP U.S. History review books and refresh their memory about the tips for taking the exam that are offered there. They could also look over the essays they have written.

Other than very light studying, the day before the test is very important in other ways as well. The evening before the exam *is* a great time for students to organize the materials they will need for the next day. They should sharpen a fistful of no. 2 pencils with good erasers for the multiple-choice section of the test, and they should set out several black or dark-blue ballpoint pens for writing the free-response essays; they should be sure to have an accurate watch and turn off any alarm—cell phones are not permitted in the exam room; they will want to have with them a piece of fruit or a snack bar and a bottle of water for the break; finally, they should be certain to have their Social Security number and whatever photo identification and admission ticket are required. Urge them to try to relax and get a good night's sleep. At this point, an extra hour of sleep is more valuable than an extra hour of study.

On the day of the examination, your students should eat a good breakfast—it is fuel for the brain and provides energy to power through the test. Point out that studies show that students who eat a hot breakfast before testing get higher grades. While food is important, they should not drink a lot of liquids, necessitating trips to the bathroom during the test. And they should wear comfortable clothes and consider taking along a sweater in case the heating or air-conditioning is erratic.

Students will most likely be very nervous before they enter the test room, only to find their anxiety increases as they wait for the test to begin. Reassure them that this is natural—it indicates how important they view the test they are about to take. Your students can take confidence and comfort in knowing that their success on the AP U.S. History exam was planned, by them and by you, well in advance.

THE AP U.S. HISTORY TEST

The more information your students have about the test, its composition, and how it is administered, the more comfortable they will feel when they take it. By this point, your students should know how the AP U.S. History exam is constructed, but a reminder cannot hurt.

Structure of the Exam

Section I has eighty multiple-choice questions. Students have fifty-five minutes to complete this section. Answer sheets for the multiple-choice questions are collected, and students are given a fifteen-minute break before they are given Section II of the exam.

Section II is made up of free-response questions, which are divided into three parts. Part A is a single document-based question (DBQ). It is mandatory. Students are given fifteen minutes for reading the documents and organizing their information. They then have forty-five minutes for writing the DBQ essay. Altogether, they have a total of sixty minutes for the DBQ.

Section II, Parts B and C have two standard free-response questions in each. Students are to write on one question from Part B and one question from Part C. They have a total of seventy minutes for writing these two essays.

When told that they will have approximately three hours in which to answer eighty challenging multiple-choice questions and write two standard free-response essays and one free-response DBQ essay, many students are thoroughly intimidated. There is no better encouragement you can give them than to prepare for the AP exam on a daily, weekly, and monthly basis. They must have a firm command of content. But an understanding of the exam's three major components—multiple-choice questions, free-response essays, and the DBQ—can give them an edge in dealing with the challenges posed by the exam.

Multiple-Choice Questions

Here are some rules of thumb to help your students work their way through the multiple-choice questions:

* **Multiple-Choice scoring.** Each correct answer is worth 1 point, and by a recent change to AP exam scoring, students will no longer lose points for incorrect answers. Therefore it is worthwhile to answer every question, even if they have to guess. There are five possible answers for each question. If the student cannot narrow down the choices at all, she or he will have a 20% chance of guessing correctly. If the student can eliminate even just one response, it will always improve the chances of guessing correctly. If the student chooses to skip a question, it is important to be careful to skip down that line on the answer sheet.

- **Read the question carefully.** Pressured for time, many students make the mistake of reading the questions too quickly or merely skimming them. By reading a question carefully, the student may already have some idea about the correct answer and can then look for it in the responses. Careful reading is especially important in EXCEPT questions.

- **Eliminate incorrect answers.** Students can write on the multiple-choice questions in the test book. Encourage your students to draw a line through any answer they are confident is wrong.

- **Read all of the possible answers, then choose the most accurate response.** AP exams are written to test the student's precise knowledge of a subject. Sometimes there are a few probable answers, but one of them is more specific. For example, a question dealing with the Open Door policy may have an answer that seems correct: "It sought to promote U.S. interests overseas." However, there may be an even better answer, one that is more specific to the topic: "To provide the U.S. access to trade in Asia." In other words, students should select the best answer.

- **Avoid absolute responses.** These answers often include the words "always" or "never." For example, the statement "Jefferson always rejected the Hamiltonian economic program" is an overstatement in that Jefferson never attempted to eliminate one of the key features of Hamilton's economic program, the Bank of the United States. Therefore, while Jefferson represented the political and economic perspectives opposite to those of Hamilton, he did not *always* reject Hamilton's ideas outright.

- **Mark and skip tough questions.** How much time should be spent on each question is a common question asked by students who are soon to take the AP exam. The answer is not as simple as dividing eighty questions by fifty-five minutes, because some questions will certainly take less time to answer than others. This is where students need to exercise common sense. If they are hung up on a question, they should mark it in the margin of the question book and, time permitting, come back to it later. Again, remind your students to be sure to skip the corresponding number on their answer sheet if they are choosing to come back to that question.

There are various kinds of multiple-choice questions. Here are some suggestions for how to approach each kind:

Classic/Best Answer Questions

This is the most common type of multiple-choice question. It simply requires the student to read the question and select the most correct answer. For example:

1. All money bills originate in
    (A)   the executive branch
    (B)   the Senate
    (C)   the House of Representatives
    (D)   the judicial branch
    (E)   the State Department

Answer: (C) This is a question that has only one correct answer. The Constitution provides for all money bills to originate in the House of Representatives.

EXCEPT Questions

In this kind of question, all but one of the answers are correct. The best way to approach these questions is as true/false. The student should mark a T or F next to each possible answer. There should be only one false answer, and that is the one to select. For example:

1. All of the following were advantages of the Union in the Civil War EXCEPT
    (A)   it needed only to fight a defensive war

(B) it was more industrialized than the South
(C) it had a larger population than the South
(D) it had a more developed railway system than the South
(E) it had a stronger navy than the South

Answer: (A) The North had to conquer the Confederacy and therefore could not wage a defensive war. Options B–E are all advantages of the Union.

List and Group Questions

In this type of question, there is a list of possible answers, and the student must select the answer that contains the correct group of responses. These questions look hard, but the student can simplify them by crossing out items from the list and then eliminating them in the answers below. For example:

1.   According to the Constitution, as amended, which of the following is directly elected by the people?

To approach the question, the student can begin by drawing a line through choice I, because the president and vice president are not elected directly but are chosen by the Electoral College. Then the student should cross out any response that contains choice I.

I.   ~~the president and vice-president~~
II.   members of the House of Representatives
III. justices of the Supreme Court
IV.   senators
    (A) ~~I and II~~
    (B) II and III
    (C) ~~I, II and III~~
    (D) ~~I and IV~~
    (E) II and IV

The student should continue to cross out items that are wrong and the responses that contain them. Justices of the Supreme Court are appointed, not elected, so the student should draw a line through III and option (B), which contains choice III. Now the possible responses have been narrowed down to one.

Answer: (E) Under the Constitution, including the Seventeenth Amendment which provides for the direct election of senators, members of the House of Representatives and Senate are elected directly.

Chart and Graph Questions

These questions require the student to examine the data on a chart or graph. Quantitative skills are an important component of any social science course, and the AP exam tests students on their ability to read and interpret charts, tables, and graphs. While these questions are no more important than any other question on the exam, warn students that they can unintentionally find themselves spending an inordinate amount of time interpreting the information on a chart or graph, especially if this is not one of their strong suits. One strategy is for students to read the question and then read the five possible answers so that they have an understanding of what they are looking for—even before attempting to decipher the chart, graph, or table. In this way, even before the students look at the visual, they may be able to eliminate some obviously incorrect answers.

For this type of question, look at the chart in *The American Pageant*, 14th ed., p. 601/15th ed., p. 543, which deals with immigration.

1.   Which of the following statements does the chart best support?
    (A) Immigration remained at the same level from 1871 to 1920.
    (B) The period 1871–1880 witnessed the largest immigration of new immigrants in the late nineteenth century.

(C)   Most immigrants came from Italy and Germany.

(D)   Between 1911 and 1920, approximately 3 million immigrants came from England, Ireland, and Germany.

(E)   The period 1891–1900 was the first decade in the late nineteenth century in which the number of new immigrants exceeded the number of old immigrants.

Answer: (E) After analyzing the table, option (A) can be eliminated because the measurement bars are not level in *any* period. Option (B) is incorrect because the total number of new immigrants in the period 1871–1880 is the lowest of any decade represented. Option (C) is also incorrect because there is no way to determine from the table what percentage of the immigrants emigrated from a specific country. Option (D) is incorrect because this decade was actually the low point of immigration from England, Ireland, and Germany (540,000 contrasted with over 2,270,000 in the period 1881–1890). Option (E) is correct because the bar representing new immigration is higher for the first time than the bar for old immigration.

Political Cartoon Questions

These questions require students to interpret a political cartoon. Every political cartoon contains symbolism and a point of view. Students are advised to examine the cartoon before they read the question and possible responses to determine what each part of the drawing represents and to identify the artist's viewpoint. Unfortunately, students often do not give as much attention to the political cartoons that appear in the textbook as they should; they assume, incorrectly, that this type of information is not necessarily important to understanding the content they are reading. However, political cartoons are obviously visual attempts to convey an opinion using recognizable icons and images, often in a way that is more powerful and incisive than words alone can convey. (Keep in mind that political cartoons, as well as graphs and charts, may appear on the DBQ.)

For this type of question, see the cartoon in *The American Pageant*, 14th ed., p. 692/15th ed., p. 629.

1.   What is the viewpoint expressed in the cartoon?

(A)   The United States rejected the Roosevelt Corollary to the Monroe Doctrine.

(B)   Under Roosevelt, the United States allowed European nations to take part in the colonization of South America.

(C)   Roosevelt brought the Caribbean under the control of the United States.

(D)   Roosevelt was protecting the Caribbean nations from U.S. intervention.

(E)   The United States in the early twentieth century began removing its military control of the Caribbean.

Answer: (C) The Monroe Doctrine was actually strengthened by the Roosevelt Corollary. Therefore, options (A) and (B) are incorrect, because one of the primary purposes of the Monroe Doctrine and the Roosevelt Corollary was to prevent European intervention in the Western Hemisphere. Because the United States consistently intervened in South American affairs, options (D) and (E) are incorrect.

Interpreting a Map

For history students, maps are used to describe not just geography but social and political organization as well. Asked to interpret a map, students can glean a considerable amount of information just by looking at the key or legend.

For this question, take a look at the map in *The American Pageant*, 14th ed., p. 262/15th ed., p. 235, titled "The Missouri Compromise and Slavery, 1820–1821."

1.   The map shows the United States

(A)   at the end of the Revolutionary War.

(B)   following the end of the Mexican-American War.

(C)   after all of the eastern Native American tribes had been moved to reservations in the West.

(D)   after the passage of the Missouri Compromise.

(E)   at the outbreak of the Civil War.

Answer: (D) At the end of the Revolutionary War, the United States comprised the thirteen original colonies; therefore option (A) is incorrect. Option (B) is incorrect for several reasons, foremost being the absence of Texas and the Mexican Cession on the map. Because there is no information on the map that indicates it has anything to do with Native American removal, option (C) is incorrect. Option (E) is incorrect because, although the map indicates free and slave states, it does not show states, such as California, Arkansas, Texas, and Oregon, that were present in 1861, when the southern states began to secede.

Free-Response Questions

The AP exam asks students to write three essays in which they respond to a question. Questions may ask to what extent a given statement is accurate, to compare and contrast particular events, or to analyze a particular direction. There is a wide variety of free-response questions that may appear on the AP exam, as you can see from the following examples:

- *Analyze* the extent to which compromise was no longer possible by the 1850s.

- *Compare and contrast* the political features of the Articles of Confederation and the United States Constitution.

- *To what extent* were the Jeffersonian Democrats and the Jacksonian Democrats similar in their political views and goals?

- *Analyze* the relationship between government, business, and labor from the end of the Civil War to the end of the nineteenth century.

- *Discuss* whether U.S. presidents in the postwar years up to 1963 were successful in containing communism. Select two of the following:

    President Truman

    President Eisenhower

    President Kennedy

- *Evaluate* the relationship between Great Britain and its American colonies prior to 1763.

- The ability and willingness the Framers had for compromise was reflected in the creation of a constitution that successfully addressed the needs of the young republic. *Explain* how two of the following reflect the validity of this statement:

    Representation

    Slavery

    Democratic rights

- *Analyze* the various groups, individuals, and movements that either challenged or presented an alternative program to President Franklin D. Roosevelt's New Deal.

- Reconstruction failed to address the social, economic, and political needs of the freed slaves. *Assess the validity* of this statement by focusing on the period 1863–1900.

- The hostilities that led to the Civil War were ultimately so significant that they led to discord. Thus the Civil War was an irreconcilable conflict. *Explain* how two of the following reflect the validity of this statement:

    The development of two distinct and incompatible civilizations in the North and South

The failure of politicians in the 1850s to establish viable political compromises

The role of territorial expansion in the antebellum period

- Evaluate the relative significance of the following factors in causing the outbreak of the American Revolution:

    British mercantilism

    British revenue-raising taxes

    The influence of colonial radicals

In constructing lucid, well-organized analytical essays, your students first need to organize their thoughts into a cogent and structured outline. This is why it is important that they make the best use of the time allotted for outlining before they write each essay—fifteen minutes for the DBQ and five minutes for each of the standard free-response questions. This is a lot to ask of students; in their minds, they hear the clock ticking. Even thirty-five minutes seems too short to construct a viable, well-structured essay, so why take five minutes—one-seventh of that time—away from writing an essay? The answer is a simple: organization. Even students who are well versed in the content and who can analyze that information may become bogged down in structuring the essay if they don't begin with an outline. In the end, appropriate information and solid analysis lose their value if presented in a way that is confusing and disorganized.

Learning how to write an essay is an ongoing process in any social science course, especially in a history course. That process begins with teaching your students how to structure an essay. You can begin by telling your students that, in writing a free-response essay, they will need the following:

- A well-developed thesis that sums up their perspective

- Effective analysis and appropriate use of information

- A cogent essay that is well-structured and lucidly written

One model for organizing an essay is as follows:

Thesis (Opinion)

↓*Supporting Arguments* (major reasons to be developed in the body paragraphs that defend or support the thesis)

A Structured Body Paragraph (includes)

A Topic Sentence (which)

  Supports the thesis

  Introduces the topic of the paragraph

Historical and Factual Information (the historical content such as)

  Facts

  Details

  Statistics

  Quotes

Analysis (which)

> Explains the separate parts of the arguments and information
>
> Explains the significance of the information presented as it relates to the thesis
>
> (Historiographic information can be used as historical content and/or as support for the analysis of the information the student presents.)

You can also recommend to students that, in constructing a strong essay, they keep the following in mind:

Frame the debate To demonstrate an understanding of the complexity of an issue or question, students should show that they are aware of both sides of the argument or perspective. This "frames" the debate for the reader. Thus, in the introduction, they might present the "other" view, the one they are _not_ supporting—but warn students not to develop the other perspective so fully that they stray from their thesis. Ultimately, the objective is to convince the reader that the student's essay has a strong thesis that is well developed with historical information and analysis.

Outline Time spent on outlining is important not only to ensure that an essay is organized; this time also provides the student with a brief brainstorming opportunity before writing the essay. Further, it helps determine one's perspective on the issue. If, after completing an outline, the student sees that the information tends to support one view over the other, then this is the perspective the student should develop.

Once the student has an outline, it is time to put pen to paper. Make sure that your students know that AP readers are looking for accurate information in straightforward, concise prose. This will disappoint your more poetic students. It will also be an important heads-up for students who might try to mask vague information with elegant prose.

Three Sample Free-Response Essays

Having established the ingredients of a free-response answer, let us now look at three sample essays—one excellent (grade: 9), one good (grade: 6), and one poor (grade: 3). Comments following each essay explain ways in which each essay succeeds or fails. All three essays respond to the following free-response question:

> **Analyze the extent to which compromise was no longer possible between the North and South by 1860.**

Sample Essay 1

By the time Abraham Lincoln was elected president in 1860, the time for compromise between the North and South had passed. Lincoln's election was the spark that ignited secession. Throughout the antebellum period, political leaders had attempted to preserve the Union through compromise and by maintaining the political balance in the Senate. As early as the Constitutional Convention, there were indications that the conflicting economies and cultures of the regions would ultimately have to be resolved, either through ongoing political compromise or through war. As late as 1858, just two years before secession, Lincoln had said, "A house divided against itself cannot stand." The outbreak of the Civil War was the tragic resolution to the sectional differences and the inability to maintain two different economic, political, and cultural systems under one government. Territorial expansion played a significant role in straining sectional relations because it involved the debate over the expansion or containment of slavery. In 1820 Congress seemed to have resolved this problem when it passed the Missouri Compromise, which prevented the expansion of slavery north of the 36° 30´ line. For a time, Congress was able to balance representation in the Senate by admitting both a slave state and a free state into the Union. For example, Missouri, a slave state, was admitted at the same time as Maine, a free state.

Compromise could address only the symptoms of the problem; it could not resolve the basic economic, political, and moral differences, especially because the two regions had completely different economic systems dominated by opposing social, economic, and political classes: the planter-slaveholder in the South and the industrial capitalist in the North. Economically, northern manufacturers and the northern economy required a protective tariff, internal improvements, and a national bank to facilitate commerce, whereas the South wanted low tariffs, state banks, and was opposed to internal improvements. The North's economy and culture rested on the wage-labor system, which was, of course, inconsistent with the South's slave economy and culture. Both sought to expand their systems for a variety of reasons: politically the North and South quarreled over the extension of slavery because the addition of a new slave state or free state meant greater political representation in Congress. This in turn meant that either region, if given the political advantage, could pass legislation that affected not only the future expansion of slavery, but other burning political issues as well, such as the tariff.

Furthermore, the North maintained that the Union had been established as a contract among the people of the United States. Southern political leaders responded that the Union was the result of a compact between the states, and that a state had the authority to nullify federal laws and even secede from the Union if necessary. These conflicting political theories made compromise even more difficult to achieve because the South claimed to have the authority to reject any federal law it deemed unconstitutional or a threat to states' rights.

Added to this was the role of northern abolitionists and southern defenders of slavery, whose justifications for or against the peculiar institution added a moral element to the already significant differences. Thus by the time Congress passed the Kansas-Nebraska Act in 1854 and the Supreme Court handed down the <u>Dred Scott</u> decision in 1857, the possibility of maintaining the Union became increasingly tenuous.

Politically, by the 1850s the two major political parties represented, for the most part, different sections: the Democrats articulated the South's objectives, whereas the Republicans represented an adversarial view. Up until the election of Lincoln, the presidency was occupied either by a southerner or by a northerner who tended to favor the South's position. Lincoln, a Republican, was an advocate of the containment of slavery, suggesting to the South that the executive branch would now become an obstacle to the South's political objectives, and that its political and economic influence would therefore wane over time. Thus by 1860 conditions for secession were already present, and the time for compromise had, for all intents and purposes, passed.

Comment: This essay effectively outlines the divisions that prevailed between the North and South in the antebellum period. While it by no means completely addresses the issue, given the time constraint (thirty-five minutes), it successfully indicates that while Lincoln's election was the event that finally shattered the Union, deep social, economic, and political divisions had been festering for decades. The writer articulates the view that the Civil War was the result of irreconcilable differences that could no longer be resolved through compromise. Although listing the features of the *Dred Scott* case would certainly help, the writer successfully synthesizes selective historical content with effective analysis to support the thesis. Grade: 9 (Excellent)

Sample Essay 2

Although there were many disputes, differences, and events that made compromise in the decades before the 1850s very difficult, political leaders such as Clay and Calhoun were able to work out solutions that politically resolved the differences between North and South and therefore prevented secession and war. Unfortunately the nation's political leaders were not up to the task in the 1850s. As early as the Constitutional Convention, the Framers developed solutions to sectional problems such as the Three-fifths Compromise and the Assumption Bill. In the early nineteenth century, with tensions high over the attempt to expand or limit the spread of slavery, congressional leaders were *able to work out the Missouri Compromise, which defined where slavery could and could not expand. In 1850 the United States could have experienced civil war had not political leaders worked out the Compromise of 1850, which strengthened the Fugitive Slave Act in the South's favor but allowed California to enter as a free state. True, the <u>Dred Scott</u> decision effectively eliminated the Missouri Compromise, but political leaders such as Senator Stephen Douglas could not create compromises that would reduce tensions. Instead, they offered the controversial Kansas-Nebraska Act.*

The idea of popular sovereignty made compromise almost impossible because Congress could no longer establish areas where slavery could expand and where it could not. Besides, the Kansas-Nebraska Act further enforced the Fugitive Slave Act, which angered northerners immensely. The only thing holding the Union together at this point was the hope on the part of the South that it could in the future continue to expand slavery. Lincoln, who was opposed to the expansion of slavery, concerned the South so much that no one in 1860 could find any way to compromise. With Lincoln's election, the South seceded. But it didn't have to come to that. The nation's political leaders had failed to do what their predecessors in Congress had been able to achieve: make effective compromises.

Comment: This essay has a clear thesis: the nation's political leaders in the 1850s were responsible for failing to reduce or resolve the sectional tensions through effective compromises that earlier political leaders had accomplished. The writer cites several important political compromises. The scope of this essay could be broader, however, in that the author does not incorporate the role of territorial expansion into the discussion. Further, the discussion is limited in that no clear differences between the sections are established. Thus the essay focuses only on the controversy over the expansion of slavery and not on its economic and political consequences for the sections. It also depicts the Compromise of 1850 as a workable solution that had no subsequent repercussions. In fact, the North was outraged by the Fugitive Slave component of the act. There is also a factual error: the Kansas-Nebraska Act did not strengthen the Fugitive Slave Act. An explanation of popular sovereignty would also add to the quality of this essay. Nevertheless, the writer exhibits a good understanding of the topic and uses information that sustains the thesis throughout the essay. Grade: 6 (Good)

Sample Essay 3

Compromise in the 1850s was impossible because the North and South no longer wanted to negotiate. They believed that only through war would their differences be settled. The Missouri Compromise was more effective than the Kansas-Nebraska Act. It prevented war, whereas the Kansas-Nebraska Act made war more possible. Popular sovereignty was not an effective solution either. Now slavery could spread anywhere and the North would be opposed to this. Lincoln was opposed to the spread of slavery, but he was not willing to break up the Union for it. Therefore a better solution to the problem could not be found. If Lincoln opposed the spread of slavery, what other option did the South have but to leave the Union? Also, the North and South viewed slavery differently. The North opposed it as inhumane, but the South claimed it was an institution that benefited both Southern whites and slaves. Had the Framers at the Constitutional Convention addressed the issue of slavery, future generations would not have to find solutions and compromises to this problem. But even if Congress did work out compromises, such as the Missouri Compromise, no one could determine what the Supreme Court would do, such as the <u>Dred Scott</u> case. Lincoln's election was not the cause of the war. True, he was a northerner, but so were other presidents. Put simply, neither the North nor the South favored compromise by the 1850s because they could not resolve their political differences.

Comment: This essay is weak in a number of areas. While it has a thesis, it is rudimentary. The thesis is not developed in the essay effectively. The writer strings together generalizations that have little connection to one another. Important issues are not explained. For instance, the writer contends that the

Missouri Compromise was more effective than the Kansas-Nebraska Act but does not explain how or why the former prevented war. The body of the essay lacks focus, analysis, and sufficient historical information to defend the thesis. Grade: 3 (Poor)

The Document-Based Question (DBQ)

The document-based question is considered by many students the most complex and challenging component of the AP exam. As its name implies, the DBQ presents the student with a wide variety of primary-source information in the form of approximately nine sources. Primary sources, which are contemporaneous with a time period or event, include everything from maps, political cartoons, photographs, and illustrations, to speeches, essays, books, documentaries, and editorials. Documents are *not* taken from secondary sources, such as textbooks.

Document-based questions run the gamut from basic "why" and "explain" questions to "support or refute" and "how and why" questions. All free-response essays require students to utilize their knowledge of the topic, but with the DBQ, the essay needs to be grounded on the documents. Thus, the goal is to demonstrate an ability to tease out the thrust and substance of each document, and then combine this information with one's own general knowledge in an analytical and evaluative essay. Thus the following are necessary ingredients for writing a quality DBQ essay:

- Background—the student's own knowledge of the topic

- Analysis—the student's ability to interpret and explain the documents

- Synthesis—the student's ability to blend outside information with the information provided in the documents to explain an issue

In order to appreciate the complexities and dimensions of interpreting, analyzing, and organizing the information associated with a document-based question, take a look at DBQ 6 in *The American Pageant*, 14th ed., pp. A79–81/15th ed. pp. A76-78.

As the directions indicate, students are expected to analyze the information in the documents and then synthesize this information with their own knowledge of the topic and period. The essential first step in approaching the DBQ is analysis of the documents themselves—the essay must be based on the documents. Once the documents are analyzed, the next step is to organize the material so that students can use the information in the documents, along with their own knowledge of the topic, to develop their response. First, students should make certain they understand what the assignment is asking them to do:

> **In the years 1830–1860, many northern Americans came to see slavery as an evil, while many southerners defended the institution as a positive good. Why did the North and South come to such different views of slavery in the years prior to the Civil War?**

> **Use these documents and your knowledge of the period from 1830 to 1860 to compose your answer.**

Two factors are apparent in the directions:

- Students are not necessarily asked to defend a thesis (for example, how legitimate each perspective is given the attitudes of the time), but to describe and discuss the conflicting arguments. This, however, does not preclude the development of a personal perspective. For example, the student can relate the sectional differences and views regarding slavery to a larger historiographic perspective—namely, that given their different modes of production, the two sections had evolved into two distinct and often incompatible civilizations that were attempting to coexist under the same government. In this way, the student can develop the views of the North and the views of the South in regard to slavery, while simultaneously using this information to develop a point of view.

- The prompt limits the time frame (1830–1860).

Of course, there were antecedents to the thinking on slavery that had been firmly established by the 1830s, and variations on these views evolved as the nation came closer and closer to separation and as war developed over time. One suggestion might be to recommend to your students that they cover the earlier interpretations (say, from the late eighteenth or early nineteenth century) in their introductory paragraph, which would provide the essay with two advantages: it establishes the origins of the debate, and it provides necessary information that helps to set up the response.

Let your students know that they do not have to use or cite every single one of the documents, but the more they use the better. They should certainly try to incorporate at least half into their essay.

Students are given a fifteen-minute reading period to go over all of the documents and, if they have time, put together a working outline before they begin writing their essay. How should your students use this time? The following three steps are essential:

- Read for comprehension.

- Take margin notes. For example, condense the meaning of the document or relate it to a historical fact or interpretation.

- Categorize the documents.

Let us now apply these steps to the documents. (Suggested margin notes are italicized in the analysis of the documents below.)

What Is the Meaning of Each Document?

Document A: Take note of the source: it was written by a member of the South Carolina legislature. South Carolina threatened to nullify federal law (the tariff) and spoke of secession as early as 1828. It was the first state to secede from the Union in 1860. This statement, by the governor of South Carolina, was made less than a decade later. *The author is contrasting the quality of life between the "comfortable" life of slaves and the miserable condition of European factory workers and peasants.*

Document B: *The author is correlating the institution of slavery with an economic imperative, the cultivation of cotton.*

Document C: Some slave-holders—for example, George Washington upon his death—did manumit (legally free) their slaves. This print shows *a black woman being restrained by a white man while another white man tears up her manumission papers.*

Document D: Garnet declares that *just as enslavement is a sin against God, so too is submission to enslavement. He exhorts slaves to resist.*

Document E: This Currier & Ives print *sums up the life of the plantation, with the planter and his wife watching as male and female slaves pick cotton, which is "ginned," baled, and transported to the riverbank for shipment by paddle wheeler to be sold in New Orleans. This print shows how important cotton was to the southern economy and idealizes plantation slavery.*

Document F: This document is an interesting counterpoint to the attitude expressed in Document B. *Lincoln is informing his audience that there is a steep political price to be paid by maintaining the economic imperatives of slavery—namely, the compromising of American freedom.*

Document G: Modeled on the set of questions and answers by which the basic principles of a religion are explained, *this catechism lays out why the slave is a slave and what the slave must do to remain in God's favor. Religion was used to keep slaves under control.*

Document H: Harriet Beecher Stowe's *Uncle Tom's Cabin*, published in 1852, was a powerful moral diatribe against chattel slavery. It touched a sensitive nerve with many northerners and southerners alike, but obviously for different reasons. *The poster reveals the popularity of the book on the eve of the Civil War and represents the extent of the moral division that plagued the nation over the institution of slavery.*

Document I: Hale declares slavery the foundation of the South. Slaves were valuable as property and as the producers of the goods that fueled not only the South's economy but those of the North and Europe. Hale sees the election of Lincoln as the North's declaration of hostilities.

Organizing the Documents

After analyzing the documents and jotting down margin notes for later reference, the next step is to organize the material.

Slavery as an evil	Slavery as a positive good
C	A
D	B
F	E
H	G
	I

Incorporating Outside or Personal Knowledge

The amount of information on the antebellum period, slavery, and the causes of the American Civil War is enormous. While the DBQ focuses on how the North and South viewed the institution of slavery, that does not necessarily reduce the number of topics, events, personalities, issues, and political developments that can be incorporated into the essay. Students must determine for themselves what information is appropriate for responding to the question. Nevertheless, you should advise your students to brainstorm before writing the essay. For example, the following information may be helpful:

- Regional economic differences—in other words, characteristics of the North and South's economies: planter-slaveholding in the South and industrial and commercial capitalism in the North.

- Attitudes in the North and South. The South's accusation that northern laborers were "wage-slaves" was an attack on the North's condemnation of slavery as well as the capitalist system as practiced in the North. For example, the ideological conflict between the South's support for slavery and corresponding condemnation of the North's socioeconomic system are seen in such works as George Fitzhugh's *Sociology for the South; or, The Failure of a Free Society* (1854) and the political platform of the North's Republican Party—"free labor, free soil, free men."

- The role of abolitionists and southern secessionists. Students can cite examples of the North's moral condemnation of slavery, such as Frederick Douglass's *Autobiography* or Harriet Beecher Stowe's *Uncle Tom's Cabin,* and the political theory of southern leaders, such as John C. Calhoun's *South Carolina Exposition and Protest,* as well as the activities and rhetoric of southern "fire-eaters," such as Edmund Ruffin.

- The debate over expanding and containing slavery and the breakdown of compromise. Students should make certain to tie together this debate with each section's belief in their opposition to or support for slavery, not merely a discussion of, say, the political features of the Missouri Compromise.

These are only suggested topics. Your instruction, assignments, and lessons will have provided your students with plenty of examples to sustain each of these topics and others as well. Given this model, students should have in place prewriting ingredients that will help them to manage their time effectively to analyze, organize, and incorporate relevant document information with their own knowledge of the topic. Continued practices over the school year can go a long way in helping them develop the skills they need to write an effective DBQ essay.

How the AP U.S. History Exam Is Scored

Grades for the AP exam are mailed out in July. They are arrived at by combining the score on the multiple-choice section and scores for the essays to arrive at a composite score. All composite scores are then ranked, and a decision is made as to where to make the grade-range breaks. The College Board uses the following criteria to evaluate a student's performance on the AP U.S. History examination:

The Free-Response Grading Rubric

In determining the quality of a student's free-response essays, the following standards are used:

8–9: Excellent The essay begins with a clear thesis. It is well written and organized, covers all aspects of the question in depth, analyzes the question effectively, and supports the thesis with sufficient and relevant historical information. There may be some minor errors.

5–7: Good The essay has a clear thesis, although it is not as well developed as in an 8–9 essay. It has clear, though not excellent, organization. The essay covers only one aspect of the question in depth, and it does not fully demonstrate an understanding of the complexity of the question or topic. The analysis is not as well developed as in an 8–9 essay, and there is limited use of relevant historical information. The essay may contain errors that do not affect the overall quality of the essay.

2–4: Fair The essay either lacks a clear thesis or has a confused—or even missing—thesis. It is not well organized, and the writing is weak. The essay does not indicate an understanding of the complexity of the question or topic, and it fails to lay out sufficient historical information and/or analysis. It may contain significant errors.

0–1: Poor The essay has no thesis, and it has poor structure and organization. It is poorly written, lacks historical information and analysis, and tends to offer rhetorical comments. It contains both major and minor errors.

Teacher Insight

Encourage students to evaluate their free-response essays on a regular basis, using the grading rubric above; they can even ask a parent or a fellow student or friend to evaluate their essays, but since objectivity (and skill) is essential in determining the quality of an essay, students should be encouraged to ask their teacher for an analysis and evaluation of their practice essays. This, in turn, will provide valuable experience in developing essays based on the College Board's criteria as well as further developing writing and editing skills.

Scoring the Multiple-Choice Section

Use the following formula to calculate the raw score on the multiple-choice section of the exam:

_____   –   (_____ x ¼) = _____ (round to nearest whole number)

number correct	*number incorrect*	*raw score*

Scoring the Free-Response Section

Use the formula below to calculate the raw score on the free-response section of the exam:

(___ x 4.5) + (___ x 2.75) + (___ x 2.75) = ____ (round to nearest whole number)

DBQ   *essay 1*   *essay 2*   *raw score*

Calculating the Composite Score

1.13 x _____ = _____ (weighted multiple-choice score: NOT rounded)

    multiple- choice

    raw score

2.73 x _____ = _____ (weighted free-response score: NOT rounded)

    free-response

    raw score

Once the calculations have been completed, add the two weighted sections and round to the nearest whole number. The result is the composite score. Students can now see where their score falls in the Composite Score Range. Remind students that this score is only a rough estimate of how they will score on the AP exam; a good score on one or two practice tests is no guarantee they will score as high on the national exam.

_____ + _____ = composite score

weighted multiple-choice score   *weighted free-response score*

AP Grades

The College Board determines final grades based on where a student's composite score falls in the range of all the composite scores. Here's one breakdown of grades by composite score range:

AP Grade	Composite Score Range
5	114–180
4	91–113
3	74–90
2	49–73
1	0–48

Note that the composite score ranges change from year to year. For example, a composite score of 109 may have earned a 5 on the 2004 AP exam, whereas it may have earned a 4 on another year's exam. For an elaboration on this and other testing questions, visit the College Board's website.

The College Board describes the meaning of its grades as follows:

AP Grade	Meaning
5	Extremely well qualified
4	Well qualified
3	Qualified
2	Possibly qualified
1	No recommendation

In the final section of this teacher's manual you will find a chapter-by-chapter guide to *The American Pageant,* Fourteenth and Fifteenth Editions. Each begins with an AP Focus section, then summarizes the textbook chapter and offers suggestions for other resources and ways you can help your students to master content and dig into the history.

PART II: College Instructor's Manual with AP* Focus Sections

CHAPTER 1

New World Beginnings, 33,000 B.C.E.–1769 C.E.

AP FOCUS

- Students should have an understanding of the pre-Columbian Americas, before European exploration.

- Worldwide exploration begins in the fifteenth century. Students need a good chronology of the voyages of Columbus and other explorers of the New World.

- European contact with the New World has an ecological impact.

- The Spanish conquer indigenous New World cultures in both North and South America, creating an enormous empire.

AP teachers should take note of the following:

1. North and South American cultures, such as the Aztec and Inca, developed prior to contact with Europe. Special attention should be given to the economic systems that shaped these cultures before the arrival of the Spaniards and other Europeans.

2. The Columbian Exchange (see the chart in *The American Pageant,* 14th ed., p. 16/15th ed., p. 14) that led to the growth of international commerce had a profound impact. For example, New World foodstuffs, crops, and even diseases entered Europe; likewise, foods, crops, minerals, and diseases indigenous to Europe were transported to the Western Hemisphere. The age of discovery and the internationalization of commerce affected the growth and development of slavery; these pertain to a number of the AP themes, especially Globalization and Slavery.

Focus on Historical Thinking:

Have students complete a Main Idea Log for each of the sections in the narrative text for this chapter. Students should write out each heading, turn it into a question, and answer that question in one clear, concise sentence. This technique allows students to look for the main idea of the section as they read it.

FOCUS QUESTIONS

1. What was Native American society like before European contact? What similarities and differences existed?

2. What factors led to Europe's increased exploration and to the discovery of the New World?

3. What is the Columbian Exchange? What are some of the results of the Columbian Exchange?

4. What was the role of *conquistadores* and *encomienda* in establishing a Spanish Empire in the New World?

5. What was the geographic extent of the Spanish Empire in the New World? What nations were challenging Spain's dominance in the New World and where?

CHAPTER THEMES

Theme: The first discoverers of America, the ancestors of the American Indians, were small bands of hunters who crossed a temporary land bridge from Siberia and spread across both North and South America. They evolved a great variety of cultures, which ranged from the sophisticated urban civilizations in Mexico and Central and South America to the largely seminomadic societies of North America.

Theme: Europe's growing demand for Eastern luxuries prompted exploration in the hopes of reducing the expense of those goods with new trade routes. Exploration occurred incrementally, beginning with the Portuguese moving around the coast of Africa and establishing trading posts. Awareness of the New World and its wealth pushed exploration across the Atlantic. Spanish exploration continued in the same fashion, first in the Caribbean islands then expanding into South and North America.

Theme: Portuguese and Spanish explorers encountered and then conquered much of the Americas and their Indian inhabitants. This "collision of worlds" deeply affected all the Atlantic societies—Europe, the Americas, and Africa—as the effects of disease, conquest, slavery, and intermarriage began to create a truly "new world" in Latin America, including the borderlands of Florida, New Mexico, and California, all of which later became part of the United States.

CHAPTER SUMMARY

Millions of years ago, the two American continents became geologically separated from the Eastern Hemisphere land masses where humanity originated. The first people to enter these continents came across a temporary land bridge from Siberia about 35,000 years ago. Spreading across the two continents, they developed a great variety of societies based largely on corn agriculture and hunting. In North America, some ancient Indian peoples like the Pueblos, the Anasazi, and the Mississippian culture developed elaborate settlements. But on the whole, North American Indian societies were less numerous and urbanized than those in Central and South America, though equally diverse in culture and social organization.

The impetus for European exploration came from the desire for new trade routes to the East, the spirit and technological discoveries of the Renaissance, and the power of the new European national monarchies. The European encounters with Africa and America, beginning with the Portuguese and Spanish explorers, convulsed the entire world. Biological change, disease, population loss, conquest, African slavery, cultural change, and economic expansion were just some of the consequences of the commingling of the Old World and the New World.

After they conquered and then intermarried with Indians of the great civilizations of South America and Mexico, the Spanish *conquistadores* expanded northward into the northern border territories of Florida, New Mexico, and California. There they established small but permanent settlements in competition with the French and English explorers who also were venturing into North America.

DEVELOPING THE CHAPTER: SUGGESTED LECTURE OR DISCUSSION TOPICS

- Using globes and maps, examine the impact of geology and geography on the prehistory and history of the Americas. Point out the areas of relatively dense Indian population and civilization before 1492 and emphasize the ways in which geography shaped the subsequent pattern of European exploration and conquest—in both South and North America.

  REFERENCE: D. W. Meinig, *The Shaping of America: A Geographical Perspective on 500 Years of Atlantic America* (1986).

- Explore what has been learned from history, anthropology, and archaeology regarding the life of American Indians before 1492. Emphasize that these societies were varied and dynamic, and had undergone significant conflicts and changes over many centuries. Perhaps select one North American Indian culture that had disappeared by the time of the Columbian encounter (e.g., the Anasazi culture that built Mesa Verde and Chaco Canyon in the Southwest) and compare their ways of life with those of the Indians that the Europeans first met when they arrived.

  REFERENCE: Brian M. Fagan, *Kingdoms of Gold, Kingdoms of Jade: The Americas Before Columbus* (1991).

- Analyze, in more depth, the condition of European societies at the beginning of the age of exploration. Consider, for example, the ways in which Europe was still medieval in its outlook around 1500 or so, and the ways in which it was being affected by more modern developments. Point out the changes in Europe that were occurring almost simultaneously with the age of discovery—particularly, the Protestant Reformation and Catholic Counter-Reformation, the Italian Renaissance, the unification of Spain, and the reign of Henry VIII—and consider their impact on the Americas.

  REFERENCE: Immanuel Wallerstein, *The Modern World-System* (1974).

- Discuss the exchanges involved in the encounter of Europeans, Native Americans, and Africans in the New World. Focus particularly on the ways in which all parties in the process—the conquerors as well as the conquered—were changed. The emphasis could be on issues of population, intermarriage, agriculture, and the like, or on the new forms of society that developed in both Hispanic America and North America as a result of the events of 1492 and after.

  REFERENCES: Karen Ordahl Kupperman, *Settling with the Indians: The Meeting of English and Indian Cultures in America, 1580–1640* (1980); Ramon A. Gutierrez, *When Jesus Came, The Corn Mothers Went Away* (1991).

FOR FURTHER INTEREST: ADDITIONAL CLASS TOPICS

- What is history? Can history change? Is there a difference between history and the past? How do you learn history? How do you learn about the past? What makes something (a piece of writing or an artifact) a good piece of information about the past? What role does bias play in recording, learning, and understanding history?

- Consider the whole story of the settlement and discovery of America from the Indians' point of view. Examine the controversies over Columbus's role in the discovery and the actions of subsequent Spanish *conquistadores*.

- Compare the development and subsequent history of the Spanish in Mexico with that of the English in North America. Consider, particularly, the impact of the *mestizo* factor in Mexican history (a result of the intermarriage of Spanish and Indians), compared with the quite different pattern of English relations with the Indians in North America.

- Discuss the different historical perspective obtained by considering the role of the Spanish borderlands of Florida, New Mexico, and California as part of the history of colonial America (as distinct from examining only the later English settlements along the Atlantic coast). How does our understanding of American history alter if we consider developments in these areas to be of equal importance?

CHARACTER SKETCHES

Christopher Columbus (1451–1506)

Although his encounter with continents and peoples previously unknown to Europeans transformed world history, Columbus, the Genoese sailor who discovered America for the Spanish monarchy, never really understood the nature or significance of his accomplishment.

Having sailed under the flags of many nations, including Portugal, Columbus was already a well-known, successful voyager when he became obsessed with the idea of reaching Cathay (China) and the Indies by sailing west. His frustrating inability to gain backing for the venture ended when Ferdinand and Isabella agreed to supply him with three ships.

The great achievement of Columbus's first voyage was not only to navigate unknown waters under unprecedented conditions but also to keep his crews from mutiny—especially when the ships were becalmed after nearly sixty days. Although well aware, during all his voyages, that he was not in China or India, Columbus became firmly convinced that he had found islands just off the Asian coast and that the rich cities of Japan and China were not far away. This notion was reinforced by his desperate need to obtain continuing funding from the Spanish rulers, who pressed ever harder for concrete economic gains from the voyages.

Quote: "The inhabitants of this and of all the other islands I have found or gained intelligence of, both men and women, go as naked as they were born, with the exception that some of the women cover one part only with a single leaf or grass with a piece of cotton, made for that purpose…. I gave away a thousand good and pretty articles which I had brought with me in order to win their affection, and that they might be led to become Christians, and be well inclined to love and serve their highnesses and the whole Spanish nation…." (Letter on the first voyage, 1493)

REFERENCE: John Stewart Wilford, *The Mysterious History of Columbus* (1991).

Moctezuma II (1466–1520)

Moctezuma II (also called Montezuma II) was the Aztec ruler who succumbed to Cortés's invasion of Mexico.

He was the tenth in the line of Aztec emperors who controlled the vast regions and diverse peoples of Mexico from their rich capital at Tenochtitlán. Like other members of the royal aristocracy, he lived in luxury and served as a high priest of the elaborate but cruel Aztec religion. He succeeded to the throne in 1502, on the death of his uncle Ahuitzotl.

Before Cortés arrived, Moctezuma had expanded the Aztec realm, yet controlling the increasingly restless subordinate peoples of the empire demanded more and more of his energy. He was particularly devoted to the god Huitzilpochtli, but also came under the influence of astrologers and readers of portents. Their pessimistic predictions about his fate evidently weakened his will to resist the Spanish invaders.

After Cortés and his men seized Moctezuma and held him under house arrest, the people of Tenochtitlán became increasingly hostile to their leader. When Moctezuma appeared in public for the first time in nearly a year in early 1520, the angry populace showered him with stones before he could retreat indoors. The Spanish claimed that the wounded ruler died shortly thereafter from the stoning, but many Aztecs believed that the Spanish killed him. The truth remains unknown.

Quote: "I have in truth seen you and have now set eyes upon your force. You have come between mists and clouds, and now it has come to pass. Now you have arrived, with much fatigue and toil. Come to our land, come and repose." (Message to Cortés as he approached Tenochtitlán, 1519)

REFERENCE: Hugh Thomas, *Conquest: Montezuma, Cortes, and the Fall of Old Mexico* (1994).

Hernán Cortés (1485–1547)

Like many *conquistadores*, Cortés was born into a noble family, but as a younger son failed to inherit extensive lands and wealth. As a youth, he was restless, ambitious, and nearly uncontrollable. In 1504, at age nineteen, he sailed for the island of Hispaniola (today's Dominican Republic and Haiti), at that time the headquarters of Spanish activity in the New World.

Cortés farmed and worked as a minor town official for six years, but he longed for greater adventures. In 1511, he joined a successful expedition to Cuba and then used a commission from the governor of Cuba, Velazquez, to assemble an expedition of eleven ships, five hundred soldiers, and sixteen horses. Although Velazquez soon changed his mind, Cortés had already sailed for Mexico. Cortés's brilliant, if treacherous, combination of military, political, and psychological tactics overcame Aztec resistance and gained him an empire larger than Spain. His reports of his conquests, contained in five lengthy letters to King Charles V of Spain, are full of fascinating detail, as well as much boasting and exaggeration.

Cortés was a talented administrator, but peaceful pursuits did not suit him, and in 1524, he headed for Honduras in search of further glory. There, he succeeded only in ruining his health and undermining his position in Mexico City. He retired to his estate in Cuernavaca, Mexico, in 1528, and in 1540, returned to Spain to die, a broken man.

Quote: "Touching Montezuma's palace and all that was remarkable in his magnificence and power, there is so much to describe that I do not know how to begin.…There could be nothing more magnificent than that this barbarian lord should have all the things of heaven to be found under his domain, fashioned in gold and silver and jewels and feathers." (Second letter to King Charles V, 1521)

REFERENCE: Jon White, *Cortés and the Downfall of the Aztec Empire: A Study in the Conflict of Cultures,* rev. ed. (1989).

QUESTIONS FOR CLASS DISCUSSION

1. How did Indian societies of South and North America differ from European societies at the time the two came into contact? In what ways did Indians retain a worldview different from that of the Europeans?

2. What role did disease and forced labor (including slavery) play in the early settlement of America? Is the view of the Spanish and Portuguese as especially harsh conquerors and exploiters valid—or is this image just another version of the English black legend concerning the Spanish role in the Americas?

3. Are the differences between Latin America and North America due primarily to the differences between the respective Indian societies that existed in the two places, or to the disparity between Spanish and English culture? What would have happened if the English had conquered densely settled Mexico and Peru, and the Spanish had settled more thinly populated North America?

4. In what ways are the early (pre-1600) histories of Mexican and the present-day American Southwest understood differently now that the United States is being so substantially affected by Mexican and Latin American immigration and culture? To what extent should this now be regarded as part of our American history?

5. Why was the Old World able to dominate the New World? What were the strengths and weaknesses of the Old World? What were the strengths and weaknesses of the New World?

MAKERS OF AMERICA: THE *CONQUISTADORES*

Questions for Class Discussion

1. Should the Spanish *conquistadores* be especially blamed for the cruelties and deaths (including those by disease) inflicted on the original Indian populations of the Americas? Is it possible to make such criticisms without falling into the traditional English fallacies of the black legend?

2. What is the long-term significance for Latin America of the immortality achieved by the *conquistadores* through intermarriage with Indian women?

Suggested Student Exercises

*   Examine the careers of Hernán Cortés and Francisco Pizarro in both Spain and the New World, and assess the reasons for their success.

*   Examine some visual portrayals of the conquests of Mexico and Peru from the past and present, and compare how, over time, artists of various political outlooks have depicted the *conquistadores* and their victims.

CHAPTER 2

The Planting of English America, 1500–1733

AP FOCUS

- Territorial expansion and imperialism, whether formal or informal, is a continuing theme in American history and appears frequently on the AP exam.

- England sets out to establish a world empire. Its first permanent North American colony is Jamestown, Virginia. Others are established in Maryland, the Carolinas, and the West Indies.

- Indigenous North American crops, such as tobacco, are extremely important.

AP teachers should take note of the following:

1. Queen Elizabeth I stimulated exploration by granting buccaneers the right to attack Spanish shipping, thereby hurting Spain's colonies. This new spirit of exploration is captured by the English writer Richard Hakluyt (*The American Pageant*, 14th ed., p. 29/15th ed., p. 25).

2. The defeat of the Spanish Armada by England helped England in the race to establish an empire.

3. England's early attempts to colonize the New World were unsuccessful—the Roanoke colonists disappeared without a trace. The variety of English colonies can be seen in the table (14th ed., p. 39/15th ed. p. 34) in the text.

4. European colonization profoundly affected Indian culture and ways of life, more often than not, in negative ways. Indian tribes reacted violently to English attempts to colonize in the Chesapeake, as expressed in the Anglo-Powhatan wars.

5. For DBQ 2 (14th ed., pp. A67–A69/15th ed., pp. A65-A66), which deals with English-Indian relations in the seventeenth century, students must keep in mind the geographical restriction—the Atlantic seaboard. Students should be alert to the various facets of the relationship between the English and the Indians. Both had their own goals and pressures, which shaped how and how much their relationship changed.

Focus on Historical Thinking:

Have students keep a Main Idea Log. For each section in the text narrative, students will write the heading, read the section, and then express the author's main idea in one clear concise sentence.

FOCUS QUESTIONS

1. What international events and domestic changes prompted England to begin colonization?

2. What was it like for the early settlers of Jamestown?

3. Why were Native Americans unable to repel the English colonization of North America?

4. What crops were important to the English colonies in the south of North America? How did the cultivation of those crops shape those colonies?

5. How did the English sugar plantations of the Caribbean differ from the English colonies in the south of North America?

6.   How did slavery develop in North America during colonization?

7.   What features were shared by Virginia, Maryland, South Carolina, North Carolina, and Georgia? What distinguished them from one another?

CHAPTER THEMES

Theme: The English hoped to follow Spain's example of finding great wealth in the New World, and that influenced the financing and founding of the early southern colonies. The focus on making the southern colonies profitable shaped colonial decisions, including choice of crops and the use of indentured and slave labor. This same focus also helped create economic and cultural ties between the early southern colonies and English settlements in the West Indies.

Theme: The early southern colonies' encounters with Indians and African slaves established the patterns of race relations that would shape the North American experience—in particular, warfare and reservations for the Indians and lifelong slave codes for African Americans.

Theme: After a late start, a proud, nationalistic England joined the colonial race and successfully established five colonies along the southeastern seacoast of North America. Although varying somewhat in origins and character, all these colonies exhibited plantation agriculture, indentured and slave labor, a tendency toward strong economic and social hierarchies, and a pattern of widely scattered, institutionally weak settlements.

CHAPTER SUMMARY

The defeat of the Spanish Armada and the exuberant spirit of Elizabethan nationalism finally drew England into the colonial race. After some early failures, the first permanent English colony was established at Jamestown, Virginia. Initially it faced harsh conditions and Indian hostility, but tobacco cultivation finally brought prosperity and population growth. Its charter also guaranteed colonists the same rights as Englishmen and developed an early form of representative self-government.

The early encounters of English settlers with the Powhatans in Virginia established many of the patterns that characterized later Indian-white relations in North America. Indian societies underwent their own substantial changes as a result of warfare, disease, trade, and the mingling and migration of Indians from the Atlantic coast to inland areas.

Other colonies were established in Maryland and the Carolinas. South Carolina flourished by establishing close ties with the British sugar colonies in the West Indies. It also borrowed the West Indian pattern of harsh slave codes and large plantation agriculture. North Carolina developed somewhat differently, with fewer slaves and more white colonists who owned small farms. Latecomer Georgia served initially as a buffer against the Spanish and a haven for debtors.

Despite some differences, all the southern colonies depended on staple plantation agriculture for their survival and on the institutions of indentured servitude and enslaved Africans for their labor. With widely scattered rural settlements, they had relatively weak religious and social institutions and tended to develop hierarchical economic and social orders.

DEVELOPING THE CHAPTER: SUGGESTED LECTURE OR DISCUSSION TOPICS

- Examine the condition of England at the time of the nation's early colonization efforts. Focus especially on the rise of the Elizabethan monarchy and the spirit of the English renaissance (for example, Shakespeare or Sir Walter Raleigh) in London and other commercial centers, as well as the social upheaval in the countryside (enclosure). Show how these factors—as well as religious rivalry with Spain—lay behind the colonization effort.

REFERENCE: Carl Bridenbaugh, *Vexed and Troubled Englishmen, 1590–1642* (1968).

- Consider the traditional Indian cultures of the south Atlantic coastal regions, and examine the transformations they underwent in response to English colonization. Explain the particular changes that affected the Powhatans of Virginia in relation to the larger patterns of English-Indian encounters that shaped subsequent American history.

REFERENCE: Helen Rountree, *The Powhatans of Virginia: Their Traditional Culture* (1989).

- Examine the issue of race relations in the early southern colonies, showing how the early patterns established there set a course for subsequent American history. Focus particularly on the policies of driving out the Indians and of importing African slaves as a solution to the labor shortages in the New World.

REFERENCE: Timothy Silver, *A New Face on the Countryside: Indians, Colonists, and Slaves in South Atlantic Forests 1500–1800* (1990).

FOR FURTHER INTEREST: ADDITIONAL CLASS TOPICS

- Contrast the pattern of English colonization with that of Spain described in Chapter 1 (or perhaps, with that of France described in Chapter 6). Examine similarities and differences in motivation, population patterns, race relations, economic development, and the like.

- Compare the legends of early English colonization with the often harsh realities: for example, the tale of John Smith and Pocahontas with the actual patterns of relations between whites and Indians in Virginia. Consider why many early settlers tried to paint a rosier portrait of the colonies than their actual conditions warranted (to satisfy investors and lure new colonists).

- Contrast other English New World settlements, particularly in the West Indies, with those on the North American mainland. Note especially how in the West Indies, many white plantation owners became absentees who spent much of their time in England, whereas the North American colonies developed as more complete, autonomous societies. (South Carolina can be used as an example of a partially West Indian pattern in North America.)

CHARACTER SKETCHES

John Smith (1580–1631)

The adventures that are popularly identified with Captain John Smith—having his life saved by Pocahontas and Smith's own rescue of the infant Jamestown colony from ruin—were first recorded by Smith himself. Whether these events were invention or fact, one thing is certain: Smith lived an extraordinarily dramatic life.

According to Smith's autobiography, he left England at an early age to become a soldier of fortune. His many escapades included being enslaved, murdering his master, and being seduced by the wife of the pasha of Turkey. The trouble with these and other of Smith's tales is that their only source is Smith himself; in fact, historians have shown that some of his stories were made up. He was, however, a talented soldier and administrator, whose efforts in organizing the Jamestown colonists and in obtaining corn from the Indians clearly helped save the colony from starvation in the winter of 1608–1609.

Smith's writings, including *The Generall Historie of Virginia, New-England, and the Summer Isles* (1624), are fascinating, even if they are more fiction than history. Actually, most historians today believe that the core of his narrative is true, but that Smith simply embellished and altered particular events to increase their dramatic effect.

Quote: "Pocahontas, the King's most dear and well-beloved daughter, being but a childe of twelve or thirteen years of age, whose compassionate, pitiful heart, of my desperate estate, gave me much cause to respect her.... After some six weeks fatting amongst those savage courtiers, at the minute of my execution, she hazarded the beating out of her own brains to save mine; and not only that, but so prevailed with her father that I was safely conducted to Jamestown, where I found about eight and thirty miserable, poor and sick creatures.... Such was the weakness of this poor Commonwealth, as had the savages not fed us, we directly had starved." (1624)

REFERENCE: Philip Barbour, *The Three Worlds of Captain John Smith* (1964).

Pocahontas (1595–1617)

Although the story of Pocahontas's rescue of John Smith from death, at the hands of her father, the great chief Powhatan, may or may not be true (most likely not), it is certain that she played an important role in the Virginia colony's early years as a kind of ambassador between the English and the Powhatan Indians—a role that Powhatan himself likely arranged. The children of powerful chiefs frequently played such intermediary roles in eastern Indian cultures. It is also known that she visited Jamestown often, sometimes to negotiate prisoner releases.

Her formal tribal name was Matoaka, meaning playful. (Pocahontas ["frolicsome"] was a pet name.) In 1613 she was kidnapped by Captain Samuel Argall and taken to live with a clergyman, though it may be that she collaborated in this arrangement as well. Shortly after, she was instructed in Christianity and baptized. She married John Rolfe, the promoter of tobacco, in 1614.

Rolfe took her to England in 1616, where she was badly affected by the climate and urban environment of London. She was presented to King James I at court, but as she boarded ship to return to Virginia, she became ill and died. Many later writers and poets—including Stephen Vincent Benét—have celebrated her brief but romantic life.

REFERENCE: Peter Lampe, *Pocahontas* (1995).

John Rolfe (1585–1622)

Rolfe was born in the county of Norfolk, England. Unhappy with his economic prospects, he sailed for Virginia in 1609 with his first wife but was shipwrecked in Bermuda, where his wife died. Rolfe pushed on to Virginia and arrived the following year. In 1612, he began experimenting with a sweeter variety of tobacco from the West Indies. (The native leaf smoked by the Powhatans of Virginia was too bitter for English tastes.) Despite the strong hostility to smoking felt by many English authorities, including King James I, the new tobacco caught on quickly and saved the colony's economy.

In 1614, Rolfe's status as the promoter of tobacco persuaded Pocahontas's father and Virginia governor Thomas Dale to grant Rolfe permission to marry the Indian princess. Before her death in England, Pocahontas gave birth to a son, Thomas, who was raised by an uncle in England.

Rolfe returned to Virginia, married again, and served on the colony's Council of State. He was killed by Indians in the Second Anglo-Powhatan War (1622). In 1640, his son, Thomas, returned to Virginia, where his many descendants continued to live.

Quote: "Likewise, add hereunto her great appearance of love to me, her desire to be taught and instructed in the knowledge of God, her capableness of understanding, and her aptness and willingness to receive any good impression, besides her own incitements stirring me up." (Letter to Governor Thomas Dale, 1614, explaining reasons for wanting to marry Pocahontas)

REFERENCE: Philip Barbour, *Pocahontas and Her World* (1970).

QUESTIONS FOR CLASS DISCUSSION

1.   What did England and the English settlers really want from colonization? Did they want national glory, wealth, adventure, a solution to social tensions, and/or new sources of goods and trade? Did they get what they wanted?

2.   How did Spanish success in the New World influence the English colonial efforts? How did England's earlier experience in Ireland influence its colonial efforts in the New World? How did different events in England (and Europe) affect England's southern colonies in the New World?

3.   Were the English colonizers crueler or more tolerant than the Spanish *conquistadores*? Why did the Spanish tend to settle and intermarry with the Indian population, whereas the English killed the Indians, drove them out, or confined them to separate territories? How did this pattern of interaction affect both white and Indian societies?

4.   Was the development of enslaved Africans in the North American colonies inevitable? (Consider that it never developed in some other colonial areas, for example, Mexico and New France.) How would the North American colonies have been different without slavery? What role did the Spanish *encomienda* system and British sugar colonies play in introducing slavery to the southern colonies?

5.   How did the reliance on plantation agriculture affect the southern colonies? Were their societies relatively loose because they were primarily rural or because they tended to rely on forced labor systems?

MAKERS OF AMERICA: THE IROQUOIS

Questions for Class Discussion

1.   It is sometimes suggested that the Iroquois Confederacy may have provided a model for the union of states into the United States of America. What similarities and differences are there between the two confederations?

2.   What role did the Iroquois play in the politics and warfare of British North America? Was the decision of most Iroquois to side with the British in the Revolutionary War the most decisive moment in their history? Why or why not?

Suggested Student Exercises

- Use a map of upstate New York to locate the traditional Iroquois lands as well as present-day areas of settlement. Examine materials on the efforts of today's Iroquois to recover lands and obtain governmental recognition in both New York state and Canada.

- Look at the conflict between Britain and the American colonies from an Iroquois perspective. Ask students to consider how subsequent history might have been different had the British defeated the Americans in the Revolution.

CHAPTER 3

Settling the Northern Colonies, 1619–1700

AP FOCUS

- The Reformation has an impact on Europe and European settlement in North America.

- The Dutch Separatists (Pilgrims) depart Holland in the *Mayflower* and establish the Plymouth Colony (1620), where they lay the foundation for a government in the form of the Mayflower Compact. The colony merges with the Massachusetts Bay Colony in 1691.

- Religious discontent and divisions stimulate the creation of other colonies, such as the one established by "dissenters" in Rhode Island and William Penn's Quaker colony in Pennsylvania.

AP teachers should take note of the following:

1. The motives and incentives for colonization were varied; however, many early English colonists were inspired to resettle in North America for religious and economic reasons.

2. Religious dissent and challenges to the religious and political status quo emerged in the Massachusetts Bay Colony. For example, Anne Hutchinson challenged the rigidity of the Puritan leadership. Banished from the Bay Colony, she helped to establish a new colony in Rhode Island.

3. The Massachusetts Bay Colony was, in a very real sense, the nucleus for later colonies, especially in New England. See the map in *The American Pageant* (14th ed., p. 52/15th ed. p. 46).

4. By the mid-seventeenth century, the middle colonies of Delaware, New Jersey, New York, and Pennsylvania were established.

Focus on Historical Thinking:

Have students make a chart comparing and contrasting the difference between northern and southern colonies.

FOCUS QUESTIONS

1. What religious turmoil in the Old World resulted in the little colony of Plymouth in the New World?

2. Why was the initial and subsequent colonization of the Massachusetts Bay Colony more successful than Plymouth?

3. How did the colony of Plymouth and Massachusetts Bay Colony contribute to the origins of American independence and government? What were the contributions to American independence and government from the New England Confederation, the Dominion of New England, and the Glorious Revolution?

4. What role did religious intolerance play in the founding of New England colonies other than Plymouth and Massachusetts Bay and in the founding of some middle colonies?

5. Besides England, what other nations influenced the colonization of the Atlantic coast of North America?

6. How did the colonization of Pennsylvania differ from the New England colonies and other middle colonies?

CHAPTER THEMES

Theme: Religious and political turmoil in England shaped settlement in New England and the middle colonies. Religious persecution in England pushed the Separatists into Plymouth and Quakers into Pennsylvania. England's Glorious Revolution also prompted changes in the colonies.

Theme: The Protestant Reformation, in its English Calvinist (Reformed) version, provided the major impetus and leadership for the settlement of New England. The New England colonies developed a fairly homogeneous social order based on religion and semicommunal family and town settlements.

Theme: Principles of American government developed in New England with the beginnings of written constitutions (Mayflower Compact and Massachusetts's royal charter) and with glimpses of self-rule seen in town hall meetings, the New England Confederation, and colonial opposition to the Dominion of New England.

Theme: The middle colonies of New Netherland (New York), Pennsylvania, New Jersey, and Delaware developed with far greater political, ethnic, religious, and social diversity, and they represented a more cosmopolitan middle ground between the tightly knit New England towns and the scattered, hierarchical plantation in the South.

CHAPTER SUMMARY

The New England colonies were founded by English Puritans. While most Puritans sought to purify the Church of England from within, and not to break away from it, a small group of Separatists—the Pilgrims—founded the first small, pious Plymouth Colony in New England. More important was the larger group of nonseparating Puritans, led by John Winthrop, who founded the Massachusetts Bay Colony as part of the great migration of Puritans fleeing persecution in England in the 1630s.

A strong sense of common purpose among the first settlers shaped the Massachusetts Bay Colony. Because of the close alignment of religion and politics in the colony, those who challenged religious orthodoxy, among them Anne Hutchinson and Roger Williams, were considered guilty of sedition and driven out of Massachusetts. The banished Williams founded Rhode Island, by far, the most religiously and politically tolerant of the colonies. Other New England settlements, all originating in Massachusetts Bay, were established in Connecticut, Maine, and New Hampshire. Although they shared a common way of life, the New England colonies developed with a substantial degree of independence.

The middle colonies took shape quite differently. New York, founded as New Netherland by the Dutch and later conquered by England, was economically and ethnically diverse, socially hierarchical, and politically quarrelsome. Pennsylvania, founded as a Quaker haven by William Penn, also attracted an economically ambitious and politically troublesome population of diverse ethnic groups.

With their economic variety, ethnic diversity, and political factionalism, the middle colonies were the most typically American of England's thirteen Atlantic seaboard colonies.

DEVELOPING THE CHAPTER: SUGGESTED LECTURE OR DISCUSSION TOPICS

- Explain Puritanism in terms of the Puritan dilemma of trying to pursue high religious ideals, while somehow remaining practically effective and involved in the world. Emphasize how the Puritans believed that their "errand into the wilderness" in New England would enable them to build an idealistic "City upon a Hill" that would inspire a corrupt world.

  REFERENCE: Andrew Delbanco, *The Puritan Ordeal* (1989).

- Examine the relationship between Puritan theology, the ideas of government its educated leaders promoted, and the religious beliefs and experience of the more ordinary settlers of the Massachusetts Bay Colony. Consider the ways in which Puritanism created both strong communal ideals, while almost guaranteeing tensions and conflicts at the boundaries of church and society.

  REFERENCE: David Hall, *Worlds of Wonder, Days of Judgment: Popular Religious Beliefs in Early New England* (1989).

- Explore the development of religious, political, and social freedom in New England and the middle colonies. Examine the role that the fight against religious intolerance in New England played in the developing ideas of American religious liberty and the particular role that dissenters, like Quakers and Baptists, played in that development in New England, Pennsylvania, and Virginia.

  REFERENCES: Carla Gardina Pestana, *Quakers and Baptists in Colonial Massachusetts* (1991).

- Consider the relations of the New England settlers and their Puritan leadership to the Indians. Examine how they adjusted, or failed to adjust, their understanding of covenant and the communal role of town government to those on the frontier of settlement. Analyze episodes like King Philip's War and the Pequot War to discover what they revealed about the roles of insiders and outsiders in defining American identity and culture.

  REFERENCE: Jill Lepore, *The Name of War: King Philip's War and the Origin of American Identity* (1998).

- Examine the origins of ethnic and social diversity in America by focusing on the early middle colonies, especially New York and Pennsylvania. Contrast the ethnic and religious diversity of those two colonies with the Anglo-Saxon, Puritan character of New England and relate this to the more turbulent politics of the middle colonies. Consider how the middle colonies' ethnic variety laid the basis for later American immigration and ethnicity.

  REFERENCE: Michael Zuckerman, ed., *Friends and Neighbors: Group Life in America's First Plural Society* (1982).

FOR FURTHER INTEREST: ADDITIONAL CLASS TOPICS

- Focus on the Thanksgiving image of the Pilgrims and Puritans and compare it with the historical reality. Consider the enduring influence of the Puritans on America and the American self-image.

- Focus on Anne Hutchinson as a complex instance of religious, political, and perhaps gender-based dissent. Consider to what extent the hostility to her religious opinions might have been strengthened because she was a woman challenging the male religious and political establishment.

- Compare the colonizing effort of the Dutch in New Netherland with that of their English neighbors. Note particularly how Peter Stuyvesant's absolutist religious and political controls differed from the much looser quality of English colonialism.

- Consider William Penn and the Quakers as a case study in religious influence on colonial origins, and compare the Quakers with the New England Puritans. Examine the influence on Pennsylvania of particular Quaker belief—such as each individual's "inner light," social equality, and nonviolence—as well as how circumstances altered the implementation of such beliefs.

CHARACTER SKETCHES

John Winthrop (1588–1649)

John Winthrop was the leader of the great Puritan migration to Massachusetts Bay in 1630 and the dominant influence in the early colony. His personality and political policies reflected the complex nature of New England Puritanism: intense, high-minded, sober, driven, intellectual, intolerant.

A very well-off country gentleman and attorney, Winthrop began to experience career difficulties in England because of his strong Puritan leanings. He grew deeply pessimistic about the future, especially after the dismissal of Parliament in 1629, and joined as one of the twelve influential Puritans who organized the migration to the New World.

Winthrop was elected governor before sailing on the *Arbella* (1630) and reelected nearly every year until his death. Pious, humorless, and extremely stern toward dissenters, he skillfully managed the colony's affairs, successfully negotiating with Puritans and others in England—while putting Massachusetts Bay on a sound economic and political footing.

Quote: "The Lord will be our God and delight to dwell among us as his own people and will command a blessing upon us all in our ways.... And he shall make us a praise and glory, that men shall say of succeeding plantations: the Lord make it like that of New England. For we must consider that we shall be as a City upon a Hill; the eyes of all people are upon us." (Sermon aboard the *Arbella*, 1630)

REFERENCE: Lee Schweninger, *John Winthrop* (1990).

Anne Hutchinson (1591–1643)

Anne Hutchinson was the strong-minded religious dissenter whose challenge to Massachusetts Bay authorities from 1636 to 1638 shook the infant colony to its foundation and led to her banishment.

The second of thirteen children of a Puritan minister, from whom she received a strong education in theology and Scripture, she married William Hutchinson, a well-to-do merchant, and bore fourteen children between 1613 and 1636, of whom eleven survived infancy.

Hutchinson's twice-weekly meetings in her home to discuss sermons and Scripture won her an enthusiastic following throughout Massachusetts Bay, and for a time, it appeared that she and her clerical allies might take over the colony. But her enemies gained control of the General Court in 1637, and she was excommunicated from the church and banished from the colony, despite her clever defense. First, she went to Rhode Island, but after her husband died in 1642, she moved with her children to Pelham, New Netherland (now in the Bronx), where she and all but one of her children were killed by Indians in 1643.

Quote:

Court: "See how your argument stands. Priscilla, with her husband, took Apollo home to instruct him privately. Therefore Mistress Hutchinson, without her husband, may teach sixty or eighty."

Hutchinson: "I call them not, but if they come to me, I may instruct them."

Court: "Yet you show us not a rule."

Hutchinson: "I have given you two places of Scripture."

Court: "But neither of them will suit your practice."

Hutchinson: "Must I show you my name written therein?"

(Excerpt from Hutchinson's trial, 1637)

REFERENCE: Amy Schrager Lang, *Prophetic Woman: Anne Hutchinson and the Problem of Dissent in the Literature of New England* (1987).

William Penn (1644–1718)

Although this English Quaker, who founded Pennsylvania, engaged in frequent quarrels with the colony's settlers, his basic policies of liberality, tolerance, and free immigration had a lasting effect on Pennsylvania and eventually on other American colonies, as well.

In his youth, Penn developed nonconformist religious leanings that angered his father, the great Admiral Sir William Penn, and eventually landed the younger Penn in the Tower of London. Reconciled to his father on Sir William's deathbed, he obtained the charter for Pennsylvania because of debts owed to his father by King Charles II.

Although Pennsylvania was a great economic success, Penn benefited little from it. His friendship with King James II caused him to lose political influence after the Glorious Revolution and his dissolute son wasted much of his fortune, so that he ended up in debtor's prison.

Penn was considered handsome, courtly, and well read—a remarkable combination of religious visionary, charming courtier, and practical statesman. In the words of a contemporary: "a man of great abilities, of an excellent disposition, quick of thought and ready of utterance, full of true discipleship, even Love, without dissimulation."

Quote: "I am sorry at heart for your animosities. For the love of God, me, and the poor country, be not so governmentish, so noisy, and so open in your dissatisfactions." (Letter to settlers, 1701)

REFERENCE: Richard and Mary Dunn, eds., *The World of William Penn* (1986).

QUESTIONS FOR CLASS DISCUSSION

1. Did the Puritans really come to America seeking religious freedom? How did they reconcile their own religious dissent from the Church of England with their persecution of dissenters like Hutchinson and Williams? Does their outlook make them hypocrites?

2. How were government and religion—or church and state—related in New England and the middle colonies? How does the colonial view of these matters compare with more recent understandings?

3. Was an American Revolution, separating the colonies from England, inevitable after the Glorious Revolution had encouraged colonists to end the Dominion of New England, England's serious attempt at enforcing royal authority? Did England's "salutary neglect" contribute to future problems in its empire? How might have England been able to successfully enforce its rule on the colonies without causing rebellion?

4. Dutch colonization efforts in New Amsterdam most closely resembled English colonization efforts in which region: New England, the middle colonies, or the southern colonies? The Dutch had a powerful presence in the East Indies, so why were the Dutch less successful in the West Indies and North America? What is the lasting influence of the Dutch in English North America?

5. How does the founding of the New England colonies compare with the origin of the middle colonies? In what ways were New England and the middle colonies each like the South, and in what ways were they different?

6. In what ways were the middle colonies more open and diverse than New England? In what ways were they less democratic?

7. How did different events in England affect the New England and middle colonies in the New World? Which was the most affected and least affected by events in the Old World: New England, middle colonies, or southern colonies?

8. What were the push and pull factors for immigrants coming to each region of English colonies (New England, the middle colonies, and the southern colonies)?

EXPANDING THE "VARYING VIEWPOINTS"

*   Thomas J. Wertenbaker, *The Founding of American Civilization* (1938).

    A view of America as the product of European culture:

    "The most stupendous phenomenon of all history is the transit of European civilization to the two American continents. For four and a half centuries Europeans have been crossing the Atlantic to establish in a new world their blood, languages, religions, literatures, art, customs. This movement, involving many nations and millions of men and women, has been termed the expansion of a new Europe in America. The Indian civilizations have been overwhelmed or subordinated, and in their place have arisen great nations speaking English, Spanish, Portuguese, or French, whose peoples profess the Christian religion, are partly or entirely European in blood, accept Shakespeare or Cervantes or Molière or even Tolstoy as their own. … Historians have been too prone to neglect the factor of inheritance in interpreting the United States, especially the multiple inheritance which makes it the child, not of England, but of Europe."

*   Gary Nash, *Red, White, and Black: The People of Early America* (1974).

    A view of America as the product of the meeting of Indian, European, and African cultures:

    "The pathways of power did not strictly dictate the history of cultural interchange—a point that is obscured if we mistakenly assume that under conditions of oppression and exploitation, acculturation occurs in only one direction. The cultures of Africans and Indians—their agricultural techniques, modes of behavior, styles of speech, dress, food preference, music, dance, and other aspects of existence—became commingled with European culture.… A New World it is…for those who became its peoples remade it, and in the process they remade themselves, whether red, white, or black."

QUESTIONS ABOUT THE "VARYING VIEWPOINTS"

1. Does J.H. Elliot's work about the New World represent more of a Eurocentric discovery and conquest history or more of a contact and adaptation history?

2. How does Wertenbaker represent the older and now generally unaccepted view that American society is essentially an extension of European civilization?

3. How does Nash combine recognition of European exploitation with a belief that all the peoples of America created a genuinely new culture?

4. How is our view of subsequent American history altered if one adopts the diversity rather than the Europeanist perspective?

CHAPTER 4

American Life in the Seventeenth Century, 1607–1692

AP FOCUS

- Social-class conflict is a key element in the revisionist interpretation of American historical development. Always under the surface of colonial societies, it erupts into full-scale civil war with Bacon's Rebellion, in Virginia. American Diversity, which takes up class, is an AP theme.

- The introduction of slavery into the New World transforms the social, economic, and political makeup of the colonies. (Slavery and Its Legacies in North America is an AP theme.) The primary source of African slaves is west-central Africa (see the map in *The American Pageant,* 14th ed., p. 73/15th ed., p. 65).

- Religious hysteria, in the form of witch trials, plague the North American colonies, especially in the New England settlements. Religion is yet another AP theme.

- European class-based customs, such as the wearing of fancy jewelry by certain segments of society, do not find fertile ground in the more democratic New World English colonies.

AP teachers should take note of the following:

1. Although initially an area where settlements barely survived, the Chesapeake colony region soon spawned a powerful industry: cultivating and selling tobacco. So important was this crop that it helped maintain the economy of the region and, because of its tendency to exhaust the soil, led to westward penetration of the Chesapeake colonies.

2. The social life and customs of the North American colonists were considerably shaped and affected by where they lived. Unique cultural traits took root in the New England, middle, and southern colonies. Despite the presence of slavery in the colonies, white settlers were not so quick to nurture the type of social stratification that prevailed in Europe.

Focus on Historical Thinking:

Pick three primary source documents from the time period and have students express the main idea of each in one clear concise sentence.

FOCUS QUESTIONS

1. How did the climate in the southern colonies influence life expectancy, family life, immigration, and economic development?

2. What role did Bacon's Rebellion play in the adoption and expansion of slavery in the southern colonies?

3. What contributions did enslaved Africans provide the colonies?

4. How was life expectancy, family life, immigration, and economic development different in New England as compared with the southern colonies?

5.   What are the differences in the legal standing of women in southern colonies and New England colonies?

6.   In what ways were all American colonists similar?

CHAPTER THEMES

Theme: In the Chesapeake region, seventeenth-century colonial society was characterized by disease-shortened lives, weak family life, and a social hierarchy that included hardworking planters at the top and restless poor whites and enslaved Africans at the bottom. Despite the substantial disruption of their traditional culture and the mingling of African peoples, slaves in the Chesapeake developed a culture that mixed African and new-world elements, and developed one of the few slave societies that grew through natural reproduction.

Theme: By contrast, early New England life was characterized by healthy, extended life spans, strong family life, closely knit towns and churches, and a demanding economic and moral environment.

CHAPTER SUMMARY

Life was hard in the seventeenth-century southern colonies. Disease drastically shortened life spans in the Chesapeake region, even for the young single men who made up the majority of settlers. Families were few and fragile, with men greatly outnumbering women, who were much in demand and seldom remained single for long.

The tobacco economy first thrived on the labor of white indentured servants, who hoped to work their way up to become landowners and perhaps even become wealthy. But by the late seventeenth century, this hope was increasingly frustrated and the discontents of the poor whites exploded in Bacon's Rebellion.

With white labor increasingly troublesome, slaves (earlier a small fraction of the workforce) began to be imported from West Africa by the tens of thousands in the 1680s and soon became essential to the colonial economy. Slaves in the Deep South died rapidly of disease and overwork, but those in the Chesapeake tobacco region survived longer. Their numbers eventually increased by natural reproduction and they developed a distinctive African American way of life that combined African elements with features developed in the New World.

By contrast with the South, New England's clean water and cool air contributed to a healthy way of life, which added ten years to the average English life span. The New England way of life centered on strong families and tightly knit towns and churches, which were relatively democratic and equal by seventeenth-century standards. By the late seventeenth century, however, social and religious tensions developed in these narrow communities, as the Salem witch hysteria dramatically illustrates.

Rocky soil forced many New Englanders to turn to fishing and merchant shipping for their livelihoods. Their difficult lives and stern religion made New Englanders tough, idealistic, purposeful, and resourceful. In later years they spread these same values across much of American society.

Seventeenth-century American society was still almost entirely simple and agrarian. Would-be aristocrats who tried to recreate the social hierarchies of Europe were generally frustrated.

DEVELOPING THE CHAPTER: SUGGESTED LECTURE OR DISCUSSION TOPICS

- Explain the search for a suitable labor supply in the plantation colonies, contrasting the relative advantages and disadvantages of white indentured servants and slaves (from the planters' point of view). Perhaps use Bacon's Rebellion as the clearest illustration of why planters feared uncontrolled laborers and turned increasingly to slavery.

REFERENCE: Edmund Morgan, *American Slavery, American Freedom* (1975).

- Explore the origins of American race relations by examining the closely linked development of slavery and racial prejudice in the seventeenth century. The emphasis might be on how slavery, once established, tended to reinforce prejudice, while prejudice justified slavery.

    REFERENCE: Winthrop Jordan, *White over Black* (1968).

- Provide a portrait of a typical New England town, focusing on the close connection between town and church and on family life, particularly the role of women and the relation of farming and trade in the region. Several towns have been studied in detail and the various social roles of men and women can be traced over time.

    REFERENCE: Stephen Innes, *Creating the Commonwealth: The Economic Culture of Puritan New England* (1995).

- Explore the Salem witch trials in more depth. The rich literature on the trials can be used to illuminate seventeenth-century New England history from numerous perspectives: town life, religion, the beliefs and actions of common people, generational conflict, and so on. Perhaps the most interesting is the light it sheds on the condition of women—both ordinary women and the extraordinary witches—and on gender relations and ideas in seventeenth-century America.

    REFERENCE: Carol F. Karlsen, *The Devil in the Shape of a Woman: Witchcraft in Colonial New England* (1987).

FOR FURTHER INTEREST: ADDITIONAL CLASS TOPICS

- Focus on the nature of colonial family life, particularly as it was affected by different demographic patterns (for example, frequent childbearing, frequent remarriage, and strong competition for women). A particular focus might be on attitudes toward children in an age of large families and infant deaths.

- Focus on the slave trade from Africa, considering how it affected those Africans who were caught in it as well as their descendants. A particular question might be that of the survival of African cultural elements among the slaves.

- Examine what happened to Africans that were imported as slaves to New World locations such as Brazil, Spanish America, the British Caribbean, and the French Caribbean. Compare that with what happened to Africans imported as slaves to England's Chesapeake and southern colonies in North America.

- Discuss women's lives in the seventeenth century, including economic functions, religion, marriage, and child raising. The focus might be on the economic and social importance of women in agrarian colonial communities, as well as on the legal and political restrictions that kept them tied to men.

- Explore the values of the traditional New Englander as both morally rigid Puritan and hard-bargaining Yankee. Examine the expansion of New England in the spread of settlements west. (Places like northern Ohio, Kansas, Oregon, and later Hawaii had a high proportion of New Englanders in their populations.)

- Review the scientific achievements that were going on in seventeenth-century Europe while the colonies were developing in North America. (Galileo, Kepler, Descartes, Pascal, Huygens, Boyle, and Newton)

CHARACTER SKETCHES

Nathaniel Bacon (1647–1676)

Although his followers were mostly poor, landless white farmers who hated the planter aristocrats, rebel leader Nathaniel Bacon was a well-off planter.

Bacon, descended from a famous English family, immigrated to Virginia in 1674 after obtaining a gentlemanly education at Cambridge University and the Inns of Court in London. After the initial phase of his rebellion, which consisted of leading unauthorized attacks on Indians, he was arrested by Governor Berkeley but then pardoned and even appointed to the colonial council in an attempt to appease him. But he and his supporters refused to be conciliated, and when Berkeley tried to suppress them, they went on a rampage that ended in the burning of Jamestown. Bacon seemed on the verge of seizing complete control of the colony when he suddenly died of illness—a development that enabled Berkeley to crush the leaderless rebels.

Quote: "For having upon specious pretences of publick works raised great unjust taxes upon the commonality for the advancement of private favorites and other sinister ends…for having wronged his Majesty's prerogative and interesting by assuming monopoly of the beaver trade…and for having protected, favored, and imboldened the Indian's against his Majesty's loyall subjects…we do demand that the said Sir William Berkeley…be forthwith delivered up or surrender [himself] within four days of this notice forthwith." (Declaration of the People, 1676)

REFERENCE: Wilcomb E. Washburn, *The Governor and the Rebel* (1957).

Cotton Mather (1662–1728)

Cotton Mather's notorious involvement in the Salem witch trials was only one episode in his long, remarkable career, but it showed many of the contradictions of his complex personality.

The influential Puritan minister's role in the Salem witch trials arose partly because of his strong scientific interest in spirits and the invisible world. Even before the trials, he took into his home a girl believed to be a victim of witchcraft so that he could study her case in detail. By seventeenth-century standards Mather was actually quite cautious about witchcraft. He believed that where witchcraft existed, it should be treated by prayer and fasting, not by prosecutions and executions. But once the Salem trials got under way, he defended them in public, despite his apparent private belief that the evidence was questionable and the executions unjust.

Mather was hot-tempered, arrogant, and power-hungry but also extremely introspective and given to anxiety and self-doubt. Although he sometimes experienced hallucinations and severe depressions, and engaged in harsh attacks on his enemies, some of his writings are brilliant.

Quote: "Albeit the business of this witchcraft may be very much transacted upon the stage of imagination, yet we know that, as in treason, there is an imagining which is a capital crime, and here also the business, though managed in imagination, yet may not be called imaginary. The effects are dreadfully real…. Our neighbors at Salem Village are blown up, after a sort, with an infernal gunpowder; the train is laid in the laws of the kingdom of darkness…. Now the question is, who gives fire to this train? And by what acts is the match applied?" (1692)

REFERENCE: Kenneth Silverman, *The Life and Times of Cotton Mather* (1984).

Rachel Clinton (1629–1694)

Clinton is one of the few Salem witches whose biography historians have been able to reconstruct. Her childhood was extremely unhappy as, evidently, was the rest of her life. After both her parents died when she was very young, she was placed under the control of her mentally unstable stepmother. Her father had left a substantial estate, but Clinton was never able to get a fair share of it because she was constantly exploited by others, including Thomas Clinton, her brother-in-law, whom she married at age thirty-six (he was twenty-two at the time). After her divorce from Thomas Clinton, she was reduced to poverty and dependency, which likely made her extremely bitter and hostile. It is known that she threw stones at people and called them names like "hellhound" and "whoremasterly rogue." Among the witchcraft activities she was accused of, even before the Salem trials, were taking away a girl's power of speech for three hours, sending animals to cross people's paths, and making beer disappear from kegs.

Although convicted in the Salem trials and imprisoned for several months, Clinton was not executed. Released from prison in 1693, she died the following year.

REFERENCE: John Demos, *Entertaining Satan* (1982).

QUESTIONS FOR CLASS DISCUSSION

1.   Why was family life in New England so different from family life in the South?

2.   Why did slavery grow to be such an important institution in colonial America? What were the effects of slavery on the Africans who were brought to the New World? What were the effects of the Africans on the New World?

3.   What was attractive and unattractive about the closely knit New England way of life?

4.   Were the Salem witch trials a peculiar, aberrant moment in an age of superstition, or did they reflect common human psychological and social anxieties that could appear in any age? How harshly should those who prosecuted the witches be condemned?

5.   Considering the extreme differences during the seventeenth century between New England and the southern colonies, was the Civil War inevitable?

MAKERS OF AMERICA: FROM AFRICAN TO AFRICAN AMERICAN

Questions for Class Discussion

1.   How did African Americans work to adapt their native traditions under the conditions of New World slavery? What kinds of traditions were most successfully preserved?

2.   What enabled African Americans in the Chesapeake region to develop societies where—unusually for the history of slavery—the population reproduced and grew through natural increase? What does this suggest about the nature of families under slavery? How might these circumstances have affected the relationship between slaves and slaveholders?

Suggested Student Exercises

•   Use photographs of art objects or other materials from one of the particular cultures or regions of Africa, from which a substantial number of slaves came to America (e.g., the Guinea Coast, Benin, Ivory Coast, or Angola), and have students consider characteristics that may have passed into African American culture.

•   Examine some of the areas along the Atlantic coast where economic and social conditions, including the density of slave populations, made for a more extensive survival of African elements within African American cultures. (The most famous and well-studied is the Gullah culture on the Georgia and South Carolina sea islands.)

CHAPTER 5

Colonial Society on the Eve of Revolution, 1700–1775

AP FOCUS

- British crown policies subordinated American capital to British capital.

- Eighteenth-century America is a melting pot of races, cultures, religions, and ethnicities—see the quote by Crèvecoeur in *The American Pageant* (14th ed., p. 90/15th ed., p. 80). Western and central Europeans dominate the early American colonies (see the map showing immigrant groups in 1775 (14th ed., p. 89/15th ed., p. 79)).

- One half of the American people, by the late eighteenth century, are English or of English descent. See the textbook for a graph showing an expanded breakdown (14th ed., p. 90/15th ed., p. 80).

- In the eighteenth century, the triangle trade (for a map, see the 14th ed., p. 95/15th ed., p. 84) is essential to trade and commerce in the colonies. Slavery and Its Legacies in North America is an AP theme.

- Challenges to the institutions and ideologies that dominated Europe and early colonial America emerge. The First Great Awakening leads to the development of American centers of higher learning. That and political and judicial developments and the advent of the American press play a pivotal role in establishing a uniquely American character—American Identity is an AP theme.

AP teachers should take note of the following:

1. The American colonies were a magnet for social, political, ethnic, and religious groups. For example, the Scots-Irish were instrumental in developing a more democratic society than they had experienced under the political disfranchisement and economic exploitation by the British.

2. Despite claims that the American colonies were more democratic and less socially stratified than Europe, a social class structure had indeed taken hold in America. Slavery had a significant impact on the level of colonial democracy, as did the increasing numbers of indentured servants and lower-class immigrants to America.

Focus on Historical Thinking:

Give students twenty major pieces of specific factual information from Chapters 1-5 (i.e. "starving time," Mayflower Compact, indentured servants, etc.). In one clear concise sentence have students both identify the term AND give its historical significance (Example – "The indentured servant system, which allowed people free passage to America in return for a set term of service, failed to adequately meet the colonial labor need, leading to the institutionalization of slavery.").

FOCUS QUESTIONS

1. How did the population growth in the eventually rebellious colonies compare with England's?

2. What ethnicities contributed to the mosaic of the thirteen colonies?

3.   How did eighteenth-century America's social hierarchy compare with seventeenth-century America's social hierarchy? How did both compare with the Old World's?

4.   What was the leading industry in eighteenth-century America? What other industries were important?

5.   How did the Great Awakening influence religion in America?

6.   Who are some of America's noteworthy artists and writers from the eighteenth century?

7.   How were the colonial governments similar and different, and how influential was England in colonial governance?

CHAPTER THEMES

Theme: Compared with its seventeenth-century counterpart, eighteenth-century colonial society became more complex and hierarchical, more ethnically and religiously diverse, and more economically and politically developed.

Theme: Colonial culture, while still limited, took on distinct American qualities in such areas as evangelical religion, education, press freedom, and self-government.

Theme: England's Atlantic sea-board colonies, with their population growth and substantial agricultural exports, grew and developed in importance to the English Empire. Thus, the relationship between England and these colonies was shifting economically, politically, and culturally. Colonists sold their agricultural abundance not only to England, but also to France and the West Indies. Royal authority was checked by colonial legislatures that sometimes refused to pay governors' salaries and the famous Zenger case. Schools and colleges emerged, and the cultural reliance on England began to fade.

CHAPTER SUMMARY

By 1775, the thirteen American colonies east of the Appalachians were inhabited by a burgeoning population of two million whites and half a million blacks. The white population was increasingly a melting pot of diverse ethnic groups, including Germans and the Scots-Irish.

Compared with Europe, America was a land of equality and opportunity (for whites), but relative to the seventeenth-century colonies, there was a rising economic hierarchy and increasing social complexity. Ninety percent of Americans remained agriculturalists. But a growing class of wealthy planters and merchants appeared at the top of the social pyramid, in contrast with slaves and "jayle birds" from England, who formed a visible lower class.

By the early eighteenth century, the established New England Congregational Church was losing religious fervor. The Great Awakening, sparked by fiery preachers such as Jonathan Edwards and George Whitefield, spread a new style of emotional worship that revived religious zeal. Colonial education and culture were generally undistinguished, although science and journalism displayed some vigor. Politics was everywhere an important activity, as representative colonial assemblies battled on equal terms with politically appointed governors from England.

DEVELOPING THE CHAPTER: SUGGESTED LECTURE OR DISCUSSION TOPICS

•   Expand on the economic activities and relationships of the different parts of the colonial social pyramid discussed in the text. Explain especially the trend toward greater hierarchy, with a wealthy elite on the top and "jayle birds" and others on the bottom. The focus might be on the concern this tendency would have aroused among the middle class of colonists.

REFERENCE: John J. McCusker and Russell R. Menard, *The Economy of British America, 1607–1789* (1991).

- Show how the Great Awakening marked a key transition from the lukewarm style of religion fostered by established (tax-supported) colonial churches to the strong commitment required by the voluntary (member-supported) churches that later became the American norm. The focus might be on how a religious revival like the Great Awakening could arouse marked fervor among some colonists, while also causing opposition among those who distrusted emotional religion. Consider the arguments regarding the role that evangelical Protestantism played in promoting the American Revolution. Consider the contentions of some historians like Jon Butler that the Great Awakening did not have the extensive influence usually attributed to it.

REFERENCES: Ronald Hoffman and Peter J. Albert, eds., *Religion in a Revolutionary Age* (1994); Jon Butler, *Awash in a Sea of Faith: Christianizing the American People* (1990).

- Examine the ordinary social lives of colonial Americans. Consider the relationship between the way average people lived in the eighteenth century and the kinds of public concerns they had in the areas of politics, religion, economics, and culture.

REFERENCES: Stephanie G. Wolf, *As Various as Their Land: Everyday Lives of 18th Century Americans* (1994); Bruce Daniels, *Puritans at Play: Leisure and Recreation in Colonial New England* (1995).

- Explain, more fully, the evolution of colonial politics and why politics was especially important to colonists jealously trying to control their own affairs. The emphasis might be on the development of a distinctively American type of opposition politics, which was anxious to preserve local liberties and fearful of centralized or corrupt governmental power—such as the royal governors represented.

REFERENCE: Bernard Bailyn, *The Origins of American Politics* (1967).

FOR FURTHER INTEREST: ADDITIONAL CLASS TOPICS

- Compare the social structure and social life of the eighteenth century with that of the seventeenth century, as described in Chapter 4. Discuss what factors caused the transition toward greater social diversity and complexity and whether the development was an inevitable result of population growth and expansion.

- Focus on the issue of racial, ethnic, and religious diversity in the colonies. The discussion might emphasize the question of how diverse the colonies really were, since the ethnic groups were all northern European—except for blacks—and the religious groups almost all Protestant.

- Select a particular colonial occupation and consider how the activities of those who performed it might differ from those of later, twentieth-century practitioners. Among the occupations that could be discussed in this way: farmer, merchant, lawyer, minister, printer, schoolteacher, and doctor. Benjamin Franklin as printer might form a good focus, with further emphasis on how he combined this role with so many others, such as scientist, politician, and diplomat.

- Use the example of Jonathan Edwards as preacher, pastor, theologian, and educator in order to explain the motivations and impact of the Great Awakening. A sermon such as "Sinners in the Hands of an Angry God" (which some students know from literature classes) might be compared with some of Edwards's other writings.

- Examine the other British colonies in the eighteenth century (Canada, the Floridas, various Caribbean islands). In what ways were they similar and different than the thirteen Atlantic seaboard colonies? What clues does this provide about why only the thirteen sought independence?

- Review the scientific achievements that were going on in eighteenth-century Europe while the colonies were developing in North America (Halley, Fahrenheit, James Bradley, Celsius, Watt). How does Benjamin Franklin compare with his European counterparts?

- Review the literary and musical achievements that were going on in eighteenth-century Europe while the colonies were developing in North America (Bach, Handel, Pope, Vivaldi, Defoe, Voltaire, Johnson, Fielding, Haydn, Mozart).

CHARACTER SKETCHES

Jonathan Edwards (1703–1758)

Edwards was the great preacher, revivalist, theologian, and philosopher of eighteenth-century New England. Even as a child he showed personal piety and intellectual brilliance: at age seven he began leading other children into the woods for prayer, and by age fourteen, he was reading John Locke and Isaac Newton.

Despite his later learned writings on subjects like the nature of the mind and its relation to the natural world, he remained a parish pastor in Northampton, Massachusetts. In 1734, his intense preaching, first considered old-fashioned, began producing emotional conversions that soon numbered thirty a week. His fame spread throughout the colonies. By 1741, he became concerned about the excesses of the Great Awakening, especially as conducted by uneducated revivalists, but he still defended it strongly.

Tall, slender, with piercing eyes and a soft but perfectly modulated voice, Edwards rose daily at 4:00 A.M. and devoted thirteen hours to study. His later years were absorbed by controversies with parishioners who objected to his strong moral demands on them. In 1750, a majority voted to dismiss him, and he was left jobless and in debt. In 1757, he was appointed president of Princeton University but died of a smallpox inoculation before taking office.

Quote: "All will allow that true virtue or holiness has its seat chiefly in the heart, rather than in the head: it therefore follows….that it consists chiefly in holy affections….Now if such things are enthusiasm, and the fruits of a distempered brain, let my brain be evermore possessed of that happy distemper! If this be distraction, I pray God that the world of mankind may be all seized with this benign, meek, beneficent, beatifical, glorious distraction!" (1742)

REFERENCE: J.E. Smith, *Jonathan Edwards: Puritan, Preacher, Philosopher* (1992).

Benjamin Franklin (1706–1790)

Franklin, the most famous American of the eighteenth century and a great cultural hero in Europe as well as in his own country, was born to a Boston soapmaker. In 1718, he became a printer's apprentice under his brother James. At age seventeen, he moved to Philadelphia, which became his permanent home.

Once Franklin had made a substantial fortune from *Poor Richard's Almanack* and other publishing business ventures, he concentrated on science, philosophy, and politics. Although largely self-taught (he learned five languages on his own), he was immensely knowledgeable in many areas. Besides electricity, he studied meteorology, hydrology (water), geology, and demographics (population).

While serving as a colonial agent in England in the 1760s, he considered permanently moving to that country, and in America, he was suspected of favoring the Stamp Act until he testified against it in Parliament. When he served as minister to France during the Revolution, his portrait was put in shop windows and on medals, rings, watches, snuffboxes, and bracelets. His charm and simple democratic manners endeared him to everyone, especially aristocratic French ladies. Practical, skeptical, coolminded, insatiably curious, sexually passionate, uninhibited, plainspoken, and above all humorous, Franklin was at ease with all kinds and levels of people, from kings to tavern maids.

Quote: "It was wise counsel given to a young man, 'Pitch upon that course of life which is most excellent, and custom will make it the most delightful.' But many pitch on no course of life at all, nor form any scheme of living, by which to attain any valuable end; but wander perpetually from one thing to another." (From *Poor Richard,* 1749)

REFERENCE: H.W. Brands, *The First American: The Life and Times of Benjamin Franklin* (2000).

Charles W. Peale (1741–1827)

Peale was one of the best-known American painters of the eighteenth century and one of the few to make his career in the United States rather than Europe. Originally apprenticed as a saddler, he was forced out of that trade because he joined the Sons of Liberty and most of his customers were Loyalists. He then became interested in art and studied under John Singleton Copley in Boston and Benjamin West in London. Besides art, he was a prominent museum curator, essayist, civic leader, silversmith, and landscape gardener. Because of his diverse talents, he was sometimes called "the American Leonardo da Vinci."

Serving as an army captain during the Revolution, he executed numerous portraits of his fellow officers. He painted Washington from life seven times and made more than fifty other portraits of him as general and president. He usually portrayed Washington more realistically and less heroically than other painters, showing his high cheekbones, sloping shoulders, and long arms and legs. Yet his portraits were very popular with Washington and others.

Quote: "A good painter of either portrait or history must be well acquainted with the Grecian or Roman statues, to be able to draw them at pleasure by memory. … these are more than I shall ever have time or opportunity to know." (1772)

REFERENCE: Charles Coleman Sellers, *Charles Willson Peale* (1969).

Phillis Wheatley (c. 1753–1784)

Wheatley, the gifted black poet who published admired verse in late-eighteenth-century America and England, was brought as a slave from Africa to Boston in 1761, when she was about eight years old, and bought by John Wheatley, a tailor. She was made Mrs. Wheatley's personal servant but quickly impressed her master with her remarkable intelligence, which he cultivated.

She began writing poems at age thirteen; the first is called "On Being Brought from Africa to America." Her first published poem (on George Whitefield's death) was composed at age seventeen, and she soon gained renown in Boston and then elsewhere. Her master's daughter took her to England in 1773, where she was introduced to many literary people.

Four years after her return to America in 1774, she contracted a disastrous marriage to John Peters, a black baker. He apparently treated her badly, and she wrote no more poems. She bore three children, two of whom died before her own death in 1784.

Quote: "On Being Brought from Africa to America"

"'Twas mercy brought me from my pagan land

Taught my benighted soul to understand

That there's a God, that there's a savior, too;

Once I redemption neither sought nor knew.

Some view our sable race with scornful eye,

'Their color is a diabolic lie.'

Remember, Christians, Negroes black as Cain

May be refined and join the angelic train."

(1766)

REFERENCE: Julian D. Mason Jr., *The Poems of Phillis Wheatley* (1966).

QUESTIONS FOR CLASS DISCUSSION

1.   How democratic was colonial American society? Why was it apparently becoming less equal?

2.   How were the various occupations and activities of colonial America related to the nature of the economy? Why were such occupations as lawyer, printer, and artisan taking on greater importance?

3.   What were the causes and effects of the Great Awakening? How did such an intense religious revival affect those who experienced conversion as well as those who did not? How did the Awakening help to create a sense of shared American identity?

4.   In what ways was colonial life attractive, and in what ways would it seem tedious and dull to the average twenty-first-century American? How were the educational, cultural, and leisured sides of colonial life affected by the basic nature of the economy?

5.   To what degree was a unique American nationality developing in the eighteenth-century colonies? Were regional differences in the colonies growing more pronounced or retreating in the eighteenth century?

6.   What shaped how ordinary colonists thought? What were important sources of influence on an ordinary colonist? Did England control these sources or did the colonists? What implications did this have for the future England and the colonies?

EXPANDING THE "VARYING VIEWPOINTS"

•   Richard Bushman, *From Puritan to Yankee* (1967).

A view of eighteenth-century society as becoming more open and democratic:

"The law and authority embodied in governing institutions gave way under the impact first of economic ambitions and later of the religious impulses of the Great Awakening…. As, in the expanding eighteenth century, merchants and farmers felt free to pursue wealth with an avidity dangerously close to avarice, the energies released exerted irresistible pressures against traditional bounds. When the Great Awakening added its measure of opposition, the old institutions began to crumble."

•   Gary Nash, *The Urban Crucible* (1979).

A view of eighteenth-century society as becoming more closed and undemocratic:

"What has led early American historians to avoid questions about class formation and the development of lower-class political consciousness is not only an aversion to Marxist conceptualizations of history but also the myth that class relations did not matter in early America because there were no classes…. By the end of the Seven Years' War, poverty on a scale that urban leaders found appalling had appeared in New York and Philadelphia. Many urban Americans, living amidst historical forces that were transforming the social landscape, came to perceive antagonistic divisions based on economic and social position; … they began to struggle around these conflicting interests; and through these struggles they developed a consciousness of class."

QUESTIONS ABOUT THE "VARYING VIEWPOINTS"

1.   Where do both viewpoints agree concerning eighteenth-century society and where do they disagree?

2.   What might each of these historians see as the social background of the American Revolution?

3.   Are these viewpoints primarily focused on society in the middle and northern colonies? How would these perspectives appear if slavery is included in the equation? Does Edmund Morgan's belief that slavery actually promoted equality and solidarity among whites offer a serious challenge to these views of colonial America?

CHAPTER 6

The Duel for North America, 1608–1763

AP FOCUS

- Competition among France, Spain, and Great Britain for North American colonies shape North American affairs. Affairs in Europe affect the North American colonies—see *The American Pageant* (14th ed., p. 114/15th ed., p. 103) for a list of the wars that, except for the Seven Years' War (called the French and Indian War in America), spread from Europe to the New World.

- France's defeat in the Seven Years' War results in the collapse of its North American empire. A military and political victory for Britain and its American colonists, the war exposes and aggravates long-standing tensions between the mother country and its colonies and between colonists and Indians.

AP teachers should take note of the following:

1. Britain, Spain, and France all vied for control of the territories west of the Appalachian Mountains. It was not until the French defeat in the Seven Years' War that Britain was able to lay claim to much of this territory. The French and their Indian allies were not so quick to abandon their forts and trading posts, however. The sites of these posts are shown on a map in the textbook (14th ed., p. 111/15th ed., p. 100).

2. American colonists participated in the war, led by such luminaries as George Washington and Benjamin Franklin. Franklin's plan for the Albany Congress laid the foundation for future colonial cooperation when tensions between Britain and its American colonies erupted into a full-scale war. Note that there was not widespread colonial support for the war with France.

Focus on Historical Thinking:

Have students draw a significant conclusion in one clear, concise sentence from Map 6.7 on page 108 (15th ed.).

FOCUS QUESTIONS

1. Where did France colonize in the New World? What was the focus of French colonization?

2. What region in the North America did both France and Britain view as critical to their colonial empires?

3. What nations were the principal adversaries in the Seven Years' War in Europe?

4. How did the Albany Congress portend the American Revolution?

5. What were the significant military engagements in North America of the Seven Years' War and what was the outcome of each?

6. In what ways did British policy during and after the Seven Years' War upset and unite the colonies?

CHAPTER THEMES

Theme: As part of their worldwide rivalry, Great Britain and France engaged in a great struggle for colonial control of North America, culminating in the British victory in the Seven Years' War (French and Indian War) that drove France from the continent.

Theme: Before the Seven Years' War, Britain and its American colonies had already been facing some tensions, as can be seen in sporadic British efforts to enforce trade laws and colonial reaction to the peace treaty in 1748. During the Seven Years' War, the relationship between British military regulars and colonial militias added to the tensions. The French defeat in the Seven Years' War created conditions for a growing conflict between Britain and its American colonies. The lack of a threatening European colonial power in North America gave the American colonists a sense of independence that clashed with new British imperial demands, such as stationing soldiers in the colonies and the Proclamation of 1763.

CHAPTER SUMMARY

Like Britain, France entered late into the American colonial scramble, eventually developing an extensive though thinly settled empire economically based on the fur trade. During much of the seventeenth and eighteenth centuries, Britain and France engaged in a bitter power struggle that frequently erupted into worldwide wars. In North America, these wars constituted an extended military duel for imperial control of the continent.

The culminating phase of this struggle was inaugurated by young George Washington's venture into the sharply contested Ohio country. After early reversals in the Seven Years' War (French and Indian War), the British, under William Pitt, revived their fortunes and won a decisive victory at Quebec, finally forcing the French from North America.

The American colonials, who had played a large part in Britain's imperial wars with France, emerged with increased confidence in their own abilities. The removal of the French and Spanish threat to British control of North America kindled increasing tensions between the colonists and Britain. The Ottawa chief Pontiac's unsuccessful uprising in 1763 convinced the British of the need to continue stationing troops in America. But with foreign threats gone, the colonists were unwilling to pay taxes for British protection and increasingly resented Britain's authority over them.

DEVELOPING THE CHAPTER: SUGGESTED LECTURE OR DISCUSSION TOPICS

- Compare the French Empire in America with those of Britain and Spain. The emphasis of the comparison might be on showing that France's Empire was like Spain's in having close relations with the Indians, like Britain's in developing settler colonization, but different from both in focusing on trade and missions rather than on precious metals or agriculture.

   REFERENCE: W.J. Eccles, *France in America* (1972).

- Explain how and why the British won the French and Indian War. The focus might be on the reasons for the early French successes (particularly the alliance with the Indians), as well as the reasons for the eventual British triumph (superior numbers, resources, leadership, and strategy—especially in the Battle of Quebec).

   REFERENCE: Francis Jennings, *Empire of Fortune: Crowns, Colonies, and Tribes in the Seven Years War in America* (1988).

- Examine the French and Indian War, and the other colonial struggles, from the perspective and the historical situation of the Indians. Consider how they viewed the struggles between European powers, and how they tried to make tensions between settlers and colonial governments work to their advantage.

REFERENCE: Richard White, *The Middle Ground: Indians, Empires, and Republics in the Great Lakes Region, 1650–1815* (1991).

- Develop, in more depth, the chapter's key paradox: that Britain's victory over France—which the British colonists officially supported—actually created new sources of tension between Americans and the mother country.

REFERENCE: Alan Rogers, *Empire and Liberty: American Resistance to British Authority, 1755–1763* (1974).

FOR FURTHER INTEREST: ADDITIONAL CLASS TOPICS

- Compare the image of the typical early French colonizer (the fur-trading *voyageur* or Jesuit priest) with the image of the typical Spanish colonizer (the *conquistador*) or English colonizer (the Puritan or tobacco planter). Consider how these images reflect the nature of each nation's colonial effort.

- Approach several of the chapter's issues from a Canadian viewpoint—especially that of a French-Canadian. Point out how the survival and growth of the aggrieved French-Canadian community reflects the losing side of the struggle for North America and discuss whether English-speaking North Americans might have ended up in the same condition had France won the French and Indian War.

- Focus on the Indian factor in the French Empire and the French and Indian War. Examine French relations with the Indians compared with British (and perhaps Spanish) and consider why most Indians supported France against Britain.

- What shaped the European alliances that formed during the eighteenth century? Why did France and Britain clash frequently? Why did France and Spain become allies a number of times? Why was Portugal no longer a major power in colonial affairs or the world?

- Examine the Seven Years' War in Europe. Assess William Pitt's statement that "America was conquered in Germany." How much did the battles and conflict in the Old World shape the fighting in the New World?

- Use the activities of the young George Washington to illustrate the double role of the colonists as both British subjects and Americans. Discuss how Washington's status as a colonial underling clashed with his status as a young Virginia aristocrat—and reflected all the colonists' frustrations with their subordinate role.

CHARACTER SKETCHES

Samuel de Champlain (1567–1635)

Before founding New France, Champlain had served as a captain in the Spanish navy in the Caribbean and had written a book containing the first proposal for a canal across the Isthmus of Panama. His first French colony was established in Acadia (Nova Scotia). When the struggling colonists there became depressed during the harsh winter, Champlain organized an "Order of Good Cheer" that required the settlers to provide food and entertainment for each other several nights a week.

The Acadia settlement was abandoned in 1607 and a year later, Champlain established Quebec. The new colony numbered only about one hundred people during its first twenty years, despite the fact that Champlain constantly lobbied the French government for stronger support. Finally, Cardinal Richelieu helped reorganize the colony and the fur trade. After 1627, about three hundred settlers a year immigrated to New France.

Quote: "It was impossible to know this country without having wintered here, for on arriving in summer everything is very pleasant owing to the woods, the fair landscape, the good fishing…but winter in this country lasts six months!" (1610)

REFERENCE: William Jay Jacobs, *Champlain* (1994).

Robert La Salle (1643–1687)

Born to a wealthy French family, La Salle, who became the greatest of the French-Canadian explorers, immigrated to New France at age twenty-three. Learning of the Ohio River from the Indians, he became convinced that it led to China. Subsequently, he talked about going to China so often that his neighbors called his estate *Le Chine* ("China").

Selling his estate to get funds for an expedition south from New France, La Salle next enlisted the support of King Louis XIV. After La Salle's venture bogged down on the Illinois River, he walked the thousand miles back to Canada to get new supplies and start over. He discovered the mouth of the Mississippi in 1682.

In 1684, Louis XIV sent La Salle back across the Atlantic to drive out the Spanish and establish a permanent settlement. But despite months of searching, he could not find the mouth of the river again. His desperate party landed instead in Texas, where La Salle was murdered by his mutinous men.

Quote: "I have chosen a life more suited to my solitary disposition, which nevertheless does not make me harsh to my people; though joined to a life among savages, it makes me, perhaps, less polished and compliant than the atmosphere of Paris requires." (Letter to France, 1683)

REFERENCE: Robert Weddle et al., eds., *La Salle, the Mississippi, and the Gulf* (2000).

George Washington (1732–1799)

Before he became the commanding general in the American Revolution and the first U.S. president, Washington was a young Virginia gentleman, surveyor, and militia officer who played an important part in the French and Indian War. We examine here only his early career (up to 1763).

Washington's father died when George was eleven, and almost nothing is known of their relationship. Washington grew up with various Virginia-gentry relatives, including his half-brother Lawrence, whose estate was at Mount Vernon. Lawrence also provided him with what little formal education he received. He learned mathematics and surveying and knew the Bible and some English literature, including contemporary novels such as *Tom Jones* and *Humphrey Clinker*. He traveled with Lawrence to Barbados, where he contracted a mild case of smallpox.

During his difficult mission into the Ohio country, he was shot at by Indians, nearly drowned crossing a river, and almost froze to death from exposure. After his service with Braddock, he married Martha Custis, a wealthy widow, and returned to managing their plantations as a twenty-seven-year-old patriarch. Solemn, soft-spoken, and extremely dignified in manner, he had a strong liking for fox hunts, fishing, cards, theatrical events, horse racing, billiards, and dancing.

Quote: "The Virginia Companies behaved like men and died like soldiers; for I believe out of the three companies that were there that day scarce thirty were left alive.…The English soldiers exposed all those who were inclined to do their duty to almost certain death; and at length, despite every effort to the contrary, [they] broke and ran as sheep before the hounds." (Letter to Governor Dinwiddie on the Battle of Fort Duquense, 1755)

REFERENCE: James Thomas Flexner, *George Washington: The Forge of Experience, 1732–1775* (1965).

QUESTIONS FOR CLASS DISCUSSION

1. Why was the French Empire ultimately so much less successful than either the Spanish or the British Empires?

2. If France, instead of Britain, had won the "duel for North America," would the thirteen colonies ever have become independent of Britain, or would they have been forced to stay within the empire for protection against France? Would Detroit, St. Louis, and New Orleans now be cities in Canada rather than in the United States?

3. How did the treatment of Americans by British officers and the military, during the war, contribute to simmering resentment against the mother country? Do the attitudes and behavior of the colonists during the war suggest that Americans felt less real patriotic loyalty to Britain and that the ties had become largely practical ones?

4. How important was William Pitt's leadership in winning the Seven Years' War? Is strong political leadership essential to military victory? Is strong political leadership or strong military leadership more important to winning a war? What about during revolutions?

5. From Britain's perspective, were stationing soldiers in the New World permanently and issuing the Proclamation of 1763 good colonial policies? What problems were these policies trying to address? How else might have Britain solved those problems while limiting colonial contempt?

6. Should the French and Indian War be considered one of the major causes of the American Revolution? Why or why not?

CHAPTER 7

The Road to Revolution, 1763–1775

AP FOCUS

- As with all conflicts, the roots of Anglo-American discord have short- and long-term causes. Students need to be able to handle both for success on the AP exam.

- The role of the state in regulating the economy has always been important in American politics, even before the American Revolution. Economic Transformations is an AP theme.

- Mercantilism is at the center of American discontent with British economic policies in the pre-1763 period, despite Britain's inability to successfully enforce mercantilist laws. A series of British acts, including the Stamp Act and the Townshend Acts, bring the British and Americans closer to conflict.

- Tensions grow significantly following the Boston Massacre. Some colonies coordinate their opposition to what they perceive as unnecessarily harsh British actions.

- Radical Bostonians challenge Britain's mercantilist policies by destroying tea belonging to the British East India Company. Britain responds harshly with the Intolerable Acts. Within a year, military conflict between British troops and colonial Minute Men at Lexington and Concord precipitate the American War for Independence.

- Twice as many American colonists oppose or are indifferent to independence from Britain than those who favor separation.

- Thinking Globally (*The American Pageant,* 14th ed., pp. 140–141/15th ed., pp. 126-127) describes how the European powers used their colonies in their imperial power struggle and explores why Britain's American colonies went to war for their independence, but Spain's American colonies did not.

AP teachers should take note of the following:

1. British mercantilism hampered the growth of American commerce—American capital interests were subordinated to those of the British. The Iron, Hat, and Wool Acts all served this purpose, as did a series of Navigation Laws, which were initiated as early as the mid-seventeenth century.

2. The ongoing military conflict with France, culminating in the Seven Years' War, strained the British Exchequer (treasury). The British government thought it reasonable that the colonists assist the mother country in alleviating its debt and paying for the cost of protecting the colonists.

Focus on Historical Thinking:

Have student list five cause/effect relationships directly discussed in the chapter.

FOCUS QUESTIONS

1. What role did mercantilism play in creating discord between British authorities and the colonists?

2. How did the colonies respond to Grenville's laws, specifically the Stamp Act?

3.   What events resulted in British soldiers landing in Boston and being involved in the Boston Massacre?

4.   How did the British respond to the Boston Tea Party?

5.   Where did the British soldiers and American colonists clash in April 1775?

6.   What were the advantages and disadvantages of Britain on the eve of the American Revolution?

7.   What were the advantages and disadvantages of the American colonists on the eve of the American Revolution?

CHAPTER THEMES

Theme: Tension between the colonies and Britain centered on the issues of mercantilism and its implementation. The British Empire attempted to more strictly enforce laws aimed at maintaining a system of mercantilism, while colonists objected to this change from the earlier salutary neglect.

Theme: The American Revolution occurred because the American colonists, who had long been developing a strong sense of autonomy and self-government, furiously resisted British attempts to impose tighter imperial controls and higher taxes after the end of the French and Indian War in 1763. The sustained conflict over political authority and taxation, enhanced by American agitators and British bungling, gradually moved Americans from asserting rights within the British Empire to openly warring with the mother country.

Theme: At the outset of the Revolutionary War, Britain appeared to be a mighty empire, but it was weaker than it seemed at first glance. Poor leadership in London, along with second-rate generals in the colonies, reduced the impact of the larger British population and its naval supremacy. Americans, on the other hand, had many advantages such as George Washington's leadership and fighting a defensive war. However, the colonists also faced disorganization, jealousy, and economic difficulties.

CHAPTER SUMMARY

The American War of Independence was a military conflict fought from 1775 to 1783, but the American Revolution was a deeper transformation of thought and loyalty that began when the first settlers arrived in America and finally led to the colonies' political separation from Britain.

One source of long-term conflict was the tension between the considerable freedom and self-government the colonists enjoyed in the American wilderness and their participation in the British Empire's mercantile system. While British mercantilism actually provided economic benefits to the colonies, along with certain liabilities, its limits on freedom and patronizing goal of keeping America in a state of perpetual economic adolescence stirred growing resentment.

The short-term movement toward the War of Independence began with British attempts to impose higher taxes and tighter imperial controls after the French and Indian War. To the British these were reasonable measures, under which the colonists would simply bear a fair share of the costs of the empire. To the colonists, however, the measures constituted attacks on fundamental rights.

Through well-orchestrated agitation and boycotts, the colonists forced repeal of the Stamp Act of 1765 as well as the Townshend Acts that replaced it, except for the symbolic tax on tea. A temporary lull in conflict between 1770 and 1773 ended with the Boston Tea Party, conducted by a network of Boston agitators reacting to the Massachusetts governor's attempt to enforce the law.

In response to the Tea Party, the British imposed the harsh Intolerable Acts, coincidentally passing the Quebec Act at the same time. These twin actions aroused ferocious American resistance throughout the colonies and led directly to the calling of the First Continental Congress and the clash of arms at Lexington and Concord.

As the two sides prepared for war, the British enjoyed the advantages of a larger population, a professionally trained militia, and much greater economic strength. The greatest American asset was the deep commitment of those Patriots who were ready to sacrifice for their rights.

DEVELOPING THE CHAPTER: SUGGESTED LECTURE OR DISCUSSION TOPICS

- Explain how the colonists had gradually developed very strong ideas of rights and liberty that differed considerably from the meaning of those terms within the context of the eighteenth-century British Empire. Show how, as a result, actions that the British considered moderate and reasonable were seen by the colonists as evidence of a vast conspiracy by a corrupt aristocracy to deprive them of their basic freedoms.

    REFERENCE: Bernard Bailyn, *Ideological Origins of the American Revolution* (1967).

- Examine the crucial issues in the conflict, perhaps focusing on the colonial cry of "No taxation without representation." Point out that this slogan actually revealed how strong a sense of self-government the colonists had already developed, since they did not really want representation in the British Parliament (even had it been offered). The same goes for the tricky distinction between internal and external taxation.

    REFERENCE: Robert Middlekauff, *The Glorious Cause: The American Revolution, 1763–1789* (1982).

- Explain, more fully, how patriotic groups like the Sons and Daughters of Liberty used boycotts, agitation, propaganda, and sometimes violence or near-violence to keep the Revolutionary movement alive, even in periods of seemingly improved relations. The focus might be on the constant spiral of action and reaction that gradually moved the conflict from an ideological and political debate to open violence and warfare.

    REFERENCES: Pauline Maier, *From Resistance to Revolution* (1972); Edward Countryman, *The American Revolution* (1987).

- Develop an appreciation of the relative strengths and weaknesses of the two sides by focusing on their typical military representatives: the British redcoats and the American minutemen (militia). Point out how the professional British army came to be seen as a hostile occupying force (for example, in the Boston Massacre), while the strong American preference for the citizen-soldier militia reflected a love of liberty and dislike of powerful authority.

    REFERENCES: Robert Gross, *The Minutemen and Their World* (1976); John Sly, *Toward Lexington: The Role of the British Army in the Coming of the American Revolution* (1965).

FOR FURTHER INTEREST: ADDITIONAL CLASS TOPICS

- Focus on the question of the inevitability of the War of Independence by asking whether independence might have come without a war. Use Canada as a counterexample to show that British colonies in America did not have to revolt but might have developed autonomy (and eventually independence) peacefully within the empire.

- Examine the issue of whether the Revolution was a true revolution in the political and social order or whether it was instead a conservative movement, in the sense of defending a status quo Americans had long ago accepted as their natural birthright. A good way to sharpen this question is to discuss whether the Revolution should be viewed primarily as a change from monarchy to republic, as a fight to preserve colonial rights, or as the separation of the colonies from England.

- Focus on one of the dramatic episodes of the early revolutionary struggle: The Stamp Act crisis, the Boston Massacre, the Boston Tea Party, or Lexington and Concord. Discuss how the particulars of the event (for example, rock throwing at British soldiers, dumping the tea) fit into the larger political context of the movement toward Revolution.

- Discuss the role of African Americans and Indians in the Revolution, both in support of the Patriot cause and as Loyalists drawn to back the British. Consider the tensions and contradictions in the Patriots' language of rights and liberty in relation to their treatment of slaves and others whom they did not consider part of their communities.

- Reexamine the conditions and events leading up to the Revolution from a British perspective, including the system of mercantilism and the imposition of taxes. Discuss why the British might have thought they were being quite generous to the colonists (for example, in defending them from France almost for free) while seeing the Americans as ungrateful and hostile to all authority.

CHARACTER SKETCHES

Samuel Adams (1722–1803)

Samuel Adams was the principal political activist for American liberty and rebellion in the early 1770s. As organizer of the committees of correspondence, he strongly influenced the movement toward American independence.

Adams came from a moderately well off and ambitious clan that included his second cousin, John Adams. Samuel failed badly after taking over his father's brewery and ended up deeply in debt. But he turned out to be as good at politics as he was bad at business. By 1763, he was the leader of the "Whipping Post Club," a political group that had a strong local influence. Adams took the democratic side against royal Governor Thomas Hutchinson and his wealthy political allies. While Adams never endorsed mob violence, he proved a master at turning popular passions to the advantage of the radical cause. When the tea crisis began, Adams organized the rousing public meetings at Faneuil Hall that culminated in the Boston Tea Party.

Although he served in both Continental Congresses, Adams possessed the skills of an agitator, not a legislator, and he rapidly lost influence once the war began. His later career was confined to Massachusetts (where he served as governor from 1794 to 1797), and he remained deeply suspicious of all forms of centralized power.

Quote: "Driven from every other corner of the earth, freedom of thought and the right of private judgment in matters of conscience direct their course to this happy country as their last asylum." (1776)

REFERENCES: Pauline Maier, *The Old Revolutionaries: Political Lives in the Age of Samuel Adams* (1980); Dennis Fradin, *Samuel Adams: The Father of American Independence* (1998).

Abigail Adams (1744–1818)

Abigail Adams was one of the most thoughtful and articulate American women of the revolutionary era and an early advocate of a larger public role for women.

The daughter of a well-known Massachusetts family, she received almost no formal education, like many women of the time, but she taught herself a good deal by reading on her own, including French and English literature. After marrying John Adams at age twenty (he was twenty-nine), she bore five children between 1765 and 1772. During the ten years of revolutionary upheaval (1773 to 1783), she and her husband, though mostly apart, maintained a constant correspondence that shows Abigail to have been astute and strong-minded. During John's absence she also managed the family businesses, including their farm in Braintree, Massachusetts.

After the war, when her husband became president, she defended his policies so actively that some of Adams's political opponents sarcastically called her "Mrs. President."

Quote: "Remember the ladies, and be more generous and favorable to them than your ancestors. Do not put such unlimited power in the hands of the husbands. Remember all men would be tyrants if they could. If particular care and attention is not paid to the ladies, we are determined to foment a rebellion, and will not hold ourselves bound by any laws in which we have not had voice or representation." (Letter to John Adams at the Second Continental Congress, 1776)

REFERENCE: Lynne Withey, *Dearest Friend: A Life of Abigail Adams* (1981).

Gilbert du Motier, Marquis de Lafayette (1757–1834)

Lafayette was the French nobleman who joined the American Revolution and promoted the Franco-American alliance. His strong sympathy for the Revolution made him an international liberal hero, while in America he has symbolized Franco-American friendship and devotion to freedom. His youthful decision to join the American cause was made partly because he was genuinely stirred by the revolutionary appeal to liberty, but also because the American war offered heroic adventure.

In his first combat, at Brandywine, the teenage general Lafayette was shot in the leg. He also commanded one of the divisions at Valley Forge. After persuading the French government to make a substantial commitment to the American cause, he played a crucial role as a commander of the Continental army in Virginia in the months preceding Cornwallis's surrender.

A leader of the early phase of the French Revolution of 1789, Lafayette lost power when the Revolution turned more radical, and he ended up in prison. His status as an honorary American citizen was used to gain his release. In 1824, he returned to America for a triumphant tour, during which huge crowds turned out everywhere and greeted him warmly.

Quote: "The moment I heard of America I loved her. The moment I knew she was fighting for freedom, I burned with a desire of bleeding for her; and the moment I shall be able to serve her, at any time or in any part of the world, will be the happiest one of my life."

REFERENCE: Jean Fritz, *Why Not, Lafayette?* (1999).

Paul Revere (1735–1818)

Paul Revere, remembered especially for his "midnight ride" in April 1775 to warn that "the British are coming," was a notable American artisan as well as an active patriot in the Revolutionary cause.

Revere's father was a French Huguenot refugee, and Paul took up his father's trade as a highly skilled silversmith. Revere fought in the French and Indian War and afterward became active in many patriotic groups such as the Sons of Liberty and the North End caucus. He became well known for his anti-British cartoons and engravings, including one of the Boston Massacre. He was one of the leaders of the Indians who carried out the Boston Tea Party.

On their famous ride, Revere and William Dawes successfully roused the colonial militia and alerted John Hancock and Samuel Adams to go into hiding to avoid arrest. Revere and Dawes were finally stopped by British patrols just before they got to Concord, but they were released. Revere later designed and printed the first Continental money and achieved the rank of lieutenant colonel in the revolutionary army.

Quote: (To a British officer) "You're too late. I've alarmed the country all the way up. We should have five hundred men at Lexington soon."

REFERENCES: JoAnn Grote, *Paul Revere: American Patriot* (2000); David Hackett Fischer, *Paul Revere's Ride* (1994).

Questions for Class Discussion

1. Evaluate the system of mercantilism. What were the benefits for Britain and for the colonies? What were the costs to Britain and to the colonies? Is the system of mercantilism sustainable or will colonies inevitably revolt?

2. Was the American Revolution inevitable? Could America have gradually and peacefully developed independence within the British Commonwealth, as Canada later did, rather than engaging in a violent revolt? At what point in time, if any, was a violent revolt inevitable? What could the British have done to stop the Revolution?

3. Were all the American grievances really justified, or were the British actually being more reasonable than most Americans have traditionally believed?

4. What was the Revolutionary movement, at its core, really all about? Was it about the amount of taxation, the right of Parliament to tax, the political corruption of Britain and the virtue of America, the right of a king to govern America, or the colonies' growing sense of national identity apart from Britain? Was the Revolution truly a radical overturning of government and society—the usual definition of a revolution—or something far more limited or even conservative in its defense of traditional rights?

5. In 1775, which side would a neutral observer have expected to win—Britain or the colonies? Why?

Suggested Student Exercises

*   Examine the biographies of some of the better-known Loyalists, and consider why they remained loyal to Britain while others in similar positions did not. Governor Thomas Hutchinson of Massachusetts and Benjamin Franklin's son William, governor of New Jersey, are good examples. (Even General Benedict Arnold came to be considered a belated Loyalist.)

*   Trace the history and continuing influence of the Loyalists who migrated to Canada after the Revolution. Examine their impact on subsequent Canadian history and political theory.

CHAPTER 8

America Secedes from the Empire, 1775–1783

AP FOCUS

- Even as late as the calling of the Second Continental Congress in May 1775, divisions still exist among moderate, conservative, and radical colonial factions. By summer, the Americans call on the king to address their concerns, but to no avail.

- George Washington is called on by the Second Continental Congress to head the American army. In late 1775, the Americans go on the offensive by invading Canada. The invasion fails, and Canada remains firmly in British hands. War and Diplomacy is an AP theme.

- The war divides Americans, many of whom remain loyal to the British crown.

- Americans are not alone in their conflict with Britain. Many European countries have grievances against Britain. See the table in *The American Pageant* (14th ed., p. 162/15th ed., p. 147).

- Despite what seemed like overwhelming odds when the conflict began, the Americans, with extensive assistance from France, finally gain their independence in 1783.

AP teachers should take note of the following:

1. The causes of the American Revolution are still debated by historians. Some see only one impulse behind the revolution: the desire for independence. Others articulate a dual-revolution thesis: that is, many American colonists wanted independence for itself and as a prerequisite for a fundamental transformation—democratization—of American society. Those who identify with the single-cause perspective repudiate the claim that the American colonies were comparatively more democratic than Britain itself; therefore, Americans sought self-determination only.

2. Many Americans perceived the conflict with Britain as an effort to replace the limitations of a monarchical system with the benefits of a republic. Few articulated this view more effectively than Thomas Paine in *Common Sense,* an excerpt of which can be found in the textbook (14th ed., p. 150/15th ed., p. 136).

Focus on Historical Thinking:

> Have students read and identify each of the three parts of the Declaration of Independence (philosophical justification for revolution, list of grievances, and declaration of independence). Have students infer why Jefferson presents the argument in this progression.

FOCUS QUESTIONS

1. What were some of the military engagements that occurred before independence was declared by the colonists and what was the outcome of each?

2. How did Thomas Paine convince colonists to fight for independence?

3. What were Thomas Paine's views on government?

4. Why was Thomas Jefferson's Declaration of Independence so inspiring at the time and for future revolutions?

5. Who were likely to be Loyalists? What types of people favored Britain? How were Loyalists treated during the war?

6. What were the major military campaigns after the colonists declared independence?

7. How was French aid secured by American diplomats?

8. How did Old World tensions contribute to the success of American diplomats in securing the Treaty of Paris and its generous provisions?

CHAPTER THEMES

Theme: When hostilities began in 1775, the colonists were still fighting for their rights as British citizens within the empire, but in 1776, they declared their independence, based on a proclamation of universal, self-evident truths. Inspired by revolutionary idealism, they also fought for an end to monarchy and the establishment of a free republic.

Theme: A combination of Washington's generalship and British bungling in 1776–1777 prevented a quick British victory and brought French assistance, which enabled the Patriots to achieve victory after several more years of struggle.

Theme: American independence was recognized by the British only after the conflict had broadened to include much of Europe. American diplomats were able to secure generous peace terms because of the international political scene: Britain's recently reorganized government that favored peace and France's inability to make good on its promises to Spain.

CHAPTER SUMMARY

Even after Lexington and Concord, the Second Continental Congress did not, at first, pursue independence. The Congress's most important action was selecting George Washington as military commander.

After further armed clashes, George III formally proclaimed the colonists in rebellion, and Thomas Paine's *Common Sense* finally persuaded Americans to fight for independence as well as liberty. Paine and other leaders promoted the Revolution as an opportunity for self-government by the people, though more conservative republicans wanted to retain political hierarchy without monarchy. Jefferson's Declaration of Independence deepened the meaning of the struggle by proclaiming its foundation in self-evident and universal human rights.

The committed Patriots, only a minority of the American population, had to fight both Loyalist Americans and the British. Loyalists were strongest among conservatives, city-dwellers, and Anglicans (except in Virginia), while Patriots were strongest in New England and among Presbyterians and Congregationalists.

In the first phase of the war, Washington stalemated the British, who botched their plan to quash the rebellion quickly at Saratoga. When the French and others then aided the Americans, the Revolutionary War became a world war.

American fortunes fell badly in 1780–1781, but the colonial army in the South held on until Cornwallis stumbled into a French-American trap at Yorktown. Lord North's ministry collapsed in Britain, and American negotiators achieved an extremely generous settlement from the Whigs.

DEVELOPING THE CHAPTER: SUGGESTED LECTURE OR DISCUSSION TOPICS

- Show how *Common Sense* and the Declaration of Independence changed the meaning of the fighting. Explain why even Patriots were, at first, reluctant to proclaim independence and how they eventually came to link their struggle for rights with the break from Britain.

    REFERENCE: Pauline Maier, *American Scripture* (1997).

- Show how Washington and his generals essentially pursued a defensive strategy in the early phase of the war, while the British had to try for a quick victory. Explain why the Battle of Saratoga was so crucial politically as well as militarily.

    REFERENCES: Bernard Bailyn, *Faces of Revolution: Personalities and Themes in the Struggle for American Independence* (1990); Piers Mackesy, *The War for America, 1775–1783* (1993).

- Consider the political dimensions of the war, particularly the civil war between Patriots and Loyalists and the politics of the French alliance. The focus might be on the role of the American military effort in swinging the neutral population to the Patriot cause.

    REFERENCE: John Shy, *A People Numerous and Armed: Reflections on the Military Struggle for American Independence* (1976).

- Consider how the Revolution has been viewed and celebrated in various periods of American history (for example, on Independence Day).

    REFERENCE: Michael Kammen, *A Season of Youth: The American Revolution and the Historical Imagination* (1988).

FOR FURTHER INTEREST: ADDITIONAL CLASS TOPICS

- Focus on Washington's dual role as practical military strategist and heroic symbol of the Patriot cause.

- Examine the Declaration of Independence as both historical document and revolutionary propaganda. Discuss the short- and long-term historical significance of the grand rhetoric in the first part and the specific indictment in the second part.

- Take the perspective of colonists loyal to the crown and write a Declaration of Loyalty. Model the document on the Declaration of Independence. Begin with a grand rhetorical statement of philosophy and proceed to a list of colonial transgressions against the crown. Determine whether Loyalists could reasonably oppose the Patriots. Discuss whether a Declaration of Loyalty would have been able to effectively counter the arguments found in the Declaration of Independence.

- Consider the role of women in the American Revolution, including both their part in revolutionary events and the new understandings that began to develop regarding their public role as "daughters of liberty" and the questions that raised.

- Compare the American Revolution to other major national revolutions. Comparisons with revolutions and struggles for independence in new nations, such as Mexico, India, and Iran, might be especially illuminating.

CHARACTER SKETCHES

Thomas Paine (1737–1809)

Paine's Revolutionary propaganda in *Common Sense* and the *Crisis* played a critical role in arousing American patriotism. Because of his later role in the French Revolution and especially his attacks on Christianity in *The Age of Reason,* Paine has long been the most controversial of the revolutionary heroes. Theodore Roosevelt, for instance, once called him a "dirty little atheist."

After the American Revolution, Paine traveled to Britain and France to promote his iron-bridge invention. He became a French citizen and was elected to the Revolutionary Convention. His stirring work, *The Rights of Man*, a reply to Edmund Burke's *Reflections on the Revolution in France,* sold hundreds of thousands of copies and made him a wanted man in Britain.

Following his return to America in 1801, even his influential friends, like Jefferson, avoided him, and he ended his life in poverty. After his death, a British admirer dug up his bones and shipped them to Britain, where they were lost.

Quote: "One of the strongest natural proofs of the folly of hereditary right in kings is that nature disapproves it, otherwise she would not so frequently turn it into ridicule by giving mankind an Ass for a Lion.... But where, some say, is the King of America? I'll tell you, friend, He reigns above, and doth not make havoc of mankind like the Royal Brute of Great Britain." (*Common Sense,* 1776)

REFERENCE: Eric Foner, *Tom Paine and Revolutionary America* (1976).

Richard Henry Lee (1732–1794)

Richard Henry Lee, the most eloquent Revolutionary orator besides Patrick Henry, was the author of the resolution declaring independence in June of 1776.

Lee came from the wealthy and influential Virginia Lee clan. Along with Henry, he gained political influence with his speeches attacking the Stamp Act and British economic domination of the colonies. He was a commanding presence at the Philadelphia Congress; John Adams was awed by him and called him a "masterly man." His brother, Francis Lightfoot Lee, also signed the Declaration of Independence.

His career declined after the Revolution, and like Henry, he was an Anti-Federalist in the fight over the Constitution. Tall and slender, Lee had receding red hair and a musical voice.

Quote: "Why then do we longer delay? Why still deliberate? Let this most happy day give birth to the American republic. Let her arise, not to devastate and conquer, but to re-establish the reign of peace and law." (Speech to Second Continental Congress, 1776)

REFERENCE: Oliver Perry Chitwood, *Richard Henry Lee: Statesman of the Revolution* (1967).

John Paul Jones (1742–1792)

A naval hero of the American Revolution, Jones is known as the founder of the United States Navy. Although he professed deep commitment to America, he was a Scottish immigrant who actually spent little time in the United States, preferring to live abroad after the Revolution.

His original name was John Paul. He added the "Jones" in 1773, evidently to conceal his identity after being accused of killing a mutineer aboard a British merchant ship he was commanding. He then came to Virginia, made influential friends like Robert Morris, and received authorization to begin a navy. The heroic fight when he lashed the *Serapis* to his *Bonhomme Richard* made him an international hero, although in Britain, he was considered a pirate because of his raids on coastal towns.

An extremely complex personality, Jones has puzzled historians and has often been the subject of novels, plays, and poems. Despite his service to America's republican cause, he was devoted to King Louis XIV of France, and near the end of his life, he became an officer in the navy of the despotic czarina of Russia, Catherine II.

Quote: "America has been the country of my fond election, from the age of thirteen, when I first saw it. I had the honor to hoist, with my hands, the flag of freedom, the first time it was displayed on the River Delaware; and I have attended it, with veneration, ever since on the ocean." (1779)

REFERENCE: Samuel Eliot Morison, *John Paul Jones* (1959).

George Rogers Clark (1752–1818)

Clark was the American frontiersman whose daring exploits won the trans-Appalachian west for the new United States.

Born in Virginia, Clark went west at age nineteen to work as a surveyor along the Ohio River. Clark became a leader of the frontier settlers, who deeply resented the British authorities' connections with Indians. Clark returned to Virginia in 1776 to receive a militia commission to attack British forts. He hoped to raise at least five hundred men, but only 175 joined him.

After his great successes in the Illinois campaign and the capture of Vincennes, he attempted to capture the British fort at Detroit in 1779 but failed. Besides his skill at frontier warfare, he proved especially adept at persuading many Indians to abandon the British and support the French and Americans or, at least, to remain neutral.

He had little success after the war. Jefferson initially offered him command of the expedition to explore Louisiana, but the position went instead to his brother William.

Quote: (Speech to Indians) "The Great Spirit has caused your old Father the French King and other nations to join the big Knife (Washington) and fight with them, so that the English have become like a deer in the woods."

REFERENCE: Lowell H. Harrison, *George Rogers Clark and the War in the West* (1969).

MAKERS OF AMERICA: THE LOYALISTS

Questions for Class Discussion

1. Why have the Loyalists been largely forgotten in American historical memory? Do they deserve to be better known? Do you agree with the text that they were often tragic figures?

2. Did the Loyalists act primarily out of conviction and feelings of patriotism toward Britain, or out of self-interest?

3. If you had been an African American, free or slave, in 1776, would you have tried to back the Patriot cause or the Loyalist cause? Why?

Questions for Class Discussion

1. What was radical and new in the Declaration of Independence and what was old and traditional? What did statements like "all men are created equal" mean in their historical context and what did they come to mean later?

2. Was military strategy or politics the key to American victory in the war? How did the two coincide?

3. If the "Model Treaty" that John Adams authored had been the basis for the American alliance with France, would the results of the Revolution have been the same? Do you agree that Benjamin Franklin's French alliance is an example of "practical self-interest trumping idealism," as the authors state? In what other situations during the Revolutionary War does practical self-interest trump idealism?

4. Did the Loyalists deserve to be persecuted and driven out of the country? What difference does it make to understand the Revolution as a civil war between Americans as well as a war against the British?

5. How important were the diplomatic relations between European nations in determining the success of the American Revolution? How significant a role did the French play in securing American independence? How significant a role did the rest of Europe play? How did the American Revolution change diplomatic relations in Europe?

6. What has the Revolution meant to later generations of Americans, including our own? Do we still think of the United States as a revolutionary nation? Why or why not?

EXPANDING THE "VARYING VIEWPOINTS"

*   Carl L. Becker, *Beginnings of the American People* (1915).

    A "progressive" view of the Revolution as the product of social conflict among colonial groups:

    "It was the opposition of interests in America that chiefly made men extremists on either side.... Those men who wished to take a safe middle ground, who wished neither to renounce their country nor to mark themselves as rebels, could no longer hold together."

*   Bernard Bailyn, *The Ideological Origins of the American Revolution* (1967).

    An "ideological" view of the Revolution as resulting from the colonists' ideas about liberty and power:

    "The colonists believed they saw emerging from the welter of events during the decade after the Stamp Act a pattern whose meaning was unmistakable....They saw about them, with increasing clarity, not merely mistaken, or even evil, policies violating the principles upon which freedom rested, but what appeared to be evidence of nothing less than a deliberate assault launched surreptitiously by plotters against liberty both in England and in America....This belief transformed the meaning of the colonists' struggle, and it added an inner accelerator to the movement of opposition.... It was this...that was signaled to the colonists after 1763, and it was this above all else that in the end propelled them to Revolution."

QUESTIONS ABOUT THE "VARYING VIEWPOINTS"

1. According to each of these viewpoints, what provided the fuel that drove the colonists from particular political disagreements to revolutionary assertion of independence?

2. How would each of these historians interpret the common view of the American Revolution as a fight for liberty?

3. How would the sequence of events leading up to the Revolution (for example, the Stamp Act and the Boston Tea Party) be treated according to each of these perspectives?

CHAPTER 9

The Confederation and the Constitution, 1776–1790

AP FOCUS

- As a consequence of the American Revolution, Americans begin to rethink their views regarding the separation of church and state, as well as the future of slavery in a democratic republic.

- The American economy is profoundly affected by the war. Along with the consequences of British mercantilist policies on the development of the American economy, the absence of a governmental structure that could address the nation's economic and judicial requirements aggravates the situation.

- The first government, the Articles of Confederation, fails to deal adequately with the problems facing the new nation. Social tensions stimulate the demand for a stronger central government, one with the power and authority to suppress domestic disturbances, such as Shays's Rebellion.

- The antecedents of the United States Constitution can be found in the political ideas, theories, and concepts associated with the state constitutions. Politics and Citizenship is an AP theme.

- The U.S. Constitution is ratified and replaces the Articles of Confederation, but not before advocates and opponents of a strong central government do political battle on the state level.

AP teachers should take note of the following:

1. Despite the inadequacies of the Articles of Confederation, the government did address a significant problem associated with disputed land claims by passing the Northwest Ordinance. The government was unable, however, to prevent British and Spanish encroachments and influences in the west. See the map in *The American Pageant* (14th ed., p. 184/15th ed., p. 167) for the locations of disputed territory and continued foreign influences.

2. Because of opposition from antifederalists, the Constitution extended certain delegated powers to the federal government, while reserving important powers to the states. Further, a Bill of Rights was later added.

Focus on Historical Thinking:

Have students identify both the successes and weaknesses of the Articles of Confederation.

FOCUS QUESTIONS

1. How did the principle of equality influence American society after the adoption of the Declaration of Independence?

2. What distinguishes constitutions in America from a constitution in the British tradition?

3. What were the shortcomings of the Articles of Confederation?

4.   What events and situations motivated a desire for a stronger central government in some Americans?

5.   What compromises were required to produce the Constitution?

6.   How did the Anti-Federalists view the proposed Constitution?

7.   What was the ratification process for the Constitution, and how did the Federalists eventually triumph?

CHAPTER THEMES

Theme: The American Revolution was not a radical transformation like the French or Russian revolutions, but it did produce political innovations and some social change in the direction of greater equality and democracy.

Theme: Compromise, on a number of important issues, was required in order to create the new federal Constitution. Adopting the new document required great political skill and involved changing the ratification process defined in the Articles of Confederation, writing persuasively in support of the stronger central government, and promising to add amendments to protect individual liberty and states' rights.

Theme: The federal Constitution represented a moderately conservative reaction against the democratic and decentralizing effects of the Revolution and the Articles of Confederation. In effect, it embedded the revolutionary ideals of liberty and popular government within a strong framework designed to advance national identity and interests against the dangers of fragmentation and disorder.

CHAPTER SUMMARY

The American Revolution did not overturn the social order, but it did produce substantial changes in social customs, political institutions, and ideas about society and government. Among the changes were the separation of church and state in some places, the abolition of slavery in the North, written political constitutions, and a shift in political power from the eastern seaboard toward the frontier.

The first weak national government, the Articles of Confederation, was unable to exercise real authority, although it did successfully deal with the western lands issue. The Confederation's weaknesses in handling foreign policy, commerce, and the Shays rebellion spurred the movement to alter the Articles.

Instead of revising the Articles, the well-off delegates to the Constitutional Convention created a permanent charter for a whole new government. In a series of compromises, the convention produced a plan that provided for a vigorous central government, a strong executive, and protection for property, while still upholding republican principles and states' rights. The pro-Constitution Federalists, generally representing wealthier and more commercial forces, frightened other groups who feared that the new government would undermine their rights and their interests.

The Federalists met their strongest opposition from Anti-Federalists in Virginia and New York, but through effective organization and argument, as well as promises to incorporate a bill of rights into the document, they succeeded in getting the Constitution ratified. By establishing the new national government, the Federalists checked the Revolutionary movement, but their conservative regime embraced the central Revolutionary values of popular republican government and liberty.

DEVELOPING THE CHAPTER: SUGGESTED LECTURE OR DISCUSSION TOPICS

- Consider the social changes brought about by the Revolution. Consider specific changes such as church-state separation in Virginia and the abolition of slavery in the North in relation to the Revolution's larger social significance.

   REFERENCE: Gordon Wood, *The Radicalism of the American Revolution* (1991).

- Analyze the structure and workings of the Articles of Confederation government, perhaps using the table in the chapter. Emphasis might be placed on the achievements of the Articles government, such as the western lands issue, as well as its obvious weaknesses.

   REFERENCE: Jack N. Rakove, *The Beginnings of National Politics* (1979).

- Address directly the "Beard interpretation" of the Constitution as a conservative counterrevolution by the propertied elite. Explain the elements of the pro-Constitution movement that support such a view as well as its limits.

   REFERENCES: Charles Beard, *An Economic Interpretation of the Constitution* (1913); Robert Brown, *Charles Beard and the Constitution* (1956); Edmund S. Morgan, *Inventing the People* (1988).

- Describe the ratification struggle as both a hard-fought political contest and a great political debate about the nature of humanity and the purposes of government. Consider, particularly, the key arguments of the Anti-Federalists, and what might or might not have been legitimate concerns of these historical losers (while remembering that the Bill of Rights is in effect a part of their legacy).

   REFERENCE: Herbert J. Storing, *What the Anti-Federalists Were For* (1981).

FOR FURTHER INTEREST: ADDITIONAL CLASS TOPICS

- Discuss the question of how revolutionary the Revolution was, measured by the social changes it caused. One issue might be why Americans have tended to think of the Revolution more in terms of liberty and political ideas than in terms of social change.

- Compare the difficulties of establishing a stable government in post–Revolutionary America with similar situations in other new nations of the modern world.

- Consider how America and American government would be different if the Articles of Confederation had remained the national government. One focus might be the extent to which the concept of the U.S. government is identified with the government of the Constitution.

- Define sovereignty. In order for a national government to be sovereign, what must it be able to do? To what extent was the national government, under the Articles of Confederation, sovereign? How much did the national government's level of sovereignty increase or decrease under the new federal Constitution? Examine the level of sovereignty in state governments under both Articles of Confederation and the Constitution.

- Discuss the reverence accorded the Constitution and the Founding Fathers in relation to the actual historical events of 1787. Examine particular provisions of the Constitution, and discuss whether they might have meant something different in the eighteenth century than they do today.

- Examine the treatment of race and slavery in the Constitutional Convention (including how and why it was mostly but not completely avoided in the actual text). Consider the question of whether directly addressing the slavery question would have made the creation of a federal union impossible—and perhaps even led to the creation of a separate proslavery confederation in 1787.

CHARACTER SKETCHES

Daniel Shays (1747–1825)

Shays was the Massachusetts Revolutionary War veteran whose rebellion, in 1786, spurred the movement for a new Constitution.

A militiaman at Lexington and Bunker Hill, Shays was typical of the ordinary Revolutionary-era Americans who left their farms to fight in the War for Independence. He rose to captain, and after the war, he was elected to various local offices.

Shays emerged as the leader of the revolt by indebted farmers when eight hundred armed men prevented a Springfield court from hearing foreclosure cases. He continually insisted that the farmers wanted only redress of grievances, not violence, but by early 1787, he was preparing to attack a state arsenal. The attack failed, and Shays fled to Vermont. He was condemned to death but pardoned the next year, and eventually, he returned to Massachusetts to live out his days in peace.

Quote: "The people assembled in arms…return for answer that, however unjustifiable the measure may be which the people have adopted in recourse to arms, various circumstances have induced them thereto.…That virtue which truly characterizes the citizens of a republican government hath hitherto marked our plans with a degree of innocence, and we wish and trust it will still be the case." (Reply to General Benjamin Lincoln's demand for surrender, 1787)

REFERENCE: David Szatmoy, *Shays's Rebellion* (1980).

James Madison (1750–1836)

Madison, the "Father of the Constitution," is generally considered the most original political thinker among the Founding Fathers. The only failure during his long career of public service was his term as president, which included the near-disastrous War of 1812.

Madison attended Princeton and considered entering the ministry. He strongly disliked religious intolerance and his first political activities were on behalf of religious disestablishment in Virginia.

Throughout his life he kept extensive journals, and his notes on the proceedings of the secret Constitutional Convention provide the only detailed record of the arguments there.

Madison's marriage to Dolley Payne Todd was a long and happy one. Since Jefferson was a widower, the Madisons' home was the social center of Washington during both the Jefferson and the Madison administrations. Although quiet, bookish, and introspective, Madison was personally warm and engaging, especially in intimate settings.

Quote: "Hearken not to the unnatural voice which tells you that the people of America, knit together as they are by so many cords of affection, can no longer…be fellow-citizens of one great, respectable, and flourishing empire, Hearken not to the voice which petulantly tells you that the form of government recommended for your adoption is a novelty in the political world.… If novelties are to be shunned, believe me, the most alarming of all novelties, the most wild of all projects, the most rash of all attempts, is that of rending us in pieces, in order to preserve our liberties and promote our happiness." (*Federalist* No. 14, 1788)

REFERENCE: Irving Brant, *The Fourth President: A Life of James Madison* (1970).

Patrick Henry (1736–1799)

Henry was the famous Revolutionary orator and five-term Virginia governor who later became the leading Anti-Federalist opponent of the Constitution.

He came from a plain frontier background rather than from the planter aristocracy. When his uncle took him to hear Samuel Davies, a famous Great Awakening preacher, young Patrick fell in love with the art of persuasive speaking.

Henry's eloquent defenses of Virginia liberty, at the time of the Stamp Act, made him the youthful leader of the radical party in that state. He made his "give me liberty or give me death!" speech during the debate over whether the Virginia assembly should take steps toward independence.

Henry's young protégé, Thomas Jefferson, succeeded him as governor during the Revolution, but Henry later demanded an investigation of Jefferson's conduct in office, which caused a bitter and lasting feud between the two. In his later years Henry was plagued with financial troubles and became increasingly conservative.

Quote: "It is now confessed that this is a national government.... The means, says the gentleman, must be commensurate to the end. How does this apply? All things in common are left with this government. There being an infinitude in the government, there must be an infinitude of means to carry it out." (Virginia debate on the Constitution, 1788)

REFERENCE: Richard R. Beeman, *Patrick Henry* (1974).

GREAT DEBATES IN AMERICAN HISTORY

GREAT DEBATE (1787–1789):

The Constitution: Should the United States adopt the new Constitution to replace the Articles of Confederation?

For: The Federalists—led by Washington, Hamilton, Madison, Jay, and Marshall; including most commercial, seacoast, urban, and upper-class groups.

Against: The Anti-Federalists—led by Patrick Henry, Samuel Adams, Richard Henry Lee, George Mason, and George Clinton; including many noncommercial, western, agrarian, and state-oriented interests.

ISSUE #1: Need for change. Does the government of the Articles need to be replaced?

Yes: Federalist Alexander Hamilton: "The faith, the reputation, the peace of the whole Union are thus continually at the mercy, the prejudices, the passions, and the interests of every member of which it is composed. Is it possible that foreign nations can either respect or confide in such a government? Is it possible that the people of America will longer consent to trust their honor, their happiness, their safety, on so precarious a

No: Anti-Federalist Patrick Henry: "The honorable gentleman said that great danger would ensue if the Convention rose without adopting this system. I ask, where is that danger? I see none. Other gentlemen have told us, within these walls, that the union is gone, or that the union will be gone.... Till they tell us the grounds of their fears, I will consider them as imaginary.... Where is the danger? If, sir, there was any, I would recur to foundation?…The Confederation…is a system so radically vicious and unsound, as to admit not of amendment but by an entire change in its leading features and characters."

the American spirit which has enabled us to surmount the greatest difficulties."

ISSUE #2: Can a republic govern a large territory and a diverse population?

Yes: Federalist James Madison: "Extend the sphere, and you take in a greater variety of parties and interests; you make it less probable that the majority of the whole will have a common motive to invade the rights of other citizens.… Hence, it clearly appears that the same advantage which a republic has over a democracy, in controlling the effects of faction, is enjoyed by a large over a small republic.…"

No: Anti-Federalist James Winthrop of Massachusetts: "It is the opinion of the ablest writers on the subject, that no extensive empire can be governed on republican principles, and that such a government will degenerate to a despotism.… No instance can be found of any free government of any considerable extent.… Large and consolidated empires may indeed dazzle the eyes of a distant spectator with their splendour, but if examined more nearly are always found to be full of misery."

ISSUE #3: Will the new constitutional government create an aristocratic power in the presidency?

No: Federalist Alexander Hamilton: "There is no comparison between the intended power of the President and the actual power of the British sovereign.… The President of the United States would be an officer elected by the people for four years; the king of Great Britain is a perpetual and hereditary prince.… What answer shall we give to those who would persuade us that things so unlike resemble each other? The same that ought to be given to those who tell us that a government, the whole power of which would be in the hands of the elective and periodical servants of the people, is an aristocracy, a monarchy and a despotism."

Yes: Anti-Federalist George Clinton of New York: "Wherein does this president, invested with his powers and prerogatives, essentially differ from the king of Great Britain (save as to the name, the creation of nobility and some immaterial incidents…)? The safety of the people in a republic depends on the share or proportion they have in the government; but experience ought to teach you, that when a man is at the head of an elective government invested with great powers, and interested in his reelection…appointments will be made by which means an imperfect aristocracy bordering on monarchy may be established."

ISSUE #4: Does the proposed Constitution protect the people's liberty?

Yes: Federalist Alexander Hamilton: "Here, in strictness, the people surrender nothing; and as they retain everything they have no need of particular reservations.... Bills of rights, in the sense and to the extent in which they are contended for, are not only unnecessary in the proposed Constitution, but would even be dangerous.... Why declare that things not be done which there is no power to do?... The truth is...that the Constitution is itself, in every rational sense, and to every useful purpose, a BILL OF RIGHTS."

No: Anti-Federalist George Mason of Virginia: "There is no declaration of rights: and the laws of the general government being paramount to the laws and constitutions of the several states, the declarations of rights, in the separate states, are no security. Nor are the people secured even in the enjoyment of the benefit of the common law, which stands here upon no other foundations than its having been adopted by the respective acts forming the constitutions of the several states."

REFERENCES: Gordon Wood, *The Creation of the American Republic, 1776–1787* (1969); Thorton Anderson, *Creating the Constitution* (1993).

QUESTIONS FOR CLASS DISCUSSION

1. Which of the social changes brought about by the Revolution was the most significant? Could the Revolution have gone further toward the principle that "all men are created equal" by ending slavery or granting women's rights?

2. Was the United States in a crisis under the Articles of Confederation, or was the crisis exaggerated by the Federalists to justify their movement? Could the United States have survived if the Articles had stayed in effect? What successes did the Articles of Confederation achieve? Was the Constitutional Convention a second American Revolution?

3. Why was the United States so uniformly held in contempt by European governments after the Revolution? Was it due more to the Articles of Confederation or to being a recently created nation?

4. What would have happened to the Constitutional Convention if Thomas Jefferson, John Adams, Thomas Paine, Samuel Adams, John Hancock, and Patrick Henry all attended?

5. Should the Founding Fathers' general elitism and indifference to the rights of people, women, African Americans, and Indians be held against them? Or should they be viewed with more understanding in their historical context?

6. What was really at stake in the debate between Federalists and Anti-Federalists? Did the Federalists win primarily because of their superior political skills or because they had a clearer view of the meaning of the Revolution and the future of the United States? What role did the ratification process play in the fight between the Federalists and Anti-Federalists (and did it favor one side or the other)?

7. Why did Americans accept the Constitution, with its strong national government and powerful executive, after, only a decade earlier, violently revolting against similar British institutions? Why did the Anti-Federalists not violently oppose the new Constitution?

EXPANDING THE "VARYING VIEWPOINTS"

- Charles Beard, *An Economic Interpretation of the Constitution* (1913).

  A view of the Constitution as a conservative "counterrevolution":

  "The concept of the Constitution as a piece of abstract legislation reflecting no group interests and recognizing no economic antagonisms is entirely false. It was an economic document drawn with superb skill by men whose property interests were immediately at stake; and as such it appealed directly and unerringly to identical interests in the country at large."

- Gordon Wood, *The Creation of the American Republic* (1969).

  A view of the Constitution as the extension of republican political theory:

  "Because new ideas had grown often imperceptibly out of the familiar, the arguments the federalists used in 1787–88 never really seemed disruptive or discontinuous. Americans had been prepared for a mighty transformation of political thought by a century and half of political experience telescoped into the rapid intellectual changes that had taken place in the three decades of the Revolutionary era.… Americans had destroyed the age-old conception of mixed government and had found new explanations for their policies created in 1776, explanations that rested on their expansion of the principle of representation. America had not discovered the idea of representation, said Madison, but it could 'claim the merit of making the discovery the basis of unmixed and extensive republics.'"

QUESTIONS ABOUT THE "VARYING VIEWPOINTS"

1. Why was Beard's view of the Constitution and the Founding Fathers so shocking when it first appeared? What would the implications be if Beard were correct?

2. Does Wood's view fit Beard's critique of those who see the Constitution as "a piece of abstract legislation reflecting no group interests"? What would Wood see as the interests of the Founding Fathers?

3. How would the holder of each of these views understand the relationship between the Revolution and the Constitution? How would each of them interpret the Anti-Federalists?

CHAPTER 10

Launching the New Ship of State, 1789–1800

AP FOCUS

- In 1794, an uprising in Pennsylvania over a federal tax on whiskey is suppressed by the militia on orders from President Washington.

- As secretary of the treasury, Alexander Hamilton has a profound impact on establishing policies that will determine the nation's economic direction and growth. Deficit spending, initiated in large part by Hamilton, endures as an economic and political tool. (It was used most famously by FDR.) Students need a good understanding of these economic issues for the AP exam.

- Politically opposed to Hamilton is Washington's secretary of state, Thomas Jefferson, a staunch opponent of Hamilton's brainchild, the Bank of the United States.

- Despite Washington's concerns about political party affiliations, the period witnesses the emergence of two political parties: the Federalists and the Democratic-Republicans.

- Washington warns the new nation about establishing alliances with foreign nations; the key to America's future, according to the first president, lies in a policy of neutrality.

- After Washington's administration, the Federalists passed legislation that restricted civil and political rights. A response, in the form of the Virginia and Kentucky Resolutions, offers a states' rights challenge to questionable federal laws.

- The American Revolution inspired France's Revolution. Thinking Globally (*The American Pageant,* 14th ed., pp. 208–209/15th. ed., pp. 188-189) looks at the similarities and differences between the two.

AP teachers should take note of the following:

1. Debate continues over the distinction made by most historians that Jefferson and Hamilton represented opposing views: Hamilton, as an advocate of a strong central government, commerce, and manufacturing; Jefferson, as a supporter of states' rights and an agrarian future for the nation. Some historians contend, however, that the two adversaries simply represented two types of wealth and class: manufacturers and planter-slaveholders.

2. Take note of the DBQ on Jefferson and philosophical consistency (14th ed., DBQ 4, pp. A73–A75/15th. ed., pp. A70-A72). Questions asking "to what extent" are common on the AP exam. Students need not fully support either the view that President Jefferson maintained his philosophy or the view that he altered it. Instead, they should discuss the degree to which he adopted one philosophical approach or another to governing.

Focus on Historical Thinking:

Have students compare the positions of Hamiltonian Federalists and Jeffersonian Republicans on at least five issues.

FOCUS QUESTIONS

1.   What important protections were added to the Constitution in the Bill of Rights?

2.   What were the components of Hamilton's economic policy, and what did he hope to accomplish with that policy?

3.   What two constitutional theories were presented by Jefferson and Hamilton when Washington asked about the constitutionality of creating a national bank?

4.   Why did Washington opt for neutrality during the French Revolution?

5.   What were the domestic and international consequences of Jay's Treaty?

6.   How did John Adams handle foreign affairs with France?

7.   What laws were being responded to in the Virginia and Kentucky resolutions, and what was Jefferson's proposed remedy?

8.   Who would likely support Hamiltonian federalists, and who would likely support Jeffersonian Republicans? What were the philosophical differences between these two political parties?

CHAPTER THEMES

Theme: Led by Washington and Hamilton, the first administration under the Constitution overcame various difficulties and firmly established the political and economic foundations of the new federal government. The first Congress under the Constitution, led by James Madison, also contributed to the new republic by adding the Bill of Rights.

Theme: The cabinet debate over Hamilton's financial measure expanded into a wider political conflict between Hamiltonian Federalists and Jeffersonian Republicans—the first political parties in America. Federalists supported a strong central government, a loose interpretation of the Constitution, and commerce (business). (Democratic) Republicans supported states' rights, a strict interpretation of the Constitution, and agriculture (farmers).

Theme: The French Revolution created a severe ideological and political division over foreign policy between Federalists and Republicans. The foreign-policy crisis coincided with domestic political divisions that culminated in the bitter election of 1800, but in the end, power passed peacefully from Federalists to Republicans. American isolationist tradition emerges as a result of Washington's strong neutrality stance and his farewell warnings about foreign alliances.

CHAPTER SUMMARY

The fledgling government faced considerable difficulties and skepticism about its durability, especially since traditional political theory held that large-scale republics were bound to fail. But President Washington brought credibility to the new government, while his cabinet, led by Alexander Hamilton, strengthened its political and economic foundations.

The government's first achievements were the Bill of Rights and Hamilton's financial system. Through effective leadership, Hamilton carried out his program of funding the national debt, assuming state debts, imposing customs and excise taxes, and establishing a Bank of the United States.

The bank was the most controversial part of Hamilton's program because it raised basic constitutional issues. Opposition to the bank from Jefferson and his followers reflected more fundamental political disagreements about republicanism, economics, federal power, and foreign policy. As the French Revolution evolved from moderation to radicalism, it intensified the ideological divisions between the pro-French Jeffersonians and the pro-British Hamiltonians.

Washington's Neutrality Proclamation angered Republicans, who wanted America to aid Revolutionary France. Washington's policy was sorely tested by the British, who routinely violated American neutrality. In order to avoid war, Washington endorsed the conciliatory Jay's Treaty, further outraging the Republicans and France.

After the humiliating XYZ affair, the United States came to the brink of war with France, but Adams sacrificed his political popularity and divided his party by negotiating peace.

These foreign-policy disagreements embittered domestic politics: Federalists passed the Alien and Sedition Acts, to which Jefferson and Madison responded with the Virginia and Kentucky resolutions.

DEVELOPING THE CHAPTER: SUGGESTED LECTURE OR DISCUSSION TOPICS

- Elaborate on the reasons for skepticism about the new government, particularly the view that factionalism would eventually destroy a republican government that extended over such a large territory. Show how Washington deliberately acted to assert the durability of the new regime.

  REFERENCE: Stanley Elkins and Eric McKitrick, *The Age of Federalism: The Early American Republic, 1788–1800* (1993).

- Explain why the French Revolution was such a dangerously divisive world event, even in America. Point out that part of the disagreement in America was over whether the French were only carrying out the principles of the American Revolution or whether they were advocating a more radical doctrine of class conflict.

  REFERENCE: Daniel Lang, *Foreign Policy in the Early Republic* (1985).

- Show how the Federalist-Republican conflict over foreign policy embittered domestic politics, since it raised charges of disloyalty on both sides. The Genêt affair, Jay's Treaty, the quasi-war with France, and the Alien and Sedition Acts might all be viewed in this light.

  REFERENCE: Leonard Levy, *Legacy of Suppression* (1960).

- Consider the Adams-Jefferson contest of 1796 in relation to both foreign- and domestic-policy disagreements. The focus might be on how, despite the depth of the conflict over issues, the Federalists and Republicans finally kept their contest within the bounds of peaceful electoral politics and the shared value of republicanism.

  REFERENCE: Lance Banning, ed., *After the Constitution: Party Conflict in the New Republic* (1989).

FOR FURTHER INTEREST: ADDITIONAL CLASS TOPICS

- Focus on the components of Washington's image as the central symbol of republican government and virtue: heroism, integrity, nonpartisanship, and reluctance to hold power.

- Compare the American political dilemmas presented by the French Revolution with those in the twentieth century caused by the Russian, Chinese, and Iranian revolutions.

- Was George Washington uniquely suited to be a successful first president under the Constitution? How might the United States be different if Alexander Hamilton, Thomas Jefferson, or Benjamin Franklin were the first president? Consider political ideas, economic issues, and foreign policy.

- What other times in American history has liberty been attacked? What situation or conditions would merit restrictions on liberty? Would they be constitutional?

- Discuss the Alien and Sedition Acts as threats to liberty. Consider, especially, their relation to the new, fragile Bill of Rights.

- Consider whether the Hamilton-Jefferson conflict was just a normal political disagreement like those between later American political parties or whether it was a more profound ideological disagreement that really threatened to destroy the new government.

CHARACTER SKETCHES

George Washington (1732–1799)

As both military leader of the Revolution and first president under the Constitution, Washington symbolized the republican ideal of Cincinnatus, the Roman citizen-soldier who only reluctantly abandoned private life to serve his country.

The only serious challenge to Washington's leadership during the Revolution came in 1777 from the "Conway cabal," a group of disgruntled officers, encouraged by some members of Congress, who plotted futilely to oust Washington from command.

In 1782, some Continental army officers proposed making Washington king of America; he was outraged when he heard of it and refused to allow anyone to mention the idea in his presence.

During his retirement from 1783 to 1787, his greatest interest was in linking the Potomac and Ohio rivers by road, and he traveled on horseback 650 miles to examine possible routes.

Quote: "My movements to the chair of government will be accompanied by feelings not unlike those of a culprit who is going to his place of execution." (1788)

REFERENCE: Garry Wills, *Cincinnatus* (1984).

Alexander Hamilton (1757–1804)

Hamilton was the political and financial genius of the early Republic whose heroic postures, personal ambition, and taste for aristocratic government made many of his contemporaries fear him, even though everyone recognized his great talents.

Born on the British West Indian island of Nevis, Hamilton came to New York at age fourteen to begin his education. The unfair attacks on him as a "bastard" arose because his mother had not obtained a legal divorce from her previous husband before establishing her union with Hamilton's father.

He became Washington's aide-de-camp in the Revolution and rose to lieutenant colonel. Extremely hot-tempered and sometimes vindictive, Hamilton denounced Washington behind his back and resigned from his staff after Washington once rebuked him for lateness.

He feuded with Aaron Burr for years in New York and helped block him from the governorship and, possibly, the presidency. He tried to avoid Burr's demand for a duel, but when Burr made Hamilton's refusal a matter of public honor, Hamilton reluctantly accepted.

Quote: "The love of fame, the ruling passion of the noblest minds, prompts a man to plan and undertake extensive and arduous enterprises for the public benefit, requiring considerable time to mature and perfect them." (*Federalist* No. 72, 1788)

REFERENCE: Gerald Stourzh, *Alexander Hamilton and the Idea of Republican Government* (1970).

John Jay (1754–1829)

Jay was one of the authors (with Madison and Hamilton) of the *Federalist Papers*. His negotiation of Jay's Treaty with Great Britain in 1795 made him a hero to Federalists and a hated symbol of American humiliation to Jeffersonian Republicans.

Although somewhat humorless and vain, Jay had a very high sense of honor. At King's College (Columbia), he was once temporarily suspended for refusing to reveal the name of a fellow student who had committed vandalism.

Washington offered him his choice of any position in the new government, and Jay chose chief justice of the United States. He carefully cultivated influential British citizens during the negotiation of the commercial treaty with Britain in order to obtain the most favorable terms, but to the Republicans, who burned him in effigy, these contacts were proof that he had sold out American interests.

Quote: "Further concessions on the part of Great Britain cannot, in my opinion, be attained. If this treaty fails, I despair of another.… If I entirely escape censure, I shall be agreeably disappointed." (Letter, 1795)

REFERENCE: Richard B. Morris, *John Jay* (1975).

John Adams (1735–1826)

Adams was the Massachusetts Revolutionary and Federalist president whose public appeal never matched his political and intellectual talents.

He originally considered becoming a minister, but "frigid John Calvin" repelled him, and he turned to law. During his frequent missions abroad, he lived very frugally and constantly complained of the extravagance of his fellow diplomats such as Franklin and Jay.

He thought that Hamilton maneuvered to get him elected to the vice presidency, which he called "the most insignificant office that ever the invention of man contrived or the mind of man conceived." Although he was prickly and cold in most situations, his diaries and letters to his wife Abigail show his warm, anxious, and generous side.

He renewed his friendship with Jefferson after both left office, and they exchanged numerous letters until they died within a few hours of each other on July 4, 1826. Adams's last words were "Thomas Jefferson still lives."

Quote: "My reputation has been so much the sport of the public, for fifty years, and will be with posterity, that I hold it a bubble, a gossamer, that idles in the wanton summer air." (Letter to Jefferson, 1813)

REFERENCE: Peter Shaw, *The Character of John Adams* (1976).

Aaron Burr (1756–1836)

Burr was the vice president of the United States who killed Alexander Hamilton in a duel and then organized a mysterious conspiracy to separate parts of the West from the United States.

A grandson of Jonathan Edwards, the Great Awakening preacher, Burr was charming and eloquent but always loved adventure and intrigue. He nearly joined the Conway cabal against Washington and helped organize the Tammany Hall political club in New York.

After killing Hamilton in the duel on July 11, 1804, he first fled but then returned to preside as vice president over the impeachment trial of Samuel Chase before embarking on his western conspiracy.

Burr's plotting was so complicated and confusing that it is still uncertain whether he wanted to set up a new western nation under himself or to form a private army to invade Mexico. Although technically acquitted in his treason trial, he was completely disgraced. He fled to France, where he lived in poverty and tried to get Napoleon to endorse his schemes for an invasion of America.

Quote: "Political opposition can never absolve gentlemen from a rigid adherence to the laws of honor....You have indulged in the use of language derogatory to my honor as a gentleman....To this I expect a definite reply which must lead to an accommodation, or the only alternative which the circumstances of the case will justify." (Dueling challenge to Alexander Hamilton, 1804)

REFERENCE: Herbert S. Parmet and Marie B. Hecht, *Aaron Burr: Portrait of an Ambitious Man* (1967).

GREAT DEBATES IN AMERICAN HISTORY

Great Debate (1791–1801):

Whose political theories and programs are more conducive to creating a strong, free Republic: Hamilton's or Jefferson's?

For Hamilton: The Federalists—led by Hamilton, Adams, Jay, Marshall, and Pickering; including merchants, urban upper classes, and conservative clergy.

For Jefferson: The Republicans—led by Jefferson, Madison, Monroe, and Burr; including farmers, westerners, and urban craft workers and tradespeople.

ISSUE #1: Loose or strict construction. Should the Constitution be interpreted loosely to grant implied powers to the federal government?

Yes: Federalist Hamilton: "The means by which national exigencies are to be provided for, national inconveniences obviated, national prosperity promoted are of such infinite variety, extent, and complexity, that there must of necessity be great latitude of discretion in the selection and application of these means. If the *end* be clearly comprehended within any of the specified powers, and if the measure have an obvious relation to the *end,* and it is not forbidden by any particular provision of the constitution, it may safely be deemed to come within the compass of the national authority."

No: Republican Jefferson: "I consider the foundation of the Constitution as laid on this ground—that all powers not delegated to the United States by the Constitution, nor prohibited by it to the states, are reserved to the states, or to the people. To take a single step beyond the boundaries thus specifically drawn around the powers of congress is to take possession of a boundless field of power, no longer susceptible of any definition."

ISSUE #2: Manufacturing versus agriculture. Should urban commerce and manufacturing be promoted as much as agriculture?

Yes: Federalist Hamilton: "The spirit of enterprise, useful and

No: Republican Jefferson: "Those who labour in the earth prolific as it is, must necessarily be contracted or expanded, in proportion to the simplicity or variety of the occupations and productions which are to be found in a society. It must be less in a nation of mere cultivators, than in a nation of cultivators and merchants; less in a nation of cultivators and merchants, than in a nation of cultivators, artificers, and merchants."

are the chosen people of God, if ever he had a chosen people, whose breasts he has made his peculiar deposit for substantial and genuine virtue.… Corruption of morals in the mass of cultivators is a phenomenon of which no age nor nation has furnished an example.… Generally speaking the proportion which the aggregate of the other classes of citizens bears in any state to that of its husbandmen, is the proportion of its unsound to its healthy parts.… The mobs of great cities add just so much to the support of pure government, as sores do to the strength of the human body."

ISSUE #3: Should the common people be trusted with government?

No: Federalist Hamilton: "All communities divide themselves into the few and the many. The first are the rich and well born; the other, the mass of the people. The voice of the people has been said to be the voice of God; and however generally this maxim has been quoted and believed, it is not true in fact. The people are turbulent and changing; they seldom judge or determine right. Give therefore to the first class a distinct, permanent share in the government. They will check the unsteadiness of the second; and as they cannot receive any advantage by a change, they therefore will ever maintain good government."

Yes: Republican Jefferson: "Whenever the people are well-informed, they can be trusted with their own government; wherever things get so far wrong as to attract their notice, they may be relied on to set them right.
"I am not among those who fear the people. They, and not the rich, are our dependence for continued freedom.
"The mass of mankind has not been born with saddles on their backs, nor a favored few booted and spurred ready to ride them legitimately, by the grace of God."

ISSUE #4: The French Revolution. Should the United States view the French Revolution with sympathy and approval?

No: Federalist Hamilton: "The cause of France is compared with that of America during its late revolution. Would to heaven that the comparison were just.

Yes: Republican Jefferson: "I still hope the French Revolution will end happily. I feel that the permanence of our own leans in some degree on that; and that a

Would to heaven that we could discern in the mirror of French affairs the same humanity, the same decorum, the same gravity, the same order, the same dignity, the same solemnity, which distinguished the cause of the American Revolution. Clouds and darkness would not then rest upon the issue as they now do. I own I do not like the comparison."

failure there would be a powerful argument to prove there must be a failure here. "My own affections have been deeply wounded by some of the martyrs to this cause, but rather than it should have failed, I would have seen half the earth desolated; were there but an Adam and Eve left in every country, and left free, it would be better than it now is."

REFERENCES: Richard Buel Jr., *Securing the Revolution: Ideology in American Politics, 1789–1815* (1972); Daniel Lang, *Foreign Policy in the New Republic* (1985).

QUESTIONS FOR CLASS DISCUSSION

1. Did the Bill of Rights satisfy the Anti-Federalists concerns? Was individual liberty and state sovereignty protected by the new amendments? What about assaults on the new Bill of Rights such as the national bank and the Alien and Sedition Acts?

2. Why did Hamilton move so rapidly to create large financial commitments by the federal government? Since we normally think of the federal debt as something bad, why did Hamilton think of it as something good and necessary for the national welfare?

3. How sympathetic should Revolutionary Americans have been to the king-killing French Revolution?

4. Why were political parties viewed as so dangerous by the Founding Fathers? Why did parties come into being at all, and why did they come to be accepted as legitimate ways to express political disagreement?

5. How wise was Washington's insistence on neutrality? What about the fact that, while this foreign policy stance may not have violated the letter of the alliance with France, it did violate the spirit of the alliance? Do you agree that, as the authors contend, "self-interest is the basic cement of alliances"? Does a nation have an obligation to maintain alliances previously established, even when it is no longer in that nation's self-interest?

6. What role did domestic politics and economic realities play in establishing an American foreign policy? How should American diplomats interact with European governments? Consider the fact that some Americans do not want diplomats to follow standard European protocol (like kissing the Queen's hand or paying bribes to speak to public officials).

7. Contrast the Hamiltonian Federalist belief that the wealthy and well educated ought to run the government with the Jeffersonian Republican belief that the common person, if educated, could be trusted to manage public affairs.

CHAPTER 11

The Triumphs and Travails of the Jeffersonian Republic, 1800–1812

AP FOCUS

- The election of Thomas Jefferson is perceived by many as a victory for the common man. The inauguration of Jefferson, a Democratic-Republican, represents the first peaceful transfer of power between differing political parties in the nation's history.

- Jefferson's foreign policy is noted for his military challenge against the Barbary pirates and for the Louisiana Purchase, which doubles the size of the United States.

- Because of violations of U.S. neutral shipping rights and other abuses, the United States declares war on Great Britain, precipitating the War of 1812.

AP teachers should take note of the following:

1. Many historians consider the election of Jefferson a revolution in political ideas, aspirations, and objectives. Others disagree, pointing to his political moderation as president; the fact that he didn't seek to destroy the Bank, but merely let its charter expire; and the fact that he represented the interests of what northerners would refer to as the "slaveocracy" of the South.

2. The Marshall Supreme Court handed down decisions that would not only establish the foundation for the judiciary's responsibilities, such as the power to determine the constitutionality of laws, but also reaffirm the separation of powers among the three branches of government.

3. The War of 1812 was unpopular in the New England states because of the cessation of commerce with a major trading partner, Great Britain. The economy was damaged, and during the war the United States was invaded, but the end of the war found the nation's worldwide image strengthened—after all, the United States had not been defeated by the powerful British military.

4. Jefferson's purchase of Louisiana was criticized as a circumvention of the Senate's power to ratify or reject treaties. It also raises the question of the political limitations placed on the president by the Constitution, a question that comes up again and again in American history.

Focus on Historical Thinking:

Have students answer the following questions to demonstrate that they understand the essence of the quotes from the following pages:
1) Philadelphia woman, page 204, 15th ed.: What is the speaker most amazed by?
2) John F. Kennedy, page 207, 15th ed.: What is Kennedy saying about Thomas Jefferson?
3) John Marshall, page 209, 15th ed.: What principle is John Marshall presenting?

FOCUS QUESTIONS

1. How did Jefferson behave as president, and how did he deal with his predecessors' federalist programs?

2.   What were the circumstances that gave birth to the principle of judicial review?

3.   How was the United States able to acquire the Louisiana territory and why did Jefferson struggle with the purchase?

4.   What foreign policy challenges did Jefferson face and how did he respond to each?

5.   Why did Madison ask Congress to declare war on Britain in 1812?

CHAPTER THEMES

Theme: Jefferson's effective, pragmatic policies strengthened the principles of a two-party republican government, even though the Jeffersonian revolution caused sharp partisan battles between Federalists and Republicans over particular issues.

Theme: Despite his intentions, Jefferson became deeply entangled in the foreign-policy conflicts of the Napoleonic era, leading to a highly unpopular and failed embargo that revived the moribund Federalist Party.

Theme: James Madison fell into an international trap, set by Napoleon, which Jefferson had avoided. Western War Hawks's enthusiasm for a war with Britain was matched by New Englanders' hostility.

CHAPTER SUMMARY

The ideological conflicts of the early Republic culminated in the bitter election of 1800 between Adams and Jefferson. Despite the fierce rhetoric of the campaign, the Revolution of 1800 demonstrated that the infant Republic could peacefully transfer power from one party to another. The election of 1800 also signaled the decline of the conservative Federalist Party, which proved unable to adjust to the democratic future of American politics.

Jefferson, the political theorist, came to Washington determined to restore what he saw as the original American revolutionary ideals and to implement his Republican principles of limited and frugal government, strict construction, and an antimilitarist foreign policy. But Jefferson, the practical politician, had to compromise many of these goals, thereby moderating the Republican-Federalist ideological conflict.

The sharpest political conflicts occurred over the judiciary, where John Marshall worked effectively to enshrine the principles of judicial review and a strong federal government. Against his original intentions, Jefferson himself also enhanced federal power by waging war against the Barbary pirates and by his dramatic purchase of Louisiana from Napoleon. The Louisiana Purchase was Jefferson's greatest success, increasing national unity and pointing to America's long-term future in the West. But in the short term the vast geographic expansion fostered schemes like Aaron Burr's to break the West away from the United States.

Nevertheless, Jefferson became increasingly entangled in the horrific European wars between Napoleonic France and Britain, as both great powers obstructed American trade and violated freedom of the seas. Jefferson attempted to avoid war through his embargo policy, which damaged the American economy and stirred bitter opposition in New England.

Jefferson's successor, James Madison, soon stumbled into a diplomatic trap set by Napoleon, and western War Hawks, hoping to acquire Canada, whooped the United States into a war with Britain in 1812. The nation went to war totally unprepared, bitterly divided, and devoid of any coherent strategy.

DEVELOPING THE CHAPTER: SUGGESTED LECTURE OR DISCUSSION TOPICS

- Focus on the rivalry between John Adams and Jefferson, examining their genuine and deeply held differences of principle regarding power, liberty, and the meaning of the new American experiment. Trace the evolution of their relationship, as it eventually revealed (in their letters) the even deeper commitments to American values that they shared.

  REFERENCE: Joseph Ellis, *Founding Brothers* (2001).

- Consider the close connection between politics and law in the early history of the Supreme Court, with Federalist Marshall contending with Republican Jefferson. Show the importance of Marshall's bold new principle that the Supreme Court has the final power to interpret the Constitution.

  REFERENCE: G. Edward White, *The Marshall Court and Cultural Change* (1988).

- Analyze the causes and consequences of the Louisiana Purchase, particularly, its long-term implications for the Federalist-Republican conflict. Consider the expansion into Louisiana in relation to Americans' increasing fascination with the West, spurred in part by the Lewis and Clark expedition.

  REFERENCE: Donald Jackson, *Thomas Jefferson and the Stony Mountain* (1981).

- Consider the puzzling problem of the causes of the War of 1812 and, particularly, the issue of maritime causes versus the Western War Hawks's frontier concerns. Examine the question of whether declaring war against Britain was essentially an emotional and irrational outburst or whether it involved a defense of central American interests and principles.

  REFERENCES: Donald R. Hickey, *The War of 1812: A Forgotten Conflict* (1989); J.C.A. Stagg, *Mr. Madison's War: Politics, Warfare, and Diplomacy in the Early American Republic* (1983).

FOR FURTHER INTEREST: ADDITIONAL CLASS TOPICS

- Focus on Jefferson as political philosopher, practical political leader, and enduring symbol of American democracy. Examine the elements of Jefferson's political ideals and compare them with his actual performance in office.

- Consider the role of the Supreme Court and judicial review in the American political system in Jefferson's time and after. Discuss particularly its apparently antidemocratic character.

- Focus on the causes and consequences of the Louisiana Purchase, particularly on its implications for the future westward movement of the United States. Examine the Lewis and Clark Expedition as both an enterprise of geographic and scientific inquiry and as a political maneuver to put an American imprint on the North American continent. (Note that Lewis and Clark traveled far beyond the Purchase territory proper, implying even further expansion.)

- Examine the background and ambitions of the young western War Hawks of 1812, including people such as Congressman Henry Clay. Consider the important place of Canada in the thinking of those who pushed for war against Britain.

CHARACTER SKETCHES

Thomas Jefferson (1743–1826)

Jefferson was, after Washington and Franklin, the most celebrated of the Founding Fathers, and the one who most completely combined intellectual genius in many fields with practical political skill.

In his youth, Jefferson was a lighthearted socialite, horseman, and violinist, but he became more serious and philosophical after an unhappy love affair and especially after the death of his young wife in 1782.

A poor public speaker, Jefferson nevertheless excelled at legislative and political work behind the scenes. His literary skill led Franklin, Adams, and the other members of the drafting committee to assign him to write the Declaration of Independence. His original version included an attack on slavery, but this was removed.

Soft-spoken and informal in manner, Jefferson liked to receive visitors at Monticello or the White House in slippers and casual clothes and drape himself across furniture as he spoke. The charge that he fathered children by one of his slaves, Sally Hemings, grew out of contemporary rumors and was published by a hostile journalist in 1802. Although Jefferson's paternity was accepted as fact within the black Hemings clan, Jefferson's admirers contended over the years that Jefferson's nephew was the father. In the late 1990s, DNA tests of Jefferson's acknowledged white descendants and descendants of Hemings confirmed the very high likelihood that Jefferson did have a liaison with Hemings. On his tombstone, Jefferson listed his three great achievements as being the author of the Declaration of Independence and the Virginia Statute for Religious Freedom and the founder of the University of Virginia.

Quote: "A government regulating itself by what is just and wise for the many, uninfluenced by the local and selfish interests of the few who direct their affairs, has not been seen, perhaps, on earth. . . . Still, I believe it does exist here in a greater degree than anywhere else, and for its growth and continuance I offer sincere prayers." (Letter to John Adams, 1813)

REFERENCES: Noble Cunningham, *In Pursuit of Reason: The Life of Thomas Jefferson* (1987); Joseph Ellis, *American Sphinx: The Character of Thomas Jefferson* (1997).

Meriwether Lewis (1774–1809)

Lewis was Jefferson's private secretary and leader of the expedition that explored the Louisiana Purchase territory.

He grew up as Jefferson's neighbor and friend. As Jefferson's presidential secretary, he supervised White House social life as well as official correspondence.

Jefferson and Lewis had planned an expedition to the west coast even before the Louisiana Purchase. William Clark was the geographer and manager of the expedition, while the better-educated Lewis carried out the scientific and cultural side of the mission. On the return trip from Oregon, Lewis was accidentally wounded by one of his men, who mistook him for a deer.

Shortly after being made governor of Louisiana, Lewis was shot to death in a remote Tennessee inn. Some people claimed he was murdered, but Jefferson said Lewis was subject to frequent bouts of depression and believed he had committed suicide.

Quote: "We were now about to penetrate a country at least two thousand miles in width, on which the foot of civilized man has not trodden; the good or evil it had in store for us was an experiment yet to determine. … Entertaining, as I do, the most confident hope of succeeding in a voyage which has formed a project of mine for the last ten years, I could but esteem this moment of departure as among the most happy of my life." (Journal, Fort Mandan, 1805)

REFERENCE: Stephen Ambrose, *Undaunted Courage* (1996).

Sacajawea (1787?–1812?)

Sacajawea was the Shoshone Indian who served as translator and negotiator on the Lewis and Clark expedition.

The daughter of a chief, she was married, along with another Indian woman, to Toussaint Charbonneau, a French-Canadian *voyageur* who lived with the Indians. Charbonneau became an interpreter for Lewis and Clark at Fort Mandan in Dakota, and Sacajawea joined the expedition even though she had given birth two months before to a son, John Baptiste.

Contrary to legend, Sacajawea did little guiding, but she did translate. When the expedition reached her own people along the Snake River, she was overjoyed and learned that her brother had become chief.

Clark became attached to her son and offered to raise him. After initially refusing, she and Charbonneau joined Clark in St. Louis, left their son with him, and returned to Dakota.

Controversy surrounds whether Sacajawea died shortly thereafter at Fort Mandan or lived to old age on the Wind River reservation in Wyoming. Because she was taken up as a heroine by American suffragists, there are more monuments to her than to any other American woman.

REFERENCE: Ella Clark and Margot Edmonds, *Sacajawea of the Lewis and Clark Expedition* (1979).

Henry Clay (1777–1852)

Clay was a Kentucky congressman and senator who, along with Webster and Calhoun, dominated congressional politics in the early nineteenth century. Beginning his career as a spokesman for the new West, he spent most of it as a Border State moderate trying to mediate between North and South.

Clay moved from Virginia to Lexington, Kentucky, in 1797 and became the state's most renowned criminal lawyer. Although initially sympathetic to Aaron Burr's schemes, he was eventually convinced by Jefferson of Burr's treasonous intentions.

Eloquent and impetuous, Clay displayed a hot western temper. His lifelong feud with Jackson began when he criticized Jackson's invasion of Florida in 1819. He maneuvered during his whole political life for the presidency but never attained it. His statement "I would rather be right than be President" can be taken with a grain of salt, since he frequently modified positions for political advantage, notably in the presidential campaign of 1844.

Like other westerners of the time, he loved horse racing, cards, liquor, and dueling—though he finally gave up the last practice.

Quote: "An honorable cause is attainable by an efficient war. . . . In such a cause, with the aid of Providence, we must come out crowned with success. But if we fail, let us fail like men, lash ourselves to our gallant tars, and expire together in one common struggle, fighting for Free Trade and Seamen's Rights." (Congressional speech, 1811)

REFERENCE: Robert Remini, *Henry Clay: Statesman for the Union* (1991).

Tecumseh (1768–1813)

Tecumseh was a Shawnee warrior who organized a major Indian confederacy against the United States just before the War of 1812.

His father, a Shawnee chief, was killed in battle with whites in 1774. Between 1805 and 1810, Tecumseh worked to organize his own people and also became well known among the Potawatomies and Kickapoos in Ohio and Indiana.

He was, at first, subordinate to his brother Tenskwatawa—commonly called the Prophet—a Shawnee shaman, or medicine man, who preached a revival of traditional Indian religion. In 1810–1811, Tecumseh expanded his influence across the whole Northwest, persuading each of the tribes not to sell land to the whites without the consent of all.

Ignoring Tecumseh's advice, his brother launched a premature battle against General Harrison at Tippecanoe and was killed. Tecumseh and his remaining warriors joined the British side in the War of 1812, but Tecumseh, too, was killed at the battle of the Thames, ending the last Indian attempt at a united front against white advance.

Quote: "The Great Spirit…gave this great island to his red children. He placed the whites on the other side of the big water. They were not content with their own, but came to take ours from us. They have driven us from the sea to the lakes. We can go no farther. They have taken upon themselves to say this tract belongs to the Miami, this to the Delawares, and so on. But the Great Spirit intended it to be the common property of all the tribes, nor can it be sold without the consent of all." (Speech, 1810)

REFERENCE: R. David Edmunds, *Tecumseh and the Quest for Indian Leadership* (1984).

QUESTIONS FOR CLASS DISCUSSION

1. In what sense, if any, is the idea of a Revolution of 1800 justified? (Note that Jefferson himself always considered that his election represented a genuine revolution—but what did he really mean or understand by that term in this context?)

2. How important was establishing the principle of judicial review? Does that principle make more sense than Jefferson's belief that the states retained the final authority on the meaning of the Constitution? How important was the failed attempt to impeach Samuel Chase in establishing an independent judiciary? What role should Supreme Court justices play in politics?

3. Why was Jefferson willing to fight for the freedom of the sea versus the pasha of Tripoli (who required tribute) but not against Britain (which was impressing American sailors)? Did Jefferson make a mistake in fighting for freedom in only one of these instances? When should America fight for its freedom and when should it not?

4. How did Jefferson's Louisiana Purchase transform America's understanding of itself and its future? Was it inevitable that the West would become part of a much greater United States, or was there real danger in efforts like Aaron Burr's to break those areas off from the country?

5. How does the period 1800–1812 look if viewed through American Indian eyes? Could the attempt of Tecumseh and the Prophet to unite western Indians against American expansion have created a different dynamic in white-Indian relations?

6. Was there any merit at all in Jefferson's embargo policy? Could some other policy have succeeded? Was Madison's ill-prepared stumble into war any better than the embargo, or was the United States simply stuck in an impossible position between Britain and France?

7. Was America controlling its own destiny in the first decade and a half of the nineteenth century or was it reacting to the destinies of foreign nations and their leaders? Consider the Barbary pirates, the sale of Louisiana, Jefferson's embargo, and the War of 1812. How influential was Napoleon on American history?

CHAPTER 12

The Second War for Independence and the Upsurge of Nationalism, 1812–1824

AP FOCUS

- Fighting against the military might of Great Britain, for the second time in less than thirty years, places significant strains on the United States politically, economically, and militarily. The Treaty of Ghent leaves in place most of the grievances that precipitated the war.

- The United States fails to conquer Canada despite two major military expeditions.

- New Englanders and the Federalist Party strongly condemn the War of 1812. The Federalists meet to discuss their grievances in Hartford, Connecticut in 1814. Many consider discussing secession at a future meeting, which, because the war ended, is never convened.

- Following the war, a spirit of increased patriotism and nationalism sweeps the nation in what has been referred to as the Era of Good Feelings.

- In order to integrate the sectional economies of the nation, Senator Henry Clay advocates what becomes known as the American System.

- As the United States expands westward, the question of containing slavery takes on an increasingly large role in the nation's political affairs.

- Concerned about possible European intervention in the affairs of the Western Hemisphere, President Monroe warns Europe that the United States will not tolerate such interference.

AP teachers should take note of the following:

1. Some historians consider the attempt to seize Canada as a reflection of early American imperialism, whereas others view it as a key aspect of American military strategy.

2. Many historians see the Monroe Doctrine as a defensive and altruistic statement by the U.S. government. On the other hand, some historians view the Monroe Doctrine as the foundation of a hegemonic policy that became the cornerstone of future U.S. foreign policy.

Focus on Historical Thinking:

Choose twenty important terms from Chapters 1 through 12. Give students ample time to prepare to write composite sentences (see the "Focus on Historical Thinking" activity in Chapter 5) on each of the terms. Quiz students on five of the terms, giving no more than two minutes for each term.

FOCUS QUESTIONS

1. What were the main military engagements in the War of 1812 and what was the outcome of each?

2. In what ways did nationalism, inspired by the War of 1812, manifest itself?

3. How did Henry Clay's American System aim to increase national unity and economic development?

4.   What were the circumstances that resulted in the Missouri Compromise?

5.   How did Chief Justice John Marshall's Supreme Court decisions strengthen federal power and defend the Constitution's economic provisions?

6.   What motivated the creation of the Monroe Doctrine and what were its main assertions?

CHAPTER THEMES

Theme: The American effort in the War of 1812 was plagued by poor strategy, political divisions, and increasingly aggressive British power. Nevertheless, the United States escaped with a stalemated peace settlement and soon turned its isolationist back to the Atlantic European world.

Theme: The aftermath of the War of 1812 produced a strong surge of American nationalism that was reflected in economics, law, and foreign policy. The rising nationalistic spirit and sense of political unity was, however, threatened by the first severe sectional dispute over slavery.

Theme: Chief Justice John Marshall's Supreme Court strengthened the federal government by supporting a loose construction of the Constitution, asserting the federal judiciary's power over state courts, and enforcing economic provisions in the Constitution (interstate commerce, sanctity of contracts).

CHAPTER SUMMARY

Americans began the War of 1812 with high hopes of conquering Canada. But their strategy and efforts were badly flawed, and before long, British and Canadian forces had thrown the United States on the defensive. The Americans fared somewhat better in naval warfare, but by 1814, the British had burned Washington and were threatening New Orleans. The Treaty of Ghent ended the war in a stalemate that solved none of the original issues. But Americans counted the war a success and increasingly turned away from European affairs and toward isolationism.

Despite some secessionist talk by New Englanders at the Hartford Convention, the ironic outcome of the divisive war was a strong surge of American nationalism and unity. Political conflict virtually disappeared during the Era of Good Feelings under President Madison. A fervent new nationalism appeared in diverse areas of culture, economics, and foreign policy.

The Era of Good Feelings was soon threatened by the Panic of 1819, caused largely by excessive land speculation and unstable banks. An even more serious threat came from the first major sectional dispute over slavery, which was postponed but not really resolved by the Missouri Compromise of 1820.

Under Chief Justice John Marshall, the Supreme Court further enhanced its role as the major force upholding a powerful national government and conservative defense of property rights. Marshall's rulings partially checked the general movement toward states' rights and popular democracy.

Nationalism also led to a more assertive American foreign policy. Andrew Jackson's military adventures in Spanish Florida resulted in the cession of that territory to the United States. American fears of European intervention in Latin America encouraged Monroe and J. Q. Adams to lay down the Monroe Doctrine.

DEVELOPING THE CHAPTER: SUGGESTED LECTURE OR DISCUSSION TOPICS

- Examine the military stalemate of the war, particularly the American failure to conquer Canada and the relative success of American naval forces on the Great Lakes.

    REFERENCE: Donald R. Hickey, *The War of 1812* (1989).

- Examine Madison's largely unsuccessful role as wartime president, in contrast with his genius as political theorist, constitution-maker, and legislative leader. Indicate the various international and domestic divisions that he proved unable to navigate in the White House.

   REFERENCE: Jack N. Rakove, *James Madison and the Creation of the American Republic* (1990).

- Explain the conflict of 1819–1820 about Missouri as the first clear indication of a deep-seated sectional division over slavery. Emphasize the two essential principles of sectional balance enshrined in the compromise: equal Senate representation of the 36°30′ line as the northern boundary of slavery.

   REFERENCE: Glover Moore, *The Missouri Controversy, 1819–1821* (1953).

- Consider the causes and consequences of the Monroe Doctrine. The emphasis might be on the difference between the doctrine's original context (the monarchist threat to the new Latin American republics) and the controversial ways in which the doctrine has sometimes been invoked in American history. Explain the relationship of the doctrine to the permanent issue of the United States' interactions with its Latin American neighbors.

   REFERENCE: James E. Lewis, *The American Union and the Problem of Neighborhood* (1998).

FOR FURTHER INTEREST: ADDITIONAL CLASS TOPICS

- Consider the War of 1812 in relation to American nationalism. Discuss the way that Andrew Jackson's victory in a battle, fought after the peace treaty had been signed, enabled Americans to emerge with flag-waving patriotism after a bungled and divisive war.

- Review the demands made in the Hartford Convention's final report. Were they reasonable remedies and thoughtful modifications to the federal government or were they simply partisan arguments for sectional self-interest?

- Analyze the Federalist opposition and the Hartford Convention. Consider whether the charge of treason was justified.

- Discuss the war in relation to Canada. Consider how it might look from a Canadian perspective.

- What might have been the official response to the Monroe Doctrine in Britain, in the continental Europe (specifically France and Spain), and in Latin America?

- Analyze one or more of Marshall's rulings—for example, *McCulloch* v. *Maryland*—in order to show how he strengthened conservative federal power against the democratizing tendencies of states' rights.

- Discuss the mixed motives behind the Monroe Doctrine and the ambiguous meanings that could be attached to it. Consider whether its primary purpose was to thwart Britain and the Old World powers, to protect the Latin American republics, or assert American security interests.

CHARACTER SKETCHES

Francis Scott Key (1779–1843)

Key was the author of "The Star-Spangled Banner" during the War of 1812.

The scion of a well-off Maryland family, he was an influential young Washington attorney at the time of the war. Having been sent aboard a British ship to negotiate the release of an American doctor, captured during the British attack on Washington, Key spent the night there when the ship began bombarding Fort McHenry. The following morning he was thrilled to see the American flag.

He wrote the poem rapidly on an envelope. A few days later it was printed in the *Baltimore American* and was soon being sung in taverns and theaters in Baltimore and elsewhere in the country to the tune of the English drinking song "To Anacreon in Heaven." Key may have had the tune in mind when he composed the poem.

He wrote only a few other light verses in his life. He later became the U.S. district attorney for the District of Columbia and carried out negotiations with southwestern Indians.

Quote: "Oh, thus be it ever, when free men shall stand

Between their loved homes, and the war's desolation

Blessed with vict'ry and peace, may the heaven-rescued land

Praise the power that hath made and preserved us a nation.

Then conquer we must, when our cause it is just

And this be our motto, 'In God is our trust.'

And the Star-Spangled Banner in triumph shall wave

O'er the land of the free and the home of the brave."

(Last verse of "The Star-Spangled Banner," 1814)

REFERENCE: George Suejda, *History of the Star-Spangled Banner from 1814 to the Present* (1969).

James Monroe (1758–1831)

Monroe was the last of the Virginia dynasty of presidents who presided over the Era of Good Feelings.

He owed much of his political rise to Jefferson, and in 1788, he purchased a new plantation in order to live closer to Monticello.

Although not present at the Constitutional Convention, Monroe was a delegate to the Virginia ratifying convention, where he opposed the Constitution. He was thus the only Anti-Federalist elected president.

As minister to France in 1794, Monroe was sharply criticized for his excessively friendly remarks to the Revolutionary National Convention. He maneuvered for the presidency as early as 1809 but backed down when Madison became the clear favorite.

He was diligent, persevering, efficient, but rather unimaginative and colorless, especially compared with the other Virginia presidents.

Quote: "The Missouri question absorbs, by its importance, and the excitement it has produced, every other.... I have never known a question so menacing to the tranquillity and even the continuance of our Union as the present one. All other subjects have given way to it and appear to be almost forgotten." (Letter to Jefferson, 1820)

REFERENCE: Harry Ammon, *James Monroe: The Quest for National Identity* (1971).

John C. Calhoun (1782–1850)

Calhoun was Monroe's secretary of war, senatorial spokesman for the South, and a brilliant political theorist and defender of slavery.

He was among Clay's young war hawks, who advocated the War of 1812, and an ardent nationalist in the years following the war. After seeking the presidency in 1824, he settled for the vice presidency under Adams and then under Jackson.

His extended feud with Jackson began when Jackson learned that Calhoun had opposed Jackson's invasion of Florida in cabinet discussions. It reached fever pitch when Calhoun's socially conscious wife snubbed Peggy Eaton, forcing Calhoun's resignation from the vice presidency.

Once he became a purely sectional figure, Calhoun spent much time writing political theory, including his doctrine of the concurrent majority. He also proposed the creation of a dual presidency, with a northern president and a southern president each having mutual veto power.

He died shortly after his last speech was read for him in the Senate during the debate over the Compromise of 1850. His last words were, "The South, the poor South."

Quote: "Our fate as a people is bound up in the question of preserving slavery. If we yield, we will be extirpated; but if we successfully resist we will be the greatest and most flourishing people of modern time. It is the best substratum of population in the world; and one on which great and flourishing commonwealths may be most easily and safely reared." (Speech, 1838)

REFERENCE: John Niven, *John C. Calhoun and the Price of Union* (1988).

John Marshall (1755–1835)

Marshall was the chief justice who originated judicial review and established the Supreme Court as an influential branch of government.

Born in a log cabin on the frontier, he was taught primarily by his father. He fought in many Revolutionary battles and served at Valley Forge, remarking that the Revolution made him "confirmed in the habit of considering America as my country and Congress as my government."

Although he moved in aristocratic Federalist circles in Washington, Marshall was the most democratic of men. He liked to drink whiskey in taverns with ordinary country people, do his own marketing, and play quoits and horseshoes with farmers. When not in his judicial robes, he wore dirty, shabby clothes and even his casual cousin Jefferson considered his appearance unkempt.

Quote: "There, Brother Story, that's the law. Now you find the precedents." (Comment to Justice Joseph Story, c. 1820)

REFERENCE: Leonard Baker, *John Marshall: A Life in Law* (1974).

QUESTIONS FOR CLASS DISCUSSION

1. Is it valid to call the War of 1812 "America's worst-fought war"? Was the cause of the failure essentially military or was it an inevitable result of the political disunity over the war's purposes? (One might compare the War of 1812 to other politically divisive conflicts like the Mexican War and the Vietnam War.)

2. Examine the Treaty of Ghent. Did the United States win this peace agreement? What international forces made this peace settlement a reality? Was the United States lucky that Britain had more important priorities than battling in the United States?

3. To what degree was the War of 1812 truly a Second War for Independence? Consider the battles, the politics, and the peace settlement. Compare it with the Revolutionary War.

4. What was significant about the strong spirit of nationalism that appeared in America from 1815 to 1824? What were its accomplishments?

5. Did the Missouri Compromise effectively deal with the sectional conflict over slavery or merely shove it out of view?

6. Did the Supreme Court decisions under John Marshall's leadership extend federal power too much? Is it appropriate that someone who was not elected should have such tremendous power to shape the government and the law? Is it appropriate that a political party's ideology be implemented through the judiciary?

7. Was the Monroe Doctrine a valuable assertion of the principles of liberty and self-determination in the Americas against potential European and monarchical intrusion or was it, in effect, an early manifestation of a patronizing and potentially imperialistic attitude by the United States toward Latin America?

MAKERS OF AMERICA: SETTLERS OF THE OLD NORTHWEST

Questions for Class Discussion

1. What historical factors worked to make the Old Northwest (today's Midwest) a distinctive region with its own identity? What perspectives divided the region's settlers?

2. Was it inevitable that the Old Northwest would eventually align itself with the Northeast in the struggles that led up to the Civil War? Why did even settlers originally from the South tend to dislike the southern plantation elite?

Suggested Student Exercises

*   Trace the patterns of settlement and institution-building across both the southern and northern tier of the states of Ohio, Indiana, and Illinois. Perhaps contrast the Western Reserve area of northern Ohio, heavily settled by Yankees, with the Ohio River counties of southern Ohio, heavily settled by pioneers from Virginia and Kentucky.

*   Use a current religious atlas of the United States to discover how persistent the original patterns of religious settlement remain in the Old Northwest states; for example, are Methodists, Baptists, and Disciples of Christ still more prominent in the southern tier and Presbyterians and Congregationalists (United Church of Christ) still stronger in the northern tier? The patterns of denominational sponsorship of colleges in the region might also be examined.

CHAPTER 13

The Rise of a Mass Democracy, 1824–1840

AP FOCUS

- Andrew Jackson handily wins the popular vote in the 1824 election but fails to win the necessary electoral votes. The U.S. House of Representatives selects his opponent, John Quincy Adams. But in 1828, Jackson easily defeats Adams, ushering in what many see as a period of democratic growth. Claiming he is attacking entrenched political forces, Jackson rewards his political supporters with patronage positions in government.

- Grassroots movements, as well as government actions and policies, help to promote democratic reforms.

- The tariff of 1832 nearly leads to military confrontation between the federal government and South Carolina. Though resolved peacefully, the conflict pits two powerful political figures against each other, President Andrew Jackson and Senator John C. Calhoun of South Carolina.

- Cherokee Indians are forced to leave their land and travel west in what becomes known as the Trail of Tears. Also, Sauk and Fox Indians are beaten in the Black Hawk War and Seminoles in Florida are defeated and removed to reservations in the West.

- Opponents of Jackson and the Democrats form a new political party in the early 1830s, the Whigs.

- Martin Van Buren succeeds Jackson. His presidency is seriously damaged by a severe depression brought on in part by Jackson's Specie Circular, which ends the Bank of the United States.

AP teachers should take note of the following:

1. The conflict over the tariffs of 1828 and 1832 revealed deepening sectional differences. Opponents of the tariff claimed that individual states could nullify federal laws deemed harmful to their interests. Jackson disagreed and threatened to use the military to enforce federal acts and laws. Calhoun, in essence, was making the claim that the United States was a confederation of states—see the excerpt in *The American Pageant* (14th ed., p. 282/15th ed., p. 254).

2. Seeing the Bank of the United States as a vestige of elite eastern control of the economy, Jackson did battle with its president, Nicholas Biddle. Jackson finally defeated the Bank of the United States with the Specie Circular. Even though the Supreme Court, in *McCulloch* v. *Maryland,* had ruled the Bank constitutional, Jackson had his way, but it precipitated an economic collapse.

Focus on Historical Thinking:

Have students complete a Main Idea Log for each of the sections in the narrative text for this chapter. Students should write out each heading, turn it into a question, and answer that question in one clear, concise sentence.

FOCUS QUESTIONS

1. How did the events related to the election of 1824 influence the election of 1828?

2. Why did the tariff issue also become an issue of nullification?

3. How were Native Americans treated during Jackson's presidency?

4. During the Bank War, how did Jackson increase the power of the presidency?

5. What happened that eventually resulted in Texan independence from Mexico and why did the United States avoid immediate annexation?

6. What distinguished the two-party system, which resulted after the 1840 election, from the earlier two-party system, and what were the philosophical and policy differences between the Democrats and the Whigs?

CHAPTER THEMES

Theme: The election to the presidency of the frontier aristocrat and common person's hero, Andrew Jackson, signaled the end of the older elitist political leadership represented by John Quincy Adams. A new spirit of mass democracy and popular involvement swept through American society, bringing new energy, as well as conflict and corruption to public life.

Theme: Jackson successfully mobilized the techniques of the New Democracy and presidential power to win a series of dramatic political battles against his enemies. But by the late 1830s, his Whig opponents had learned to use the same popular political weapons against the Democrats, signaling the emergence of the second American party system.

Theme: Amidst the whirl of democratic politics, issues of tariffs, financial instability, Indian policy, and possible expansion in Texas indicated that difficult sectional and economic problems were festering beneath the surface and not being very successfully addressed.

CHAPTER SUMMARY

Beginning in the 1820s, a powerful movement celebrating the common person and promoting the New Democracy transformed the earlier elitist character of American politics. The controversial election of the Yankee sophisticate John Quincy Adams in 1824 angered the followers of Andrew Jackson.

Jackson's sweeping presidential victory in 1828 represented the political triumph of the New Democracy, including the spoils-rich political machines that thrived in the new environment. Jackson's simple, popular ideas and rough-hewn style reinforced the growing belief that any ordinary person could hold public office. The Tariff of Abominations and the nullification crisis with South Carolina revealed a growing sectionalism and anxiety about slavery that ran up against Jackson's fierce nationalism.

Jackson exercised the powers of the presidency against his opponents, particularly, Calhoun and Clay. He made the Bank of the United States a symbol of evil financial power and killed it after a bitter political fight. Destroying the bank reinforced Jacksonians' hostility to concentrated and elite-dominated financial power, but also left the United States without any effective financial system.

Jackson's presidency also focused on issues of westward expansion. Pursuing paths of civilization, Native Americans of the Southeast engaged in extensive agricultural and educational development. But pressure from white settlers and from the state governments proved overwhelming, and Jackson finally supported the forced removal of all southeastern Indians to Oklahoma along the Trail of Tears.

In Texas, American settlers successfully rebelled against Mexico and declared their independence. Jackson recognized the Texas Republic but, because of the slavery controversy, he refused its application for annexation to the United States.

Jackson's political foes soon formed themselves into the Whig party, but in 1836, they lost to his handpicked successor, Van Buren. Jackson's ill-considered economic policies came home to roost under the unlucky Van Buren, as the country plunged into a serious depression following the panic of 1837.

The Whigs used these economic troubles and the political hoopla of the new mass democratic process to elect their own hero in 1840, following the path of making a western aristocrat into a democratic symbol. The Whig victory signaled the emergence of a new two-party system, in which the two parties' genuine philosophical differences and somewhat different constituencies proved less important than their widespread popularity and shared roots in the new American democratic spirit.

DEVELOPING THE CHAPTER: SUGGESTED LECTURE OR DISCUSSION TOPICS

- Analyze the rise of mass politics and popular democracy. Focus on the increasing democratic American celebration of the people in opposition to entrenched elites, as well as specific political innovations: the end of property qualifications, political conventions, political machines, and the spoils system.

    REFERENCE: Harry L. Watson, *Liberty and Power: The Politics of Jacksonian America* (1990).

- Contrast Adams and Jackson as symbols of the old and new politics. Show how the Jacksonians used the elitist and corrupt election of 1824 to arouse popular feelings for their sweeping democratic victory in 1828.

    REFERENCES: Samuel Bemis, *John Quincy Adams and the Union* (1956); Robert V. Remini, *Andrew Jackson and the Course of American Freedom* (1981).

- Develop the theme of rising sectionalism in the late 1820s and 1830s. Show how the assertion of states' rights and nullification in the tariff controversies reflected growing southern fears of northern political and economic power.

    REFERENCE: William J. Cooper, *The South and the Politics of Slavery, 1828–1856* (1978).

- Connect Jackson's political battles with the emergence of the second two-party system. Show how Jackson especially appealed to plain people who distrusted eastern bankers and capitalists, while the Whigs grew out of the various groups that disliked Jackson and the Democrats.

    REFERENCE: Robert V. Remini, *Andrew Jackson and the Course of American Democracy, 1833–1845* (1984).

- Explain both the Indian removal and the Texas rebellion as products of the expansionism and land hunger of the time. The emphasis might be on how, in both cases, the U.S. government essentially reacted to local political developments.

    REFERENCES: Michael Green, *The Politics of Indian Removal* (1982); Anthony Wallace, *The Long, Bitter Trail: Andrew Jackson and the Indians* (1993).

- Show how the Whigs turned the Democrats' own political techniques against them in the log-cabin and hard-cider campaign of 1840.

    REFERENCE: Robert G. Gunderson, *The Log-Cabin Campaign* (1957).

FOR FURTHER INTEREST: ADDITIONAL CLASS TOPICS

- Contrast the earlier elitist method of selecting presidents (reflected in the four-way election of 1824) with the new, more democratic political methods, including national conventions and noisy popular campaigns.

- Discuss the political machines and the spoils system. Consider the advantages and disadvantages of Jackson's democratic belief that any citizen could hold public office without special qualifications.

- Focus on Jackson's personality, particularly his fierce animosities against his enemies and the secrets of his appeal as a symbol of democracy and the common person.

- Provide more material on the Five Civilized Tribes, particularly the Cherokees, and discuss their fate during and after the Trail of Tears.

- Examine the dramatic events of the Texas revolution, such as the Alamo and San Jacinto, in relation to the broad historical context of the Texas revolt. Explain the reasons so many northerners regarded the Texas revolt as a slaveholders' conspiracy. Consider how the Texas developments might have looked from a Mexican perspective.

CHARACTER SKETCHES

David ("Davy") Crockett (1786–1836)

Davy Crockett, the frontier congressman and hero who died at the Alamo, has remained a half-legendary symbol of western democracy and humor.

Crockett's father was an Irish immigrant and revolutionary soldier who frequently beat his son, causing him to run away from home on several occasions. The young Crockett attended school for six months in order to please a girlfriend but left when she jilted him and never returned to school.

He became a legendary hunter in frontier Tennessee, once killing 105 bears in nine months. Crockett also served with Jackson in the Indian wars and became a justice of the peace, though barely able to read and write. He considered spelling and grammar "contrary to nature."

The suggestion that he run for Congress was first made as a joke, but he was so popular with his pioneer neighbors that he was elected to three terms. A Whig who strongly opposed Jackson and defended the Indians in the Cherokee removal, he became a national hero during his tour of the North from 1834 to 1835, when he regaled big-city audiences with his frontier anecdotes. He headed for frontier Texas and the Alamo because of disappointment over his defeat in a bid for reelection to Congress.

Quote: "What a miserable place a city is.… I sometimes wonder they don't clear out to a new country where every skin hangs by its own tail." (Comment during his tour of the North, 1835)

REFERENCE: Walter Blair, *Davy Crockett* (1955).

John Quincy Adams (1767–1848)

Adams was the secretary of state who proposed the Monroe Doctrine, the sixth president, and a noted opponent of slavery in the House of Representatives.

He grew up at his father's side and, early on, began keeping detailed diaries that form a memorable record of his thoughts and experiences. In 1794, he became minister to the Netherlands, the first of his numerous diplomatic assignments.

Regarded as a traitor by Federalists for supporting Jefferson's embargo, he also aroused Jackson's hatred, even though he was Old Hickory's only cabinet supporter in the Monroe administration.

After leaving the presidency, he planned to retire to write history but was elected to Congress and returned for eight successive terms. "Old Man Eloquent" was contentious and sarcastic in his speeches against the gag rule. In 1841, he won the famous *Amistad* court case on behalf of black slaves who had revolted and taken command of a slave ship.

Quote: "When I came to the Presidency the principle of internal improvement was swelling the tide of public prosperity.… The great object of my life therefore as applied to the administration of the government of the United States has failed. The American Union as a moral person in the family of nations is to live from hand to mouth, to cast away instead of using for the improvement of its own condition, the bounties of Providence, and to raise to the summit of power a succession of Presidents the consummation of whose glory will be to growl and snarl with impotent fury against a money broker's shop, to rivet into perpetuity the clanking chain of the slave, and to waste in boundless bribery to the West the invaluable inheritance of the public lands." (Letter, 1837)

REFERENCE: Samuel Bemis, *John Quincy Adams and the Union* (1956).

Daniel Webster (1782–1852)

Webster, a Massachusetts senator and U.S. secretary of state, was considered the greatest orator and lawyer of his time.

In childhood, fragile health compelled him to stay indoors and read much of the time. When he attended Dartmouth, "Black Dan" was frequently thought to be an Indian because of his swarthy appearance.

Not only was Webster's law practice lucrative, often bringing in $65,000 a year or more, but he was also liberally subsidized by Massachusetts textile-mill owners. He lived in splendor and entertained lavishly at his estate at Marshfield, Massachusetts.

The debate with Robert Hayne came one month after Webster's second marriage to New York socialite Caroline LeRoy. His eloquence was so renowned that huge crowds gathered for even minor occasions, and generations of schoolchildren memorized his most famous utterances.

Quote: "When my eyes shall be turned to behold for the last time the sun in heaven, may I not see him shining on the broken and dishonored fragments of a once glorious Union; on states dissevered, discordant, belligerent; on a land rent with civil feuds, or drenched, it may be, in fraternal blood! Let their last feeble and lingering glance rather behold the glorious ensign of the republic, now known and honored throughout the earth, still full high advanced, its arms and trophies streaming in their original luster, not a stripe erased or polluted, nor a single star obscured...." (Webster-Hayne debate speech, 1831)

REFERENCE: Irving Bartlett, *Daniel Webster* (1978).

Nicholas Biddle (1786–1844)

Biddle was the wealthy, learned financier who fought and lost the Bank War with President Jackson.

He graduated from Princeton as valedictorian in 1801, with honors in the classics. Although he became a lawyer, Biddle spent most of his time on literary endeavors, including writing a history of the Lewis and Clark expedition and composing poetry.

Having left the scholarly life for government service in 1819, at the request of his friend President Monroe, in 1822 he became president of the Second Bank of the United States. The charges of corruption against him arose partly because he represented the interests of the bank's private stockholders as well as the government.

After losing the bank battle, he retired to Andalusia, his Delaware estate, and pursued his interest in classical Greece. He also wrote works on economics, in which he advocated such progressive policies as shorter hours and higher wages for workers.

Quote: "My own course is decided—all the other Banks and all the merchants may break, but the Bank of the United States shall not break." (1834)

REFERENCE: Thomas P. Govan, *Nicholas Biddle* (1959).

Black Hawk (1767–1838)

Black Hawk was the Sauk chief who led his people to defeat in Black Hawk's War of 1832.

His bitterness toward Americans developed when William Henry Harrison obtained a treaty ceding the Indians' land along the Mississippi by getting two lesser Sauk chiefs drunk. Black Hawk fought beside Tecumseh in the War of 1812 and after the war continued to seek British aid against Americans.

In 1831, he formed a war alliance with a Winnebago shaman, White Cloud, but when U.S. troops were called up, Black Hawk withdrew to Iowa. After his attempted recrossing of the Mississippi ended in disaster, he was imprisoned and taken to meet President Jackson. Those who saw them together claimed that the two old chieftains resembled each other.

While in federal custody Black Hawk dictated his life story to an interpreter. A journalist wrote it up and it became a minor classic.

Quote: "I surveyed the country that had caused us so much trouble, anxiety, and blood, and that now caused me to be a prisoner of war. I reflected upon the ingratitude of the whites, when I saw their fine houses, rich harvests…and recollected that this land had been ours, for which I and my people had never received a dollar, and that the whites were not satisfied until they took our villages and our grave yards from us and removed us across the Mississippi." (Autobiography, 1835)

REFERENCES: Donald Jackson, ed., *Black Hawk: An Autobiography* (1964); Cecil Eby, *"That Disgraceful Affair": The Black Hawk War* (1973).

Sam Houston (1793–1863)

Houston was the military hero of Texas independence and later president of the Texas Republic.

He grew up with his widowed mother near Cherokee country in Tennessee, learning the Cherokee customs and language as a boy. Throughout his life, he had a strong sympathy for Indians.

In 1827, he became governor of Tennessee. In 1829, he married, but his bride returned to her parents after three months, and the subsequent scandal and divorce ruined his political career.

Houston first headed to Indian territory, where he became an Indian trader and married an Indian woman. In 1835, he moved to Texas and became commander of the tiny Texas army. Only six of his 783 men were killed in the decisive Battle of San Jacinto; Houston was badly wounded in the leg.

As U.S. senator from 1846 to 1860, he was almost the only southerner to support sectional compromise, even on slavery. As governor in 1861, he refused to recognize the authority of the secession convention or to swear allegiance to the Confederacy; he was therefore forced to resign the office.

Quote: "While an enemy to your independence remains in Texas the work is incomplete; but when liberty is firmly established by your patience and valor, it will be fame enough to say, 'I was a member of the army of San Jacinto.' " (Message to Texas army, 1836)

REFERENCE: John Hoyt Williams, *Sam Houston* (1993).

Martin Van Buren (1782–1862)

Van Buren was the New York politician who helped engineer Jackson's presidential victories in 1828 and 1832, before being elected to his own unsuccessful term as president.

A tavern keeper's son, Van Buren rose to power amid the fiercely competitive factional politics of New York. His own political machine, the Albany Regency, eventually achieved dominance by perfecting the techniques of patronage and spoils.

Van Buren was Jackson's most intimate political associate and the only cabinet member to back him completely in the Peggy Eaton affair. In 1830, Jackson suggested that if Van Buren would become his vice president, he, Jackson, would resign and let Van Buren become president.

Although badly beaten in 1840 after his unsuccessful presidency, Van Buren probably could have been renominated in 1844 if he had not come out against annexing Texas. In 1847, he and other Barnburner New York antislavery Democrats broke away from the proslavery Hunkers who controlled the party. In 1848, he accepted the nomination of the Free Soil party for president.

Quote: "Why the deuce is it that they have such an itching for abusing me? I try to be harmless and positively good-natured, and a most decided friend of peace." (Comment on newspapers, 1822)

REFERENCE: John Niven, *Martin Van Buren and the Romantic Age of American Politics* (1983).

QUESTIONS FOR CLASS DISCUSSION

1. What were the advantages and disadvantages of the new politics of mass democracy? Were such things as the spoils system, party machines, and hoopla-driven campaigns inevitable accompaniments of popular democracy, or could the people have been mobilized by a more open and less partisan system?

2. Did John Quincy Adams's cold personality make him a less competent president than popular hero Andrew Jackson? Why did Americans come to expect their presidents to be charismatic "men of the people" as well as skilled political leaders or administrators? What American presidents fit well into the Jackson mold?

3. Which side fared better as a result of the nullification crisis: the national government (and federal supremacy) or South Carolina (and states' rights)? Why?

4. How dramatically did President Jackson change the balance of power between the three branches of government? Did he dramatically expand the power of the executive branch?

5. How would the following Founding Fathers assess Andrew Jackson's presidency: George Washington, Alexander Hamilton, and Thomas Jefferson? Consider Jackson's democratic views, his reaction to the nullification issue, his support for expansion, and his attack on the Bank of the United States.

6. How was Jackson able to make the Bank War such an effective symbol of democracy and of his presidency? Why were his opponents, like Clay and Biddle, unable to counter his appeals, even when their arguments appeared to have economics and stability on their side?

7. What were the causes and consequences of the Texas revolt? Why did Texas remain for a time an independent nation rather than become a state of the Union?

8. How did the log-cabin and hard-cider campaign of 1840 demonstrate the nature of the two-party system in the New Democracy?

MAKERS OF AMERICA: MEXICAN OR TEXICAN?

Questions for Class Discussion

1. In what ways were the original Texas settlers like other westward-moving American pioneers and in what ways were they different?

2. How have its unique beginnings made Texas different from most other American states?

Suggested Student Exercises

- Examine a map of Texas for Hispanic place names. Find the parts of the state where such names are common and where they appear less often.

- The text notes that many of the Texas pioneers were originally Scots-Irish. Consider which of their qualities may have derived from their Scots-Irish ancestry. (See "Makers of America: The Scots-Irish," Chapter 5.)

EXPANDING THE "VARYING VIEWPOINTS"

- Arthur M. Schlesinger Jr., *The Age of Jackson* (1945).

  A view of Jacksonian democracy as a product of class conflict:

  "During the Bank War, laboring men began slowly to turn to Jackson as their leader, and his party as their party.… This conversion of the working classes to the hard-money policy injected new strength and determination into the hard-money party.… From it would come the impetus to carry through the second stage in the national struggles of Jacksonian democracy."

- Lee Benson, *The Concept of Jacksonian Democracy: New York as a Test Case* (1961).

  A view of Jacksonian democracy as a product of ethnic and cultural conflict:

  "A composition portrait of their [Whigs' and Democrats'] social and economic backgrounds reveals striking similarities. Their most significant difference is that several Democratic leaders claimed Dutch or German ancestry, while the Whigs invariably claimed British ancestry (mostly by way of New England)."

QUESTIONS ABOUT THE "VARYING VIEWPOINTS"

1. What does each of these historians see as the fundamental difference between the two major parties of the Jacksonian era?

2. Why would Schlesinger think of the political conflicts of the day as real and critical to the national future, while Benson would tend to regard them as largely symbolic?

3. How would each of these historians approach an event like Andrew Jackson's attack on the Bank of the United States?

4. How does Daniel Walker Howe's synthesis support or challenge both Schlesinger's and Benson's views on the Jacksonian era?

CHAPTER 14

Forging the National Economy, 1790–1860

AP FOCUS

- Americans look to the western territories and states for new economic opportunities. Profound innovations in transportation make distant markets accessible. As a result, the North and West are tied economically. See *The American Pageant* (14th ed., pp. 330, 331/15th ed., pp. 298, 299) for maps showing canal and railroad networks. The West also absorbs large numbers of immigrants, many from Ireland and Germany. Economic Transformations and Demographic Changes are AP themes.

- In this period, the population increases tenfold. See the textbook (14th ed., p. 309/15th ed., p. 279) for statistics.

- With industrialization, comes despair for the wage laborer, which gives rise to labor organizing. Because they are a cheap form of labor, women penetrate the industrial workplace.

- The nation's economy matures and diversifies as people are increasingly tied to trade, industry, and commercial farming. Historians refer to this development as the Market Revolution.

AP teachers should take note of the following:

1. Arriving in huge numbers in the antebellum period, Irish and German immigrants coalesced into voting blocks, allowing them to play a significant role in the nation's municipal, state, and federal elections. Concurrently, organizations and political parties, such as the Know-Nothings, formed to fight what they considered a weakening of American culture because of immigration.

2. Industrialization was mainly a northern phenomenon. The southern economy was comparatively stagnant and lacked diversity. Consequently, the two dominant classes, the industrial and merchant capitalist in the North and the planter-slaveholder in the South, wanted political and economic regulations and laws contrary to the other's needs. For example, northern manufacturers favored a high protective tariff, which was not in the interest of the planter-slaveholders.

3. The economic interdependence between the Northeast and the West would play a role in the debate over the expansion of slavery. This relationship grew so strong that the regions would ally against the Confederacy—keep in mind, the AP theme Slavery and Its Legacies in North America.

Focus on Historical Thinking:

Create a twenty to twenty-five question matching quiz which matches causes with effects. Examples: failure of the indentured servant system/institutionalization of slavery; declining Puritan church membership/Halfway Covenant, etc.

FOCUS QUESTIONS

1. How fast was the population of America growing and what were the sources of its population growth?

2. What were important developments in American manufacturing?

3.   How did the developing factory system impact women and children?

4.   What technological advances improved agricultural production?

5.   What transportation innovations developed and how did they change sectional relationships?

CHAPTER THEMES

Theme: The importance of the West grew in the early nineteenth century. Cheap land attracted immigrants and natives alike, and after some technological innovations, the West became an agricultural giant. The increased output also spurred transportation developments to tie this developing region to the rest of the United States.

Theme: In the era of Jacksonian democracy, the American population grew rapidly and changed in character. More people lived in the raw West and in the expanding cities, and immigrant groups, like the Irish and Germans, added their labor power to America's economy, sometimes arousing hostility from native-born Americans in the process.

Theme: In the early nineteenth century, the American economy developed the beginnings of industrialization. The greatest advances occurred in transportation, as canals and railroads bound the Union together into a continental economy with strong regional specialization.

CHAPTER SUMMARY

The youthful American republic expanded dramatically on the frontier in the early nineteenth century. Frontier life was often crude and hard on the pioneers, especially women.

Westward-moving pioneers often ruthlessly exploited the environment, exhausting the soil and exterminating wildlife. Yet the wild beauty of the West was also valued as a symbol of American national identity, and eventually, environmentalists would create a national park system to preserve pieces of the wilderness.

Other changes altered the character of American society and its workforce. Old cities expanded, and new cities sprang up in the wilderness. Irish and German immigrants poured into the country in the 1830s and 1840s, and the Irish, in particular, aroused nativist hostility because of their Roman Catholic faith.

Inventions and business innovations, such as free incorporation laws, spurred economic growth. Women and children were the most exploited early factory laborers. Male workers made some gains in wages and hours but generally failed in unionization attempts.

The most far-reaching economic advances before the Civil War occurred in agriculture and transportation. The early railroads, despite many obstacles, gradually spread their tentacles across the country. Foreign trade remained only a small part of the American economy, but changing technology gradually created growing economic links to Europe. By the early 1860s, the telegraph, railroad, and steamship had gone far toward replacing older means of travel and communication such as the canals, clipper ships, stagecoach, and pony express.

The new means of transportation and distribution laid the foundations for a continental market economy. The new national economy created a pattern of sectional specialization and altered the traditional economic functions of the family. There was growing concern over the class differences spawned by industrialization, especially in the cities. But the general growth of opportunities and the increased standard of living made America a magnetic land of opportunity to many people at home and abroad.

DEVELOPING THE CHAPTER: SUGGESTED LECTURE OR DISCUSSION TOPICS

- Focus on the Irish and German immigrants and the nativist reaction to them. Show why nativists thought that immigrant poverty and Catholicism posed a threat to American democracy. Consider the important role that the Catholic Church played in the lives of Irish and German Catholic immigrants, despite the opposition of nativists.

  REFERENCES: Kerby Miller, *Emigrants and Exiles: Ireland and the Irish Exodus to North America* (1985); Jay P. Dolan, *The Immigrant Church* (1975).

- Examine the effects of early industrial development on labor and society. Show how the change from a subsistence to a market economy affected workers, farmers, and especially women.

  REFERENCES: Herbert Gutman, *Work, Culture, and Society in Industrializing America* (1976); Mary Blevitt, *Men, Women, and Work* (1988).

- Consider the various stages of the market and transportation revolutions. Focus on the particular significance of the steamboat and the canal and their gradual replacement by the railroad.

  REFERENCE: Charles Sellers, *The Market Revolution: Jacksonian America, 1815–1846* (1992).

- Analyze the relation between the growing national economy and the regional economic specialization of the Northeast, South, and Midwest. Point out the paradoxical way in which economic development both united and divided the sections.

  REFERENCE: W. Elliot Brownlee, *Dynamics of Ascent* (1974).

FOR FURTHER INTEREST: ADDITIONAL CLASS TOPICS

- Discuss the roots of Irish immigration to America. Consider the changing historical image of Irish-Americans and their culture from the nineteenth century to the present and the relationship between popular stereotypes (Irish police, St. Patrick's Day) and the actual experience of Irish-Americans.

- Discuss one or more of the early inventions and their relation to economic growth, for example, the cotton gin, the sewing machine, the mechanical reaper, and the telegraph. Consider how much technological progress depends on the proper social and economic conditions.

- Compare the early-nineteenth-century American economy with those of developing Third World countries today. Discuss the absolutely crucial role that developing a basic infrastructure—particularly transportation and communication facilities—plays in the early stages of industrial development.

- Focus on the lives of early factory workers, perhaps using the female textile workers of Lowell, Massachusetts, as a case study.

CHARACTER SKETCHES

Eli Whitney (1765–1825)

Whitney was the American inventor whose two major innovations—the cotton gin and the system of interchangeable parts—revolutionized the American economy.

He did not care for school, preferring to spend his time making and fixing things in his father's shop. Whitney once took his father's watch completely apart and reassembled it without his father discovering the deed. For a time, he supported himself by manufacturing nails and hatpins.

He earned money to attend Yale by fixing things around the college. One campus carpenter allegedly said, "There was a good mechanic spoiled when you went to college."

He built the first cotton gin in ten days and a larger model in a year. The original machine was stolen and imitations were produced; it took Whitney many years of legal battles to gain the sole patent for the device.

Quote: "There were a number of very respectable Gentlemen at Mrs. Greene's who all agreed that if a machine could be invented which would clean the cotton with expedition, it would be a great thing both to the country and to the inventor.… I concluded to relinquish my school and turn my attention to perfecting the Machine. I made one before I came away which required the labor of one man to turn it and with which one man will clean ten times as much cotton as he can in any other way before known.…" (Letter to his father, 1793)

REFERENCE: Constance M. Green, *Eli Whitney and the Birth of American Technology* (1956).

Robert Fulton (1765–1815)

Fulton is best known in America for his development of the steamboat, but he was also a successful artist and an inventor of the submarine and the torpedo.

As a boy, Fulton became a skilled gunsmith, and in school, he made his own pencils. He liked to fish but hated to row boats, so at fourteen, he devised a paddle wheel to move the boat by foot.

A talented artist, he studied in London under Benjamin West and was earning a successful living by painting before he turned to mechanics and engineering.

He first worked in Britain on iron aqueducts and bridges, and then went to France, where he built a diving boat, the *Nautilus,* which could stay underwater for four hours. But Napoleon lost interest in the device when it proved unable to sink British shipping.

His first steamboat sank on the Seine, but a second model, built in 1803, was successful. This became the prototype for the *Clermont.*

Quote: "When [the *Clermont*] came so near that the noise of the machine and paddles were heard…some prostrated themselves and besought Providence to protect them from the approach of the horrible monster which was marching on the wave and lighting its path by spitting fire." (Newspaper account of the *Clermont*'s first voyage, 1807)

REFERENCE: Kirkpatrick Sale, *Fire of His Genius: Robert Fulton and the American Dream* (2001).

Samuel F. B. Morse (1791–1872)

Morse, the inventor of the telegraph, was also a superb American painter and was, for a time, a leader of nativist agitation.

He studied painting in England, with some of his work winning prizes in the Royal Academy competitions. He returned to Boston in 1815 but discovered that he could earn a living only by painting portraits. After Congress rejected his plan to paint the Capitol rotunda, he reluctantly abandoned art and turned to inventing.

From his time in Europe, he had developed a strong dislike of Catholicism, and in the 1830s, he was a leader of American anti-Catholic agitation.

He developed the first ideas for the telegraph from hearing lectures on electricity. But it took several years of experimentation to perfect the sending and receiving devices and to develop his Morse code for communicating messages by short and long signals. He was in continual poverty and was nearly at the point of abandoning the project when Congress finally authorized funds for the successful Baltimore-to-Washington line.

Quote: "If the presence of electricity can be made visible in any part of an electric circuit closed by an electromagnet, I see no reason why intelligence may not be transmitted instantaneously by electricity." (1832)

REFERENCE: Carleton Mabee, *American Leonardo: A Life of Samuel F.B. Morse* (1943).

QUESTIONS FOR CLASS DISCUSSION

1.   How does the image of the frontier compare with the reality of pioneer life as described in the chapter?

2.   Review the push factors that forced Europeans (specifically the Irish and Germans) from their home countries. What were the pull factors that attracted them to the United States? Why was the United States more appealing than other locations for European immigrants?

3.   Why was transportation—particularly the canals and the railroads—so important in the early stages of industrialization? Would industrialization have occurred more quickly if the federal government had been unimpeded in offering financial assistance to transportation projects?

4.   Which technological innovation was most important for early-nineteenth-century economic development?

5.   Compare the life of factory workers to that of slaves in the South. Is "wage slave" an appropriate description for factory workers?

6.   What effects did the movement from a subsistence to a market economy have on American society, including farmers, laborers, and women? What were the advantages and disadvantages of the change?

7.   To what degree was American industrialization made possible by foreign contributions, such as immigration and stolen mill plans?

MAKERS OF AMERICA: THE IRISH

Questions for Class Discussion

1.   In what ways were the Irish similar to other immigrants from the British Isles, such as the English (Chapter 3) and the Scots-Irish (Chapter 5) and in what ways were they different?

2.   How did the Irish particularly shape the history of American politics, urban life, and religion? What factors contributed to their success in America and what made it difficult for them to get ahead?

Suggested Student Exercises

•   Use your local yellow pages to find the names of Irish businesses or professions.

•   Examine some well-known Irish-Americans (for example, John F. Kennedy, Mayor Richard Daley, Eugene O' Neill, Al Smith). Consider why more Irish-Americans have achieved prominence in the twentieth century than in the nineteenth.

MAKERS OF AMERICA: THE GERMANS

Questions for Class Discussion

1. Compare the historical experience of German immigrants, both before and after immigration, with that of the Irish. How did the patterns of German settlement compare with those of the Irish?

2. What elements of American culture have been influenced by the German presence? Is that presence more visible in certain regions of the country than in others?

Suggested Student Exercises

- Use maps of Pennsylvania and Wisconsin, or of cities like Cincinnati or Milwaukee, to identify German place names.

- Consider the rather harsh persecution of German-Americans during World War I as a contrast to their generally benign experience in America. (See Chapter 33 in the text.)

CHAPTER 15

The Ferment of Reform and Culture, 1790–1860

AP FOCUS

- The Second Great Awakening releases a torrent of religious fervor, combining a belief in moral self-improvement and a wish to expand democracy by means of evangelicalism. Religion and Reform are among the new AP themes.

- From the 1830s to 1850s, the nation experiences a burst of reform activity. Various movements set out to democratize the nation further by combating what they see as institutions and ideas that thwart the expression of democratic values and principles.

- The Hudson River School of art celebrates, mostly through landscape painting, the nation's endless opportunities, uniqueness, and promise. Transcendentalism, a philosophical and literary movement, shapes the cultural outlook of the nation by pointing out the limitations of empirical evidence and encouraging individuals to rely on their senses and emotions to achieve moral improvement. Culture is another AP theme.

AP teachers should take note of the following:

1. Historians debate whether the term *Jacksonian democracy* is accurate. Some see Jackson as a representative of the common man and at the center of the era's democratizing spirit. Others see Jackson as indifferent to some reform movements (such as women's suffrage), opposed to others (abolitionism—he was a slave owner), or unaware of others (possibly urban reform). They hold that grassroots movements in the 1830s, 1840s, and 1850s were the primary impetus for reform.

2. Some reform movements advocated challenging the social, economic, and ideological status quo. Advocates of women's rights, for example, challenged the stereotypes that associated women with a "cult of domesticity." Abolitionists challenged the institution of slavery. For their part, temperance advocates fumed that American civilization and culture were being undermined by "demon rum."

Focus on Historical Thinking:

Create a list of twenty-five important terms. Have students correctly place them in one of the following chronological time periods: pre-Columbian to 1607; 1607-1754; 1754-1800; 1800-1848.

FOCUS QUESTIONS

1. How did Deism, the Second Great Awakening, continued denominational fragmentation, and Mormons shape American religious life?

2. What educational developments occurred in the first half of the nineteenth century?

3. Who led the various reform movements in the early half of the nineteenth century?

4. How did Americans contribute to the advance of science during this time?

5. Who were America's foremost artistic and literary figures in the first half of the nineteenth century?

CHAPTER THEMES

Theme: The spectacular religious revivals of the Second Great Awakening reversed a trend toward secular rationalism in American culture and helped to fuel a spirit of social reform. In the process, religion was increasingly feminized, while women, in turn, took the lead in movements of reform, including those designed to improve their own condition.

Theme: The attempt to improve Americans' faith, morals, and character affected nearly all areas of American life and culture, including education, the family, literature, and the arts—culminating in the great crusade against slavery.

Theme: Intellectual and cultural development in America was less prolific than in Europe, but they did earn some international recognition and became more distinctly American, especially after the War of 1812.

CHAPTER SUMMARY

In early nineteenth century America, movements of moral and religious reform accompanied the democratization of politics and the creation of a national market economy. After a period of growing rationalism in religion, a new wave of revivals, beginning about 1800, swept out of the West and effected great change not only in religious life, but also in other areas of society. Existing religious groups were further fragmented, and new groups like the Mormons emerged. Women were especially prominent in these developments, becoming a major presence in the churches and discovering, in reform movements, an outlet for energies that were often stifled in masculinized political and economic life.

Among the first areas to benefit from the reform impulse was education. The public elementary school movement gained strength, while a few women made their way into still tradition-bound colleges. Women were also prominent in movements for improved treatment of the mentally ill, peace, temperance, and other causes. By the 1840s, some women also began to agitate for their own rights, including suffrage. The movement for women's rights, closely linked to the antislavery crusade, gained adherents even while it met strong obstacles and vehement opposition.

While many reformers worked to improve society as a whole, others created utopian experiments to model their religious and social ideals. Some of these groups promoted radical sexual and economic doctrines, while others appealed to high-minded intellectuals and artists.

American culture was still quite weak in theoretical sciences and the fine arts, but a vigorous national literature blossomed after the War of 1812 with the works of Washington Irving and James Fenimore Cooper. In New England, the literary renaissance encouraged truly "American" literature and was closely linked to the philosophy of transcendentalism promoted by Emerson , Henry David Thoreau and Margaret Fuller, the editor of the *Dial*. Many of the great American writers, such as Walt Whitman, reflected the national spirit of utopian optimism, but a few dissenters, such as Hawthorne and Melville, explored the darker side of life and of their own society.

Imitative portraiture and historical painting gave way to the emerging romanticism of the Hudson River School that glorified nature and began to examine human interaction with the environment.

DEVELOPING THE CHAPTER: SUGGESTED LECTURE OR DISCUSSION TOPICS

- Explain the revivals of the Second Great Awakening and their broad cultural implications. Emphasize how the spirit of social reform grew out of individual conversion and how religious change was linked to the wider democratic movements in American society.

REFERENCES: Nathan Hatch, *The Democratization of American Christianity* (1989); Robert Abzug, *Cosmos Crumbling: American Reform and the Religious Imagination* (1994).

- Examine the nature of the nineteenth-century family and its relation to society, stressing particularly how the cult of domesticity and women's separate sphere gave women a specially defined role in society. Examine how some female reformers began to advocate their own rights as well as the betterment of others.

  REFERENCE: Carl Degler, *At Odds: Women and the Family in America from the Revolution to the Present* (1980).

- Examine the early women's movement as one of the most important reforms and explain the obstacles it faced. Show the relationship between women's growing activism and the broader reforms of the antebellum era.

  REFERENCE: Lori Ginzburg, *Women and the Work of Benevolence* (1990).

- Explore the perfectionist and utopian quality of early American culture, as revealed in both the utopian communal experiments and philosophical movements like transcendentalism. Point out the involvement of many writers in reform movements and experiments such as Brook Farm.

  REFERENCE: Anne C. Rose, *Transcendentalism as a Social Movement, 1830–1850* (1981).

FOR FURTHER INTEREST: ADDITIONAL CLASS TOPICS

- Use popular contemporary texts such as *McGuffey's Readers* or *Godey's Lady's Book* to illuminate early American character and values. Discuss how the messages that were especially aimed at children or women reveal prevalent social attitudes, as well as the nature and purposes of nineteenth-century education.

- Examine the story of the Mormons. In what way is it an American story (individualism, fighting religious persecution, and pioneering)? In what ways is it an un-American story (others' intolerance, communalism, and polygamy)?

- Analyze one or more of the utopian communities, such as the Shaker communes, New Harmony, Oneida, or Brook Farm. Consider how the success or failure of such efforts should be judged.

- Listen to the music of Stephen Foster. Compare it with contemporary European music by Beethoven, Brahms, Verdi, and Wagner. Why the difference?

- Review American works of literature of this time (Thoreau, Alcott, Poe, Hawthorne, and Melville). Find contemporary European authors and works of literature (Dickens, Hugo, and Dumas). Are the American works distinct and unique when compared with the European ones?

CHARACTER SKETCHES

Charles G. Finney (1792–1875)

Finney was the most influential revivalist of the Second Great Awakening and a president of Oberlin College, a center of abolitionism and reform.

Although he was a successful attorney before turning to preaching, Finney never attended college or law school. Despite his dislike of conventional churches, he underwent a total conversion to religion after reading the Bible on his own. He then abandoned his law practice entirely, saying that he had a "retainer from the Lord to plead His cause."

Finney was ordained by the Presbyterians but was often at odds with them and conducted revivals completely on his own. Besides the anxious bench, some of his other new methods included praying by name for the conversion of sinners in the community, holding extended nightly meetings for a week or more, and encouraging women to pray and speak publicly. He also used theatrical gestures, movement, and emotional rhetoric to rouse his listeners.

Quote: "A revival is not a miracle, or dependent on a miracle in any sense. It is a purely philosophical result of the right use of the constituted means." (*Lectures on Revivalism,* 1835)

REFERENCE: William G. McLoughlin, *Modern Revivalism: Charles Grandison Finney to Billy Graham* (1959).

Joseph Smith (1805–1844)

Smith was the founder and original prophet of the Mormon Church.

The poor New York frontier family in which he grew up frequently moved during his childhood. He experienced his first vision of the angel Moroni in 1820, followed by subsequent encounters that led to the discovery of the Book of Mormon. The Book of Mormon recounts the coming of Old Testament people to America and the battles of the good Nephites with the evil Lamanites (American Indians).

The Mormon Church was organized very hierarchically, with Smith as "Seer, Translator, Prophet, Apostle of Jesus Christ, and Elder of the Church." He gave numerous new revelations before his martyrdom in Carthage, Illinois. The most famous was that allowing polygamy; Smith himself had twenty-seven wives at the time of his death. He had also announced his plan to run for president of the United States in 1844.

A magnetic personality, Smith was down-to-earth, clever, physically vigorous, and virile.

Quote: "We believe in the literal gathering of Israel and in the restoration of the Ten Tribes; that Zion will be built upon this continent; that Christ will reign personally upon the earth; and that the earth will be renewed and receive its paradisaical glory." (Statement of Faith, 1843)

REFERENCE: Richard Bushman, *Joseph Smith and the Beginnings of Mormonism* (1984).

Catharine Beecher (1800–1878)

Beecher was a prominent women's educator and writer and a member of the famous Evangelical family.

Catharine, the oldest of four Beecher daughters, was very close to her father, and when her mother died, sixteen-year-old Catharine took over much of the responsibility for managing the household and the younger children.

Her plans to marry an unchurched man in 1822 came to naught when he died four months after their engagement, and she took the death as a divine judgment on her. The following year, she opened the first of her female seminaries.

Beecher insisted that the young ladies in her schools take up physical exercise and attacked the confining clothing and social norms that restricted women. But she opposed higher education for women and attacked women's involvement in abolitionism and other social reforms. Her popular *Treatise on Domestic Economy,* written with her sister Harriet Beecher Stowe, contained practical tips on child-rearing, cooking, family health, and other matters that would enable women to run their homes effectively.

Quote: "Any activity that throws woman into the attitude of a combatant, either for herself or others, lies outside her appropriate sphere." (*An Essay on Slavery and Abolitionism,* 1837)

REFERENCE: Kathryn Kish Sklar, *Catharine Beecher: A Study in American Domesticity* (1973).

Elizabeth Cady Stanton (1815–1902)

Stanton, the cofounder (with Lucretia Mott) of the Seneca Falls Convention, was the most influential nineteenth-century American feminist.

Her father was a lawyer, and she took great interest in his work. When he said to her, "Oh, my daughter, I wish you were a boy," she set out to show him that girls were as good as boys.

She wrote the "Declaration of Sentiments" for the Seneca Falls Convention and pushed through the demand for woman suffrage. For a few years, she wore Amelia Bloomer–style pants outfits in protest against women's confining clothing.

After 1851, she worked in close collaboration with Susan B. Anthony. Anthony was the traveler and organizer who focused almost exclusively on suffrage, while Stanton was the writer and theorist who advocated a broader feminism and many other radical causes. She was lively, humorous, well read, and a very popular speaker.

Quote: "I should feel exceedingly diffident to appear before you at this time, having never before spoken in public, were I not nerved by a sense of sacred right and duty [and]…did I not believe that woman herself must do this work; for woman alone can understand the height, the depth, the length and the breadth of her degradation." (Speech to the Seneca Falls Convention, 1848)

REFERENCE: Alma Lutz, *Created Equal: A Biography of Elizabeth Cady Stanton* (1973).

Mary Lyon (1797–1849)

Lyon was a pioneering women's educator and the founder of Mt. Holyoke Seminary (later Mt. Holyoke College).

One of her male schoolteachers told her that the general belief in women's mental inferiority was wrong and the girls could absorb as much advanced learning as they had an opportunity to obtain. She opened her first girls' school in 1824 but spent much time pursuing knowledge on her own by attending lectures at all-male Amherst College.

She raised the first thousand dollars for Mt. Holyoke on her own and took no salary until the venture was under way. The original name for the school was to be Pangynaskean (Greek for "whole-woman-making"), but this was dropped after press ridicule. Mt. Holyoke was unique among female seminaries because the young ladies were taught the same academic subjects as men and because the students managed their own cooking, housekeeping, and laundry.

A very religious woman, Lyon often encouraged campus revivals. She was hardworking, friendly, and very popular with students and faculty. So indifferent was she to dress that her students bought her stylish hats to replace the unfashionable ones she usually wore.

Quote: "During the past year my heart has so yearned over the female youth…that it has sometimes seemed as if there was a fire shut up in my bones." (1834)

REFERENCE: Anne Rose, *Voices of the Marketplace: American Thought and Culture* (1995).

Henry David Thoreau (1817–1862)

Thoreau was the writer and friend of Emerson whose works on nature and civil disobedience have had a continuing influence on American culture.

He was born in Concord, Massachusetts. The death of his older brother, John, at a young age deeply affected Henry and contributed to the lonely and tragic side of his character.

After resigning from school teaching after a few weeks because he refused to discipline the children, he later organized a progressive school, where classes were held outdoors and children were encouraged to develop their own interests.

Emerson agreed to allow Thoreau to build his cabin on Emerson's property at Walden Pond if Thoreau would clear the land and put in a garden. Thoreau moved there on the Fourth of July, 1845, and stayed two years and two months. During that time he wrote his two masterpieces, *Walden* and *A Week on the Concord and Merrimack Rivers.*

Quote: On his deathbed, Thoreau was asked if he had made his peace with God. He replied, "I did not know that we had ever quarreled."

REFERENCE: Robert D. Richardson, *Thoreau: A Life of the Mind* (1986).

Ralph Waldo Emerson (1803–1882)

Emerson was the most famous American writer and philosopher of the early nineteenth century, whose transcendentalist theories shaped the golden age of New England literature.

He came from a long line of New England clergymen but eventually abandoned both the pulpit and conventional religion. His speech to the Harvard Divinity School in 1838, which questioned the value of historical Christianity, aroused ministerial opposition and prevented his returning to Harvard until 1865.

Emerson was popular in the local community of Concord, where he was once elected Hogreeve (the town official in charge of rounding up stray pigs). After his "American Scholar" lecture, he was in great demand as a speaker and traveled thousands of miles to deliver his addresses—which he repeated many times. His booming platform voice belied his generally quiet and mild-mannered demeanor.

Quote: "Books are for the scholar's idle times. When he can read God directly, the hour is too precious to be wasted in other men's transcripts of their readings." ("American Scholar" address, 1837)

REFERENCES: Joel Porte, *Representative Man: Emerson in His Time* (1979); Robert D. Richardson, *Emerson: The Mind on Fire* (1995).

QUESTIONS FOR CLASS DISCUSSION

1. What particular qualities did Evangelical religion give to the early American culture? Why did so many of its energies move toward the reform of society? Were there elements of American religion that resisted the reform impulse?

2. How important is a free public education to a republic? If it is important, why then was early education so poor? If it is not important, why did it begin? Do you agree that public education was "an insurance premium that the wealthy paid for stability and democracy," as the authors assert? Is it important to a republic to have compulsory public education?

3. Were the cult of domesticity and the rise of the child-centered family signs of an improvement or a restriction on women's status and condition? Was the new family a progressive reflection of American democratic ideals or a restriction on them?

4. Why did America produce so many reform and utopian movements? What did they contribute to American culture?

5. What made women such prominent leaders in the religious and reform movements? How did the women's rights movement compare with the other movements of the period? What obstacles did

women reformers face? Why did women often have more difficulty working on their own behalf than they did advocating other causes?

MAKERS OF AMERICA: THE ONEIDA COMMUNITY

Questions for Class Discussion

1. What were the fundamental human and social problems that Noyes's radical ideas attempted to address? Why was he able to put them into practice in antebellum America?

2. Was the Oneida experiment doomed to failure from the start? Or should its nearly thirty years of existence be considered a rather remarkable success, especially in its challenge to traditional Victorian patterns of marriage gender relations, considering the very short life span of most utopian communes?

Suggested Student Exercises

*   Locate Putney, Vermont, and Oneida, New York, on maps. Compare the pattern of Noyes's communal migrations with those of other utopian groups that challenged conventional patterns of monogamous marriage—especially Joseph Smith's Mormons and Mother Ann Lee's Shakers. Consider why such groups frequently migrated toward the frontier.

*   Examine some of Noyes's own statements and writings. Consider whether his sexual and communal experimentation was really a movement toward freedom or whether it really represented a kind of cultlike control by the founder himself that was resented by the younger generation reared in the commune.

EXPANDING THE "VARYING VIEWPOINTS"

*   David Donald, *Lincoln Reconsidered* (1956).

    A view of reformers as motivated by cultural anxiety:

    "In these plebeian days they could not be successful in politics; family tradition and education prohibited idleness; and agitation allowed the only chance for personal and social self-fulfillment.... What they did question, and what they did rue, was the transfer of leadership to the wrong groups in society, and their appeal for reform was a strident call for their own class to re-exert its former social dominance.... Leadership of humanitarian reform may have been influenced by revivalism or by British precedent, but its true origin lay in the drastic dislocation of Northern society."

*   Nancy Cott, *The Bonds of Womanhood: "Women's Sphere" in New England, 1780–1835* (1977).

    A view of social reform as a reflection of women's social ties:

    "Women who joined maternal associations thus asserted their formative power over their children's lives, took up evangelical goals, and complemented the private job of child rearing by approaching their occupation cooperatively with their peers. Women joined moral reform societies to accomplish different immediate aims, but with similar reasoning.... Like maternal associations, moral reform societies focused women's energies on the family arena in order to solve social problems."

QUESTIONS ABOUT THE "VARYING VIEWPOINTS"

1. How do the proponents of these two viewpoints each explain the relationship between the reformers' backgrounds and their reform activities?

2.   How might these different views of reformers' motives affect our judgments about the value of social reform?

3.   How might each of these historians interpret the temperance movement or the career of Dorothea Dix?

CHAPTER 16

The South and the Slavery Controversy, 1793–1860

AP FOCUS

- The South in the antebellum period is dominated by the planter-slaveholder class, which comprises only a small percentage of the South's white population—approximately two-thirds of southern whites own no slaves. See the chart in *The American Pageant* (14th ed., p. 375/15th ed., p. 341) for a breakdown of slave ownership.

- So important is cotton to the South's—and, some contend, the nation's—economy that it is referred to as King Cotton. See a British visitor's comment (14th ed., p. 375/15th ed., p. 340). The textbook has maps (14th ed., pp. 376, 377/15th ed., pp. 342, 343) showing the centers of cotton production and the growth in production from 1820 to 1860.

- The life of freed slaves, while appreciably better than that of their enslaved brethren, is precarious. Freed slaves did not find a panacea to their problems and treatment in the North either.

- Abolitionism takes hold. Abolitionists, however, are not particularly popular in the North because they are seen as troublemakers and rabble-rousers.

- Thinking Globally (14th ed., pp. 388–389/15th ed., pp. 354-355) charts the struggle to abolish slavery, spearheaded by the British, and how it played out in other countries around the world.

AP teachers should take note of the following:

1. Abolitionists came in varieties. Most favored gradualism, which, for some, meant resettling freed slaves in Africa and compensating slaveholders. Others would settle for nothing short of an immediate end to slavery, even if violence was needed to achieve their goal. Lincoln initially identified with gradualism. William Lloyd Garrison and John Brown identified with the second, although they differed over the methods to be used: Garrison advocated an end to slavery through legislation, and John Brown believed that slavery could be defeated only through violent means. Former slaves, like Frederick Douglass, Harriet Tubman, and Sojourner Truth, who had experienced the degradation of slavery firsthand, passionately and articulately expressed their disdain for the "peculiar institution."

2. The American Colonization Society (formed in the early nineteenth century) was at the forefront of the movement to resettle freed slaves in Africa. Although ultimately it was not a viable remedy to the problem, the society resettled thousands of emancipated slaves on land purchased in Africa.

Focus on Historical Thinking:

Reproduce Figure 16.1 on p. 341, Map 16.1 on p. 342, and Table 16.1 on p. 355 (15th ed.) without captions. Ask students to write one clear, concise sentence explaining the significance of each.

FOCUS QUESTIONS

1. What are the rungs on the social ladder of the South?

2.   Where and how did slaves live in the South?

3.   What did slaves do to resist the "peculiar institution"?

4.   Who were prominent abolitionists, and what distinguished one from another?

5.   How did the South react to the growing agitation of abolitionists?

CHAPTER THEMES

Theme: The explosion of cotton production fastened the slave system deeply upon the South, creating a complex, hierarchical racial and social order that deeply affected whites as well as blacks.

Theme: The economic benefits of an increasing production of cotton due to the cotton gin and slavery were shared between the South, the North, and Britain. The economics of cotton and slavery also led to bigger and bigger plantations, since they could afford the heavy investment of human capital.

Theme: The emergence of a small but energetic radical abolitionist movement caused a fierce proslavery backlash in the South and a slow but steady growth of moderate antislavery sentiment in the North.

CHAPTER SUMMARY

Whitney's cotton gin made cotton production enormously profitable and created an ever-increasing demand for slave labor. The South's dependence on cotton production tied it economically to the plantation system and racially to white supremacy. The cultural gentility and political domination of the relatively small plantation aristocracy concealed slavery's great social and economic costs for whites as well as blacks.

Most slaves were held by a few large planters. But most slaveowners had few slaves, and most southern whites had no slaves at all. Nevertheless, except for a few mountain whites, the majority of southern whites strongly supported slavery and racial supremacy because they cherished the hope of becoming slaveowners themselves, and because white racial identity gave them a sense of superiority to the blacks.

The treatment of the economically valuable slaves varied considerably. Within the bounds of the cruel system, slaves yearned for freedom and struggled to maintain their humanity, including family life.

The older black colonization movement was largely replaced in the 1830s by a radical Garrisonian abolitionism demanding an immediate end to slavery. Abolitionism and the Nat Turner rebellion caused a strong backlash in the South, which increasingly defended slavery as a positive good and turned its back on many of the liberal political and social ideas gaining strength in the North.

Most northerners were hostile to radical abolitionism and respected the Constitution's evident protection of slavery where it existed. But many also gradually came to see the South as a land of oppression and any attempt to extend slavery as a threat to free society.

DEVELOPING THE CHAPTER: SUGGESTED LECTURE OR DISCUSSION TOPICS

- Analyze the complex relations among the different elements of southern society: planter-aristocrats, small planters, poor whites, slaves, and free blacks. Contrast the dominant slaveholding elite with the mass of poorer whites who nevertheless supported slavery.

  REFERENCES: Bruce Collins, *White Society in the Antebellum South* (1985); Ira Berlin, *Slaves Without Masters* (1975).

- Examine the nature of slavery. Explain how slavery was both an economic institution and a social system that shaped whites and blacks alike, including their social and family life.

  REFERENCE: Brenda Stevenson, *Life in Black and White: Family and Community in the Slave South* (1996).

- Describe the lives of blacks under slavery. Show both the burdens of the system and the slaves' struggles to survive and maintain their humanity.

  REFERENCE: Eugene Genovese, *Roll, Jordan, Roll* (1976).

- Explain the various responses to slavery, from radical abolitionism to the defense of slavery as a positive good, and why the abolitionists had such a great impact even though they were an unpopular minority.

  REFERENCE: Lewis Perry and Michael Fellman, *Antislavery Reconsidered* (1979).

FOR FURTHER INTEREST: ADDITIONAL CLASS TOPICS

- Describe the operation of a typical large plantation or the working life of a typical large-plantation owner, including relations with overseers and slaves.

- Examine the black family and black religion. Consider how slavery affected both white and black views of women, family, and sexuality.

- Examine the paradox that slavery often involved intimate and personal relationships between individual whites and blacks (exemplified by the photo of the slave nurse with white child), even while it maintained a strict and often violent system of control over the slaves as a group. Ask why this paternalistic element of American slaveholding was so important to southerners' self-justification of slavery.

- Review the creation of the Republic of Liberia. Determine if the colonization or relocation concept would have worked at any point in pre–Civil War America.

- Investigate the actions of the Royal Navy's West African Squadron. What issues arise when one nation acts to enforce its laws (in this case, prohibition on the slave trade) on an international stage?

- Review the case of the *Amistad*, specifically, the arguments made by John Quincy Adams before the Supreme Court.

- Explore the British efforts to free slaves in the West Indies. Why was Britain successful in 1833 in ending slavery in the West Indies when it was still going strong in the United States?

- Discuss the northern debate over the means of ending slavery by contrasting Garrison's radical abolitionism with the moderate no-expansion position of a politician like Lincoln.

CHARACTER SKETCHES

Theodore Dwight Weld (1803–1895)

Weld was the leader of the abolitionist Lane rebels, the West's most influential antislavery preacher, and the author of *American Slavery as It Is*, the most important abolitionist propaganda book besides *Uncle Tom's Cabin*.

He was converted by Charles Finney and joined Finney's holy band of young men who wanted to "convert the world." Weld's first causes were temperance and manual labor, but the English abolitionist Charles Stuart converted him to antislavery.

He and his fellow antislavery Lane Seminary students worked in the poverty-stricken black community of Little Africa in Cincinnati. After he led the Lane rebels out of the seminary, he traveled and lectured constantly on behalf of the antislavery cause.

In 1838, he married Angelina Grimké, who, with her sister Sarah, had left South Carolina to become a prominent abolitionist. Angelina helped Weld write *American Slavery as It Is,* but they both eventually retired from active crusading to raise their family and organize a school in New Jersey.

Quote: "Slavery, with its robbing of body and soul from birth to death, its exactions of toil unrecompensed, its sunderings from kindred, its frantic orgies of lust, its intellect levelled with dust, its baptisms of blood, and its legacy of damning horrors to the eternity of the spirit—slavery in this land of liberty, and light, and revivals of millenial glory—its days are numbered and well-nigh finished.... The nation is shaking off its slumbers to sleep no more." (1934)

REFERENCE: Robert Abzug, *Passionate Liberator: Theodore Dwight Weld and the Dilemma of Reform* (1980).

William Lloyd Garrison (1805–1879)

Garrison was the most famous American abolitionist, an advocate of nonresistance, and editor of *The Liberator.*

His father, a Canadian sea captain who drank heavily, deserted the family when Garrison was a child. Garrison received little education and practiced a number of trades before becoming a printer in Maryland.

He first crusaded for nationalism and temperance, then for moderate abolition, before being converted to radical abolition. Besides attacking slavery, *The Liberator* promoted many other causes, including peace, women's rights, temperance, and abolition of capital punishment.

Garrison eventually denounced the northern churches and the Constitution for their compromises with slavery. He was often threatened by antiabolitionist mobs, and several southern states offered rewards for his arrest. Despite his pacifism, he supported the Civil War as a means to end slavery.

Quote: "I am earnest—I will not equivocate—I will not excuse—I will not retreat a single inch—and *I will be heard.*" (*The Liberator,* 1831)

REFERENCE: Henry Mayer, *All on Fire: William Lloyd Garrison and the Abolition of Slavery* (2000).

Frederick Douglass (1817–1895)

Douglass was a former slave who became the leading pre–Civil War black abolitionist and the most influential African American of the nineteenth century.

Douglass's original name was Frederick Bailey. His father was white and his mother a black slave from whom he was separated at an early age. His first escape attempt failed and he landed in jail. He was trained as a ship caulker in Baltimore and escaped to New York in 1838 by disguising himself as a sailor.

He moved to Boston, changed his name to Douglass to avoid capture, and worked as a common laborer for three years. After a speech before an antislavery meeting, he became an abolitionist agent. He eventually split with Garrison and formed his own paper, *The North Star.* After the Civil War, he was prominent in Republican politics and served in various federal positions, such as minister to Haiti from 1889 to 1891.

Quote: "I have been frequently asked how I felt when I found myself in a free state.... It was a moment of the highest excitement I ever experienced.... This state of mind, however, very soon subsided; and I was again seized with a feeling of great insecurity and loneliness. I was yet liable to be taken back, and subjected to all the tortures of slavery. This in itself was enough to damp the ardor of my enthusiasm." (*Narrative of the Life of Frederick Douglass,* 1845)

REFERENCE: William McFeely, *Frederick Douglass* (1990).

Martin Delany (1812–1885)

Delany was the pioneering black nationalist and author who advocated that African Americans leave the United States.

He was born a free man in Virginia. His grandfather was said to have been an African chief who was captured and sold to America, and traditions and memories of Africa remained alive in Delany's family.

Delany moved to Pennsylvania, became involved in the black convention movement, and started a black newspaper. For a time, he worked with Garrison and Douglass but despaired of abolitionism after the Fugitive Slave Act of 1850 and began working to encourage blacks to leave America.

In 1856, he moved to a fugitive-slave community in Canada. Before his exploratory trip to Africa in 1859–1860, Delany communicated with African Americans in Liberia. Upon his return to the United States, he served in the army during the Civil War. He later became involved in Republican politics in South Carolina during Reconstruction.

Quote: "I care but little what white men think of what I say, write or do; my sole desire is to benefit the colored people. This being done I am satisfied—the opinion of every white person in the country or the world to the contrary notwithstanding." (Letter to Frederick Douglass, 1852)

REFERENCE: Victor Ullman, *Martin R.. Delany: The Beginnings of Black Nationalism* (1971).

GREAT DEBATES IN AMERICAN HISTORY

Great Debate (1830–1860):

Slavery: Is slavery an intolerable institution?

Yes: Antislavery forces: abolitionists, led by Garrison, Weld, and the Grimké sisters; Free Soil and Republican politicians, led by Lincoln, Seward, and Sumner.

No: Proslavery forces: white southerners, led by Calhoun, Davis, and Butler; northern moderates, led by Webster, Douglas, and Buchanan.

ISSUE #1: Is slavery a violation of fundamental moral and religious principles?

Yes: Antislavery leader Angelina Grimké: "The great fundamental principle of abolitionists is, that man cannot rightfully hold his fellow man as property…. It matters not what *motive* he may give for such a monstrous violation of the laws of God. The claim to him as *property* is an annihilation of his right to himself, which is the foundation upon which all his other rights are built. It is high-handed robbery of Jehovah; for he has declared, 'All souls are mine.'"

No: Proslavery Senator Andrew Butler of South Carolina: "Inequality seems to characterize the administration of the providence of God. I will not undertake to invade that sanctuary, but I will say that the abolitionists cannot make those equal whom God has made unequal, in human estimation. That He has made the blacks unequal to the whites, human history…has pronounced its uniform judgment."

ISSUE #2: Is slavery incompatible with the most fundamental American principles?

Yes: Antislavery leader Abraham Lincoln: "There is no reason in the world why the negro is not entitled to all the natural rights enumerated in the Declaration of Independence—the right to life, liberty, and the pursuit of happiness. I hold that he is as much entitled to these as the white man. I agree with Judge Douglas that he is not my equal in many respects.... But in the right to eat the bread, without the leave of anybody else, which his own hand earns, he is my equal and the equal of Judge Douglas, and the equal of every living man."

No: Proslavery Senator Stephen A. Douglas: "At the time the Constitution was framed there were thirteen states in the Union, twelve of which were slaveholding states and one a free state.... For one, I am opposed to negro citizenship in any and every form. I believe this government was made on the white basis. I believe it was made by white men for the benefit of white men and their posterity forever, and I am in favor of confining citizenship to white men...instead of conferring it upon negroes, Indians, and other inferior races...."

ISSUE #3: Would the attempted abolition of slavery threaten the foundations of the Union?

No: Antislavery leader William Seward: "Hitherto the two systems have existed in different states, but side by side within the American Union. This has happened because the Union is a confederation of states. But in another aspect the United States constitute only one nation.... It is an irrepressible conflict between opposing and enduring forces, and it means that the United States must and will, sooner or later, become either entirely a slaveholding nation or entirely a free-labor nation.... Our forefathers knew it to be true, and unanimously acted upon it when they framed the constitution of the United States."

Yes: Proslavery Senator Alfred Iversen of Georgia: "Sir, I believe that the time will come when the slave states will be compelled, in vindication of their rights, interests, and honor, to separate from the free states and erect an independent confederacy.... At all events, I am satisfied that one of two things is *inevitable;* either that the slave states must surrender their peculiar institutions or separate from the North.... No union or no slavery will sooner or later be forced upon the choice of the southern people."

ISSUE #4: Should slavery be allowed to expand into the territories if the people of those territories want it?

No: Antislavery leader Abraham Lincoln: "I believe we shall not have peace upon the question until the opponents of slavery arrest the further spread of it and place it where the public mind shall rest in the belief that it is in the course of ultimate extinction.... Now I believe if we could arrest the spread, and place it where Washington and Jefferson and Madison placed it, it would be in the course of ultimate extinction and the public mind would, as for eighty years past, believe that it was in the course of ultimate extinction.... The crisis would be past and the institution might be let alone for a hundred years—if it should live so long—in the states where it exists, yet it would be going out of existence in the way best for both the black and the white races."

Yes: Proslavery Senator Stephen A. Douglas: "Whenever it becomes necessary, in our growth and progress, to acquire more territory, I am in favor of it, without reference to the question of slavery, and, when we have acquired it, I will leave the people free to do as they please, either to make it slave or free territory, as they prefer.... If they prohibit slavery, it shall be prohibited. They can form their institutions to please themselves, subject only to the Constitution; and I, for one, stand ready to receive them into the Union."

REFERENCES: Don E. Fehrenbacher, *Prelude to Greatness: Lincoln in the 1850s* (1962); J. Jeffrey Auer, ed., *Antislavery and Disunion, 1858–1861: Studies in the Rhetoric of Compromise and Conflict* (1963).

QUESTIONS FOR CLASS DISCUSSION

1. How did slavery affect whites—those who owned slaves and those who did not?

2. How did blacks respond to the condition of slavery?

3. Why did the South move from viewing slavery as a "necessary evil" to proclaiming it a "positive good"?

4. How effective were the abolitionists in achieving their goals? Did they hasten or delay the end of slavery?

5. Was Britain being hypocritical by freeing their slaves in the West Indies while openly importing cotton from the slave-owning South? What role, if any, should have other nations taken in America's slave question?

6. Were basic freedoms jeopardized or forfeited with regard to congressional action about the question of slavery (Gag Resolution, mail restrictions)? Were the decisions of Congress justified?

EXPANDING THE "VARYING VIEWPOINTS"

*   Stanley Elkins, *Slavery* (1959).

    A view of slavery as a totalitarian system that destroyed blacks' personalities:

    "Both [the Nazi concentration camp and slavery] were closed systems from which all standards based on prior connections had been effectively detached. A working adjustment to either system required a childlike conformity, a limited choice of 'significant others.'… Absolute power for [the master] meant absolute dependency for the slave—the dependency not of the developing child but of the perpetual child.… The result would be something resembling 'Sambo.'"

*   Eugene Genovese, *Roll, Jordan, Roll* (1972).

    A view of slavery as a paternalistic system within which blacks could maintain their humanity:

    "Thus, the slaves, by accepting a paternalistic ethos and legitimizing class rule, developed their most powerful defense against the dehumanization implicit in slavery. Southern paternalism may have reinforced racism as well as class exploitation, but it also unwittingly invited its victims to fashion their own interpretation of the social order it was intended to justify. And the slaves, drawing on a religion that was supposed to assure their compliance and docility, rejected the essence of slavery by projecting their own rights and value as human beings."

QUESTIONS ABOUT THE "VARYING VIEWPOINTS"

1. How does the holder of each of these viewpoints see the relationship between masters and slaves?

2. How does each of these historians connect the nature of slavery with its effect on blacks?

3. What might each of these historians say about the long-term effects of slavery on African Americans?

4. Do Genovese's contentions contradict Frank Tannebaum's arguments?

CHAPTER 17

Manifest Destiny and Its Legacy, 1841–1848

AP FOCUS

- A member of the Democratic Party, John Tyler, becomes the Whig's vice-presidential candidate in 1840. When President William Henry Harrison dies just one month into his term, Tyler, much to the distress of Whig party loyalists, such as Henry Clay, is elevated to the presidency.

- Manifest Destiny, the belief that the United States is divinely inspired to spread across the continent, becomes the rationale for widespread territorial expansion. Critics repudiate it as nothing short of unbridled imperialism.

- "Oregon fever" seizes Americans who flock to the Willamette Valley and other areas in the Northwest, opening yet another border dispute with Britain.

- Texas enters the union in 1845.

- James K. Polk becomes a spokesman for those lured to the West. During his one term as president, the Oregon boundary dispute is settled, but tensions with Mexico ultimately lead to war.

- The Mexican-American War is a disaster for the Mexicans, who lose nearly half of their nation to the United States for compensation of a mere $15 million.

AP teachers should take note of the following:

1. Some veterans of the Mexican-American War, among them Robert E. Lee and Ulysses S. Grant, would later play a role in the American Civil War.

2. The entrance of Texas into the Union and the Mexican-American War stirred often-heated debates. Many northerners and Whigs were angered by what they saw as an unjust war and a blatant attempt to expand slavery. Congressman Abraham Lincoln demanded from President Polk a justification for war. See Lincoln's comment on the Mexican-American War in *The American Pageant* (14th ed., p. 408/15th ed., p. 370).

3. Justifications for territorial expansion were often expressed in racist terms. See the diatribe in a major New York newspaper (14th ed., p. 411/15th ed., p. 373) in regard to land taken from Mexico.

Focus on Historical Thinking:

Have student identify five cause/effect relationships concerning territorial acquisition.

FOCUS QUESTIONS

1. Why were Whigs, like Clay and Webster, unhappy with Tyler's accession to the presidency?

2. What issues caused tension between Britain and the United States?

3. Why was Texas annexed into the United States at the time that it was? Why not earlier or later?

4. What circumstances resulted in the peaceful settlement of the Oregon dispute between Britain and the United States?

5. What was Polk's four-point program as president and how successful was he in accomplishing each part of his plan?

6. Why did the United States and Mexico go to war in 1846?

7. Who led the major military campaigns during the Mexican War and how successful was each campaign?

8. What were the provisions of the Treaty of Guadalupe Hidalgo?

9. How did the Wilmot Proviso reveal strong sectional differences?

CHAPTER THEMES

Theme: American expansionism gained momentum in the 1840s, leading first to the acquisition of Texas and Oregon, and then to the Mexican War, which added vast southwestern territories to the United States and ignited the slavery question.

Theme: American international prestige grows as the United States expands. Successful military campaigns against Mexico along with well-negotiated treaties with Britain force Europe to respect America more, while Latin America begins to be wary of the Colossus of the North.

CHAPTER SUMMARY

As Tyler assumed the presidency after Harrison's death, the United States became engaged in a series of sharp disputes with Britain. A conflict over the Maine boundary was resolved, but British involvement in Texas revived the movement to annex the Lone Star Republic to the United States.

The Texas and Oregon questions became embroiled in the 1844 campaign, as the Democrats nominated and elected the militantly expansionist Polk. After Texas was added to the Union, conflicts with Mexico over California and the Texas boundary erupted into war in 1846.

American forces quickly conquered California and New Mexico. Winfield Scott's and Zachary Taylor's invasion of Mexico was also successful, and the United States obtained large new territories in the peace treaty.

Besides adding California, New Mexico, and Utah to American territory, the Mexican War trained a new generation of military leaders and aroused long-term Latin American resentment of the United States. Most important, it forced the slavery controversy to the center of national debate, as first indicated by the Wilmot Proviso.

DEVELOPING THE CHAPTER: SUGGESTED LECTURE OR DISCUSSION TOPICS

• Explain the movement toward expansion in relation to the theories of American Manifest Destiny and mission. The focus might be on how the drives to acquire Oregon, Texas, and California arose from the general belief that America should expand across the continent.

REFERENCE: Ray Billington, *Westward Expansion* (1974).

• Examine the role of women in the westward expansion of the 1840s to Oregon and elsewhere. Compare their outlooks and concerns with those that dominated the Manifest Destiny ideology.

REFERENCE: Susan Butuille, ed., *Women's Voices from the Oregon Trail* (1994).

• Consider the origins of the Mexican War in relation to Polk's desire for California and the narrow issue of the Texas boundary. Analyze the charges by the war's opponents that Polk's essential aim was to add new slave territory to the United States. Consider the long-term results of the Mexican War.

REFERENCE: Patricia Nelson Limerick, *The Legacy of Conquest* (1987).

- Examine the Mexican War in relation to broader patterns of ethnic and racial conflict in the Southwest.

REFERENCE: Reginald Horsman, *Race and Manifest Destiny* (1981).

FOR FURTHER INTEREST: ADDITIONAL CLASS TOPICS

- Discuss whether the Mexican War would have happened without the annexation of Texas.

- Focus on the Manifest Destiny campaign of 1844. Discuss whether Polk had a mandate for expansionism and, if so, whether he successfully fulfilled the American majority's goals in the West. If Clay had been elected in 1844, would America have expanded in the same manner?

- Use Lincoln's spot resolutions or Thoreau's "Civil Disobedience" essay to highlight the opposition to the war, particularly the charge that Polk had maneuvered to bring on the fighting.

- Consider the Mexican War from a Mexican perspective. Discuss the long-term consequences of acquiring the Spanish borderlands for both Mexicans and Americans.

- Why was the United States able to expand without European intervention? Also, why was Mexico unable to gain the support of either France or Britain in defending its territories? Why did France and Britain remain uninvolved during the Mexican War?

CHARACTER SKETCHES

Thomas Hart Benton (1782–1858)

Benton, the most prominent Jacksonian Democratic senator of the early nineteenth century, was a grand spokesman for national greatness and the common person.

Having grown up on the Tennessee frontier, he moved to St. Louis in 1815 and became editor of the second newspaper printed west of the Mississippi. In his youth, he was involved in numerous duels, including one in which he and his brother nearly killed Andrew Jackson. He later became one of Jackson's closest political allies.

Benton was a huge man with great energy and long-winded speaking capacity. When not orating in the Senate, he undertook speaking tours of up to a thousand miles on horseback, and huge crowds gathered to hear him talk for two or three hours. Mark Twain used one of Benton's visits to Hannibal, Missouri, as the basis for an episode in *Tom Sawyer*.

Like most Jacksonians, Benton tried to divert national attention away from the slavery issue, thinking that it would disappear. But he harshly condemned southerners who threatened secession over slavery.

Quote: "I shall not fall on my sword, as Brutus did… but I shall save it, and save myself, for another day, and for another use—for the day when the battle of the disunion of these states is to be fought—not with words but with iron—and for the hearts of the traitors who appear in arms against their country." (Senate speech, 1844)

REFERENCE: William Chambers, *Old Bullion Benton: Senator from the New West* (1956).

James K. Polk (1795–1849)

Polk was the dark-horse presidential winner of 1844, who carried out his ambitious program of Manifest Destiny.

The scion of a stern Scots-Irish family, he was very serious and fanatically hardworking, never able to relax or get away from politics.

He was Andrew Jackson's leader in the House of Representatives during the Bank War. Although called a dark-horse nominee in 1844, Polk was actually a very well-known Democrat and would probably have been the vice-presidential candidate with Van Buren in 1844 if the former president had not opposed the Texas annexation.

During his presidency, Polk operated almost entirely alone, having no personal friends, and his diaries show that he was often secretive and manipulative. He exhausted himself with overwork and died only a few months after leaving office.

Quote: "After repeated menaces, Mexico has passed the boundary of the United States, has invaded our territory, and shed American blood upon American soil. She has proclaimed that hostilities have commenced, and that the two nations are at war.... War exists, and notwithstanding all our efforts to avoid it, exists by the act of Mexico herself...." (War Message to Congress, 1846)

REFERENCE: Sam W. Haynes, *James K. Polk and the Expansionist Impulse* (1997).

Antonio López de Santa Anna (1795–1876)

Santa Anna was the Mexican military dictator who lost both the Texas war for independence and the Mexican War.

The uneducated son of a minor Spanish bureaucrat, Santa Anna emerged from the turmoil of the independence movement to dominate Mexican politics. He was an unscrupulous manipulator and opportunist who ruled by granting favors to the army and exploiting the peasant masses. When not at war, Santa Anna spent most of his time in cockfighting and gambling. He loved to stage fantastic, expensive public entertainments, which he would attend with his numerous mistresses.

He lost a leg defending Vera Cruz against a French raid in 1838 and used this sacrifice as proof of his patriotism when it was questioned. He was frequently driven into exile in Cuba and Colombia but usually managed to return to power when civilian politicians led the country to chaos.

Quote: "Mexicans! You have a religion—protect it! You have honor—free yourself from infamy! You love your wives, your children—then liberate them from American brutality!" (Appeal to the Mexican populace, 1847)

REFERENCE: Oakah L. Jones, *Santa Anna* (1968).

Winfield Scott (1786–1866)

Scott, the American commander in the Mexican War, was the most important U.S. military leader between the Revolution and the Civil War.

Scott first became a national hero as a young officer in the War of 1812, when he was wounded in the Battle of Lundy's Lane. He fought in several Indian wars in the 1830s before becoming head of the army in 1841. He was called "Old Fuss and Feathers" because of his love for military pomp and detailed regulations. His campaign from the coast at Vera Cruz over the mountains to Mexico City is still considered a military masterpiece. During the year in which he ruled the city under military occupation, he was considered very fair and just by the Mexicans.

Although he had a decent understanding of politics from a military perspective, his Whig candidacy for the presidency in 1852 was doomed by sectional conflict within the party. He was still holding on as the aged commander of the U.S. army at the outbreak of the Civil War, but was shortly replaced.

Quote: "The object of all our dreams and hopes, toils and dangers—once the gorgeous seat of the Montezumas. That splendid city will soon be ours!" (Speech to troops, 1847)

REFERENCE: James McCaffrey, *Army of Manifest Destiny* (1992).

QUESTIONS FOR CLASS DISCUSSION

1. Was American expansion across North America an inevitable development? How was the idea of Manifest Destiny used to justify expansionism?

2. Why was the Texas annexation so controversial? What would have happened had Texas remained an independent nation?

3. How did rivalry with Britain affect the American decision to annex Texas, the Oregon dispute, and lesser controversies of the period?

4. What caused the Mexican War? Did Polk provoke the Texas-boundary conflict in order to gain California or expand slavery, as war opponents such as Lincoln charged?

5. What were the benefits and costs of the Mexican War both immediately and in the longer run of American history?

MAKERS OF AMERICA: THE CALIFORNIOS

Questions for Class Discussion

1. What distinctive features of Spanish and Mexican society and culture affected the early history of settlement in California?

2. In what ways was the Californios' experience of being forcibly incorporated into the United States similar to that of voluntary immigrants and in what ways was it different?

Suggested Student Exercises

*   Use a map of California to discover Spanish place names. Consider why it is misleading to assume that all such names derive from the pre-1848 Californios.

*   Compare this early history of California settlement with the later image of California as a golden land of youth and excitement. Consider which features of the Californios' actual historical experience have been incorporated into this romantic vision of California and which have not.

CHAPTER 18

Renewing the Sectional Struggle, 1848–1854

AP FOCUS

- The California Gold Rush tempts miners from around the world to try their luck panning in the Sierra Nevada Mountains. Few hit it rich, but overnight, the population of the area swells. In less than two years, California is ready for statehood. Plans for a transcontinental railroad follow shortly, spurred by the imperative to connect the East with territories newly taken from Mexico.

- Always just under the surface, the slavery issue once again takes hold of the nation as new territories, such as California, prepare to enter the Union. The series of acts that ultimately become the Compromise of 1850 provide concessions that both North and South can grudgingly accept, at least for another decade: a stricter fugitive slave law is instituted, and California enters the Union as a free state, giving control of the Senate to the North.

- Not content with the land gained from Mexico, southerners look to Central America and the Caribbean for possible slave states. Central America is also seen as an ideal location for a canal connecting the Pacific and Atlantic Oceans, a project a future generation will undertake.

- The Kansas-Nebraska Act, orchestrated by Senator Stephen A. Douglas for political as well as personal reasons, further polarizes the nation. Northerners conclude that, with popular sovereignty, there will be no limitations placed on the expansion of slavery.

AP teachers should take note of the following:

1. The expansion of slavery brought together seemingly disparate factions. Disenchanted Democrats, Free-Soilers, Know-Nothings, and others groups, concerned about political developments in regard to slavery expansion, ultimately coalesced into a new political party, the Republicans.

2. From the 1820s to the 1850s, the South had dominated the executive branch, either through presidents who were themselves slave-owners or supporters of the South or through "doughface" presidents—northerners with southern sympathies.

Focus on Historical Thinking:

In one clear, concise sentence have students indicate the major historical significance of the following: the Compromise of 1850; the California gold rush; the Fugitive Slave Law; the Kansas-Nebraska Act; the death of Zachary Taylor. (Note: answers may vary.)

FOCUS QUESTIONS

1. How did the California gold rush result in inflaming strong sectional disputes?

2. Who supported and who opposed the Compromise of 1850, what were its main provisions, and how did it pass?

3. What section benefited the most from the Compromise of 1850? Why?

4. What foreign policy agreements were made with regard to Latin America and Asia?

5.   What were the explicit provisions and implicit understandings of the Kansas-Nebraska Act and what were some of the consequences of its passage?

CHAPTER THEMES

Theme: The sectional conflict over the expansion of slavery that erupted after the Mexican War was temporarily quieted by the Compromise of 1850, but Douglas's Kansas-Nebraska Act of 1854 exploded it again.

Theme: In the 1850s, American expansionism in the West and the Caribbean was extremely controversial because it was tied to the slavery question.

Theme: Commercial interests guided American foreign policy in Asia and contributed to sectional tension within the United States, as regions tried to secure the terminus to a transcontinental railroad.

CHAPTER SUMMARY

The acquisition of territory from Mexico created acute new dilemmas concerning the expansion of slavery, especially for the two major political parties, which had long tried to avoid the issue. The antislavery Free Soil party pushed the issue into the election of 1848. The application of gold-rich California for admission to the Union forced the controversy into the Senate, which engaged in stormy debates over slavery and the Union.

After the timely death of President Taylor, who had blocked a settlement, Congress resolved the crisis by passing the delicate Compromise of 1850. The compromise eased sectional tension for the moment, although the Fugitive Slave Law aroused opposition in the North.

As the Whig Party died, the Democratic Pierce administration became the tool of proslavery expansionists. Controversies over Nicaragua, Cuba, and the Gadsden Purchase showed that expansionism was closely linked to the slavery issue.

The desire for a northern railroad route led Stephen Douglas to ram the Kansas-Nebraska Act through Congress in 1854. By repealing the Missouri Compromise and making new territory subject to popular sovereignty on slavery, this act aroused the fury of the North, sparked the rise of the Republican Party, and set the stage for the Civil War.

DEVELOPING THE CHAPTER: SUGGESTED LECTURE OR DISCUSSION TOPICS

- Discuss the conflicts created by the Mexican War acquisitions and explain how the Compromise of 1850 tried to resolve them. The focus might be on the extreme delicacy of the sectional adjustment.

  REFERENCE: David Potter, *The Impending Crisis, 1848–1861* (1976).

- Assess the breakup of the second two-party system in relation to the slavery controversy. Show how the Whig demise and Democratic divisions paved the way for the Republicans.

  REFERENCE: Bruce Levine, *Half Slave and Half Free: The Roots of the Civil War* (1992).

- Show the connection between the proslavery expansionist schemes, particularly the Cuban affair and the Gadsden Purchase and the sectional controversy. Emphasize southern hopes and northern fears of potential slavery expansion to the Caribbean or Central America.

  REFERENCE: Robert May, *The Southern Dream of a Caribbean Empire* (1973).

- Examine the Kansas-Nebraska Act and explain why it aroused such wrath in the North. Particular attention might be paid to the railroad-promoting Douglas, with his theory of popular sovereignty and to the rise of the free soil ideology in the North.

   REFERENCE: Richard Sewell, *A House Divided* (1988).

FOR FURTHER INTEREST: ADDITIONAL CLASS TOPICS

- Consider the characters and drama of the Senate debates over the Compromise of 1850, especially the roles of Webster, Clay, Seward, and Douglas.

- Discuss the Fugitive Slave Law and the Underground Railroad as running sores in the sectional conflict. The life of Harriet Tubman might provide a focus.

- Examine the various filibustering efforts in connection with the issues of Cuba and Central America, and relate them to the southern dream of expanding slavery by acquiring new territory to the South.

- Focus on Douglas as a typical northern Democrat—one who did not really like slavery but thought it a secondary issue that should not disrupt such important matters as railroads.

CHARACTER SKETCHES

Zachary Taylor (1784–1850)

Taylor was the military hero of the Mexican War and the Whig president whose political ineptitude nearly blocked the Compromise of 1850.

He came from a slaveholding Kentucky family and fought in the War of 1812, the Black Hawk War, and the Seminole wars before his performance in the Mexican War made him a national hero.

Using daring and risky troop movements, Taylor defeated Santa Anna's much larger army at Buena Vista. Polk was jealous of Taylor's appeal but failed to stop the public and journalistic celebration of "Old Rough and Ready."

While Taylor had long supported the Whigs, he was so politically ignorant that he nearly ruined his 1848 candidacy by writing blunt letters. At the time of his death, Whig politicians were despairing of Taylor's incompetence and trying to persuade prominent figures to enter the cabinet and keep him under control.

Quote: "I am a Whig, but not an ultra Whig. If elected I would not be the mere President of a party. I would endeavor to act independent of party domination. I should feel bound to administer the government untrammeled by party schemes." (1848)

REFERENCE: K. Jack Bauer, *Zachary Taylor: Soldier, Planter, Statesman of the Old Southwest* (1985).

Harriet Tubman (1821–1913)

Tubman was a fugitive slave and black abolitionist who led many slaves out of the South.

She was born a slave in Maryland and, as a child, suffered a severe head injury that affected her throughout her life. She worked as a field hand, displaying tremendous physical stamina.

In 1844, her master forced her to marry another slave against her wishes. Five years later, she escaped across the Pennsylvania border, traveling only by night.

She began making raids back into the South and eventually led out an estimated three hundred slaves, including her elderly parents. Between trips, she worked as a cook and used much of her income to help the fugitives get a start or move to Canada.

Tubman was illiterate but learned to speak before abolitionist groups. During the Civil War, she went south with the Union army and worked as a cook, laundress, nurse, and spy.

Quote: "Jes' so long as he [God] wanted to use me, he would take keer of me, an' when he didn't want me no longer, I was ready to go. I always tole him, I'm gwine to hole stiddy on you, an' you've got to see me trou'." (Comment, 1868)

REFERENCE: Sarah Bradford, *Harriet Tubman: The Moses of Her People* (1974).

Stephen A. Douglas (1813–1861)

Douglas was the Democratic senator whose Kansas-Nebraska Act helped bring on the Civil War that ruined his party and dashed his once-high presidential hopes.

Born in Vermont, he made his way to frontier Illinois, where he taught school and learned law. Although only briefly a judge on the state supreme court, he was always called "Judge Douglas." Douglas was first elected to the Illinois legislature in 1836, along with young Abraham Lincoln.

Douglas's first wife inherited a southern plantation with many slaves, and this became a political liability for Douglas. His second wife was related to Dolley Madison and was well connected in Washington high society, where the Douglases were very prominent in the late 1850s.

Once Douglas realized he had no hope of winning the 1860 election, he concentrated on rallying Democratic support for the Union and against secession. Although he and Lincoln had been longtime political rivals, he held Lincoln's hat at his inaugural and publicly defended him in the secession crisis. Douglas died of typhoid fever in 1861.

Quote: "I hold that under the Constitution of the United States each state of this Union has a right to do as it pleases on the subject of slavery. In Illinois we have exercised that right by abolishing slavery.... It is none of our business whether slavery exists in Missouri. Hence I do not choose to occupy the time allotted to me in discussing a question that we have no right to act upon." (Lincoln-Douglas debates, 1858)

REFERENCE: Robert W. Johannsen, *Stephen A. Douglas* (1973).

William Walker (1824–1860)

Walker was the American filibusterer and adventurer who attempted to add a Central American slave empire to the American commonwealth before the Civil War.

A graduate of the University of Nashville, Walker earned a medical degree, practiced law, and edited a New Orleans newspaper, but his boredom with ordinary pursuits constantly drove him into exotic and dangerous schemes. He first attempted to set up a republic with himself as president in Lower California (part of Mexico) in 1853, but he was arrested and acquitted of violating neutrality laws.

His briefly successful dictatorship in Nicaragua in 1855 began to collapse when he attempted to seize control of overland transit in the country from Cornelius Vanderbilt's company. An angry Vanderbilt helped turn other Central American countries and U.S. authorities against Walker, and his southern friends in the American navy proved unable to save him from capture and execution.

Quote: "That which you ignorantly call 'filibustering' is not the offspring of hasty passion or ill-regulated desire. It is the fruit of the supreme instincts that act in accord with fixed laws as old as creation." (Autobiography, 1860)

REFERENCE: Laurence Greene, *The Filibuster: The Career of William Walker* (1937).

QUESTIONS FOR CLASS DISCUSSION

1. Was the Compromise of 1850 a wise effort to balance sectional differences or a futile attempt to push the slavery issue out of sight? Could a better compromise have been met if California had not skipped the regular territorial phase?

2. Why did the North so strongly resent the Fugitive Slave Law and why did the South resent northern resistance to enforcing it?

3. Is there a significant difference in the leadership of Old Guard senators such as Clay, Webster, and Calhoun when compared with the Young Guard of Douglas and Seward?

4. Did the North, South, or West benefit most from the Compromise of 1850? Why?

5. Why was the issue of acquiring Cuba so controversial in the 1850s? Could some of the Caribbean islands or parts of Central America have become incorporated as slave states with the United States? How would American designs for expansion into the Caribbean and Central America effect U.S. relations with Latin America? Did European turmoil in the late 1840s and early 1850s encourage American expansionist dreams?

6. Would the sectional conflict have been reheated had Douglas not pushed through the Kansas-Nebraska Act? Why or why not?

CHAPTER 19

Drifting Toward Disunion, 1854–1861

AP FOCUS

- In their attempt to take the White House, the Republicans are defeated when John Frémont loses to Democrat James Buchanan. Nativists, concerned by German and Irish immigration, organize the American, or Know-Nothing, Party, which probably takes votes from the Republicans.

- In March 1857, the Supreme Court rules that Dred Scott is not a citizen because of his race. The decision goes even further, stating that Congress has no authority to exclude slavery from any part of the nation or its territories. The Missouri Compromise is therefore ruled unconstitutional.

- The financial crash of 1857 primarily affects the North and West. The South is essentially unaffected because of high cotton prices. Southerners cite this as an example of the superiority of their economic system over the North's, which exploits the "wage-slaves."

- Abraham Lincoln returns to politics in 1858 by running against Senator Stephen A. Douglas, an Illinois Democrat. In a series of debates, Lincoln challenges Douglas to reconcile support for popular sovereignty with the Supreme Court's *Dred Scott* decision (which Douglas does in his Freeport Doctrine). Lincoln loses the election, but not before becoming a national figure.

- Senator James Henry Crittenden offers a plan to convince southerners to return to the Union. It is, however, condemned by the North for giving too many concessions to the South. For a southern perspective on the Crittenden Compromise, see *The American Pageant* (14th ed., p. 457/15th ed., p. 414).

AP teachers should take note of the following:

1. Senator Stephen A. Douglas's repudiation of the Lecompton Constitution lost him the support of the South and whatever hope he had of becoming president.

2. That sectional fury in the late 1850s is shown by the near-fatal attack on Senator Charles Sumner of Massachusetts by Congressman Preston Brooks of South Carolina. Sumner had given a harsh speech in which he excoriated slave-owners in general and insulted Brooks's uncle, Senator Andrew Butler of South Carolina. Southerners did not generally condemn Brooks's attack. Note the differing opinions of the attack in the North and the South, highlighted in the textbook (14th ed., p. 443/15th ed., p. 401).

Focus on Historical Thinking:

Reproduce Table 19.1 on p. 410 and Map 19.3 on p. 411 (15th ed.) without explanatory captions. Ask students to analyze how Lincoln was able to secure such a majority of electoral votes despite getting under 40% of the popular vote.

FOCUS QUESTIONS

1. Who authored literature related to slavery that aroused sympathy in the North and ire in the South?

2. How did events unfold in Kansas after the passage of the Kansas-Nebraska Act?

3.   What was the decision of the Supreme Court in the Dred Scott case?

4.   How did John Brown's actions further entrench sectional differences?

5.   Who were the candidates for president in 1860, where did each get most of his support, and what were the results of the election?

6.   What happened in the time between the election of 1860 and the inauguration of the new president?

CHAPTER THEMES

Theme: A series of major North-South crises in the late 1850s culminated in the election of the antislavery Republican Lincoln to the presidency in 1860. His election caused seven southern states to secede from the union and form the Confederate States of America.

CHAPTER SUMMARY

The 1850s were punctuated by successive confrontations that deepened sectional hostility, until it broke out in the Civil War.

Harriet Beecher Stowe's *Uncle Tom's Cabin* fanned northern antislavery feeling. In Kansas, proslavery and antislavery forces fought a bloody little preview of the Civil War. Buchanan's support of the proslavery Lecompton Constitution alienated moderate northern Democrats such as Douglas. Congressman Brooks's beating of Senator Sumner aroused passions in both sections.

The 1856 election signaled the rise of the sectionally based Republican Party. The Dred Scott case delighted the South, while northern Republicans pledged defiance. The Lincoln-Douglas debates of 1858 deepened the national controversy over slavery. John Brown's raid on Harpers Ferry made him a heroic martyr in the North but caused outraged southerners to fear a slave uprising.

The Democratic Party split along sectional lines, allowing Lincoln to win the four-way 1860 election. Seven southern states quickly seceded and organized the Confederate States of America.

As southerners optimistically cast off their ties to the hated North, lame-duck President Buchanan proved unable to act. The last-minute Crittenden Compromise effort failed because of Lincoln's opposition.

DEVELOPING THE CHAPTER: SUGGESTED LECTURE OR DISCUSSION TOPICS

- Explain how the events of the late 1850s developed in a chain reaction, with each crisis deepening sectional hatreds, thus paving the way for another critical event.

   REFERENCE: David M. Potter, *The Impending Crisis, 1848–1861* (1976).

- Analyze the Kansas conflict as a small-scale rehearsal for the Civil War. The focus might be on the way sectional violence fed on itself, producing extremist figures such as Brown and the border ruffians.

   REFERENCE: James A. Rawley, *Race and Politics: "Bleeding Kansas" and the Coming of the Civil War* (1969).

- Use the Lincoln-Douglas debates to explain the rise of Lincoln and the Republican Party, and the issues in the northern debate about how to deal with slavery. Focus on Lincoln's rise to national prominence in relation to the slavery issue.

   REFERENCE: Don E. Fehrenbacher, *Prelude to Greatness: Lincoln in the 1850s* (1962).

- Examine the 1860 election and its consequences. Emphasize the Democratic split, the sectional character of the voting, and the Deep South's clear determination to secede as soon as Lincoln won, even before he took office.

  REFERENCE: Steven A. Channing, *Crisis of Fear* (1970).

FOR FURTHER INTEREST: ADDITIONAL CLASS TOPICS

- Use Stowe's *Uncle Tom's Cabin,* and the southern reaction to it, to demonstrate the growing division of outlook between the sections. Compare and contrast the criticisms and their effects of Stowe's *Uncle Tom's Cabin* and Helper's *The Impending Crisis of the South.*

- Focus on John Brown as a crucial character in two of the major events of the decade, bleeding Kansas and Harpers Ferry.

- Trace the rise of Lincoln through the events of the decade, from the Kansas-Nebraska Act to the Lincoln-Douglas debates to the 1860 election.

- Consider the southern decision to secede and the last-minute Crittenden Compromise effort.

- Assess the textbook authors' assertion that it was fortunate that Republican presidential candidate Fremont did not win in 1856 because the "North was more willing to let the South depart in peace than in 1860."

- Did lame duck President Buchanan or President-elect Lincoln have any responsibility to act once South Carolina announced its secession after the election? What options did each have in dealing with the crisis? What results seemed likely from each option?

- Was civil war inevitable by 1850? Was there a point in time after 1850 where something different might have prevented civil war, or would civil war just have been delayed?

CHARACTER SKETCHES

Harriet Beecher Stowe (1811–1896)

A member of the famous Beecher family, Stowe wrote *Uncle Tom's Cabin,* the book that more than anything else deepened northern hostility to slavery.

Stowe was closer to her brother Henry, later a famous preacher, than to her father or her older sister Catharine. She was very fond of her parents' free black servants, particularly one kind woman who may have been a model for characters in *Uncle Tom's Cabin.*

Although she had published a few stories before marrying Calvin Stowe, a professor at her father's seminary, she then gave up writing. For eighteen years, she was a housewife who struggled to raise her seven children on a very limited income. She visited slaveholding areas of Kentucky during that time and knew abolitionists at her father's seminary but at first was not very sympathetic to them.

Her brother urged her to write against slavery, and she submitted *Uncle Tom's Cabin* in serial form to a magazine. Although the magazine paid her only $300, the book sold 10,000 copies the first week, 300,000 the first year, and eventually millions in the United States and abroad.

Quote: "As long as the baby sleeps with me nights I can't do much of anything—but I shall *do it at last.* I shall write it if I live...." (Letter to Calvin Stowe, 1850)

REFERENCE: Joan Hedrick, *Harriet Beecher Stowe: A Life* (1994).

John Brown (1800–1859)

Brown was the militant abolitionist whose violent attacks at Osawatomie, Kansas, and Harpers Ferry, Virginia, helped to bring on the Civil War.

An unsuccessful tanner, cattle driver, and sheep raiser, Brown was frequently in financial difficulty. He had twenty children—seven by his first wife and thirteen by his second.

For a time, he lived in a black community in New York on land donated by abolitionist Gerrit Smith. After five of his sons migrated to Kansas in 1855, he joined them with a wagonload of guns and ammunition and then hacked five proslavery settlers to death in the Osawatomie massacre.

After Osawatomie, he solicited money and supplies from some New England intellectuals and began planning to lead a slave uprising. He rented a farm near Harpers Ferry in the summer of 1859 and gradually accumulated weapons and his little army of twenty-one men. He could have escaped after raiding the armory, but his plans were too confused. Two of his sons died in the fighting.

Quote: "I John Brown am now quite certain that the crimes of this guilty land will never be purged away, but with blood. I had, as I now think, vainly flattered myself that without very much bloodshed it might be done." (Statement before hanging, 1859)

REFERENCE: Stephen B. Oates, *To Purge This Land with Blood: A Biography of John Brown* (1970).

Dred Scott (1795–1858)

Scott was the slave whose attempt to secure his freedom was denied by the Supreme Court, which declared that blacks "have no rights that white men are bound to respect."

Born a slave in Virginia, Scott was later purchased by a U.S. Army doctor, who took him for three years to Illinois (a free state) and two years to Wisconsin (a free territory).

After the doctor died, Scott passed into other hands, but his former owner's sons sympathized with him and helped carry his case through the state and federal courts.

After he lost the case, the doctor's sons bought Scott and freed him. Although unskilled and illiterate, he was intelligent and proud of his notoriety. Scott was married, had several children, and ended his days as a janitor in a St. Louis hotel.

Quote: "I have no money to pay anybody at Washington to speak for me.… Will nobody speak for me at Washington, even without hope of other reward than the blessings of a poor black man and his family?… I can only pray that some good heart will be moved by pity to do that for me which I cannot do for myself; and that if the right is on my side it may be so declared by the high court to which I have appealed." (Pamphlet containing Scott's appeal for aid, 1854)

REFERENCE: Don E. Fehrenbacher, *The Dred Scott Case* (1978).

QUESTIONS FOR CLASS DISCUSSION

1. How did each of the major crisis events of the 1850s contribute to the advent of the Civil War?

2. How could a fanatical and violent man like John Brown come to be regarded as a hero by millions of northerners?

3. Why did Douglas's popular sovereignty approach to the slavery question prove to be unworkable in Kansas and elsewhere?

4. What did the Supreme Court decide in the Dred Scott case? Did the Court do too much in its ruling or was it within its traditional constitutional boundaries? What effect did the decision have in the territories, in the North, and in the South?

5. Why was sectional compromise impossible in 1860, when such compromises had previously worked in 1820 and 1850? Since Lincoln had guaranteed to protect slavery in the states where it existed, why did the seven southern states secede as soon as he was elected?

EXPANDING THE "VARYING VIEWPOINTS"

*   Charles and Mary Beard, *The Rise of American Civilization* (1927).

    A view of the Civil War as an economic and social revolution:

    "At bottom, the so-called Civil War…was a social war, ending in the unquestioned establishment of a new power in the government, making vast changes in the arrangement of class, in the accumulation and distribution of wealth, in the course of industrial development, and in the Constitution inherited from the Fathers.… If the series of acts by which the bourgeois and peasants of France overthrew the king, nobility, and clergy is to be called the French Revolution, then accuracy compels us to characterize by the same term the social cataclysm in which the capitalists, laborers, and farmers of the North and West drove from power in the national government the planting aristocracy of the South.… The so-called civil war was in reality a Second American Revolution, and in a strict sense, the First."

*   David M. Potter, *The Impending Crisis, 1848–1861* (1976).

    A view of the 1850s as a time of irreconcilable conflict between North and South over the central issue of slavery:

    "Thus slavery suddenly emerged as a transcendent sectional issue in its own right, and as a catalyst of all sectional antagonisms, political, economic, and cultural.… The slavery question became the sectional question, the sectional question became the slavery question, and both became the territorial question.…From the sultry August night in 1846 when Wilmot caught the chairman's eye, the slavery question steadily widened the sectional rift until an April dawn in 1861 when the batteries along the Charleston waterfront opened fire on Fort Sumter.…"

*   Michael Holt, *Forging a Majority: The Formation of the Republic Party in Pittsburgh, 1848–1860* (1969).

    A view of the 1850s as a time when many issues besides slavery dominated national politics:

    "Politics did not revolve around [slavery and the South] just as politics today does not revolve around communism, although most people dislike it. Instead, social, ethnic, and religious considerations often determined who voted for whom between 1848 and 1861. Divisions between native-born Americans and immigrants and between Protestants and Catholics, rather than differences of opinion about the tariff or the morality of slavery, distinguished Whigs and Republicans from Democrats.… Interpreting the rise of the Republican party in the North solely in terms of hostility to slavery or economic issues is, therefore, too simplified."

QUESTIONS ABOUT THE "VARYING VIEWPOINTS"

1. How does each of these views see the relationship between slavery and sectional feeling?

2. What does each of these views see as the relationship between slavery and other issues in the 1850s?

3. How would each of these historians interpret the decline of the Whigs and the rise of the Republicans in the 1850s?

CHAPTER 20

Girding for War: The North and the South, 1861–1865

AP FOCUS

- The long coexistence of two conflicting economic systems—planter-slaveholding and industrial capitalism—under one government ends with the outbreak of war.

- A month after taking the oath of office, Lincoln is confronted with a serious question: whether to supply Fort Sumter, a major U.S. military installation in South Carolina still in federal hands.

- Maryland, Kentucky, Delaware, and Missouri, slave states that border both free and slave states, stay loyal to the government, although their citizens have divided loyalties. They provide many troops for both sides, but probably more for the federal army than for the Confederacy.

- When the Civil War breaks out, the South's advantages are martial spirit and excellent military leadership. The North's advantages are industrial might, population, and resources. See the table in *The American Pageant* (14th ed., p. 470/15th ed., p. 425) comparing the manufacturing capabilities and investments by section in 1860. War and Diplomacy is an AP theme.

- Britain and France remain neutral despite Lincoln's fear that both will recognize the Confederacy and even break the Union blockade. The Emancipation Proclamation makes the war a moral crusade to eradicate slavery, an endeavor that the European powers hesitate to oppose.

- At the end of the war, the North is experiencing a boom fueled by its growing industrial sector, whereas much of the South lies in ruins. Tie this to the AP theme Economic Transformations.

AP teachers should take note of the following:

1. The North's military strategy, the Anaconda plan, was designed to divide the Confederacy and to employ a naval blockade to cut off its ability to import and export goods. The Union capture of Vicksburg in 1863 and other strategic points in the western military theatre separated the trans-Mississippi states from the rest of the Confederacy. Sherman's march to the sea divided the Confederacy yet again, and the Union blockade dramatically reduced the South's ability to trade.

2. On two separate occasions, the Confederate Army of Northern Virginia, commanded by General Robert E. Lee, invaded the North: at Antietam in 1862 and at Gettysburg in 1863. Both times, Lee and his army were turned back.

3. An excellent DBQ (14th ed., DBQ 7, pp. A82–A84/15th ed., pp. A79-A82) deals with Lincoln's primary objective: preserving the Union while emancipating the slaves. The documents fall in the period 1862–1863. Students should incorporate, in their essay, Lincoln's earlier views on slavery—Lincoln's response to the 1854 Kansas-Nebraska Act shows his desire to contain slavery but, at that time, and unwillingness to advocate abolition. The necessities of war convinced him to adopt emancipation as a war aim.

Focus on Historical Thinking:

Have students create a timeline of what they consider to be the twenty-five most important bits of specific factual information from 1607 to 1865.

FOCUS QUESTIONS

1.   What did Lincoln do that provoked South Carolina to bombard Fort Sumter, and what did Lincoln do immediately following the attack?

2.   Which states were Border States and how did they influence Lincoln's statements and actions?

3.   At the outbreak of war, what advantages did the South have and what advantages did the North have?

4.   Why did the South believe they would be able to enlist foreign intervention and why were they unable to do so?

5.   What incidents threatened peaceful relations between the Union and Britain?

6.   How did the war impact the economy in the North and the economy in the South?

CHAPTER THEMES

Theme: The North effectively brought to bear its long-term advantages of industrial might and human resources to wage a devastating total war against the South. The war helped organize and modernize northern society, while the South, despite heroic efforts, was economically and socially crushed.

Theme: Lincoln's skillful political leadership helped keep the crucial Border States in the Union and maintain northern morale, while his effective diplomacy kept Britain and France from aiding the Confederacy.

CHAPTER SUMMARY

South Carolina's firing on Fort Sumter aroused the North for war. Lincoln's call for troops to suppress the rebellion drove four upper South states into the Confederacy. Lincoln used an effective combination of political persuasion and force to keep the deeply divided Border States in the Union.

The Confederacy enjoyed initial advantages of upper-class European support, military leadership, and a defensive position on its own soil. The North enjoyed the advantages of lower-class European support, industrial and population resources, and political leadership.

The British upper classes sympathized with the South and abetted Confederate naval efforts. But effective diplomacy and Union military success thwarted those efforts and kept Britain, as well as France, neutral in the war.

Lincoln's political leadership proved effective in mobilizing the North for war, despite political opposition and resistance to his infringement on civil liberties. The North eventually mobilized its larger troop resources for war and ultimately turned to an unpopular and unfair draft system.

Northern economic and financial strengths enabled it to gain an advantage over the less-industrialized South. The changes in society opened new opportunities for women, who had contributed significantly to the war effort in both the North and South. Since most of the war was waged on Southern soil, the South was left devastated by the war.

DEVELOPING THE CHAPTER: SUGGESTED LECTURE OR DISCUSSION TOPICS

- Analyze the Sumter crisis and the secession of the upper South. The focus might be on Lincoln's success in maneuvering South Carolina into firing the first shot, thereby arousing the North for a war it had previously been reluctant to fight.

  REFERENCE: Richard Current, *Lincoln and the First Shot* (1963).

- Explain the various internal political conflicts in the North, focusing on Copperheadism and the 1864 campaign. Point out how crucial it was for Lincoln to achieve military success in order to overcome such opposition, since any political settlement would have meant recognition of the Confederacy.

  REFERENCE: James A. Rawley, *The Politics of Union* (1974).

- Examine Lincoln the wartime leader and Lincoln the martyr and hero. Contrast the many contemporary criticisms of his leadership with those qualities that now constitute his greatness.

  REFERENCE: David H. Donald, *Lincoln* (1995).

- Explain the role of women both on the home front and in such new areas as battlefield nursing. Compare and contrast the situations and ideologies of northern and southern women.

  REFERENCES: Catherine Clinton and Nina Silber, eds., *Divided Houses* (1992); Drew Gilpin Faust, *Mothers of Invention: Women of the Slaveholding South in the American Civil War* (1996).

FOR FURTHER INTEREST: ADDITIONAL CLASS TOPICS

- Identify the significance of the Border States to both the North and the South, and examine how they influenced decisions of the Union and the Confederacy.

- Focus on the ordinary soldiers, North and South. Point out the differences (for example, in supplies) as well as the similarities in the experiences of Billy Yank and Johnny Reb.

- Discuss different interpretations of the Civil War. Point out how its meaning has varied according to changes in North-South and black-white relations.

- Focus on the might-have-beens that could have resulted in a Confederate victory. Specifically examine the need for the South to secure foreign intervention. If the South had been able to quickly realize the failure of King Cotton, what could it have done instead to procure foreign recognition and/or intervention?

- Discuss the effects of the Civil War on the homefront, North and South, including ways the war affected women.

CHARACTER SKETCHES

Abraham Lincoln (1809–1865)

Born in a log cabin in Kentucky, Lincoln, who would become our sixteenth president, had only vague but fond memories of his mother, Nancy, who died when he was nine. His father was a stocky, heavyset, hard-drinking frontier drifter. Lincoln became estranged from him and did not attend his final illness or funeral, even though he was only seventy miles away at the time.

The story that Lincoln's one true love was the beautiful Ann Rutledge rests solely on the report of his law partner William Herndon following Lincoln's death, thirty years after the supposed romance. Lincoln did know Ann Rutledge, but he never mentioned her, and Mary Todd Lincoln emphatically denied the Herndon story.

His natural melancholy was much deepened by the deaths of his children, especially eleven-year-old Willie in 1862. He thought a good deal about the afterlife, and at his wife's instigation, brought spiritualist mediums into the White House and attended séances to communicate with the dead.

Quote: "The dogmas of the quiet past are inadequate to the stormy present.… As our case is new, so we must think anew, and act anew. We must disenthrall ourselves, and then we shall save our country." (Message to Congress, 1862)

REFERENCE: David Herbert Donald, *Lincoln* (1995).

Elizabeth Blackwell (1821–1910)

Blackwell was the first American female physician and a pioneer in developing medical knowledge and health care for women and children.

Blackwell was born in Bristol, England, into a family of twelve children. Her father, a charming sugar refiner and social reformer, believed in women's rights and was a great influence on Elizabeth. He died when she was eleven, shortly after the family immigrated to America.

She was turned down by many medical schools before being accepted by Geneva College—though the acceptance was initially considered a joke by the male students.

After graduation from Geneva and further study in England, she opened a clinic on Bleecker Street in New York and began treating poor women. In 1868, she opened her own women's medical college. She later wrote extensively on "the human element in sex," and attempted to combat ignorance and prejudice concerning women's sexuality.

Quote: "The idea of acquiring a doctor's degree gradually assumed the aspect of a great moral struggle, and the moral fight possessed great attraction for me." (Memoir, 1879)

REFERENCE: Dorothy Clarke Wilson, *Lone Woman: The Story of Elizabeth Blackwell* (1970).

Clara Barton (1821–1912)

Barton was the Civil War nurse who founded and led the American Red Cross for twenty-three years.

Born in Massachusetts of old Yankee stock, Barton was close to her family, including her older brother David, whom she nursed through a two-year illness. Shy and lonely, she attempted school-teaching, but gave it up to become a clerk in the U.S. Patent Office in Washington—one of the first female federal employees.

When she saw the lack of medical facilities after the Battle of Bull Run, she organized her friends to provide first aid, using her own house as a store room. Scorned at first, she eventually won the respect of military officers and men.

She suffered a nervous breakdown after the war and went to Europe for relief, where she learned of the newly formed Red Cross in Switzerland. She returned to the United States and waged a long, difficult campaign to found the American branch of the organization in 1881.

Quote: "The paths of charity are over the roadways of ashes, and he who would tread them must be prepared to meet opposition, misconstruction, jealousy, and calumny. Let his work be that of angels, still it will not satisfy all." (Speech, 1887)

REFERENCE: Stephen B. Oates, *A Woman of Valor: Clara Barton and the Civil War* (1995).

QUESTIONS FOR CLASS DISCUSSION

1. How justified were Lincoln's wartime abridgments of civil liberties and his treatment of the Copperheads?

2. What were the advantages of the South during the Civil War? What were the advantages of the North? What advantage proved most important to each side? What were the disadvantages of each side? Which disadvantage proved most troublesome to each side?

3. To what degree did Britain get involved in the American Civil War? Assess the importance of that degree of involvement to the North and to the South. Review key events involving the British (cotton, grain, Trent affair, Alabama, and Laird rams).

4. How did the American Civil War reshape the Americas? What did European powers do in the Americas during the American Civil War?

5. How was the impact of the Civil War different for the soldiers and civilians of the North and South?

6. Did the results of the Civil War justify its cost? Does the answer to that question depend partly on whether you are a Northerner or a Southerner, black or white?

7. What made Lincoln a great president? Was it primarily his political leadership or his personal qualities and character?

CHAPTER 21

The Furnace of Civil War, 1861–1865

AP FOCUS

- In the early stages of the war, Lincoln is disappointed with the performance of his generals, especially those who commanded the eastern Army of the Potomac. General George McClellan, despite abundant resources at his disposal and an army larger than his foe's, fails to capture Richmond, Virginia, the capital of the Confederacy, in 1862.

- The war provides both free blacks and runaway slaves the opportunity to take part in a personal crusade to destroy slavery. Over 180,000 black men serve in the Union army.

- In 1863, Lincoln issues the Emancipation Proclamation, ending slavery in states in open rebellion.

- The most important battle on North American soil is fought at Gettysburg, Pennsylvania, when Union forces repulse the Confederacy's second and final major invasion of the North.

- With the capture of Vicksburg, Mississippi, the North controls the Mississippi River, effectively dividing the Confederacy.

- The 1864 election in the North is a pivotal historical event; in the midst of a civil war, an election is held to determine whether the incumbent administration will be reelected. It is, providing Lincoln a mandate to continue the war, despite considerable opposition in the North. Interestingly, Lincoln's Democratic opponent is his former military commander, George McClellan.

AP teachers should take note of the following:

1. One of history's most important naval battles occurred in 1862. Attempting to break the Union blockade, the Confederacy sent into battle an ironclad ship, the *Merrimack* (or *Virginia*). It soon engaged the North's ironclad vessel, the *Monitor,* at Hampton Roads, Virginia. The battle was a draw, but from that point on, wooden ships would be considered obsolete fighting vessels.

2. The war settled the decades-old debate over whether the states or the federal government was supreme; the compact theory, the foundation of nullification and secession, was repudiated.

Focus on Historical Thinking:

Have students list five major outcomes of the Civil War, including political, economic, and social outcomes. In one additional sentence have students explain the importance of that outcome.

FOCUS QUESTIONS

1. How successful was McClellan as commander of the Army of the Potomac?

2. What are some of the pivotal battles of the Civil War and what was the outcome of each?

3. What did the Emancipation Proclamation do and how did it affect the Union cause?

4. How successful was Lee as commander of the Confederate army?

5. Once he was put in charge of the entire Union army, how did Grant prosecute the war until its end?

6.   What was the political situation as the election of 1864 approached, and how did Lincoln win a reelection?

7.   What were the costs of the Civil War?

CHAPTER THEMES

Theme: The Civil War, begun as a limited struggle over the Union, eventually became a total war to end slavery and transform the nation.

Theme: After several years of seesaw struggle, the Union armies under Ulysses Grant finally wore down the Southern forces under Robert E. Lee and ended the Confederate bid for independence, as well as the institution of slavery.

CHAPTER SUMMARY

The Union defeat at Bull Run ended Northern complacency about a quick victory. George McClellan and other early Union generals proved unable to defeat the tactically brilliant Confederate armies under Lee. The Union naval blockade put a slow but devastating economic noose around the South.

The political and diplomatic dimensions of the war quickly became critical. In order to retain the Border States, Lincoln first deemphasized any intention to destroy slavery. But the Battle of Antietam, in 1862, enabled Lincoln to prevent foreign intervention and turn the struggle into a war against slavery. Blacks and abolitionists joined enthusiastically in a war for emancipation, but white resentment in part of the North created political problems for Lincoln.

The Union victories at Vicksburg in the West and Gettysburg in the East finally turned the military tide against the South. Southern resistance remained strong, but the Union victories at Atlanta and Mobile assured Lincoln's success in the election of 1864 and ended the last Confederate hopes. The war ended the issues of disunion and slavery, but at a tremendous cost to both North and South.

DEVELOPING THE CHAPTER: SUGGESTED LECTURE OR DISCUSSION TOPICS

- Examine how the different political and military perspectives and respective advantages that the North and the South (see Chapter 20) brought to the war affected their respective strategies. Show why the failure of McClellan's Peninsular Campaign almost guaranteed a long and bloody struggle.

  REFERENCE: James M. McPherson, *Battle Cry of Freedom* (1988).

- Explain why the North won the Civil War and why the South lost. The factors of military strategy, political leadership, and economic resources might be related to key turning points of the war, such as Vicksburg and Gettysburg.

  REFERENCES: Herman Hattaway and Archer Jones, *How the North Won* (1983); Richard E. Beringer, Herman Hattaway, Archer Jones, and William N. Still Jr., *Why the South Lost the Civil War* (1986).

- Examine the politics of the war, especially the way Lincoln gradually turned it from being strictly a "war to preserve the Union" into a war for black emancipation. Show how Lincoln first kept the war aims limited to appease the Border States but later used the Emancipation Proclamation to strengthen the North's moral position.

  REFERENCE: James M. McPherson, *Ordeal by Fire: The Civil War and Reconstruction* (1982).

- Consider the role of slavery and the race question in the changing politics of the Civil War. The career of Frederick Douglass provides a good window on the racial question during the war.

  REFERENCE: David W. Blight, *Frederick Douglass' Civil War* (1989).

FOR FURTHER INTEREST: ADDITIONAL CLASS TOPICS

- Consider the various crucial What Ifs? of the Civil War in relation to the possibilities of a) a Confederate victory or negotiated settlement and b) a war that might have preserved the Union but not ended slavery. Critically analyze the text's assertion that even though Vicksburg and Gettysburg were the decisive military battles of the war, Antietam was probably the political and diplomatic turning point.

- The South had long hoped for international intervention in its fight with the North. If the South had been able to secure international aid, what would have been most beneficial? What did the South need from other nations in order to win the war (or at least force a peace settlement)?

- Compare and contrast the various Union leaders that Lincoln went through (McClellan and Meade specifically) before settling on Grant.

- Compare Grant and Lee as military leaders. The focus might be on Lee as the greatest of the traditional strategists, whereas Grant represented the new age of total war.

- Use Lincoln's First Inaugural Address, Gettysburg Address, Emancipation Proclamation, and Second Inaugural Address to examine the changing interpretations that he gave to secession, the Union, and the issue of slavery.

- Examine the effects of the use of black soldiers on the Union military effort and on public opinion. (The film *Glory* might be used as a resource and starting point for discussion.)

CHARACTER SKETCHES

Clement Vallandigham (1820–1871)

Vallandigham was the Copperhead Democratic politician who was convicted of treason and exiled by Lincoln, only to return and continue his peace agitation.

Vallandigham's family originally came from Virginia, and they romanticized the South as a land of noble social ideals and order. As an Ohio politician and congressman, he was a bitter foe of Republicans and abolitionists. In 1859, he interviewed John Brown in prison and came away convinced that there was a widespread abolitionist conspiracy to bring about a civil war.

He was given direct military orders to stop his calls for resistance to the war before he was arrested, convicted, and exiled to the South. He used a disguise with a false mustache and a pillow to sneak back across the border from Canada in 1864. The government decided not to rearrest him, and he helped push through the peace plank at the 1864 Democratic convention.

Quote: "Yes, it is amazing that our people—Americans, proud, boastful, free—should have submitted to usurpation and despotism.... I am a Democrat—for the Constitution, for law, for the Union, for liberty—this is my only crime." (1863)

REFERENCE: Frank Clement, *Copperheads in the Middle West* (1972).

Robert E. Lee (1807–1870)

Lee was the son of "Light-Horse Harry" Lee, a cavalry hero of the revolution and a member of the great Lee family of Virginia. When Robert was still a boy, his father sank into debtor's prison and disgrace, and eventually left the family.

An 1829 graduate of West Point, where he was a distinguished student, the younger Lee married Mary Custis, a great-granddaughter of Martha Washington, and became master of the Custis estate at Arlington. Lee became a military hero in the Mexican War and later commanded the soldiers who captured John Brown at Harpers Ferry in 1859.

Politically a strong Whig, Lee was initially very unsympathetic to secession. He always said, however, that he would follow the decision of his home state regarding secession. When offered the field command of the Union Army, he turned it down, and instead assumed command of Confederate forces.

Lee had only 7,800 fully armed troops left with him when he surrendered at Appomattox. Most of them wept when he rode by them on his horse Traveler to say farewell. After the war, he served as president of Washington College, which was later renamed "Washington and Lee College."

Quote: "After four years of arduous service, marked by unsurpassing courage and fortitude, the Army of Northern Virginia has been compelled to yield to overwhelming numbers and resources…. Feeling that valor and devotion could accomplish nothing that could compensate for the loss that would have attended the continuation of the contest, I have determined to avoid the useless sacrifice of those whose past services have endeared them to their countrymen." (Farewell Speech to Confederate Troops, 1865)

REFERENCES: Emory Thomas, *Robert E. Lee: A Biography* (1995); George W. Gallagher, *Lee the Soldier* (1996).

Ulysses S. Grant (1822–1885)

Grant was a national hero as the commanding Union general in the Civil War, but his reputation suffered badly from his two unfortunate terms as president.

Born in a log cabin in Ohio, Grant inherited his mother's strong, silent, fiercely determined character but not her marked religious bent. Although officially "Hiram Ulysses," he changed his name to "Ulysses Hiram" at West Point because he was afraid he would be laughed at for his initials "HUG." Later, a military error substituted "Simpson" for "Hiram," and he left it that way.

Grant's drinking bouts in California were partly caused by his having served a horrendous tour of duty in Panama and by his separation from his family. He was totally devoted to his wife, Julia, who often advised him during his years in politics.

After leaving the presidency, he took a grand tour of Europe for two years and lived so lavishly that he was soon poverty-stricken. He completed his memoirs, which are still greatly admired, while dying of cancer of the throat.

Quote: "I saw an open field…so covered with dead that it would have been possible to walk across the clearing, in any direction, stepping on dead bodies, without touching a foot on the ground." (After the Battle of Shiloh, 1862)

REFERENCE: William McFeely, *Grant* (1981).

Salmon P. Chase (1808–1873)

Chase was Lincoln's politically ambitious secretary of the treasury.

He made his career as an antislavery lawyer in Ohio. Although he aided many fugitive slaves as Ohio attorney general, Chase was actually fearful of large black migrations to the North and hoped that emancipation would keep blacks in the South.

In the 1860 Republican convention, Chase had forty-nine votes before throwing them to Lincoln. He always considered Lincoln a weak leader and in December 1862, he conspired with some radical Republicans in Congress to try to take control of the cabinet. But Lincoln invited the conspirators into a cabinet meeting, where Chase was forced to express his support of the president.

He wanted the nomination in 1864 but ran the other way when the movement collapsed. After being extremely unhappy as chief justice of the United States, in 1868, he maneuvered for the Democratic nomination. Chase was self-righteous, opinionated, and difficult to get along with.

Quote: "I think a man of different qualities from those the President has will be needed for the next four years. I am not anxious to be regarded as that man. I am quite willing to leave [the choice] to the decision of those who think some such man should be chosen." (Diary, 1864)

REFERENCES: John Niven, *Salmon P. Chase: A Biography* (1995); David Donald, ed., *Inside Lincoln's Cabinet: The Civil War Diaries of Salmon P. Chase* (1954).

John Wilkes Booth (1838–1865)

Booth was the prominent Shakespearean actor who assassinated Abraham Lincoln.

Booth's father was Junius Brutus Booth, one of the most famous actors of his time. Junius Booth eventually went insane, and John Wilkes was always high-strung, moody, and emotionally unstable. Although probably not actually insane, he did experience periods of wild fantasy and irrationality. He would sometimes go into a rage at the sight of cats and occasionally killed them.

The younger Booth was dark, handsome, and always wore a long black cloak. He was especially popular with women and was said to have had numerous affairs. His favorite roles were Hamlet and Macbeth, but he also played popular melodramas.

He had planned to abduct Lincoln as early as 1864. Several of those he gathered for the assassination plot were feebleminded. He visited Lincoln's box the afternoon before the performance to arrange the assassination. The barn where he hid after fleeing was set on fire by Union soldiers, and Booth then evidently shot himself.

Quote: "I am not a murderer. I have done nothing that a soldier on the battlefield would not do. I do not regret what I have done." (Statement to physician aiding him, April 15, 1865)

REFERENCE: Albert Furstwangler, *Assassin on Stage* (1991).

QUESTIONS FOR CLASS DISCUSSION

1. Why did the North win the Civil War? How might the South have won?

2. Rank the following battles in order of importance and justify the ranking: Antietam, Gettysburg, and Vicksburg.

3. Should the Civil War be seen primarily as a war to save the Union or as a war to free the slaves? Why? What name would you give to the conflict?

4. What role did race and racism play in the Civil War? How did the war itself reflect and affect American attitudes toward race? Why were the black Union soldiers so critical in this regard? What impact did Lincoln's Emancipation Proclamation have on the war and society?

5. How does the popular image of the Civil War compare with the historical reality? Discuss the different perceptions and memories of the war in the North and South (for example, the popular images of Lee or Sherman in the two sections).

EXPANDING THE "VARYING VIEWPOINTS"

- T. Harry Williams, *Lincoln and His Generals* (1952).

  A view of Northern victory focused on military leadership:

  "Fundamentally Grant was superior to Lee because in a modern total war he had a modern mind, and Lee did not. Lee looked to the past in war as the Confederacy did in spirit.… What was realism to Grant was barbarism to Lee. Lee thought of war in the old way as a conflict between armies and refused to view it for what it had become—a struggle between societies. To him, economic war was needless cruelty to civilians. Lee was the last of the great old-fashioned generals, Grant the first of the great moderns."

- Allan Nevins, *The War for the Union* (1971).

  A view of Northern victory focused on political leadership:

  "One cardinal deficiency of the Confederacy…lay in the lack of a chief national executive possessing some of the energy, foresight, and firm decision exhibited by those other leaders of a newborn republic at war, Washington, Cromwell, or Masaryk. It is impossible for a student of the great rebellion to avoid comparing the character, talents, and sagacity of Lincoln with the parallel gifts of Jefferson Davis, greatly to the disadvantage of the latter. This broad subject…must always be kept in mind as an essential element of the war."

- Thomas C. Cochran, "Did the Civil War Retard Industrialization?" *Mississippi Valley Historical Review* (1961).

  A view of the Civil War actually slowed capitalist economic transformation:

  "Collectively these statistical estimates support a conclusion that the Civil War retarded American industrial growth.… Economically the effects of war and emancipation over the period 1840 to 1880 were negative.… If factory industry and mechanized transportation be taken as the chief indexes of early industrialism, its spread in the United States was continuous and rapid during the entire nineteenth century.… Few economists would see a major stimulation to economic growth in the events of the Civil War."

- James McPherson, *Battle Cry of Freedom* (1988).

  A view of the Civil War as expanding national power and Northern economic dominance:

  "The old federal republic in which the national government had rarely touched the average citizen except through the post-office gave way to a more centralized polity that taxed the people directly and created an internal revenue bureau to collect these taxes, drafted men into the army, expanded the jurisdiction of the federal courts, created a national currency and a national banking system, and established the first national agency for social welfare—the Freedmen's Bureau.… These changes in the federal balance paralleled a radical shift of political power from South to North.… The accession to power of the Republican party, with its ideology of competitive, egalitarian, free-labor capitalism, was a signal to the South that the northern majority had turned irrevocably toward this frightening, revolutionary future. Union victory in the war destroyed the southern vision of America and ensured that the northern vision would become the American vision."

QUESTIONS ABOUT THE "VARYING VIEWPOINTS"

1. How does Williams alter the usual judgment concerning Lee's superior military leadership? Does his definition of military leadership differ from the common one?

2. Are the political failings that Nevins sees in Davis similar to the military failings that Williams sees in Lee?

3. How might each of these historians interpret such turning points of the war as the Emancipation Proclamation, Vicksburg, and Gettysburg?

CHAPTER 22

The Ordeal of Reconstruction, 1865–1877

AP FOCUS

- The Union victory is significant in transforming and diversifying the South's production. It also represents the defeat of the planter-slaveholder and the continued rise of the industrial capitalist.

- In the aftermath of the war, especially in those southern states that reenter the Union under Johnson's lenient plan, Black Codes again segregate and subordinate the South's blacks. Organizations, such as the Ku Klux Klan and the Knights of the White Camellia, use violence and intimidation to deny blacks access to institutions, such as voting, that would improve their lives. Blacks are reduced to a form of slavery without chains, in that they are economically dependent and subservient to the owner of the land on which they are sharecroppers.

- President Johnson wrangles with the Radical Republicans over who will administer Reconstruction. The conflict is not resolved until Johnson is impeached. He barely survives the trial by the Senate, but the Radical Republicans dominate until he leaves office.

- Under the Radical Republicans, the South is placed under military rule in order to enforce blacks' rights and prepare states for readmission to the Union. Take note of the map and table in *The American Pageant* (14th ed., p. 525/15th ed., p. 476), which show the order of readmission.

- One legacy of Reconstruction is the passage of three amendments: the thirteenth (abolishing slavery), the fourteenth (defining citizenship rights), and the fifteenth (defining voting rights).

AP teachers should take note of the following:

1. Lincoln premised his lenient Reconstruction plan on the belief that the southern states had not seceded but had been pulled out of the Union by their political, economic, and military leaders.

2. Even though Reconstruction lasted little more than a decade, it provided blacks and their white supporters with valuable experience in establishing grassroots civil rights movements and developing organizational skills. When Reconstruction ended in 1877, blacks were reduced to a state of political and economic subordination and social submissiveness in a nation that, constitutionally at least, had granted them citizenship rights.

Focus on Historical Thinking:

Have students construct a chart listing the successes and failures of Reconstruction, including at least five successes and five failures.

FOCUS QUESTIONS

1. How did blacks respond to freedom, and what black organizations flourished?

2. How had Lincoln hoped to accomplish Reconstruction, and what modifications did Johnson make to Lincoln's original plan?

3. In what ways was Congressional Reconstruction different that Presidential Reconstruction?

4.   After gaining suffrage, how successful were blacks politically?

5.   What circumstances led to the impeachment and trial of President Johnson and what was the outcome?

CHAPTER THEMES

Theme: Johnson's political blunders and Southern white recalcitrance led to the imposition of congressional military Reconstruction on the South. Reconstruction did address difficult issues of reform and racial justice in the South and achieved some successes, but was ultimately abandoned, leaving a deep legacy of racial and sectional bitterness.

Theme: During Reconstruction, the Constitution was strengthened with the Fourteenth (citizenship and equal protection of the laws) and Fifteenth (black voting rights) Amendments, but it was also tested with the conflicts between the president and Congress that culminated in an impeachment process.

Theme: Southern resistance to Reconstruction began immediately with the sending of ex-rebels to be seated in Congress and continued with the creation of violently oppressive groups like the Ku Klux Klan. Although forced to make some concessions, Southern Redeemers successfully outlasted the congressional Reconstruction efforts.

CHAPTER SUMMARY

With the Civil War over, the nation faced the difficult problems of rebuilding the South, assisting the freed slaves, reintegrating the Southern states into the Union, and deciding who would direct the Reconstruction process.

The South was economically devastated and socially revolutionized by emancipation. As slave-owners reluctantly confronted the end of slave labor, blacks took their first steps in freedom. Black churches and freedmen's schools helped the former slaves begin to shape their own destiny.

The new President Andrew Johnson was politically inept and personally contentious. His attempt to implement a moderate plan of Reconstruction, along the lines originally suggested by Lincoln, fell victim to Southern whites' severe treatment of blacks and his own political blunders.

Republicans imposed harsh military Reconstruction on the South after their gains in the 1866 congressional elections. The Southern states reentered the Union with new radical governments, which rested partly on the newly enfranchised blacks, but also had support from some sectors of southern society. These regimes were sometimes corrupt but also implemented important reforms. The divisions between moderate and radical Republicans meant that Reconstruction's aims were often limited and confused, despite the important Fourteenth and Fifteenth Amendments.

Embittered whites hated the radical governments and mobilized reactionary terrorist organizations, such as the Ku Klux Klan, to restore white supremacy. Congress impeached Johnson but failed narrowly to convict him. In the end, the poorly conceived Reconstruction policy failed disastrously.

DEVELOPING THE CHAPTER: SUGGESTED LECTURE OR DISCUSSION TOPICS

- Analyze in more detail the condition of the South at the end of the Civil War, particularly, the economic and social revolution caused by the end of slavery. The focus might be on the great difficulty of working out a new system of racial relations, and on blacks' efforts to make their own way under harsh conditions.

  REFERENCE: Leon Litwack, *Been in the Storm So Long* (1979).

- Compare the mild presidential Reconstruction plans of Lincoln and Johnson with the harsher congressional Reconstruction, perhaps emphasizing how Johnson's blunders and severe treatment of blacks in the South handed the radical Republicans their chance.

  REFERENCE: James McPherson, *Ordeal by Fire: The Civil War and Reconstruction* (1982).

- Explain the actual impact of Reconstruction in the South. Particular consideration might be given to the limitations of the Republican governments and the Freedmen's Bureau, especially in altering fundamental economic and social conditions.

  REFERENCE: Eric Foner, *Reconstruction: America's Unfinished Revolution, 1863–1877* (1988).

- Examine the impeachment and acquittal of Johnson in relation to the overreaching of the radical Republicans and the declining support for military Reconstruction in the North.

  REFERENCES: Michael Les Benedict, *Impeachment and Trial of Andrew Johnson* (1973); Hans Trefousse, *The Impeachment of a President* (1975).

FOR FURTHER INTEREST: ADDITIONAL CLASS TOPICS

- Discuss the new circumstances and experiences of the ordinary freed African Americans. Consider such developments as the westward-migrating Exodusters and the newly powerful black churches. What obligation, if any, did the federal government have to the African Americans that it recently freed from slavery?

- Look at the Ku Klux Klan in relation to its historical significance in the 1870s and its enduring presence as a symbol of white racism and illegal violence.

- Focus on the character of Andrew Johnson, and particularly, his difficulty as a "poor Southern white" in the White House during Republican Reconstruction. Perhaps contrast him with his great enemy Thaddeus Stevens.

- Compare the enormous gap between the still widely held popular image of Reconstruction and the more complicated historical reality described in the text. The D. W. Griffith film *Birth of a Nation* would be a good starting point, since it helped to fix the general image of the period more than any other work.

- Why were women's rights ignored during the period of Reconstruction? What does the failure to include sex in the Fourteenth and Fifteenth Amendments suggest about the nation's commitment to equality?

CHARACTER SKETCHES

Andrew Johnson (1808–1875)

Even after Johnson's wife taught him to read as an adult, he frequently misspelled words. He once said, "It is a man of small imagination that cannot spell his own name in more than one way."

As a representative of poor mountain whites, he hated slaveholders, blacks, and abolitionists. Even though he hated slavery, he opposed emancipation because, he said: "What will you do with two million Negroes in our midst? Blood, rape, and rapine will be our portion."

The attacks on Johnson during his "swing around the circle" were partly orchestrated by Republican newspapers, which played up his vulgar language and behavior. Once they discovered that Johnson would go out of control, radical hecklers baited him at every stop.

Johnson remained a political hero to the plain whites of Tennessee following his departure from the presidency. After several tries, he was reelected to the Senate in 1875 but attended only one session before he died.

Quote: (In reply to hecklers' shouts of "Judas!"): "There was a Judas, and he was one of the twelve apostles…. If I have played Judas, who has been my Christ that I have played Judas with? Was it Thad Stevens? Was it Wendell Phillips? Was it Charles Sumner?" (Swing around the circle, 1866)

REFERENCE: Hans Trefousse, *Andrew Johnson: A Biography* (1989).

Oliver O. Howard (1830–1909)

Howard was the Civil War general who became head of the Freedmen's Bureau during Reconstruction.

In the Battle of Fair Oaks, Howard lost his right arm. His Civil War record was somewhat mixed: he bungled several operations and once refused to obey an order from General Hooker. Considered a "Christian officer," he was shocked by the destruction inflicted on Georgia by Sherman's army, even though he justified it as militarily necessary.

After leaving the Freedmen's Bureau, he founded Howard University in Washington, D.C., and served as its president from 1869 to 1874. He caused a split in his church in Washington by demanding the admission of black members.

Howard later returned to active military duty and commanded the 1877 expedition against the Nez Percé Indians in the West. He wrote frequently for newspapers and magazines and was a popular lecturer.

Quote: "A brief experience showed us that the negro people were capable of education, with no limit that men could set on their capacity. What white men could learn or had learned, they, or some of them, could learn." (Autobiography, 1907)

REFERENCE: William S. McFeely, *Yankee Stepfather: General O. O. Howard and the Freedmen* (1968).

Hiram Revels (1822–1901)

Revels, a clergyman, became one of the two black senators from Mississippi during Reconstruction.

Born a free man in Kentucky, Revels was of black and Indian ancestry. He first worked as a barber but then attended Knox College in Illinois and became a minister of the African Methodist Church.

He organized two black regiments in Maryland during the Civil War and then traveled widely in the South promoting religion and education for blacks. He was first elected an alderman in Natchez, Mississippi, despite his concern about mixing religion and politics. Many whites, as well as blacks, liked him, and he was elected to take Jefferson Davis's seat in the Senate. During his brief term, he supported the moderate Republicans and not the radicals.

He later came under white Democratic influence and joined in the overthrow of Republican Reconstruction in 1875. Quiet and mild-mannered, he disliked political conflict.

Quote: "The colored members, after consulting together on the subject, agreed to give their influence and votes for one of their own race, as it would in their judgment be a weakening blow against color line prejudice, and they unanimously elected me for their nominee…. Some of the Democracy favored it because they thought it would seriously damage the Republican party." (1884)

REFERENCE: Julius Thompson, *Hiram R. Revels, 1827–1901: A Biography* (1973).

Thaddeus Stevens (1792–1868)

Stevens was the Republican congressman who led radical Reconstruction and engineered the impeachment of Andrew Johnson.

Often sickly as a child, Stevens was partially physically disabled as an adult. He hated slavery from an early age and occasionally purchased fugitive slaves in order to give them their freedom.

In Congress, Stevens constantly attacked Southerners in scurrilous language, and some of his speeches nearly provoked riots on the floor of the House. As soon as the Civil War broke out, he advocated arming the slaves and encouraging a slave insurrection. His hatred of the South was increased when Confederate soldiers destroyed his ironworks during Lee's invasion of Pennsylvania.

Stevens was well read and eloquent but relied heavily on vituperation and sarcasm and seemed in a constant state of barely suppressed rage. He died shortly after the Johnson trial, but only his nephew and his black housekeeper attended his funeral. He chose to be buried in a black cemetery.

Quote: "I repose in this quiet and secluded spot, not from any natural preference for solitude, but, finding other cemeteries limited by charter rules as to race, I have chosen this, that I might illustrate in my death the principle which I have advocated through a long life—Equality of Man before his Creator." (Inscription on Stevens's tombstone, written by himself, 1868)

REFERENCE: Hans Trefousse, *Thaddeus Stevens: Nineteenth-Century Egalitarian* (1997).

QUESTIONS FOR CLASS DISCUSSION

1. Could presidential Reconstruction have succeeded if politically skilled Abraham Lincoln, instead of politically inept Andrew Johnson, had been president?

2. How truly radical was radical Reconstruction?

3. How did both Southern and Northern racial attitudes shape Reconstruction, and what effect did Reconstruction have on race relations and the conditions of blacks? Did Reconstruction really address the problems of race?

4. Was Reconstruction a noble experiment that failed, a vengeful Northern punishment of the South, a weak effort that did not go far enough, or the best that could have been expected under the circumstances? What has been the historical legacy of Reconstruction? (Consider, particularly, the Fourteenth and Fifteenth Amendments.)

EXPANDING THE "VARYING VIEWPOINTS"

*   William A. Dunning, *Reconstruction: Political and Economic* (1907).

    A view of Reconstruction as a national disgrace:

    "Few episodes of recorded history more urgently invited thorough analysis than the struggle through which the southern whites, subjugated by adversaries of their own race, thwarted the scheme which threatened permanent subjection to another race.... The most rasping feature of the new situation to the old white element of the South was the large predominance of northerners and negroes in positions of political power.... The most cunning and malignant enemy of the United States could not have timed differently this period of national ill-repute; for it came with the centennial of American independence...."

*   Kenneth Stampp, *The Era of Reconstruction* (1965).

    A favorable view of Reconstruction:

"Finally, we come to the idealistic aim of the radicals to make southern society more democratic, especially to make the emancipation of Negroes something more than an empty gesture. In the short run this was their greatest failure.... Still, no one could quite forget that the Fourteenth and Fifteenth Amendments were now part of the federal Constitution.... Thus Negroes were no longer denied equality by the plain language of law, as they had been before radical reconstruction, but only by coercion, by subterfuge, by deceit, and by spurious legalisms.... The blunders of that era, tragic though they were, dwindle into insignificance. For if it was worth four years of civil war to save the Union, it was worth a few years of radical reconstruction to give the American Negro the ultimate promise of equal civil and political rights."

QUESTIONS ABOUT THE "VARYING VIEWPOINTS"

1. What does each of these historians see as the fundamental goals of Reconstruction? How well does each think it achieved those goals?

2. According to each of these viewpoints, what were the roles of Northern whites, Southern whites, and blacks in Reconstruction?

3. How would each of these historians interpret the overturning of Reconstruction and its continuing meaning for American society?

CHAPTER 23

Political Paralysis in the Gilded Age, 1869–1896

AP FOCUS

- The post–Civil War era is rife with corruption, graft, and influence-peddling. Corruption is rampant at the local and state levels as well. The infamous New York City political party machine, known as the Tweed Ring, for example, bilks the city and state out of millions of dollars.

- In an attempt to clean their own house, the Republicans take steps to lower the protective tariff, which many consider unreasonably high and beneficial to specific industries. In addition, to address the problem of nepotism and favoritism in attaining government employment, the Republicans pass modest civil-service reform legislation, such as the Pendleton Act.

- A devastating depression hits the nation in 1873, adding to the already significant political woes of President Grant and his Republican Party.

- Farmers begin organizing in response to their economic woes; they form the Grange.

AP teachers should take note of the following:

1. An effect of the Civil War, the weakening of the Democratic Party during this period, would have a long-term effect. Indeed, only two Democrats were elected president between 1860 and 1912.

2. While he himself was honest to a fault, President Grant's administration was riddled with political figures who viewed their position in government as a means to acquire ill-gotten wealth. Some people who were not government officials found ways to penetrate the federal government to benefit themselves. For example, financial speculators Jay Gould and Jim Fisk cornered the gold market. Their unscrupulous acts were uncovered, but not before ruining many unsuspecting investors and businessmen and further tarnishing the already tainted Grant administration.

3. With the end of Reconstruction, Jim Crow laws brought a new form of subordination and degradation for southern blacks. Relegated again to a position of dependence, many former slaves turned to sharecropping, one of the few options open to them. Millions of blacks scratched out a meager existence while locked into a system that made them indebted to the owners of the land on which they worked. In many cases, those landowners were their former masters. The maps in *The American Pageant* (14th ed., p. 548/15th ed., p. 497) show how this new dependency worked.

Focus on Historical Thinking:

Reproduce without captions the painting on p. 487, the political cartoon on p. 490, the chart on p. 497, and the map on p. 507 (15th ed.). Have students construct a single sentence for each that clearly expresses its main purpose.

FOCUS QUESTIONS

1. Why were the political times so prone to political corruption in the post–Civil War Era?

2. What were the main issues surrounding the election of 1876? Did the Compromise of 1877 resolve those issues?

3. What were the biggest challenges facing the post–Reconstruction South?

4.   What were the main reasons for Chinese immigration in the second half of the nineteenth century?

5.   What were some of the reasons for the depression of 1893 and how did Cleveland deal with it?

CHAPTER THEMES

Theme: Even as post–Civil War America expanded and industrialized, political life in the Gilded Age was marked by ineptitude, stalemate, and corruption. Despite their similarity at the national level, the two parties competed fiercely for offices and spoils, while doling out "pork-barrel" benefits to veterans and other special interest groups.

Theme: The serious issues of monetary and agrarian reform, labor, race, and economic fairness were largely swept under the rug by the political system, until revolting farmers and a major economic depression beginning in 1893 created a growing sense of crisis and demands for radical change.

Theme: The Compromise of 1877 made reconstruction officially over and white Democrats resumed political power in the South. Blacks, as well as poor whites, found themselves forced into sharecropping and tenant farming; what began as informal separation of blacks and whites in the immediate postwar years evolved into systematic state-level legal codes of segregation known as Jim Crow laws.

CHAPTER SUMMARY

After the soaring ideals and tremendous sacrifices of the Civil War, the post–Civil War era was generally one of disillusionment. Politicians from the White House to the courthouse were often surrounded by corruption and scandal, while the actual problems afflicting industrializing America festered beneath the surface.

The popular war hero Grant was a poor politician and his administration was rife with corruption. Despite occasional futile reform efforts, politics in the Gilded Age was monopolized by the two patronage-fattened parties, which competed vigorously for spoils while essentially agreeing on most national policies. Cultural differences, different constituencies, and deeply felt local issues fueled intense party competition and unprecedented voter participation. Periodic complaints by "Mugwump" reformers and "soft-money" advocates failed to make much of a dent on politics.

The deadlocked contested 1876 election led to the sectional Compromise of 1877, which put an end to Reconstruction. An oppressive system of tenant farming and racial supremacy and segregation was thereafter fastened on the South, enforced by sometimes lethal violence. Racial prejudice against Chinese immigrants was also linked with labor unrest in the 1870s and 1880s.

Garfield's assassination by a disappointed office seeker spurred the beginnings of civil-service reform, which made politics more dependent on big business. Cleveland, the first Democratic president since the Civil War, made a lower tariff the first real issue in national politics for some time. But his mild reform efforts were eclipsed by a major economic depression that began in 1893, a crisis that deepened the growing outcry from suffering farmers and workers against a government and economic system that seemed biased toward big business and the wealthy.

DEVELOPING THE CHAPTER: SUGGESTED LECTURE OR DISCUSSION TOPICS

•   Analyze the corruption of the Gilded Age in relation to the increasingly low moral and political standards of the time. Contrast the quality of politicians with those of the previous age—Clay, Jackson, Webster, and Lincoln.

    REFERENCE: Mark Summers, *The Era of Good Stealings* (1993).

- Examine the impact of the new political alignments in the South. Consider the role of "redeemers," poor whites, and blacks in the post–Reconstruction era.

  REFERENCES: Otto Olsen, *Reconstruction and Redemption in the South* (1980); Michael Perman, *The Road to Redemption* (1984).

- Consider the link between racial and labor conflict, especially in places like California, where the "racially different" Chinese were seen as threats to the advances of white (often Irish or other immigrant) working people.

  REFERENCE: Alexander Saxton, *The Indispensable Enemy: Labor and the Anti-Chinese Movement in California* (1975).

- Examine the depression of the 1890s as the immediate context for the growing sense of class crisis in America. Consider the different but related grievances of western and southern farmers and (largely) northern and eastern industrial workers.

  REFERENCES: Charles Hoffman, *The Depression of the Nineties* (1970); Paul Krause, *The Battle for Homestead, 1880–1892* (1992); Robert McMath, *American Populism* (1993).

FOR FURTHER INTEREST: ADDITIONAL CLASS TOPICS

- Focus on the Tweed scandal as both event and symbol of the generally corrupt atmosphere of the times. Thomas Nast political cartoons make a good starting point.

- Discuss Grant's failures as president in contrast with his success as a general. Contrast his performance with that of other general-presidents such as Washington or Jackson who were successful politicians.

- Consider the Compromise of 1877 in relation to race and sectional conflict. Ask whether a Republican unwillingness to compromise by ending Reconstruction might have led to renewed sectional violence.

- Examine the "corrupt" J.P. Morgan gold deal of 1895 as a symbol of what many Americans saw as the capture of the federal government by big business. Consider Morgan himself as an important political as well as economic figure, and ask whether he deserved the villainous treatment he received from critics and protestors.

- Have students read the following novel: Erik Larson, *The Devil in the White City – Murder, Magic, and Madness at the Fair That Changed America*, New York: Vintage Books, 2003. A true story about the lives of two men—the architect behind the 1893 World Fair in Chicago and the serial killer who used the World Fair to lure his victims to their death. #1 National Bestseller and National Book Award Finalist.

- Have the students read Mark Twain and Charles Dudley Warner's novel *The Gilded Age* (1873). Use the novel to illustrate the level of political corruption in the post–antebellum era.

- Conduct a class debate over the following topics: for example, Excluding Chinese Immigrants Runs Counter to the Spirit of America; primary source readings will come from the following book *Opposing Viewpoints in American History—Volume II: From Reconstruction to the Present*, San Diego, CA: Greenhaven Press, 1996. Another good source of debate topics is Larry Madaras and James M. SoRelle, *Taking Sides—Clashing Views on Controversial Issues in American History, Volume II: Reconstruction to the Present*, Connecticut: McGraw-Hill, 2000.

CHARACTER SKETCHES

William Marcy Tweed (1823–1878)

Tweed was the New York political boss whose grand-scale corruption symbolized the low political standards of the Gilded Age.

He got his start in politics with volunteer fire companies, which were closely tied to Tammany Hall, and he soon learned tricky devices such as running "dummy" candidates to divide the opposition. The City Council during his service was known as the "Forty Thieves."

Tweed offered $5 million to the *New York Times* if it would not print the information on his corruption and $500,000 to Nast if he would stop his anti-Tweed cartoons. Tweed was treated luxuriously in prison, even being allowed to take carriage rides. He escaped and fled to Cuba and Spain disguised as a sailor but was recognized and returned to harsher jail treatment.

Always genial and friendly, Tweed held no personal grudges against Thomas Nast and others who brought him down. He said he was only surprised that they wouldn't take his bribes.

Quote: (When asked how his ring had managed to keep the scandals hidden for so long): "Well, we used money wherever we could." (1869)

REFERENCE: Alexander Callow, *The Tweed Ring* (1966).

Horace Greeley (1811–1872)

Greeley was the most famous newspaper editor of the nineteenth century, whose eccentric involvements in reform and politics made him an object of humor and anger.

He started on a Vermont newspaper at age fourteen and in 1841 launched the *New York Tribune* in close association with Whig politicians Thurlow Weed and William Seward.

At various times, he supported Fourierism, ending capital punishment, prohibition, cooperative labor unions, women's rights (though not suffrage), and homesteading. He once spent a few months in an unsuccessful farming venture and then published a book called *What I Know of Farming*.

He had a high, squeaky voice and whiskers and always wore a broad-brimmed hat and white socks. He tried numerous times for political office, but except for a few months in Congress, he always failed. He had often been satirized but took personally the attacks on him in the 1872 campaign: one cartoon depicted him shaking hands with Booth over Lincoln's body. He already showed signs of mental instability before the election and died shortly thereafter.

Quote: "We are henceforth to be one American people. Let us forget that we fought. Let us remember only that we have made peace." (1872)

REFERENCE: Lurton D. Ingersoll, *The Life of Horace Greeley* (1974).

James G. Blaine (1830–1893)

Blaine was the colorful Republican politician, presidential candidate, and secretary of state during the Gilded Age.

Blaine married his wife secretly because she was a schoolteacher who was supposed to remain single. She came from a well-off Maine family, and they helped him get his start in politics there.

Although he had the grand platform manner of earlier politicians, Blaine excelled at personal contact and humorous banter. He could easily remember thousands of names and connect each of them with an anecdote about the person.

By dramatically producing and reading the "Mulligan letters," which supposedly proved his involvement in railroad corruption, he convinced many people of his innocence. Although never charged with crime, he became wealthy by trading favors with the owners of railroads and other interests.

Quote: "This letter requires no answer. After reading it file it away in your most secret drawer or give it to the flames.… Do not say a word…no matter who may ask you." (Letter to Sherman, 1884)

REFERENCE: R. Hal Williams, *Years of Decision* (1978).

QUESTIONS FOR CLASS DISCUSSION

1. Why did politics in the Gilded Age seemingly sink to such a low level? Did the Gilded Age party system have any strengths to compensate for its weaknesses?

2. Was the Compromise of 1877 another cynical political deal of the era or a wise adjustment to avoid a renewal of serious sectional conflict?

3. What were the short- and long-term results of the "Jim Crow" system in the South? Why was the sharecropping system so hard to overcome? Were blacks worse off or better off after the Civil War?

4. Why was the political system so slow to respond to the economic grievances of farmers and workers, especially during the hard economic times of the 1890s? Were the Populists and others more effectively addressing the real problems that America faced, or was their approach fatally crippled by their nostalgia for a simpler, rural America?

MAKERS OF AMERICA: THE CHINESE

Questions for Class Discussion

1. How was the Chinese immigrant experience similar to that of such European groups as the Irish (Chapter 14), and how was it different? What effect did the racial distinctiveness of the Chinese have on their experience in America?

2. What were the greatest problems the Chinese-Americans experienced? How did they attempt to overcome them?

Suggested Student Exercises

*   Consider various prejudicial stereotypes of Chinese-American immigrants from the movies or elsewhere (for example, Charlie Chan). Compare these images with the actual experiences of Chinese-Americans.

*   Consider how the history of California and the West Coast was significantly affected by the presence of even the relatively small number of Chinese immigrants. Examine whether that history has a new significance today, when modern China has again become a great power and new generations of Asian-American immigrants have arrived.

EXPANDING THE "VARYING VIEWPOINTS"

*   Richard Hofstadter, *The Age of Reform* (1955).

    A view of the Populists as backward-looking and irrational reactionaries:

    "In the attempts of the Populists … to hold on to some of the values of agrarian life, to save personal entrepreneurship and individual opportunity and the character type they engendered, and to maintain a homogeneous Yankee civilization, I have found much that was retrograde and delusive, a little that was vicious, and a good deal that was comic. … Such tendencies in American life as isolationism and the extreme nationalism that often goes with it, hatred of Europe and Europeans, racial, religious, and nationalist phobias, resentment of big business, trade-unionism, intellectuals, the Eastern seaboard and its culture—all these have been found not only in opposition to reform but also at times oddly combined with it."

- Lawrence Goodwyn, *Democratic Promise: The Populist Moment in America* (1976).

  A view of the Populists as forward-looking and rational:

  "For the triumph of Populism—its only enduring triumph—was the belief in possibility it injected into American political consciousness.… Tactical errors aside, it was the élan of the agrarian crusade, too earnest ever to be decisively ridiculed, too creative to be permanently ignored, that lingers as the Populist residue.… The creed centered on concepts of political organization and uses of democratic government that—even though in a formative stage—were already too advanced to be accepted by the centralizing, complacent nation of the Gilded Age.… The issues of Populism were large. They dominate our world."

QUESTIONS ABOUT THE "VARYING VIEWPOINTS"

1. What does each of these historians see as the essential character of populism?

2. How does the holder of each of these viewpoints see the relationship between populism and the new corporate industrial order of the late nineteenth century?

3. How would each of these historians likely interpret the fact that populism disappeared as a political force but has remained a strong undercurrent in American political thinking?

CHAPTER 24

Industry Comes of Age, 1865–1900

AP FOCUS

- Enormous immigration, mass production, and the presence of low-skill jobs drive down workers' wages.

- A catalyst for postwar industrial and economic expansion is the railroad industry, which not only facilitates trade, commerce, and transportation, but also makes locomotive production a major industry. The government plays a major role in the industry's development and importance by providing the companies with millions of acres of free land—a giveaway, some say.

- By the turn of the twentieth century, important industries necessary to the health and prosperity of the nation and its citizens are controlled by economically and politically powerful trusts and other types of business combinations, which undermine the foundation of capitalism: competition.

- The Gilded Age is dominated by key industrialists and financiers. So enormous are their own wealth, control of business capital, and political influence that many refer to them as Robber Barons. See the political cartoons in *The American Pageant* (14th ed., pp. 572, 576, 578, 579/15th ed., pp. 518, 521, 523, 524). Many aspects of the Gilded Age pertain to the AP theme Economic Transformations.

AP teachers should take note of the following:

1. Justifications for the enormous disparity in wealth were expressed in philosophy, literature, and the social and behavioral sciences. One novelist, Horatio Alger, established a format for his works of fiction that repeatedly expressed the same theme: industry, self-discipline, sacrifice, and hard work ultimately lead to financial success, regardless of the obstacles. Culture is an AP theme.

2. Industrial development was uneven, especially in the South. Some industries, such as textile production, flourished while others, such as the steel industry, lagged behind those of the North.

3. Industrial development had a human toll, as many laborers, including women and children, worked long hours under oppressive conditions for very low wages. Not surprisingly, many workers attempted to unionize in order to engage in collective bargaining. Most capitalists refused to recognize the legitimacy of the unions and balked at even the thought of negotiating. Often-intense and costly strikes, such as the Railroad Strike of 1877, shaped the period. It is important to note that President Hayes called out the army to suppress the Railroad Strike, a harbinger of what was to come, as business interests and the federal and state governments allied in their opposition to organized labor. Economic Transformations, including labor and unions, is an AP theme.

4. The DBQ on the capitalists (14th ed., DBQ 8, pp. A86–A88/15th ed., pp. A83-A85) offers two interpretations of late nineteenth–century American capitalists and asks students to evaluate which of the two is more accurate. In supporting a particular thesis, students can provide information that supports one designation and also provide information that refutes the other designation.

Focus on Historical Thinking:

Have students complete a Main Idea Log for each section in the text narrative. Students should write out each heading, turn it into a question, and answer that question in one clear, concise sentence.

FOCUS QUESTIONS

1.   What were the main reasons for the increase in railroad construction? What were some of the positives and negatives of this revolution?

2.   What were the main principles of the Gospel of Wealth and Social Darwinism? In what ways did they attempt to deal with (and justify) the concentration of wealth?

3.   What were some of the main ways in which the government tried to deal with the trusts? How did the Interstate Commerce Act and the Sherman Anti-Trust Act deal with monopolies? Were they successful?

4.   What were some of the biggest challenges facing labor in the second half of the nineteenth century?

CHAPTER THEMES

Theme: America accomplished heavy industrialization in the post–Civil War era. Spurred by the transcontinental rail network, business grew and consolidated into giant corporate trusts, as epitomized by the oil and steel industries.

Theme: Industrialization radically transformed the practices of labor and the condition of the American working people. But despite frequent industrial strife and the efforts of various reformers and unions, workers failed to develop effective labor organizations to match the corporate forms of business.

Theme: With the concentration of capital in the hands of a few, new moralities arose to advance justifications for this social and economic phenomenon. A "survival of the fittest" theory emerged, a popular theory based on the thought of Herbert Spencer and William Graham Sumner, which argued that millionaires were products of natural selection. Another theory known as the "Gospel of Wealth" argued that well-to-do societies had to prove themselves morally responsible.

CHAPTER SUMMARY

Aided by government subsidies and loans, the first transcontinental rail line was completed in 1869, soon followed by others. This rail network opened vast new markets and prompted industrial growth. The power and corruption of the railroads led to public demands for regulation, which was only minimally begun.

New technology and forms of business organization led to the growth of huge corporate trusts. Andrew Carnegie and John D. Rockefeller led the way in the steel and oil industries. Initially, the oil industry supplied kerosene for lamps; it eventually expanded by providing gasoline to fuel automobiles. Cheap steel transformed industries from construction to rail building, and the powerful railroads dominated the economy and reshaped American society.

The benefits of industrialization were unevenly distributed. The South remained in underdeveloped dependence, while the industrial working class struggled at the bottom of the growing class divisions of American society. Increasingly transformed from independent producers and farmers to dependent wage earners, America's workers became vulnerable to illness, industrial accidents, and unemployment.

Workers' attempts at labor organization were generally ineffective. The Knights of Labor disappeared after the Haymarket bombing. Gompers founded the AF of L to organize skilled craft laborers but ignored most industrial workers, women, and blacks.

DEVELOPING THE CHAPTER: SUGGESTED LECTURE OR DISCUSSION TOPICS

- Explain the central role the railroads played in late-nineteenth-century America. Show how they not only moved goods and people but also dominated politics, employed workers, promoted farms and cities, and created the models for American big business. Perhaps use the building of the transcontinental railroad as a key symbolic event of the age.

  REFERENCE: David Bain, *Empire Express: Building the First Transcontinental Railroad* (1999).

- Examine the dramatic impact of "big business" and the new industrial corporations on the American economy and American life generally. Use Andrew Carnegie and John D. Rockefeller as examples of how the new corporate industrial organizers became widely celebrated heroes as well. Consider their effects not only on the economy but also on American culture.

  REFERENCE: Alan Trachtenberg, *The Incorporation of America: Culture and Society in the Gilded Age* (1982).

- Consider the impact of industrialization on the nature of work and the lives of workers. Point out how most workers went from being self-employed or working in small enterprises to being employed in large, impersonal corporate enterprises.

  REFERENCE: Herbert Gutman, *Power and Culture: Essays on the American Working Class* (1987).

- Analyze the growing place of wage-earning women in the late-nineteenth-century industrial economy. Compare and contrast men's and women's attitudes toward work, family, and labor unions.

  REFERENCE: Alice Kessler-Harris, *Out to Work: A History of Wage-Earning Women in the United States* (1982).

- Analyze the goals of the New South and consider to what extent these goals were realized following Reconstruction.

  REFERENCES: W.J. Cash, *The Mind of the South* (1941, revised 1991); C. Van Woodward, *Origins of the New South, 1877–1913* (1971).

FOR FURTHER INTEREST: ADDITIONAL CLASS TOPICS

- Discuss the railroads as both romantic enterprise (for example, the golden spike, the luxurious Pullman cars) and as controversial exploitative business (for example, the corruption of legislatures, price-fixing).

- Examine the benefits and drawbacks of industrialization for various groups (business, labor, women, minorities, immigrants).

- Using Edison as a symbol of the emerging technological and industrial age, show how his inventions were quickly taken up and incorporated into huge new industries.

- Use the Haymarket affair to illustrate the growing class conflicts in industrial America and to highlight the debates over how American workers should respond to the new industrial conditions.

- Conduct a class debate over the following topics: for example, Concentrations of Wealth Harm America, The Organization of Labor into Unions Is Dangerous, A Populist Prescription for Social Reform, A New Industrial South Is Rising; readings will come from the following book: *Opposing Viewpoints in American History—Volume II: From Reconstruction to the Present*, San Diego, CA: Greenhaven Press, 1996. Another good source of debate topics is Larry Madaras and James M. SoRelle, *Taking Sides—Clashing Views on Controversial Issues in American History, Volume II: Reconstruction to the Present*, Connecticut: McGraw-Hill, 2000.

- Have the students read selections from Thorstein Veblen's *The Theory of the Leisure Class* (1899) in David A. Hollinger and Charles Capper's (Editors), *The American Intellectual Tradition: Volume II—1865 to the Present*, New York: Oxford University Press, 2001.

CHARACTER SKETCHES

Thomas Edison (1847–1931)

Edison was the inventive genius of American industrialization who symbolized the modern fusion of science, technology, and industry.

Edison was regarded as a very slow student, and consequently, his formal education lasted only three months. Still a boy, he turned to selling newspapers on the streets of Port Huron, Michigan, handing over some of the money to his family but spending the rest on books and chemicals. At age fifteen, he went to work for the telegraph. His first inventions were electrical stock tickers and vote recorders.

He took out over a thousand patents in his life. Among his lesser-known inventions were synthetic chemicals, waxed paper, portland cement, the mimeograph machine, and light sockets and fixtures.

Although celebrated as a solitary genius, Edison actually developed the new forms of team research and systematic technological innovation. His laboratory at Menlo Park, New Jersey, was set up in 1880 and employed teams of researchers financed by industry.

Quote: "The first step is an intuition—and comes with a burst, then difficulties arise.... 'Bugs,' as such little faults and difficulties are called—show themselves, and months of anxious watching, study, and labor are requisite.... I have the right principle and am on the right track, but time, hard work, and some good luck are necessary, too...." (Letter, 1878)

REFERENCE: Paul Israel, *Edison: A Life of Invention* (1998).

Andrew Carnegie (1835–1919)

Carnegie was a Scottish immigrant who became the leading industrialist of the American steel industry and a prominent philanthropist.

His parents, Scottish hand-loom weavers, were well informed and very interested in education. The family came to the United States when Carnegie's father was thrown out of work by the new textile mills. Carnegie's boyhood dream was to dress his mother in silks, and she lived long enough for him to shower her with expensive gifts.

Carnegie decided early in his career that he should eventually give away most of his money. He spent much of his time associating with literary people and writing magazine articles and books. Eventually, he gave away an estimated $350 million, including $60 million to American libraries.

Charming, smooth, and polished, Carnegie was generally popular with the public.

Quote: "Thirty-three, and an income of $50,000 per annum.... Beyond this never earn—make no effort to increase fortune, but spend the surplus each year for benevolent purposes...." (Memo to himself, 1868)

REFERENCE: Joseph Frazier Wall, *Andrew Carnegie* (1970).

John D. Rockefeller (1839–1937)

Rockefeller was the industrialist who organized the Standard Oil Company and became the leading symbol of American capitalism.

His mother was harsh, austere, and religious, and Rockefeller inherited these qualities from her. He was generally frugal and humorless. As a young man, he taught Sunday school and always remained a committed member of the Baptist Church.

Rockefeller avoided serving in the Civil War to devote himself to business. He began his career by working with a Cleveland merchant and bought his first refinery for $72,000.

He retired from active control of Standard Oil in 1897. By the 1920s his net worth was probably a billion dollars.

Quote: "In speaking of the real beginnings of the Standard Oil Company, it should be remembered that it was not so much the consolidation of the firms in which we had a personal interest, but the coming together of the men who had the combined brainpower to do the work.… It is not merely capital and plans and the strictly material things that make up a business, but the character of the men behind these things.…" (1909)

REFERENCE: Ron Chernow, *Titan: The Life of John D. Rockefeller, Sr.* (1998).

Samuel Gompers (1850–1924)

Gompers was the American labor leader who organized the American Federation of Labor and promoted the strategy of conservative craft organization.

Almost entirely self-educated, Gompers gained much of his knowledge by reading and attending lectures in New York City. He was very well acquainted with European socialist thinkers and even learned German so he could read Karl Marx in the original. But he always believed the marxists and socialists were wrong and worked to develop arguments against them.

Gompers loved drama and pageantry but kept the "secret brotherhood" approach out of the AF of L unions. He disliked reformers and intellectuals, calling them "industrially impossible." Although strongly patriotic, after World War I Gompers and the AF of L were often accused of being "un-American" for promoting labor organization and strikes.

Quote: "The trusts are our employers, and the employer who is fair to us, whether an individual or a collection of individuals in the form of a corporation or a trust, matters little to us as long as we obtain fair wages." (1912)

REFERENCES: Harold Livesay, *Samuel Gompers and Organized Labor in America* (1987); David Montgomery, *The Fall of the House of Labor* (1987).

QUESTIONS FOR CLASS DISCUSSION

1. What were the costs and benefits of the industrial transformation of the post–Civil War era?

2. Should industrialists such as Vanderbilt, Carnegie, and Rockefeller be viewed as "robber barons" or "captains of industry"?

3. Was the growing class division of the time a threat to American democracy? Why or why not?

4. Why did American workers have such trouble responding to the new industrial conditions of labor? Why were business and the middle-class public generally hostile to allowing workers to organize as industry did? Why did the AF of L survive while the Knights of Labor failed?

5. Does the government regulation of the economy disprove the belief that capitalism is a morally superior economic theory? Why or why not?

MAKERS OF AMERICA: THE KNIGHTS OF LABOR

Questions for Class Discussion

1. What was admirable and "progressive" in the Knights' outlook? What was largely nostalgic and doomed to failure?

2. What was the appeal of the Knights' emphasis on secrecy, ritual, and "brotherhood"? What elements of the Knights' emphasis on social solidarity remained part of the labor movement, and what disappeared?

Suggested Student Exercises

- Examine the Knights' role in the great industrial strikes of 1886. Explain why they experienced a boom in membership, especially with the advocacy of the eight-hour day, and then suddenly collapsed and soon disappeared.

- Examine the biographies of the Knights' two most prominent leaders, Terence Powderly and "Mother" Jones. Perhaps compare their "utopian"- and "producer"-oriented outlook with that of more pragmatic unionists such as Samuel Gompers and socialists such as Eugene V. Debs.

EXPANDING THE "VARYING VIEWPOINTS"

- Matthew Josephson, *The Robber Barons: The Great American Capitalists, 1861–1901* (1934).

  A view of industrialization focused on business:

  "The members of this new ruling class were generally, and quite aptly, called 'barons,' 'kings,' 'empire-builders,' and even 'emperors.' They were aggressive men, as were the first feudal barons; sometimes they were lawless; in important crises, nearly all of them tended to act without those established moral principles which fixed more or less the conduct of the common people of the community. At the same time … many of them showed volcanic energy and qualities of courage which, under another economic clime, might have fitted them for immensely useful social constructions, and rendered them glorious rather than hateful to their people."

- Herbert Gutman, *Work, Culture, and Society in Industrializing America* (1976).

  A view of industrialization focused on labor and society:

  "In the half-century after 1843 industrial development radically transformed the earlier American social structure, and during this Middle Period…a profound tension existed between the older American preindustrial social structure and the modernizing institutions that accompanied the development of industrial capitalism…. In each of these distinctive stages of American society, a recurrent tension also existed between native and immigrant men and women fresh to the factory and the demands imposed upon them by the regularities and disciplines of factory labor."

QUESTIONS ABOUT THE "VARYING VIEWPOINTS"

1. What does each of these historians see as the most crucial feature of the new industrialization?

2. How does each of them see the relationship between industrial capitalism and the moral and cultural values of society?

3. How would each of them likely interpret the labor conflicts and strikes of the period—for example, the Haymarket affair and the decline of the Knights of Labor?

CHAPTER 25

America Moves to the City, 1865–1900

AP FOCUS

- Industrialization sparks urbanization, and cities become magnets for immigrants. Those who can afford to leave behind the hustle and bustle of urban life move to the budding suburbs. See the table in *The American Pageant* (14th ed., p. 598/15th ed., p. 540). Demographic Changes is an AP theme.

- The late nineteenth century sees a surge of immigration, now from eastern and southern Europe. Most encounter living and working conditions not appreciably better than what they had left. The tenement floor plan (14th ed., p. 599/15th. ed., p. 542) shows typical living conditions for impoverished urban workers.

- As it was for earlier immigrants, those who immigrate in the post–Civil War era are generally not welcomed by those whose families established roots in America in an earlier period. Asians, Eastern and Southern Europeans, and Jews often face hostility from those who consider themselves culturally superior and who maintain that American culture is being weakened by these new immigrants. Take note of President Grover Cleveland's critique of this exclusionary sentiment (14th ed., p. 609/15th ed., p. 551), and keep in mind that American Diversity is an AP theme.

- Disappointed with the premature end of Reconstruction and the continuing struggle of blacks to achieve social acceptance and political and economic equality, black leaders suggest various ways to defeat racism. Some black leaders, such as Booker T. Washington, advocate a gradualist approach, while W. E. B. Du Bois is committed to a more aggressive, confrontational approach.

- Incensed by the expanding gap between wealth and poverty, corruption in government, and a host of other social, economic, and political concerns, reformers put pen to paper and educate millions of Americans about these problems. Books and journals, such as *The Nation*, provide readers an alternative perspective to more widely known mainstream political ideas. Reform is an AP theme.

- The foundations of the twentieth-century women's rights movement are laid in the nineteenth century by advocates, such as Victoria Woodhull and Jane Addams. The struggle over women's suffrage is one facet of the strain between those who identified with the notion of Victorian womanhood and those who celebrated the new, modern American woman.

AP teachers should take note of the following:

1. The prohibition movement attracted those who claimed that alcohol consumption was immoral and unchristian. Some contemporaneous critics of the movement refuted this perspective as a veiled attempt to impose a set of social of social and cultural values on society.

2. In 1909, W. E. B. Du Bois helped found a black civil rights organization that is still in existence, the National Association for the Advancement of Colored People (NAACP).

Focus on Historical Thinking:

> Distribute a list of 50 important historical terms from the beginning of the year to this point. Give students the opportunity to review these terms and then create a matching quiz, randomly selecting 25 of the terms.

FOCUS QUESTIONS

1. What were some of the reactions to the New Immigration? How were these immigrants different from the previous generations of American immigrants?

2. What were the major challenges faced by the increased urban population?

3. What were some of the challenges to traditional thought during the second half of the nineteenth century? How did the religious and secular elements in American society deal with those?

4. What were some of the major reform movements during the second half of the nineteenth century?

5. Who were some of the significant artistic and literary figures of the Gilded Age? What contributions did they make to American society?

CHAPTER THEME

Theme: In the late nineteenth century, American society was increasingly dominated by large urban centers. Explosive urban growth was accompanied by often disturbing changes, including the New Immigration, crowded slums, new religious outlooks, and conflicts over culture and values. While many Americans were disturbed by the new urban problems, cities also offered opportunities to women and expanded cultural horizons.

Theme: African Americans suffered the most as the south lagged behind other regions of the country with regard to educational improvements and opportunities. Two schools of thought emerged as to the best way to handle this problem. Booker T. Washington advocated that blacks should gain knowledge of useful trades. With this would come self-respect and economic security—Washington avoided the issue of social equality. W.E.B. Du Bois demanded complete equality for blacks, both social as well as economic.

CHAPTER SUMMARY

The United States moved from the country to the city in the post–Civil War decades. Mushrooming urban development was exciting but also created severe social problems, including overcrowding and slums. Attempts to remedy the growing problems of urbanization, such as the "City Beautiful" movement, were undertaken by people like Frederick Olmstead and Daniel Burnham.

After the 1880s, the cities were flooded with the New Immigrants from southern and eastern Europe. With their strange customs and non-Protestant religions, the newcomers sometimes met with nativist hostility and discrimination.

Religion had to adjust to social and cultural changes. Roman Catholicism and Judaism gained strength, while conflicts over evolution and biblical interpretation divided Protestant churches.

American education expanded rapidly, especially at the secondary and graduate levels. Blacks and immigrants tried, with limited success, to use education as a path to upward mobility.

Significant conflicts over moral values, especially relating to sexuality and the role of women, began to appear. The new urban environment provided expanded opportunities for women but also created difficulties for the family. Families grew more isolated from society, the divorce rate rose, and the average family size shrank.

American literature and art reflected a new realism and regionalism, while popular amusement became a big business. The art of Thomas Eakins and Winslow Homer moved away from romanticism toward a more realistic view of life. Similarly, literature began to focus on the "coarse comedy" of human life. The novels of Henry James and Edith Wharton explored the psychological themes of modern life with an eye toward scientific objectivity. Symphony orchestra, operas, and ragtime reflected musical appeal to different segments of society.

DEVELOPING THE CHAPTER: SUGGESTED LECTURE OR DISCUSSION TOPICS

- Explain the strong connection among the new forces of industrialization, urbanization, and immigration. Show how each one tended to reinforce the others, creating a significantly new kind of urban environment.

  REFERENCE: Eric Monkkonen, *America Becomes Urban* (1988).

- Describe the experience of the New Immigrants and explain why they were often regarded with suspicion or hostility. The emphasis might be on the factors that made them different from most earlier immigrants—particularly their "strange" cultures, religions, poverty, and the fact that they crowded into urban slums.

  REFERENCE: John Bodnar, *The Transplanted: A History of Immigrants in Urban America* (1985).

- Relate the cultural conflicts over religion and values to the new social and cultural environment of the city. Show how urban life tended to undermine traditional standards of belief and behavior (for example, about drinking or divorce) while creating new institutions and values, including popular culture.

  REFERENCE: Gunther Barth, *City People: The Rise of Modern City Culture in Nineteenth-Century America* (1980).

- Consider the complicated effects of urbanization on women's roles and family—new opportunities arose but they imposed new strains on marriage and child-rearing.

  REFERENCES: Elaine May, *Great Expectations: Marriage and Divorce in Post-Victorian America* (1983); Steven Mintz, *A Prison of Expectations: The Family in Victorian Culture* (1985).

FOR FURTHER INTEREST: ADDITIONAL CLASS TOPICS

- Use Jane Addams's experiences to demonstrate how some Americans encountered the problems of new industrial metropolises like Chicago.

- Examine the myths and the realities of immigration. A good starting point might be Emma Lazarus's Statue of Liberty poem, which says, "Give me your tired, your poor, your huddled masses yearning to breathe free," but also called the immigrants "wretched refuse."

- Analyze the impact of urban life, immigration, Darwinism, and biblical higher criticism (literary scholarship) on religion, including the "immigrant religions" such as Roman Catholicism, Eastern Orthodoxy, and Judaism.

- Consider the impact and meaning of new "popular amusements" such as the circus, baseball, vaudeville, and so on.

- Conduct a class debate over the following topics, for example, Blacks Should Stop Agitating for Political Equality and Racial Segregation Is Constitutional; primary source readings will come from the following book: *Opposing Viewpoints in American History—Volume II: From Reconstruction to the Present*, San Diego, CA: Greenhaven Press, 1996. Another good source of debate topics is Larry

Madaras and James M. SoRelle, *Taking Sides—Clashing Views on Controversial Issues in American History, Volume II: Reconstruction to the Present*, Connecticut: McGraw-Hill, 2000.

- Have students read William James, *Pragmatism* (1907). Use the book to explore the criticisms James had of both the transcendental and rational traditions in American philosophy; in this work, James argues for the concept that any idea must have validity only in terms of its practical consequences.

- Have students read Edward Bellamy's *Looking Backward: 2000–1887* (1888). Use the novel to explore a number of key issues of late-nineteenth-century economic and political thought: the proper role of government, the nature of humanity, cooperation versus competition, the practicality of utopian thought, and the merits of socialism.

- Have students look at art slides from the American Realists tradition, especially, Winslow Homer, *The Gulf Stream* (1899), Thomas Eakins, *The Gross Clinic* (1875), George Bellows, *The Lone Tenement* (1909), *Pennsylvania Station Excavation* (1906), *Cliff Dwellers* (1913), *Stag at Sharkey's* (1909), and *Tennis at Newport* (1920). Use the slides as visual primary sources—have students discuss the ways in which artists used visual critiques as guides to implement change within society.

- Have students read Jacob A. Riis, *How the Other Half Lives* (1890). "Long ago it was said that 'one half of the world does not know how the other half lives.' That was true then. It did not know because it did not care."

- Have the students read selections from W.E.B. Du Bois's *The Souls of Black Folk* (1903) in David A. Hollinger and Charles Capper's (Editors), *The American Intellectual Tradition: Volume II—1865 to the Present*, New York: Oxford University Press, 2001.

- Have the students read Oliver Wendell Holmes Jr., "Natural Law" (1918) in David A. Hollinger and Charles Capper's (Editors), *The American Intellectual Tradition: Volume II—1865 to the Present*, New York: Oxford University Press, 2001.

CHARACTER SKETCHES

Jane Addams (1860–1935)

Addams, the founder of Hull House and the profession of social work, was the leading female reformer of the progressive era.

Her father was a prominent Illinois businessman and politician who had served in the state legislature with Lincoln. Her mother died when she was two, and she remained deeply devoted to her father until he suddenly died when she was twenty-one.

For the next eight years, she underwent a prolonged personal crisis, marked by physical ailments and deep depression. Her decision to open Hull House with her friend Ellen Gates Starr came partly out of her growing awareness of urban problems, but it also ended her personal struggles and gave meaning to her life.

Addams first used her own money for Hull House but later became a highly skilled fund-raiser. Her opposition to World War I lost her considerable popularity in the 1920s. Addams was benevolent, thoughtful, and modest but somewhat cool, aloof, and formal in personal relations.

Quote: "I found myself…with high expectations and a certain belief that whatever perplexities and discouragement concerning the life of the poor were in store for me, I should at least know something at firsthand and have the solace of daily activity…. I had at last finished with the ever-lasting 'preparation for life,' however ill-prepared I might be."

REFERENCE: Allen F. Davis, *American Heroine: The Life and Legend of Jane Addams* (1973).

Dwight L. Moody (1837–1899)

Moody was the most prominent evangelical revivalist of the post–Civil War era and the founder of Moody Bible Institute and other schools.

After growing up in rural New England, in 1856, he moved to Chicago and became a successful shoe salesman. He began taking slum dwellers to church with him and in 1858 organized a Sunday school for Chicago street kids.

He traveled to Britain to study evangelical methods and conducted spectacularly well-received revivals there. His musician and choir leader, Ira D. Sankey, contributed greatly to Moody's success with his popular, sentimental hymns.

Never officially ordained, Moody spoke the plain language of the ordinary person. His organization was large and sophisticated but developed techniques like the "conference room" to give each convert a sense of personal concern.

Quote: "Water runs down hill, and the highest hills are the great cities. If we can stir them, we can stir the whole nation.… There is misery in the great city, but what is the cause of it? Why, the sufferers have become lost from the Shepherd's care." (1876)

REFERENCE: Lyle Dorsett, *A Passion for Souls: The Life of D.L. Moody* (1997).

Booker T. Washington (1856–1915)

A former slave who became the dominant American black leader in the period from 1890 to 1910, Washington was popular with whites but extremely controversial among blacks.

He was born in Virginia; his father was a white man from a neighboring plantation. As a boy, Washington lived in a one-room, floorless cabin and slept on the ground.

After emancipation, he and his mother walked over a hundred miles to Charleston, West Virginia, so that he could go to school. He was taken under the wing of whites at Hampton Institute and eventually was sent to organize Tuskegee Institute.

His 1895 speech at the Atlanta Exposition accepting segregation made him a national figure, but many blacks disagreed strongly. He eventually built up a large "machine" in the black community and controlled newspapers, jobs, and substantial patronage. His famous autobiography, *Up from Slavery*, was ghostwritten by a journalist and excluded many harsh facts of his life, especially in relation to his treatment by whites.

Quote: "The wisest among my race understand that the agitation of questions of social equality is the extremist folly.… The opportunity to earn a dollar in a factory just now is worth infinitely more than the opportunity to spend a dollar in an opera house." (1895)

REFERENCES: Louis R. Harlan, *Booker T. Washington: The Making of a Black Leader* (1975); *Booker T. Washington: The Wizard of Tuskegee, 1901–1915* (1986).

Charlotte Perkins Gilman (1860–1935)

Gilman was the feminist theorist and writer whose work on economics influenced the early women's movement and whose ideas and writings have attracted renewed attention since the revival of American feminism in the 1960s.

Gilman was a descendant of the famous Beecher family of American clergymen and writers. Her father abandoned the family, and her mother struggled to raise the family alone. Charlotte's unhappy marriage to Charles Stetson, an artist, led to a "nervous collapse" and depression. This experience was eventually described in her short story, "The Yellow Wall-Paper," published after her divorce from Stetson.

Gilman's major work, *Women and Economics,* differed from most progressive feminism in emphasizing the need for new communal social systems of child-rearing, cooking, and home maintenance, if women were ever to attain full economic and social equality. Her belief that women were morally superior to men was presented in her utopian novel *Herland,* in which she presented a perfect all-female society.

Quote: "In the school [the child] learns something of social values, in the church something, in the street something…but in the home he learns…every day and hour, that life, this deep, new, thrilling mystery of life consists mainly of eating and sleeping, of the making and wearing of clothes." (*The Home,* 1903)

REFERENCE: Mary A. Hill, *Charlotte Perkins Gilman: The Making of a Radical Feminist* (1980).

Edward Bellamy (1850–1898)

Bellamy was an American author and socialist, whose novel *Looking Backward* earned him immediate fame and vaulted him into an elite circle of literary figures.

Bellamy was born in Chicopee Falls, Massachusetts, in a long line of Baptist ministers. He first attended Union College, but did not graduate. He spent time over in Europe (especially Germany); when he returned to the United States he took up the study of law and was admitted to the Massachusetts bar. Bellamy was unsatisfied with the legal profession (he quit after one case) and turned his attention to writing, first journalism, then as a novelist.

Bellamy's novel *Looking Backward* told the story of unsuspecting time traveler Julian West, who falls asleep in the later part of the nineteenth century and awakes one hundred years into the future. Boston is very different now, instead of being a capitalist society, the United States is a socialist utopia. The novel was extremely popular. Bellamy's sequel, *Equality,* fell dead on the presses. It never achieved the same level of success and popularity as *Looking Backward.*

Quote: "So long as competition continues to be the ruling factor in our industrial system, the highest development of the individual cannot be reached, the loftiest aims of humanity cannot be realized." ("Declaration of Principles" *The Nationalist,* May 1889; quoted in *Edward Bellamy Speaks Again!,* 1937)

REFERENCE: Arthur E. Morgan, *Edward Bellamy* (1944).

QUESTIONS FOR CLASS DISCUSSION

1. Did the development of American cities justify Jefferson's claim that "when we get piled up in great cities we will become as corrupt as Europe"?

2. Compare the "heroic" story of immigration, as illustrated in the Statue of Liberty, with the historical reality. What explains the ambivalence toward the New Immigrants reflected in Lazarus's poem?

3. Did urban life cause a decline in American religion or just an adjustment to new forms?

4. Why did urban life alter the condition of women and bring changes like birth control and rising divorce rates to the family?

MAKERS OF AMERICA: THE ITALIANS

Questions for Class Discussion

1. In what ways was the Italian experience typical of that of other New Immigrant groups, such as the Polish, Greeks, Jews, and others? (See Chapter 26 text.)

2. Why did so many Italian-Americans initially intend to return to Italy after a time? How does that fact fit with the common understanding of immigration to America?

Suggested Student Exercises

*   Compare the ethnic "Little Italy" enclaves in various American cities with the "Chinatowns" established by the Chinese-Americans (Chapter 24). Consider what functions these communities served for the new immigrants, and how they affected other Americans' perceptions of the immigrants.

*   Examine biographies of some recently prominent Italian-Americans (for example, Congresswoman Geraldine Ferraro, New York Governor Mario Cuomo, Supreme Court Justice Antonin Scalia, actor Al Pacino, historian Eugene Genovese). Explore how their parents' and grandparents' experience fits into the general history of Italian immigration to America.

MAKERS OF AMERICA: THE EARLY PRAGMATISTS

Questions for Class Discussion

1. Assess the validity of the following quote, "pragmatism offers … a philosophy of life built on experimentation, ethical commitment, and open-ended democratic debate."

2. Why is pragmatism considered the quintessential American philosophy? Do you agree with that assessment? Why or why not?

3. Historically speaking, what was so appealing about pragmatism and what was so repugnant about it? Does this philosophical worldview have anything to offer twenty-first century Americans?

Suggested Student Exercise

*   Have students read Louis Medand's *The Metaphysical Club*, New York: Farrar, Straus and Giroux, 2001.

CHAPTER 26

The Great West and the Agricultural Revolution, 1865–1896

AP FOCUS

- Federal land grants entice whites to seek out new lives in the West, which brings them into conflict with the Indians, many of whom had earlier been pushed west by the U.S. government. See the sardonic observation made by one Indian in *The American Pageant* (14th ed., p. 635/15th ed., p. 577), and the maps (14th ed., p. 642/15th ed., p. 584) showing the Indians' vanishing lands.

- By the end of the century, the frontier is closed—all of the land in the continental United States is settled or can no longer be considered frontier, according to the Census Bureau.

- As commercial farming overtakes the smaller family farm, the nation dramatically expands its agrarian sector, producing a bounty of crops while driving out smaller farms. Small farmers and others are hurt by a deflationary cycle, which drives many into debt and ultimately foreclosure.

- Outraged that their profits are consumed by unregulated and unrestrained railroad companies, grain storage and elevator operators, as well as the government's failure to address the deflationary cycle that has ruined many of them, farmers in the West establish the Grange. The Grange and other grassroots organizations coalesce into a political party, the Populists.

- One key political conflict of the post–Civil War era, especially late in the century, is over currency. Debtors, farmers, the Democratic Party, and others favor silver-backed specie, which is inflationary. Gold-backed specie is favored by, among others, businessmen and the Republican Party. William Jennings Bryan, an opponent of the gold standard, passionately advocates the silver standard in his famous Cross of Gold speech. The textbook quotes one scathing view, British (14th ed., p. 662/15th ed., p. 603). A map (14th ed., p. 663/15th ed., p. 603) shows how the country voted in the 1896 presidential election; the Republicans captured the more heavily populated Northeast, which was essential to their victory.

AP teachers should take note of the following:

1. Adding to the already considerable woes of the nation's Indian population, the Dawes Severalty Act of 1887 compelled Indians to relinquish legal control of their land.

2. Coxey's Army was a dramatic, if not necessarily effective, illustration of the plight of the nation's unemployed in the midst of the deepest depression the nation had yet experienced.

Focus on Historical Thinking:

Have students identify and explain five important factors that drew people to settle in the West.

FOCUS QUESTIONS

1. Describe the clashes between the white population and that of the Native Americans.

2. Explain how the West "comes of age" and how agriculture becomes a global enterprise.

3.   Explain how the growing discontent of the farmers gets transformed into the Populist Party. What are the main objectives of the populist?

4.   Describe the main issues of the Election of 1896. How did McKinley and Bryan each accurately represent their parties major issues?

CHAPTER THEMES

Theme: After the Civil War, whites overcame the Plains Indians' fierce resistance and settled the Great West, bringing to a close the long frontier phase of American history.

Theme: The farmers who populated the West found themselves the victims of an economic revolution in agriculture. Trapped in a permanent debtor dependency, in the 1880s, they finally turned to political action to protest their condition. Their efforts culminated in the Populist Party's attempt to create an interracial farmer/labor coalition in the 1890s, but William Jennings Bryan's defeat in the pivotal election of 1896 signaled the triumph of urbanism and the middle class.

CHAPTER SUMMARY

At the close of the Civil War, the Great Plains and Mountain West were still occupied by Indians who hunted buffalo on horseback and fiercely resisted white encroachment on their land and way of life. But the whites' railroads, mining, and livestock broke up Indian territory, while diseases undercut their strength and numbers. A cycle of environmental destruction and intertribal warfare eventually overcame Indian resistance and soon threatened Native Americans' very existence. The federal government combined a misconceived treaty program with intermittent warfare to force the Indians onto largely barren reservations.

Attempting to coerce Indians into adopting white ways, the government passed the Dawes Act, which eliminated tribal ownership of land, while often insensitive humanitarians created a network of Indian boarding schools that further assaulted traditional culture.

The mining and cattle frontiers created colorful chapters in Western history. Farmers carried out the final phase of settlement, lured by free homesteads, railroads, and irrigation. The census declared the end of the frontier in 1890, concluding a formative phase of American history. The frontier was less of a safety valve than many believed, but the growth of cities actually made the West the most urbanized region of the United States by the 1890s.

Beginning in the 1870s, farmers began pushing into the treeless prairies beyond the 100th meridian, using techniques of dry farming that gradually contributed to soil loss. Irrigation projects, later financed by the federal government, allowed specialized farming in many areas of the arid West, including California. The closing of the frontier in 1890 signified the end of traditional westward expansion, but the Great West remained a unique social and environmental region.

As the farmers opened vast new lands, agriculture was becoming a mechanized business dependent on specialized production and international markets. Once declining prices and other woes doomed the farmers to permanent debt and dependency, they began to protest their lot, first through the Grange and then through the Farmers' Alliances, the prelude to the People's (Populist) Party.

The major depression of the 1890s accelerated farmer and labor strikes and unrest, leading to a growing sense of class conflict. In 1896, pro-silverite William Jennings Bryan captured the Democratic Party's nomination, and led a fervent campaign against the goldbug Republicans and their candidate William McKinley. McKinley's success in winning urban workers away from Bryan proved a turning point in American politics, signaling the triumph of the city, the middle class, and a new party system that turned away from monetary issues and put the Republicans in the political driver's seat for two generations.

DEVELOPING THE CHAPTER: SUGGESTED LECTURE OR DISCUSSION TOPICS

- Place the dramatic Indian wars in the context of both irresistible white encroachment and the postwarfare history of American Indians. The Sioux experience—from Little Big Horn to Wounded Knee and after—might provide a good focus.

  REFERENCE: Robert Utley, *The Indian Frontier of the American West, 1846–1890* (1984).

- Examine the successive phases of economic activity in the Great West: mining, cattle raising, agriculture. Show how in each case an early little person era was ended by the coming of big business and new technology, and how the entry of corporate and investment capital shaped later western development.

  REFERENCE: Patricia Nelson Limerick, *Legacy of Conquest: The Unbroken Past of the American West* (1987).

- Examine the unique roles of women in the West, including the more typical pioneer farming women of the Great Plains, as well as the more unusual women who made their way in the mining towns and later cities of the Far West. Consider how their experience was similar to that of males in the West, and how it was different.

  REFERENCE: Glenda Riley, *The Female Frontier: A Comparative View of Women on the Prairie and Plains* (1988).

- Focus on the bitter labor conflicts of the decade, including the Homestead strike and the Pullman strike. Explain why the use of federal troops in the Pullman strike and the use of Pinkerton's antilabor agents in the Homestead strike embittered many workers against both industry and the government's executive and judicial authority.

  REFERENCE: Paul Krause, *The Battle for Homestead, 1880–1892* (1992).

- Examine the 1896 election as a crucial election in American history. Show how Mark Hanna and McKinley effectively organized the forces of the new urban industrialism against Bryan's agrarian-based crusade.

  REFERENCE: Stanley L. Jones, *The Presidential Election of 1896* (1964).

FOR FURTHER INTEREST: ADDITIONAL CLASS TOPICS

- Focus on one of the notable Indian chiefs (for example, Sitting Bull, Chief Joseph, or Geronimo). Examine their roles as leaders of their people both in resistance to white conquest and under the forced circumstances of reservation life. Consider their subsequent role as continuing symbols in later American history and culture.

- Discuss the validity of the frontier thesis first advanced by Frederick Jackson Turner in 1893. (See *Expanding the "Varying Viewpoints"* for an excerpt from Turner's famous essay.) Consider how his use of the word *frontier* contrasts with common understanding, in which the term refers almost entirely to the post–Civil War frontier of the Great West.

- Examine the life of the typical homesteader on the Great Plains, perhaps drawing on literary works such as those of Ole Rolvaag or Willa Cather. Consider why such a person might be led to join the Farmers' Alliances. Perhaps compare the condition of pioneer farmers with those in the South, white and black.

- Consider the rapid rise and fall of the Populists in both the West and the South. Consider the attempt by Populists such as Tom Watson to overcome racial division, and explain the reasons he and other disillusioned reformers later turned to a vicious racism.

- Examine Hanna's free-spending policies in the 1896 election. Assess what role campaign spending (and other political tactics) may have had in defeating Bryan, compared with the deeper social and political forces that kept most of the urban working class from supporting the pro-silver campaign.

- Analyze the long-term significance of the Republican victory in 1896. Consider McKinley as a symbol of triumphant urban industrial capitalism and the harbinger of an age of Republican political domination.

- Have the students read Frederick Jackson Turner's "The Significance of the Frontier in American History" (1893) in David A. Hollinger and Charles Capper's (Editors), *The American Intellectual Tradition: Volume II—1865 to the Present*, New York: Oxford University Press, 2001.

CHARACTER SKETCHES

Sitting Bull (1834–1890)

Sitting Bull was the Sioux chief and shaman (medicine man) who organized the Indian coalition that defeated Custer at the Battle of Little Big Horn.

His Indian name was Ta-tan-ka I-yo-ta-ke, which translates literally as "Sitting Bull." As a young warrior he had led the Sioux against their traditional enemies, the Crow. He was friendly for a time with Father Pierre-Jean DeSmet, a Catholic priest who tried unsuccessfully to convert him to give up warfare.

Sitting Bull brought together over four thousand Sioux, Cheyenne, Arapahoe, and others in a single encampment before Little Big Horn. He did not fight in the battle himself because his job as shaman was to create the good medicine that would bring Indian victory.

After his return from Canada and surrender, he remained extremely hostile to whites. He participated in the Ghost Dance revival and agitation on a Sioux reservation and was shot by Indian police sent to arrest him.

Quote: "I don't want a white man over me. I don't want an agent.... I want to do right by my people, and cannot trust anyone else to trade with them or talk with them." (1882)

REFERENCE: Robert Utley, *The Lance and the Shield: The Life and Times of Sitting Bull* (1993).

Chief Joseph (1840–1904)

Chief Joseph was the Nez Percé leader whose campaign against the U.S. Army in 1877 is considered a military classic.

Joseph's Indian name was Hinmaton-Yalaktit, meaning "Thunder-Coming-Across-the-Water-onto-Land." He had maintained peaceful relations with whites for years, but when some white civilians killed some Nez Percé, a group of young braves retaliated by killing whites, and the army under General O.O. Howard (former head of the Freedmen's Bureau) was sent after Chief Joseph.

His maneuvers in defeating and eluding the army for over fifteen hundred miles were carried out with women and children in tow. He compelled his warriors to fight only against soldiers and not to kill or steal from white civilians. General Howard and other military personnel who met him after his surrender were all impressed by his intelligence and humanity.

His tribe was first moved to Oklahoma, where many of its members died, and then to the Colville reservation in Washington.

Quote: "I am tired of fighting. Our chiefs are killed.… It is cold and we have no blankets. The little children are freezing to death.… From where the sun now stands, I will fight no more forever." (Statement of surrender, 1877)

REFERENCE: Merrill D. Beal, *"I Will Fight No More Forever": Chief Joseph and the Nez Percé War* (1963).

Helen Hunt Jackson (1830–1885)

Jackson was the writer and advocate of Indian rights, whose book *A Century of Dishonor* was one of the first to advocate more humane policies toward Native Americans.

A vivacious, intelligent, charming New Englander, Jackson turned to writing after her first husband was killed and her two young sons died. She became a very popular poet and novelist. Her novel *Mercy Philbrick's Choice* was based partly on the life of her schoolmate and friend Emily Dickinson.

She became interested in Indians after moving to Colorado with her second husband. Although Jackson did a good deal of research for *A Century of Dishonor,* she really understood little of Indian culture. Her subsequent novel about California Indians, *Ramona,* was a greater popular success. She also carried on a public controversy over Indian policy with Secretary of the Interior Carl Schurz.

Quote: "[This Congress] could cover itself with the lustre of glory as the first to cut short our nation's record of cruelties and perjuries—the first to attempt to redeem the United States from the shame of a century of dishonor!" (*A Century of Dishonor,* 1881)

REFERENCE: Siobhan Senier, *Voices of Indian Assimilation and Resistance: Helen Hunt Jackson, Sarah Winnemucca, and Victoria Howard* (2001).

Mark Hanna (1837–1904)

Hanna was the Cleveland businessman who engineered McKinley's election in 1896 and later became a prominent Republican senator.

He came from a strong antislavery Quaker background, which jeopardized his marriage to his first wife because she was an equally strong Democrat. Hanna made his fortune in coal and iron but focused much of his energy on forging an alliance between business and politics.

McKinley's political fortunes had declined for a time, until Hanna became interested in his ideas and began to promote McKinley for Ohio governor. He also got other business leaders to substantially aid McKinley's personal finances. Hanna was later elected senator by a very narrow margin amid charges of bribery of state legislators.

Hanna was genial and popular with both businesspeople and politicians, whom he liked to bring together. Although a staunch conservative on most issues, he favored labor unions and was so generous to workers that his own companies never had a strike.

Quote: "I am glad that there is one member of the Convention who has the intelligence to ascertain how this nomination was made. By the people. What feeble efforts I have contributed to the result, I am here to lay at the feet of my party.…" (Statement after McKinley's nomination, 1896)

REFERENCE: Wayne Morgan, *William McKinley and His America* (1963).

Eugene V. Debs (1855–1926)

Debs was a railway union leader who became the top socialist in the United States and the frequent presidential candidate of the Socialist Party.

Debs's parents were French immigrants who settled in Indiana. During one period, he worked three full-time jobs—as a grocery clerk, as a city clerk, and as secretary-treasurer of the Brotherhood of Locomotive Firemen.

When Debs was released from jail after the Pullman strike, there was a huge celebration in Chicago. He was always much-loved in his home town of Terre Haute, even by most people who disliked his socialism. A heavy drinker, Debs often had to be pulled away from his liquor by fellow socialists.

He was passionate, warmhearted, eloquent, and simple. Workers everywhere loved him and thronged to watch him jab his bony finger in the air and denounce capitalism, even if they did not vote for him.

Quote: "While there is a lower class I am in it.… While there is a soul in prison I am not free."

REFERENCE: Nick Salvatore, *Eugene V. Debs: Citizen and Socialist* (1982).

William Jennings Bryan (1860–1925)

Bryan was the eloquent three-time-losing presidential candidate who later became Wilson's secretary of state and the prosecuting attorney in the Scopes evolution trial.

He began his career as a small-town Nebraska lawyer and journalist and retained a small-town outlook throughout his career. When not campaigning for president, he traveled widely as a Chautauqua lecturer. Two of his most popular lectures on religion were "The Prince of Peace" and "The Value of an Ideal." His voice was a remarkable instrument, which could carry with perfect clarity to the back of a crowd of thousands.

Although he became secretary of state, Bryan knew almost nothing about foreign policy or the world beyond the United States. On a visit to Turkey, he once asked the foreign-service officers, "Where are the Balkans?"

Bryan had long been an active crusader in Fundamentalist causes before becoming involved in the Scopes trial. He was deeply humiliated by Darrow in the trial and died shortly afterward.

Quote: "The poor man who takes property by force is called a thief but the creditor who can by legislation make the debtor pay a dollar twice as large as he borrowed it is lauded as the friend of sound currency. The man who wants the people to destroy the government is an anarchist but the man who wants government to destroy the people is a patriot." (Congressional speech, 1893)

REFERENCE: Paolo Coletta, *William Jennings Bryan* (3 Vols., 1964–1969).

John Peter Altgeld (1847–1902)

Altgeld was the Illinois governor whose pardon of the Haymarket anarchists and support for organized labor made him a hero to reformers and a hated figure among conservatives and businessmen.

Altgeld was born in Germany and spent most of his youth as a poverty-stricken farm laborer in Ohio and elsewhere in the Midwest. He essentially educated himself by reading, especially in the law, and began a career as a prosecuting attorney and judge in Missouri and Illinois.

In 1892, Altgeld was elected the first Democratic governor of Illinois since the Civil War. The case of the Haymarket anarchists came to him for review shortly afterward, and his thorough study of the trial and the evidence convinced him that justice had not been done. The political furor set off by his pardon of three of the convicted men escalated when he protested President Cleveland's use of federal troops in the 1894 Pullman strike as unnecessary and unconstitutional. Aroused Republicans mounted a strong campaign against him in 1896, and his political career was ended by his defeat.

Quote: "There is no situation in Illinois which warrants the sending of federal troops. It is not soldiers that the railroads need so much as it is men to operate trains." (Statement, 1894)

REFERENCES: Harry Barnard, *Eagle Forgotten: The Life of John Peter Altgeld* (1938); Paul Avrich, *The Haymarket Tragedy* (1984).

GREAT DEBATES IN AMERICAN HISTORY

Great Debate (1890–1896):

Government, finance, and the farmer: Should the government adopt monetary and other measures to aid American farmers and laborers?

Yes: Reformers: Populists led by Ignatius Donnelly, Jerry Simpson, and others; writers like Henry George and Henry Demarest Lloyd; free-silver Democrats like William Jennings Bryan and Richard Bland.

No: Conservatives: most Republican businesspeople and politicians like William McKinley and Mark Hanna; gold Democrats like Cleveland; most eastern newspapers and economists.

ISSUE #1: Free silver. Should the United States adopt free coinage of silver and thereby inflate the currency to aid farmers?

Yes: Reform Democrat William Jennings Bryan: "To recapitulate, there is not enough of either metal to form the basis for the world's metallic money; both metals must therefore be used as full legal tender primary money.... If metallic money is sound money, then we who insist upon a base broad enough to support a currency redeemable in coin on demand are the real friends of sound money.... If all the currency is built upon the small basis of gold those who hold the gold will be the masters of the situation."

No: Conservative Republican William McKinley: "Now they tell you that free silver is the panacea for all our ills.... As free wool degraded your industry so free silver will degrade your money.... We do not propose now to inaugurate a currency system that will cheat labor of its pay. The laboring men of this country whenever they give one day's work to their employers want to be paid in full dollars good everywhere in the world. We want in this country good work, good wages, and good money."

ISSUE #2: The tariff. Should the government maintain high protective tariffs against foreign imports?

No: Reform Populist Congressman "Sockless Jerry" Simpson of Kansas: "The enormous amount collected for this extraordinary privilege ... fell heavily upon the agricultural classes. They are the consumers of sugar and window glass and of all those things that the four hundred and fifty trusts that

Yes: Conservative Republican William McKinley: "[The protective system] has dignified and elevated labor; it has made all things possible to the man who works for a living and cares for what he earns; it has opened to him every gateway to opportunity. We observe its triumphs on every hand: we see have been formed under your protective system produce, and that is what has brought the agricultural interests of this country to poverty and bankruptcy today."

the mechanic become the manufacturer, the workman the proprietor, the employee the employer. Is this not worth something? Is it not worth everything? The Republican Protectionist would give the first chances to our people, and would so levy duties upon the products of other nations as to discriminate in favor of our own."

ISSUE #3: Trusts. Should the federal government act more forcefully to control trusts?

Yes: Reform Democrat William Jennings Bryan: "Every trust rests upon a corporation, and every corporation is a creature of law. The corporation is a man-made man.... My contention is that the government that created must retain control, and that the man-made man must be admonished, 'Remember now thy creator.'... What government gives, the government can take away. What the government creates it can control.... In my judgment a government of the people, by the people, and for the people will be impossible when a few men control all the source of production and dole out daily bread to all the rest on such terms as the few may prescribe.... It will be a government of the syndicates, by the syndicates, and for the syndicates."

No: Conservative Democrat W. Bourke Cockran: "For the same reason I would suppress the monopoly built on favor I would protect the monopoly created by excellence. There is no way to suppress a monopoly arising from conspicuous merit except by the suppression of merit. If the producer of the best commodity may not dominate the market for that particular article, neither should the possessor of particular ability in any other department of human endeavor.... Mr. Bryan's position is that monopoly in private hands is always oppressive. Instead of distinguishing between corporations which dominate the market by excellence and those dominating it by favor, he appears to distinguish between those which are successful and those which are not."

ISSUE #4: Government aid to farmers. Should the federal government adopt measures such as the subtreasury plan to provide economic aid to indebted farmers?

Yes: Texas Populist Harry Tracy: "Now if the government can loan these bankers money at one percent on collaterals, why can't the government loan it to the people on their collaterals? If the government can bridge the

No: Conservative Democrat Secretary of Agriculture J. Sterling Morton: "The free and independent farmers of this country...are not mendicants; they are not wards of the Government to be treated to bankers over a close money market and keep them from having to sacrifice their collateral, why can't the government do the same by the people? What a burlesque on democratic government for 4000 men, because they are rich, to enjoy privileges that are denied 65,000,000 people."

annuities, like Indians upon a reservation.... Legislation can neither plow nor plant. The intelligent, practical, and successful farmer needs no aid from the Government. The ignorant, impractical, and indolent farmer deserves none."

REFERENCE: Paul Glad, *McKinley, Bryan, and the People* (1964).

QUESTIONS FOR CLASS DISCUSSION

1. Why has the Plains Indians' resistance to white encroachment played such a large part in the popular American view of the West? How is that mythical past related to the Indians' actual history?

2. What was romantic about the final phases of frontier settlement, and what was not?

3. Why was the "passing of the frontier" in 1890 a disturbing development for many Americans? Was the frontier more important as a particular place or as an idea?

4. Was the federal government biased against farmers and workers in the late nineteenth century? Why or why not?

5. Was McKinley's election really a conservative one, or was it Bryan and the Populists who represented the agrarian past resisting a progressive urban American future?

MAKERS OF AMERICA: THE PLAINS INDIANS

Questions for Class Discussion

1. Compare the Plains Indians' history and culture, especially before the coming of the whites, to that of the Iroquois (see Chapter 2). How does this comparison prove the assertion that the cultures of various Indian peoples differed greatly?

2. In what ways did the Plains Indians benefit by the transformation of their way of life brought about by the horse? In what ways were they harmed?

Suggested Student Exercises

- Examine some photographs or artistic representations of Plains Indians from the late nineteenth century. Discuss what features of their culture are portrayed.

- Use the map of Indian reservations in the text (p. 642) to consider where the Plains Indians were particularly concentrated after the era of warfare ended. Consider what areas of the United States still have substantial populations of such plains peoples as the Sioux, Cheyenne, Kiowa, Crow, and Comanche. (Remember that the Oklahoma Indian territory included many originally eastern Indian peoples such as the Cherokee and the Choctaw.)

EXPANDING THE "VARYING VIEWPOINTS"

- Frederick Jackson Turner, "The Significance of the Frontier in American History" (1893).

A view of the West as a place permanently shaping the formerly European American character:

"The existence of an area of free land, its continuous recession, and the advance of American settlement westward explain American development.... This perennial rebirth, this fluidity of American life, this expansion westward with its new opportunities, its continuous touch with the simplicity of primitive society, furnish the forces dominating American character.... In this advance, the frontier is the outer edge of the wave—the meeting point between savagery and civilization...."

- Richard White, *The Middle Ground* (1991).

A view of the West as the product of the interaction of whites and Indians:

"[The West] is not a traditional world either seeking to maintain itself unchanged or eroding under the pressure of whites. It is a joint Indian-white creation.... The real crisis came...when Indians ceased to have power to force whites onto the middle ground. Then the desire of whites to dictate the terms of the accommodation could be given its head.... Americans invented Indians and forced Indians to live with the consequences."

QUESTIONS ABOUT THE "VARYING VIEWPOINTS"

1. What does each of these historians understand to be the essential characteristics of the West?

2. How does White's assessment differ from Turner's view of the frontier as a "meeting point between savagery and civilization"?

3. How would each of these historians interpret the Plains Indian wars and the confinement of Indians on reservations?

CHAPTER 27

Empire and Expansion, 1890–1909

AP FOCUS

- Thinking Globally (*The American Pageant,* 14th ed., pp. 694–695/15th ed., pp. 632-633) looks at how the United States came late to empire-building, which European powers had used to colonize large parts of the world in the nineteenth century.

- Social Darwinism is one key justification for U.S. territorial expansion.

- Having expanded to the Pacific Ocean by the late nineteenth century, the United States will go on to establish a global empire. The first step is to defeat Spain and take over its crumbling empire. This is accomplished in the Spanish-American War, when the United States ostensibly comes to the aid of Cubans who are seeking to break the chains of Spanish imperialism. Having defeated the Spaniards and wrested from them their empire in the Caribbean and the Pacific, the United States faces an insurgency by people who earlier were its allies, notably the Cubans and Filipinos, who bridle at what they see as a new hegemonic power.

- Despite nearly coming to blows over the Venezuelan boundary dispute, the United States and Britain establish a cordial relationship that has endured. War and Diplomacy is an AP theme.

- To protect U.S. economic interests in China, Secretary of State John Hay proposes the Open Door policy to guarantee equal trading and commercial rights in China for all. The Chinese, however, are not consulted; this exacerbates tensions between China and the western powers. Globalization is an AP theme.

- McKinley's assassination thrusts Theodore Roosevelt into the spotlight and the Oval Office—a man whom most conservative Republicans distrust. Many advocates of U.S. imperialism are not disappointed by Roosevelt's policies, such as the construction of the Panama Canal and a corollary to the Monroe Doctrine that strengthens U.S. hegemonic influence in Latin America.

AP teachers should take note of the following:

1. Hawaii came under U.S. control when the reigning monarch, Queen Lilioukalani, opposed American economic and political presence in her island country.

2. The Spanish-American War facilitated the reconciliation of the North and South as both sections now had a common foreign-policy objective. An example of this development is that ex-Confederate General Joseph Wheeler fought in a war that was in part orchestrated by Lincoln's former aide, later McKinley's secretary of state, John Hay.

Focus on Historical Thinking:

Have students compare and contrast U.S. expansionism during New Imperialism and the era of Manifest Destiny. Be certain they look for both similarities and differences.

FOCUS QUESTIONS

1. What were the main reasons for America turning outward (i.e., becoming an international or global power)?

2.   Describe the biggest challenges facing America with the acquisition of their island territories?

3.   Explain the main issues in the election of 1900. What change in focus occurred from the previous election?

4.   What are the main features of Teddy Roosevelt's Big Stick policy and the Roosevelt Corollary?

5.   In what ways did the events in China and Japan force America to take on a more international or global attitude?

CHAPTER THEMES

Theme: In the 1890s, a number of economic and political forces sparked a spectacular burst of imperialistic expansionism for the United States that culminated in the Spanish-American War—a war that began over freeing Cuba and ended with the highly controversial acquisition of the Philippines and other territories.

Theme: In the wake of the Spanish-American War, President Theodore Roosevelt pursued a bold and sometimes controversial new policy of asserting America's influence abroad, particularly in East Asia and Latin America.

CHAPTER SUMMARY

Various developments provoked the previously isolated United States to turn its attention overseas in the 1890s. Among the stimuli for the new imperialism were the desire for new economic markets, the sensationalistic appeals of the yellow press, missionary fervor, Darwinist ideology, great-power rivalry, and naval competition.

Strong American intervention in the Venezuelan boundary dispute of 1895–1896 demonstrated an aggressive new assertion of the Monroe Doctrine and led to a new British willingness to accept American domination in the Western Hemisphere. Longtime American involvement in Hawaii climaxed in 1893, in a revolution against native rule by white American planters. President Cleveland temporarily refused to annex the islands, but the question of incorporating Hawaii into the United States triggered the first full-fledged imperialistic debate in American history.

The splendid little Spanish-American War began in 1898 over American outrage about Spanish oppression of Cuba. American support for the Cuban rebellion had been whipped up into intense popular fervor by the yellow press. After the mysterious *Maine* explosion in February 1898, this public passion pushed a reluctant President McKinley into war, even though Spain was ready to concede on the major issues.

An astounding first development of the war was Admiral Dewey's naval victory in May 1898 in the rich Spanish islands of the Philippines in East Asia. Then in August, American troops, assisted by Filipino rebels, captured the Philippine city of Manila in another dramatic victory. Despite mass confusion, American forces also easily and quickly overwhelmed the Spanish in Cuba and Puerto Rico.

After a long and bitter national debate over the wisdom and justice of American imperialism, which ended in a narrow pro-imperialist victory in the Senate, the United States took over the Philippines and Puerto Rico as colonial possessions. Regardless of serious doubts about imperialism, the United States had strongly asserted itself as a proud new international power.

America's decision to take the Philippines aroused violent resistance from the Filipinos, who had expected independence. The brutal war that ensued was longer and costlier than the Spanish-American conflict.

Imperialistic competition in China deepened American involvement in Asia. Hay's Open Door policy helped prevent the great powers from dismembering China. The United States joined the international expedition to suppress the Boxer Rebellion.

Theodore Roosevelt brought a new energy and assertiveness to American foreign policy. When his plans to build a canal in Panama were frustrated by the Colombian Senate, he helped promote a Panamanian independence movement that enabled the canal to be built. He also altered the Monroe Doctrine by adding a Roosevelt Corollary that declared an American right to intervene in South America.

Roosevelt negotiated an end to the Russo-Japanese War but angered both parties in the process. Several incidents showed that the United States and Japan were now competitors in East Asia.

DEVELOPING THE CHAPTER: SUGGESTED LECTURE OR DISCUSSION TOPICS

- Explain more fully the different views of the causes of imperialism, including the idea of expansion as a way to create new economic markets. Show how these factors affected the Spanish-American War and the decision to take the Philippines.

  REFERENCE: Walter LaFeber, *The New Empire* (1963).

- Analyze the complicated mix of idealism and realism in the Spanish-American War, and explain why some Americans were deeply concerned about the oppressed Cubans while others were more interested in the war as an occasion to demonstrate and spread America's new national power abroad.

  REFERENCE: Ernest May, *Imperial Democracy* (1961).

- Demonstrate how the political impact of the war was much greater than the impact of the actual chaotic fighting. The focus might be on the ways in which the war raised up new heroes (Theodore Roosevelt and George Dewey) and created a new sense of the United States as a great world power.

  REFERENCE: David Trask, *The War with Spain in 1898* (1981).

- Consider why the question of whether to hold on to the Philippines was so controversial and why the pro-imperialist forces were able to win by a narrow margin. The discussion might center on both the short- and long-term consequences of the Philippine acquisition.

  REFERENCE: H. W. Brands, *Bound to Empire: The United States and the Philippines* (1992).

- Show how the United States after the Spanish-American War was increasingly acting like a great power in world affairs, especially in Asia, and how Roosevelt energetically promoted this involvement despite the traditional belief in American isolationism.

  REFERENCES: Marilyn Young, *The Rhetoric of Empire: America's China Policy, 1895–1901* (1968); Charles E. Neu, *Troubled Encounter: The United States and Japan* (1975).

- Explain why the Philippine-American War was the most serious consequence of the Spanish-American War. Consider the disturbing questions it raised about America's new international involvements, especially imperial control of a distant, hostile people.

  REFERENCE: Richard E. Welsh, *Response to Imperialism: The United States and the Philippine-American War, 1899–1902* (1975).

- Examine Roosevelt's aggressive determination to build the Panama Canal in relation to America's growing international assertiveness, particularly in Latin America. Show how American involvement in the Panama coup and the Roosevelt Corollary to the Monroe Doctrine aroused sharp Latin American opposition.

REFERENCE: Richard H. Collin, *Theodore Roosevelt's Caribbean: The Panama Canal, the Monroe Doctrine, and the Latin American Context* (1990).

- Discuss the role of Asian immigration and the fear of the yellow peril in shaping America's relations with East Asia in the early twentieth century.

  REFERENCE: Alexander DeConde, *Ethnicity, Race, and American Foreign Policy* (1992).

- Examine the relationship between racial ideology and the new imperial attitude of American foreign policy.

  REFERENCE: Eric T. L. Love, *Race over Empire: Racism and U.S. Imperialism* (2004).

- Examine the history of American acquisitions; discuss the similarities and differences between these acquisitions with regard to American foreign policy. At what point in American foreign policy does a fundamental shift occur from domestic power to international power?

  REFERENCE: Walter Nugent, *Habits of Empire: A History of American Expansion* (2008).

FOR FURTHER INTEREST: ADDITIONAL CLASS TOPICS

- Examine Teddy Roosevelt as a central character in the events of the chapter: as imperialist advocate, assistant secretary of the navy, Rough Rider, legendary war hero, governor of New York, vice president, and then president.

- Analyze the yellow press: explain what yellow journalism is, why it had such great appeal and popular impact in the late nineteenth century, how it sensationalized and distorted issues, how important it was (or was not) in really influencing President McKinley and others.

- Focus on Cuba and America: discuss why, from the pre–Civil War era forward, Americans were concerned with Cuba; how they viewed the Cuban rebels; what issues dominated American debates about Cuban readiness for independence (for example, the Teller and Platt amendments); and what links developed to the subsequent history of American-Cuban relations.

- Consider the Philippines: discuss where they are (point out that most Americans, even government officials, did not know their location in 1898), who the Filipino people were and are, why the islands have been viewed as strategically and commercially important (especially in relation to China). Discuss the nature of the Filipino rebellion against Spain, which became a rebellion against America. Perhaps tie in the subsequent history of American-Philippine relations.

- Examine Roosevelt's theory and practice of the big stick in foreign policy, especially in his relations with Latin America.

- Examine the role of American missionaries in shaping U.S. foreign policy in this period, especially in China.

- Take up the question of gender in relation to American foreign policy and American imperialism, particularly the idea that aggressive overseas action was one way for men (including Theodore Roosevelt) to assert their masculinity in an era of growing feminine influence in society and culture.

- Conduct a class debate over the following topics: for example, America Should Retain the Philippines; primary source readings will come from the following book *Opposing Viewpoints in American History—Volume II: From Reconstruction to the Present*, San Diego, CA: Greenhaven Press, 1996. Another good source of debate topics is Larry Madaras and James M. SoRelle, *Taking Sides—Clashing Views on Controversial Issues in American History, Volume II: Reconstruction to the Present*, Connecticut: McGraw-Hill, 2000.

- Show students the following video: *The Century—America's Time* (ABC Video in association with The History Channel), *Volume I: The Beginning: Seeds of Change.* "In an era of innocence and prosperity, the American landscape is set in motion for a new century of unimaginable change—a time when the promise of electricity, automobiles, moving pictures and air flight was just over the horizon."

- Have the students read Henry Adams, *The Education of Henry Adams* (1918). Use the book as an example of political and philosophical autobiography. Adams reflects on his search for order and unity in a world that is obsessed with self-destruction and complexity.

CHARACTER SKETCHES

Queen Liliuokalani (1838–1917)

The refusal by Liliuokalani, the native ruler of Hawaii, to accept the white planters' revolt of 1893, and her eloquent pleas to President Cleveland, helped delay American annexation of Hawaii until 1898. Her devotion to her people and her resistance to white assimilation has made Liliuokalani a romantic symbol of traditional Hawaiian culture down to the present.

She became queen of Hawaii in 1891, at age fifty-two, after the death of her brother, King Kalakaua. She was a conscientious Christian with strong charitable interests, but she also had a disdain for Protestant moralism. Despite her tireless efforts to preserve the power of the monarchy, she was deposed following the 1893 uprising, in which American troops openly aided the rebellious white minority.

A contemporary newspaper described Liliuokalani's face as "strong and resolute." She spoke a pure and graceful English, and her voice was musical and well modulated. Throughout her life, she composed beautiful Hawaiian songs, including the famous "Aloha Oe" ("Farewell to Thee").

Quote: "Some of my subjects, aided by aliens, have renounced their loyalty and revolted against the constitution and government of my kingdom. … Upon receiving incontestable proof that His Excellency the Minister of the United States aided and abetted their unlawful movements, and caused United States troops to be landed for that purpose, I submitted to force." (To President Grover Cleveland, 1893)

REFERENCE: Helena Allen, *The Betrayal of Liliuokalani: Last Queen of Hawaii, 1838–1917* (1982).

William Randolph Hearst (1863–1951)

Hearst's sensationalistic yellow journalism and bombastic warmongering in 1897–1898 have long provoked the debatable charge that he was personally responsible for the Spanish-American War—a view to which Hearst himself was willing to subscribe. "You furnish the pictures and I'll furnish the war," Hearst allegedly responded to the assertion of artist-correspondent Frederic Remington (who covered Cuba during the war) that Remington had witnessed little evidence of Spanish cruelty. (Although the statement was reported by another correspondent, there is no proof that Hearst ever actually said it.)

A native San Franciscan, Hearst had been raised primarily by his mother and given an elite education, but he was expelled from Harvard (where he worked on the humor magazine *Lampoon*) for a stunt that involved sending chamber pots to professors. In 1887, he used family wealth to take control of the *San Francisco Examiner,* which he turned into a commercially successful paper. In 1895, he acquired the *New York Journal* and entered a fierce circulation war with Pulitzer's *New York World.* In June 1898, Hearst personally sailed to Cuba, where he helped round up Spanish prisoners while writing headline-grabbing stories.

Ever an extremely flamboyant and controversial figure, Hearst was active in politics and remained a dynamic force in journalism for many decades.

Quote: "The journalism that talked was a great advance from no journalism at all. But the future belongs to the journalism that acts." (1898)

REFERENCES: David Nasaw, *The Chief: The Life of William Randolph Hearst* (2000).

Theodore Roosevelt (1858–1919)

Although Roosevelt was a great president, a skilled international diplomat, and a gifted writer, it was his brief actions during the Spanish-American War that created the enduring Roosevelt legend the public always loved best: Teddy the Rough Rider charging up San Juan Hill. Roosevelt himself never regretted that these exploits overshadowed his more substantive achievements, because he too loved the image of the rugged hero.

After graduation from Harvard in 1880, Roosevelt began his public life by writing lively works of naval and western history. An assistant secretary of the navy under William McKinley, he pushed for a big navy and expansionism. His famous order to Commodore George Dewey, issued when Secretary of the Navy Long was away for a weekend, led to the American victory at Manila Bay and the conquest of the Philippines, which Roosevelt and his friends strongly desired. Although lacking military experience, Roosevelt used his political connections to obtain his army commission for service in Cuba and, along with writer Richard Harding Davis, effectively promoted the legend of the Rough Riders that made him "the most famous man in America."

Quote: "There comes a time in the life of a nation, as in the life of an individual, when it must face great responsibilities, whether it will or no. We have now reached that time.… The guns of our warships in the tropic seas of the West and the remote East have awakened us to the knowledge of new duties."

REFERENCES: Edmund Morris, *The Rise of Theodore Roosevelt* (1979); John M. Cooper Jr., *The Warrior and the Priest* (1983).

John Hay (1838–1905)

Hay was Abraham Lincoln's private secretary, secretary of state under McKinley and Roosevelt, and a noted poet and historian.

Hay's uncle's law office in Springfield, Illinois, was next to Lincoln's, and Hay's childhood friend John Nicolay arranged for Hay to become Lincoln's private secretary, even though Hay was only twenty-three. He performed many personal chores for the Lincolns at the White House and was sometimes awakened by a sleepless Lincoln, who would tell him jokes. Hay and Nicolay later wrote a ten-volume biography of Lincoln that presents the president in a highly favorable light but reflects serious scholarship rather than mythologizing the national hero.

In the 1870s, Hay became a celebrated literary figure. His poetry, such as *Pike County Ballads and Other Pieces,* was quite popular, but his novels were mostly attacks on labor unions. Hay was the closest friend of historian Henry Adams, and the two built adjoining houses across the street from the White House. Hay appreciated Adams's philosophical distance from politics but could not accept his friend's dark pessimism about public affairs.

Quote: "I need not tell you the lunatic difficulties under which we labor.… All the powers treat us as a central Hello Office, and we strive to please the public. If I looked at things as you do, in the light of reason, history, and mathematics, I should go off after lunch and die." (Letter to Henry Adams about Open Door policy, 1900)

REFERENCE: Tyler Dennett, *John Hay: From Poetry to Politics* (1933).

Philippe Bunau-Varilla (1859–1940)

Bunau-Varilla was the French engineer who energetically promoted the Panama Canal and the Panamanian revolution, and negotiated the Hay–Bunau-Varilla Treaty with the United States.

As a young engineering student, Bunau-Varilla had come under the spell of Suez Canal builder Ferdinand Lesseps, and Bunau-Varilla became convinced that his mission in life was to complete Lesseps's work by building the canal across Panama. Besides distributing stamps showing Nicaraguan volcanoes, he bombarded senators with favorable information about Panama, while carefully concealing the overwhelming problems the French builders had experienced there in nearly twenty years of effort.

He played a key role in fomenting the revolution in Panama, having obtained assurances that the United States would intervene as soon as independence was declared. He wrote the constitution and designed the flag of the new republic, and he gave both to one of the plotters.

Quote: "I have been exposed to calumny in my long fight against ignorance and falsehood.… I have served the Republic of Panama, and her interests are coincident with those of the canal. Once the treaty is ratified, I will have fulfilled the pledge I made to myself twenty-three years ago."

REFERENCE: G. A. Anguizola, *Philippe Bunau-Varilla: The Man Behind the Panama Canal* (1980).

George Goethals (1858–1928)

Goethals was the American engineer who built the Panama Canal.

Although a career military officer in the Army Corps of Engineers, Goethals never fired a weapon except in basic training. After the first two engineers assigned to the canal job resigned, Goethals was given near-absolute power over the Canal Zone in order to speed up the job.

Besides planning and supervising the construction, he managed over thirty thousand employees and their families, and created social institutions such as jails, courts, hospitals, and so on. He set aside every Sunday morning to hear individual complaints from the workers.

Goethals was a tough, unsmiling, chain-smoking martinet. Someone once asked a family member how Goethals amused himself, and the reply was, "He does not amuse himself."

Quote: "The real builder of the Panama Canal was Theodore Roosevelt. It could not have been more Roosevelt's triumph if he had personally lifted every shovelful of earth in its construction." (1919)

REFERENCE: David McCulloch, *The Path Between the Seas* (1977).

GREAT DEBATES IN AMERICAN HISTORY

Great Debate (1899):

American imperialism. Should the United States become an imperialist power by keeping the Philippine Islands?

For: The pro-imperialists—led by expansionists like Theodore Roosevelt, Henry Cabot Lodge, and Albert Beveridge; some business publications like the *Review of Reviews* and business spokespersons like Mark Hanna; and some religious leaders like the Rev. J.H. Barrows and the

Against: The anti-imperialists— led by writers like William James and Mark Twain; some business spokespersons like Andrew Carnegie; some labor leaders like Samuel Gompers; and some clergymen like the Rev. Charles Ames and the Rev. Henry Van Dyke.

Rev. Josiah Strong.

ISSUE #1: Manifest Destiny. Is overseas expansion, and therefore control of the Philippines, part of the inevitable manifest destiny of the United States?

For: Pro-imperialist Theodore Roosevelt: "Our whole national history has been one of expansion. Under Washington and Adams we expanded westward to the Mississippi. Under Jefferson we expanded across the continent to the mouth of the Columbia.... The same will be true of the Philippines. Nations that expand and nations that do not expand may ultimately go down, but the one leaves heirs and a glorious memory, and the other leaves neither."

Against: Anti-imperialist Carl Schurz: "Whenever there is a project on foot to annex a foreign territory to this republic the cry of 'manifest destiny' is raised to produce the impression that all opposition to such a project is a struggle against fate. The fate of the American people is in their own wisdom and will. If they devote their energies to the development of what they possess within their present limits...their 'manifest destiny' will be the preservation of the exceptional and invaluable advantages they now enjoy...."

ISSUE #2: Democracy. Would ruling another nation be compatible with basic American ideals of democracy and self-government?

For: Pro-imperialist *New York Tribune:* "Cannibals govern themselves. The half-ape creatures of the Australian bush govern themselves. The Eskimo governs himself, and so do the wildest tribes of darkest Africa. But what kind of a government is it?"

Against: Anti-imperialist Rev. Henry Van Dyke: "How can we pass by the solemn and majestic claim of our Declaration of Independence, that 'government derives its powers from the consent of the governed'? How can we face the world as a union of free states holding vassal states in subjection, a mighty mongrel nation in which a republic is tied to an empire, and democracy bears children not to be distinguished from the offspring of absolutism?"

ISSUE #3: Economic benefit. Is acquiring the Philippines essential for America's economic health and future trade with Asia?

For: Pro-imperialist *American Wool and Cotton Exporter:* "Annexation is important because the contingencies of our China trade bid fair to be such as to make the Philippines exceedingly valuable to us as a basis for operations in the continent of China."

Against: Anti-imperialist Carl Schurz: "I agree that we cannot have too many foreign markets. But can such markets be opened only by annexing to the United States the countries in which they are situated?"

ISSUE #4: Race. Should the dark-skinned Filipinos be brought under the rule of white-skinned Americans?

For: Pro-imperialist *The Textile Record:* "Supremacy in the world appears to be the destiny of the race to which we belong, the most competent governor of inferior races.... The clear path of duty for us appears to be to bring to the people of the Spanish islands in the Pacific and the Atlantic an opportunity to rise from misery and hopelessness to a promise of just government and commercial success."

Against: Anti-imperialist Henry Labouchère: [A parody of Rudyard Kipling's "The White Man's Burden." See text.] "Pile on the brown man's burden
Nor do not deem it hard
If you should earn the rancor
Of those ye yearn to guard.
The screaming of your eagle
Will drown the victim's sob
Go on through fire and slaughter
There's dollars on the job.
Pile on the brown man's burden
And through the world proclaim
That ye are freedom's agent—
There's no more paying game!
And should your own past history
Straight in your teeth be thrown
Retort that Independence
Is good for whites alone."

REFERENCES: E. Berkeley Tompkins, *Anti-Imperialism in the United States: The Great Debate, 1890–1920* (1970); Richard Welch, ed., *Imperialists vs. Anti-Imperialists* (1972).

QUESTIONS FOR CLASS DISCUSSION

1. What were the causes and consequences of the Spanish-American War? Did the results of the war (particularly the acquisition of the Philippines) flow from the nature of the war, or were they unexpected?

2. How was American expansionism overseas similar to previous continental expansion westward, and how was it different?

3. Was the taking of Hawaii, Puerto Rico, and the Philippines really a violation of fundamental American ideals of self-government and democracy?

4. What were the elements of idealism and realism in American expansionism in the 1890s? How have Americans incorporated both of these seemingly contradictory philosophies in their foreign policy?

5. Why was the Philippine-American War such a brutal affair, and why is it not as well remembered as the less costly Spanish-American War?

6. Did Roosevelt more often speak softly or use the big stick? Was his approach to foreign policy aggressive or simply energetic?

7. How did the Roosevelt Corollary distort the Monroe Doctrine? What were the consequences of the Roosevelt Corollary for American relations with Latin America?

8. Was the United States essentially acting as a white, Western imperialist power, or did American democratic ideals substantially restrain the imperialist impulse?

MAKERS OF AMERICA: THE PUERTO RICANS

Questions for Class Discussion

1. How has Puerto Rico's special relationship to the United States made Puerto Ricans unique among all immigrant groups?

2. Compare the experience of Puerto Ricans with that of other Latino immigrants, especially the Mexicans (see Chapter 42).

Suggested Student Exercises

- Examine the continuing debate over Puerto Rico's relationship with the United States. Consider how Puerto Rican statehood or independence would affect Puerto Ricans in the mainland United States.

- Consider the particularly important role that Puerto Ricans have played in the life of New York City in the twentieth century and the transformations their community has undergone there. Daniel Patrick Moynihan and Nathan Glazer, *Beyond the Melting Pot* (1963) is an older sociological work that examines Puerto Ricans in New York; Virginia Sanchez Korral, *From Colonia to Community: The History of Puerto Ricans in New York City* (1983) is a good study of the evolution of the Puerto Rican community.

MAKERS OF AMERICA: THE FILIPINOS

Questions for Class Discussion

1. Compare the Philippine immigration to America with that of the Chinese (see Chapter 23). How did American imperial ownership of the Philippines make the Filipinos' experience different from that of other Asians?

2. Even though more immigrants have come from the Philippines than from China or Japan, it seems that most Americans do not regard Filipinos as they view other Asian immigrants. Why might that be so? Is the awareness of the Filipino presence greater in Hawaii and the West Coast than in other parts of the country?

Suggested Student Exercises

- Analyze the political history of American-Philippine relations as described in this chapter of the text. Consider its relation to the history of Filipino immigration described here.

- Compare the old Filipino immigration described here with the new post–World War II immigration from the Philippines.

EXPANDING THE "VARYING VIEWPOINTS"

- Julius Pratt, *Expansionists of 1898* (1951).

  A traditional view of imperialism:

  "The Manifest Destiny of the 1840s had been largely a matter of emotion. Much of it had been simply one expression of a half-blind faith in the superior virility of the American race and the superior beneficence of American political institutions. In the intervening years, much had been done to provide this emotional concept with a philosophic backing.... Far-fetched and fallacious as their reasoning may appear to us, it nevertheless carried conviction.... The observation must be made that the rise of an expansionist philosophy in the United States owed little to economic influences.… The need of American business for colonial markets and fields for investment was discovered not by businessmen but by historians and other intellectuals, by journalists and politicians."

- William Appleman Williams, *The Tragedy of American Diplomacy* (1959).

A revisionist view of imperialism as a product of economic expansionism:

"Men like McKinley and other national leaders thought about America's problems and welfare in an inclusive, systematized way that emphasized economics. Wanting democracy and social peace, they argued that economic depression threatened those objectives, and concluded that overseas economic expansion provided a primary means of ending that danger. They did not want war per se, let alone war in order to increase their own personal fortunes. But their conception of the world ultimately led them into war in order to solve the problems in the way that they considered necessary and best."

QUESTIONS ABOUT THE "VARYING VIEWPOINTS"

1. Which of these two interpretations better explains (a) the war with Spain, (b) the decision to keep the Philippines, and (c) the U.S. involvement as a great power in world affairs?

2. Which historian would see American imperialism more as inevitable, and which would see it more as a matter of choice?

3. Which of the two would judge American imperialism more harshly as a violation of moral principles and a threat to American democracy?

CHAPTER 28

Progressivism and the Republican Roosevelt, 1901–1912

AP FOCUS

- Corporate abuses and the government's attempt at patchwork reforms—Reform is an AP theme—over the previous decades convince progressives that stronger action is needed.

- Muckrakers galvanize Americans through exposés and novels describing, for example, the abuses of major corporations. President Roosevelt, however, is not enamored of these writers—see the quote in *The American Pageant* (14th ed., p. 704/15th ed., p. 640). Culture is another AP theme.

- The American political system undergoes a revolutionary transformation that will lead to women getting the right to vote in 1920 (Nineteenth Amendment). Also, election of senators by state legislatures is replaced by the much more democratic direct election (Seventeenth Amendment).

- Wisconsin becomes the model for reform at the state level, with Governor Robert M. La Follette in the vanguard. Again, Reform is an AP theme.

- Legislation had been passed to protect the American worker, though widespread abuse continues, sparking strikes. One of the most important is the Anthracite Coal Strike, and it is significant because the federal government does not instinctively take the side of management.

- Roosevelt spearheads efforts to impose regulations on corporations and eliminate unfair competition, but his record as a trust-buster is uneven, as a political cartoon suggests (14th ed., p. 715/15th ed., p. 649).

- Roosevelt is a unique political leader, especially when it comes to his interest in protecting the nation's resources through conservation. Take note of a point in his message to Congress (14th ed., p. 716/15th ed., 651).

- Conflict between Roosevelt and William Howard Taft, once political allies, divides the Republican Party.

AP teachers should take note of the following:

1. Upton Sinclair, author of a novel that exposed abuses at a meatpacking plant, had written *The Jungle* to awaken Americans to socialist ideas, but had to settle for the public's outrage at the abuses he described in vivid and graphic detail, which led to the passage of the Meat Inspection Act, Pure Food and Drug Act, and other consumer safety legislation.

2. At times, it took a tragedy to awaken the American people to the exploitation and dangerous working conditions that workers faced on a daily basis. A haunting image (14th ed., p. 711/15th ed., p. 646) of the burned and broken bodies of the mostly young female victims of the Triangle Shirtwaist Fire in New York (1911) is one vivid reminder that laws were necessary to protect vulnerable workers.

Focus on Historical Thinking:

>   Choose twenty important terms from Chapters 1 through 28. Give students ample time to prepare to write composite sentences (see "Focus on Historical Thinking" activity in Chapter 5) on each of the terms. Quiz students on five of the terms, giving no more than two minutes for each term.

FOCUS QUESTIONS

1.   What were the roots of the Progressive movement in the United States?

2.   Describe how the Muller and Lochner cases contributed to or hurt the Progressive movement.

3.   What were the three C's of Roosevelt's political platform? How were these implemented?

4.   Explain the differences between Taft and Roosevelt. How did this difference split the Republican Party in the election of 1912?

5.   What was Taft's dollar diplomacy?

CHAPTER THEMES

Theme: The strong progressive movement successfully demanded that the powers of government be applied to solving the economic and social problems of industrialization. Progressivism first gained strength at the city and state level, and then achieved national influence in the moderately progressive administrations of Theodore Roosevelt.

Theme: Roosevelt's hand-picked successor, William H. Taft, aligned himself with the Republican Old Guard, causing Roosevelt to break away and lead a progressive third-party crusade.

CHAPTER SUMMARY

The progressive movement of the early twentieth century became the greatest reform crusade since abolitionism. Inaugurated by Populists, socialists, social gospelers, female reformers, and muckraking journalists, progressivism attempted to use governmental power to correct the many social and economic problems associated with industrialization.

Progressivism began at the city and state level, and first focused on political reforms before turning to correct a host of social and economic evils. Women played a particularly important role in galvanizing progressive social concern. Seeing involvement in such issues as reforming child labor, poor tenement housing, and consumer causes as a wider extension of their traditional roles as wives and mothers, female activists brought significant changes in both law and public attitudes in these areas.

At the national level, Roosevelt's Square Deal used the federal government as an agent of the public interest in the conflicts between labor and corporate trusts. Rooseveltian progressivism also acted on behalf of consumer and environmental concerns. Conservatism became an important public crusade under Roosevelt, although sharp disagreements divided preservationists from those who favored the multiple use of nature. The federal emphasis on rational use of public resources generally worked to benefit large enterprises and to inhibit action by the smaller users.

Roosevelt personally selected Taft as his political successor, expecting him to carry out "my policies." But Taft proved to be a poor politician who was captured by the conservative Republican Old Guard and rapidly lost public support. The conflict between Taft and pro-Roosevelt progressives finally split the Republican Party, with Roosevelt leading a third-party crusade in the 1912 election.

DEVELOPING THE CHAPTER: SUGGESTED LECTURE OR DISCUSSION TOPICS

- Analyze the roots of progressivism and the various elements that made up the progressive coalition. Show particularly the role of muckraking journalists and female reformers in arousing public opinion in favor of reform.

    REFERENCE: William L. O'Neill, *The Progressive Years: America Comes of Age* (1975).

- Examine the critical role of women in progressive reform, and show how their efforts were largely—although not entirely—focused and successful in areas that seemed consistent with their social roles as protectors and nurturers of the family.

    REFERENCE: Robyn Muncy, *Creating a Female Dominion in American Reform* (1991).

- Discuss consumer protection and environmental conservation as examples of middle-class concerns that progressivism and progressive political leaders such as Roosevelt promoted.

    REFERENCES: Elmo Richardson, *The Politics of Conservation* (1968); James Harvey Young, *Pure Food: Securing the Federal Food and Drug Act of 1906* (1989).

- Discuss the contrast between Roosevelt's regulatory New Nationalism and Wilson's more libertarian New Freedom in the campaign of 1912.

    REFERENCE: Morton Keller, *Regulating a New Economy: Public Policy and Economic Change in America, 1900–1933* (1990).

FOR FURTHER INTEREST: ADDITIONAL CLASS TOPICS

- Consider one city or state as a case study in the actual conflicts and achievements of progressivism. Cincinnati or Cleveland are good urban examples, and Wisconsin is the best state example.

- Use excerpts from the work of some muckrakers, such as Lincoln Steffens or Ida Tarbell, to show how journalists aroused public concern and promoted involvement in progressive reform.

- Discuss Roosevelt as both personality and progressive political leader.

- Examine the rise of conservationism as a national concern to (a) Roosevelt's concern to preserve rugged American values and (b) the increasing needs of an urban populace for escape and revival in nature.

- Conduct a class debate over the following topics: for example, American Women Should Have the Right to Vote. Primary source readings will come from the following book: *Opposing Viewpoints in American History—Volume II: From Reconstruction to the Present*, San Diego, CA: Greenhaven Press, 1996. Another good source of debate topics is Larry Madaras and James M. SoRelle, *Taking Sides—Clashing Views on Controversial Issues in American History, Volume II: Reconstruction to the Present*, Connecticut: McGraw-Hill, 2000.

- Have students read selections from Herbert Croly's *The Promise of American Life* (1909). A systematic study of American culture at the beginning of the twentieth-century, Croly envisions a society moving away from the individualistic liberalism to a more organized and planned society.

- Have students read Upton Sinclair's *The Jungle* (1906). Use the novel as a way to explore the ways in which literature can bring about real change within a society. How accurately does literature have to represent the truth—how accurate was Sinclair's depiction of the meat-packing industry, and what kinds of changes took place as a result of Sinclair's novel.

CHARACTER SKETCHES

Lincoln Steffens (1866–1936)

Steffens was the muckraking journalist who helped stir the nation to progressive reform and, in the 1930s, wrote an influential autobiography claiming to show the limits of progressivism.

After growing up in a moderately affluent San Francisco family, Steffens spent some years randomly studying and traveling in Europe. He had difficulty finding a career, but a young German student whom he had met in Europe died and left Steffens his substantial estate, enabling Steffens to live independently and pursue unconventional journalism.

Steffens's *The Shame of the Cities* was so shocking because he used massive documentation to supposedly demonstrate that practically everyone was not merely corrupt but abusing power for his or her private interests. After a disillusioning fling with Christian reform, Steffens turned toward tougher movements and wrote favorably about revolutionary Mexico, Mussolini's Italy, and Lenin's Russia. When he returned from Russia in 1919, he said, "I have seen the future, and it works."

Quote: "I was not the original muckraker—the prophets of the Old Testament were ahead of me.... I did not intend to be a muckraker; I did not know that I was one till President Roosevelt picked the name out of Bunyan's *Pilgrim's Progress* and pinned it on us." (Autobiography, 1931)

REFERENCE: Justin Kaplan, *Lincoln Steffens: A Biography* (1974).

Ida Tarbell (1857–1944)

Tarbell was the muckraking journalist and reformer whose critical articles on Standard Oil helped bring about the breakup of Rockefeller's giant petroleum trust.

Tarbell's father made wooden kegs for the infant Pennsylvania oil industry. When she was researching the Standard Oil articles, she learned that one of her father's business partners had committed suicide after being squeezed out by Rockefeller oil interests.

Originally an ardent feminist who traveled to France to write about the role of women in the French Revolution, Tarbell later turned against feminism and suffragism, perhaps because she felt that feminism had deprived her of marriage and motherhood.

She was a very popular biographer and lecturer and wrote best-selling books about Lincoln, Napoleon, and Madame Roland. Despite her sharp criticism of Rockefeller, she admired much of American business and looked favorably on Henry Ford and scientific management.

Quote: "[Rockefeller] has never lowered [the price of oil] a point if it could be avoided, and in times of public stress he has taken advantage of the very misery of the poor to demand higher prices.... Does it pay the public to trust the control of a great necessity of life to such a man?" (1904)

REFERENCE: Kathleen Brady, *Ida Tarbell: Portrait of a Muckraker* (1984).

Upton Sinclair (1878–1968)

Sinclair was the reform-minded journalist and novelist whose works helped inspire consumer protection and other progressive movements.

Raised in an aristocratic southern family, impoverished by the Civil War, Sinclair moved to the Lower East Side of New York and worked his way through the City College of New York by writing hack journalism.

He was an enthusiast who got carried away by almost any cause with which he came in contact. Sinclair spent months in the stockyards researching *The Jungle* and donated the proceeds to a utopian commune.

He founded the Intercollegiate Socialist Society with Jack London and wrote many more muckraking novels attacking financiers (*The Moneychangers*), coal mines (*King Coal*), the petroleum industry (*Oil!*), and so on. By age eighty-four, he had written seventy-nine books.

In 1934, he ran for governor of California on a tax and pension program called EPIC (End Poverty In California). The campaign was unsuccessful but attracted much national attention.

Quote: "And as for the other men who work in tank rooms full of steam, where there were open vats near the level of the floor, their peculiar trouble was that they fell into the vats; and when they were fished out, there was never enough of them left to be worth exhibiting—sometimes they would be overlooked for a day, till all but the bones of them had gone out to the world as Durham's Pure Beef Lard." (*The Jungle*, 1906)

REFERENCE: Leon Harris, *Upton Sinclair: American Rebel* (1975).

Robert M. La Follette (1855 – 1925)

Nicknamed "Fighting Bob," Robert La Follette was an American politician who served in the U.S. Congress, the U.S. Senate, and as governor of Wisconsin. He ran for the presidency in the election of 1924, accepting the nomination of the Progressive Party.

La Follette was best known for his strong opposition to American involvement in World War I. He also supported child labor laws, social security, women's suffrage, and other progressive reforms.

Quote: "It is well for us to remember that war is always cruel; that its iron tread means destruction and devastation, whether its march is across Europe or from Atlanta to the sea; that war arouses all the fiercest human passions; that there are always cases of brutality and outrage—and that usually there is quite as much of it on one side as upon the other. … Believing in democracy, in the right of self-government— ready to defend the precious heritage of our own sovereignty—let us here and now resolve and declare that we will never permit the armed forces of the United States to be used to despoil our sister republics of their property, interfere with their right to govern themselves according to their own standards or violate their sovereignty—as sacred to them as American sovereignty is to us. … I am not an extremist, I do not say there may not be supreme principles for which men must fight to the death as a last resort. But I do believe that as organized society in its slow evolution has developed more rational means of settling individual differences than brute force, so must the nations of the world ultimately find other ways of deciding their disagreements than war." (*The Political Philosophy of Robert M. La Follette*, 1920)

REFERENCES: Robert M. La Follette, *A Personal Narrative of Political Experiences* (1913); Nancy C. Unger, *Fighting Bob La Follette– The Righteous Reformer* (2000).

MAKERS OF AMERICA: THE ENVIRONMENTALISTS

Questions for Class Discussion

1.   What really caused the sudden upsurge in concern for preserving America's environment at the beginning of the twentieth century? To what extent was this concern motivated by nostalgia for an older America, and to what extent by a desire to preserve nature and natural resources for future generations?

2.   What were the underlying issues in the debate between rational use environmentalists and the more thoroughgoing preservationists? How did the rise of modern ecological science tilt that debate?

Suggested Student Exercises

1.   Examine a comprehensive map of all of American's national parks, wildlife preserves, and national forests, along with the dates they were established. See what patterns can be discovered regarding

the relationship between areas set aside for preservation and recreation and changing American society (for example, where and when were preserved areas established near to major urban populations, and where and when were very remote lands set aside).

2. Examine the ideas and actions of some of the major national figures who shaped American environmental awareness, for example, Henry David Thoreau, John Muir, Gifford Pinchot, Ansel Adams, Rachel Carson, or others. Compare and contrast their different approaches to nature and preservation, and consider what tensions as well as shared outlooks have shaped the environmental movement.

QUESTIONS FOR CLASS DISCUSSION

1. Why did the progressives believe that strong government action was the only way to tackle the social and economic problems of industrialization? How did this approach differ from traditional American emphasis on voluntary solutions to social problems?

2. Why were women so critical to the successes of the progressive movement? Were there any weaknesses in their ideas and approaches to social reform?

3. Why was Roosevelt such a popular progressive leader? In what ways did he sound like a more ardent reformer than he really was?

4. To what extent was progressivism really a middle-class reform effort that did not really reflect the interests or concerns of the poor and working classes it claimed to benefit? How did some of the progressive concern for conservation and environment reflect the perspectives of more affluent Americans?

5. Did the progressive movement make any long lasting contributions to American society?

CHAPTER 29

Wilsonian Progressivism at Home and Abroad, 1912–1916

AP FOCUS

- A split in the Republican Party between supporters of Theodore Roosevelt and of President William Howard Taft gives the Democrats' Woodrow Wilson victory in the 1912 election.

- An idealist by nature and experience, President Wilson soon addresses some of the burning concerns of his time: the high protective tariff, the power of the trusts, and banking monopolies. He also uses his rhetorical skills and academic experience to convince the public and Congress that the plight of impoverished and exploited farmers and wage laborers must be addressed.

- Wilson alters foreign policy in Latin America. Roosevelt waved the Big Stick; Taft advocated what became known as dollar diplomacy to protect and attract U.S. investments. Wilson, on the other hand, recoils from imperial pretensions. But events in Haiti, the Dominican Republic, and Mexico convince him to modify his objections to imperialism and use of the U.S. military.

- As militarism, nationalism, and imperialism strain relations among European countries, Wilson maintains a precarious policy of neutrality. Germany's use of U-boats to starve Britain into submission leads to what the United States considers serious violations of its shipping and maritime rights. War and Diplomacy is an AP theme.

AP teachers should take note of the following:

1. Despite his reputation as a progressive and advocate for the downtrodden and often-forgotten worker and farmer, Wilson was, at best, indifferent, often opposed, to black rights. Wilson instituted segregation in the federal government. A product of the Civil War and Reconstruction South, he held attitudes on black rights in stark contrast to his zeal for reform in other areas.

2. The sinking of the passenger liner *Lusitania,* which resulted in the loss of nearly 1,200 lives, including 128 U.S. citizens, outraged Americans. However, today many historians are convinced that the ship was carrying war material to Britain, a violation of the U.S.'s own neutral stance.

3. The DBQ on the United States as a world power (*The American Pageant,* 14th ed., DBQ 11, pp. A96–A98/15th ed., pp. A93-A95) limits students to only one of two options: was U.S. foreign policy based on idealism or on self-interest? The documents for this DBQ demonstrate the wide variety of sources that can appear in a DBQ.

Focus on Historical Thinking:

Have students construct a three-part chart which lists progressive attempts to regulate big business, democratize the political system, and look after the social welfare of the people. Then have students rank progressive success in each category by placing a "1" beside the most successful category, a "2" beside the second most successful category, and a "3" beside the least successful. Have students explain their ranking. This activity should incorporate material from both Chapters 28 and 29.

FOCUS QUESTIONS

1. What were the main issues in the election of 1912 and how was Woodrow Wilson a minority president?

2. What was the "triple wall of privilege" that Wilson set out to deal with in his first term as president?

3. How was Wilson's foreign policy different from that of Roosevelt and Taft?

4. What events happened in Mexico that challenged Wilson's foreign policy?

5. What were the circumstances surrounding Wilson's reelection win in 1916? What major challenges did the president face as Europe entered World War I?

CHAPTER THEMES

Theme: After winning a three-way election, focused on different theories of progressivism, Woodrow Wilson successfully pushed through a sweeping program of domestic economic and social reform in his first term.

Theme: Wilson's attempt to promote an idealistic progressive foreign policy failed, as dangerous military involvements threatened Latin America, the North Atlantic, and Europe.

CHAPTER SUMMARY

Wilson and his New Freedom defeated Roosevelt and his New Nationalism in a contest over alternative forms of progressivism. Eloquent, idealistic former professor Wilson successfully carried out a broad progressive economic reform of the tariff, finances, and the trusts. He also achieved some social reforms that benefited the working classes, but not blacks.

Wilson's attempt to implement progressive moral goals in foreign policy was less successful, as he stumbled into military involvements in the Caribbean and revolutionary Mexico. The outbreak of World War I in Europe also brought the threat of American involvement, especially from German submarine warfare.

Wilson temporarily avoided war by extracting the precarious *Sussex* pledge from Germany. His antiwar campaign of 1916 narrowly won him reelection over the still-quarreling Republicans.

DEVELOPING THE CHAPTER: SUGGESTED LECTURE OR DISCUSSION TOPICS

*   Examine Wilson's complex personality and explain how it influenced both his great successes and his failures in politics.

    REFERENCE: August Mecksher, *Woodrow Wilson* (1991).

*   Examine Wilson's idealistic approach to both domestic and foreign policy. Show how he used his eloquence and moral appeals to arouse the public and achieve his goals at home, and explain why this approach was not as successful abroad.

    REFERENCE: John Morton Blum, *Woodrow Wilson and the Politics of Morality* (1956).

*   Consider how Wilson's attempt to promote American-style democracy in Mexico led him into military intervention and near-war. The focus might be on the difficulties even well-intentioned policies encountered in the face of a revolutionary upheaval such as Mexico was experiencing.

    REFERENCE: P. Edward Haley, *Revolution and Intervention: The Diplomacy of Taft and Wilson with Mexico, 1910–1917* (1970).

- Analyze why Wilson found himself headed to the brink of war with Germany over the submarine. Show how America's traditions, geography, and interests tended to create sympathy for the Allies, while the barbarous new weapon struck directly at Wilson's moral approach to foreign policy.

  REFERENCE: John M. Cooper Jr., *The Vanity of Power: American Isolation and the First World War, 1914–1917* (1969).

- Explore the party platforms of the Republicans, Democrats, Progressive Party, and the Socialist Party and other issues surrounding the election of 1912. Consider how this election defined the vision of Progressivism.

  REFERENCE: Brett Flehinger, *The 1912 Election and the Power of Progressivism—A Brief History with Documents* (2003).

FOR FURTHER INTEREST: ADDITIONAL CLASS TOPICS

- Examine the events in Europe before and after the outbreak of World War I, and discuss how both Germany and the Allies tried to influence the United States.

- Compare and contrast Wilson's and Roosevelt's policies in Latin America. Consider how each policy might have looked from a Latin American standpoint.

- Examine the role of both British and German propaganda in the United States in the years before American entry into World War I. Consider the extent to which these attempts to shape American public opinion affected both official and popular views of the two sides (including among different ethnic groups).

- Consider women's issues in relation to Roosevelt's and Wilson's progressivism, especially such prominent figures as Jane Addams and Lillian Wald.

- Conduct a class debate over the following topics: for example, Immigrants Harm American Society and New Nationalism v. New Freedom. Primary source readings will come from the following book: *Opposing Viewpoints in American History—Volume II: From Reconstruction to the Present*, San Diego, CA: Greenhaven Press, 1996. Another good source of debate topics is Larry Madaras and James M. SoRelle, *Taking Sides   Clashing Views on Controversial Issues in American History, Volume II: Reconstruction to the Present*, Connecticut: McGraw-Hill, 2000.

- Have the students read George Santayana's "The Genteel Tradition in American Philosophy" (1913) in David A. Hollinger and Charles Capper's (Editors), *The American Intellectual Tradition: Volume II—1865 to the Present*, New York: Oxford University Press, 2001.

- Have the students read Woodrow Wilson's 'The Ideals of America' (1902) in David A. Hollinger and Charles Capper's (Editors), *The American Intellectual Tradition: Volume II—1865 to the Present*, New York: Oxford University Press, 2001.

CHARACTER SKETCHES

Louis Brandeis (1856–1941)

Brandeis was the progressive lawyer who became the first Jewish justice of the Supreme Court.

His parents came to the United States as refugees from the failed liberal revolution in Hungary in 1848. The family strongly emphasized culture and education, and Louis returned to Europe several times to travel and study at leading institutions.

Although he was a star student at Harvard Law School and a successful private attorney, the Homestead Steel strike turned Brandeis toward involvement in labor and progressive causes, to which he donated his legal services. His Brandeis brief on behalf of women workers in *Muller* v. *Oregon* made him nationally famous. His efforts on behalf of eastern European Jewish garment workers led him to a rediscovery of his own Jewish heritage and a growing involvement in Zionism.

He was frequently a Supreme Court dissenter in the 1920s, but later many of his views became accepted as law. He endorsed New Deal legislation in the 1930s but opposed Roosevelt's Court-packing plan.

Quote: "Refuse to accept as inevitable any evil in business (e.g., irregularity of employment). Refuse to tolerate any immoral practice (e.g., espionage).... [Democracy] demands continuous sacrifice by the individual and more exigent obedience to the moral law than any other form of government." (1922)

REFERENCE: Philippa Strum, *Louis D. Brandeis: Justice for the People* (1984).

Woodrow Wilson (1856–1924)

Wilson was an influential academic scholar and administrator before he became president. He held public office for only two years before his election to the White House.

Brought up under the close guidance of his Presbyterian pastor father, Wilson seldom played with his childhood peers. He failed as a lawyer before pursuing graduate studies in political science at Johns Hopkins. His book, *Congressional Government* (1885), was a classic study of the American legislative process.

As president of Princeton after 1902, he battled against the snobbish eating clubs and tried to establish a more democratic system on campus but was defeated.

Wilson first fell seriously ill during the Paris Conference in April 1919. There is now substantial medical evidence that he suffered a series of minor strokes over several years before the massive stroke that nearly killed him on his western tour. After his collapse, his second wife kept him in virtual isolation from all advisers, including his most intimate friend, Colonel House.

Quote: "Those senators do not understand what the people are thinking. They are far from the people, the great mass of the people." (1919)

REFERENCE: Kendrick Clements, *The Presidency of Woodrow Wilson* (1992).

Francisco ("Pancho") Villa (1878–1923)

Villa was the so-called Robin Hood of the Mexican Revolution, whose raids into the United States provoked Wilson to intervene in Mexico.

Born to a poor peasant family, Villa became a thief and cattle rustler who was accused of several murders. He eventually headed up a large gang of desperadoes, but in 1910, he announced that he was joining the Mexican Revolution's fight for social justice against oppressive landlords and foreign interests.

He did sometimes redistribute land and goods to the peasants, but he also became wealthy himself through questionable means. Among his enterprises were meat-packing plants and gambling casinos. Villa was at first friendly with Americans and was even rumored to have received funds from powerful Americans such as Hearst. Because of his thorough knowledge of northern Mexico, he successfully eluded Pershing, but he finally laid down his arms in 1920. Three years later, he was gunned down in his home village by unknown assassins.

Quote: "It is unfair for some to have a lot when others have nothing. The poor who work but earn too little have a claim on the wealth of the rich." (1915)

REFERENCES: Manuel Machado, *Centaur of the North: Francisco Villa, the Mexican Revolution, and Northern Mexico* (1988); Clarence C. Clendenen, *The United States and Pancho Villa* (1961).

QUESTIONS FOR CLASS DISCUSSION

1. Were Wilson's progressive legislative achievements in his first term consistent with his New Freedom campaign? Why or why not?

2. How was Wilson's progressive presidency similar to Theodore Roosevelt's, and how was it different? Were the differences ones of personality or policy?

3. Why did Wilson fail in his attempt to develop a more moral, less imperialistic policy in Latin America? Were his involvements really an attempt to create a new mutual relationship between the United States and the neighboring republics, or was it just an alternative form of American domination?

4. Was the United States genuinely neutral during the first years of World War I, or was it biased in favor of the Allies and against Germany? Was it possible for the United States to remain neutral? Why or why not?

EXPANDING THE "VARYING VIEWPOINTS"

- Richard Hofstadter, *The Age of Reform* (1955).

A view of progressives as backward-looking individualists:

"Progressivism, at its heart, was an effort to realize familiar and traditional ideals under novel circumstances…. At the core of their conception of politics was a figure quite as old-fashioned as the figure of the little competitive entrepreneur who represented the most commonly accepted economic ideal. This old-fashioned character was the Man of Good Will, the same innocent, bewildered, bespectacled, and mustached figure we see in the cartoons today labeled John Q. Public—a white collar or small business voter-taxpayer with perhaps a modest home in the suburbs."

- Gabriel Kolko, *The Triumph of Conservatism* (1963).

A view of progressivism as a victory for business conservatism:

"The New Freedom, in its concrete legislative aspects, was little more than the major demands of politically oriented big businessmen. They had defined the issues, and it was they who managed to provide the direction for change…. In its larger outlines it was they who gave progressivism its essential character. By the end of 1914 they had triumphed, and to the extent that the new laws were vague and subject to administrative definitions by boards and commissions, they were to totally dominate the extensive reign of political capitalism that had been created in the United States by 1915."

- Robert Wiebe, *The Search for Order, 1877–1920* (1967).

A view of progressives as forward-looking bureaucrats:

"Experts in administration supported by a variety of professionals sought solutions to the city's problems through proper procedures and continuous enforcement…. A blend of many ideas, the new political theory borrowed its most revolutionary qualities from bureaucratic thought…. Trained, professional servants would staff a government broadly and continuously involved in society's operations…. This revolutionary approach to government, incomplete as it was, eventually dominated the politics of the early twentieth century."

QUESTIONS ABOUT THE "VARYING VIEWPOINTS"

1. According to each of these historians, who were the progressives, and what were their central values?

2.   How would each of these historians relate the progressive constituency to the basic progressive approach to government?

3.   How would each interpret the progressive attack on political bosses and the establishment of independent regulatory commissions to monitor businesses such as the railroads, meat packing, and banking?

CHAPTER 30

The War to End War, 1917–1918

AP FOCUS

- With U.S.-German relations strained, what is left of the rapport erodes with the disclosure of the Zimmerman telegram in March 1917. In it, the German government promises that if Mexico agrees to an alliance with Germany, it will regain the territory it lost to the U.S. in the Mexican-American War. The following month, President Wilson asks and receives from Congress a declaration of war. Opposition to U.S. entry into the war is strong in the Midwest and Southwest; the Zimmerman telegram, however, infuriates residents of Texas, Arizona, and New Mexico.

- Envisioning a postwar world in which nations would cooperate and respect one another's right to self-determination and recognize and enforce international law, President Wilson delivers what becomes known as the Fourteen Points in a speech to Congress.

- Leaving nothing to chance, and aware that the war is not popular with all Americans, the government enacts legislation to stifle opposition to the war.

- By and large, mainstream unions, such as the AFL, support the war effort and do not press their demands during the conflict. Radical unions, such as the IWW (Wobblies), have no such reservations; indeed, they see the war itself as contributing to what they consider the exploitative nature of capitalism. For many workers, however, real wages climb during the war.

- With Germany's capitulation in November 1918, the war to end war, as it is optimistically referred to, ends. Wilson goes to Europe to hammer out a plan to establish peace and cooperation for the future. Hoping for a "peace of right," as opposed to a "peace of might," Wilson is soon disappointed. All of this material pertains to the AP theme War and Diplomacy.

AP teachers should take note of the following:

1. To reconcile the knee-jerk reaction of the victors to engage in an imperialist dissection of the Central Powers' empires, with his own political and moral idealism, Wilson seeks to replace colonialism with trusteeships. Conquered territories would be administered by the League of Nations, Wilson's brainchild and one of his most enduring, if not necessarily successful, legacies.

2. Despite his valiant effort to convince the American people and the Senate to ratify the Versailles Treaty (and with it U.S. membership in the League of Nations), Wilson fails to accomplish this goal. The treaty goes down to defeat in the Senate, and with it, Wilson's health. Incapacitated by a stroke, the president is forced to relinquish many of his responsibilities and powers to others.

Focus on Historical Thinking:

Create a twenty to twenty-five question matching quiz that matches causes with effects. Examples: Compromise of 1877/end of Reconstruction; Chesapeake-Leopard Affair/The Embargo; etc.

FOCUS QUESTIONS

1. What were the steps that lead America to enter World War I?

2. After his campaign promise of keeping America out of the war in 1916, how did Wilson garner American support for the war?

3.   How did America convert from a peacetime economy to a wartime economy?

4.   What were the reasons for the failure of both the League of Nations and the Treaty of Versailles?

5.   What were the reasons for the conflict between Wilson and the U.S. Senate, especially Lodge?

CHAPTER THEMES

Theme: Entering World War I in response to Germany's unrestricted submarine warfare, Wilson turned America's participation into a fervent ideological crusade for democracy that successfully stirred the public to a great voluntary war effort, but at some cost to traditional civil liberties.

Theme: After America's limited but important contribution to the Allied victory, a triumphant Wilson attempted to construct a peace based on his idealistic Fourteen Points. But European and senatorial opposition, and especially his own political errors, doomed American ratification of the Versailles Treaty and participation in the League of Nations.

CHAPTER SUMMARY

Germany's declaration of unlimited submarine warfare, supplemented by the Zimmerman note proposing an alliance with Mexico, finally caused the United States to declare war. Wilson aroused the country to patriotic heights by making the war an idealistic crusade for democracy and permanent peace based on his Fourteen Points.

Wartime propaganda stirred voluntary commitment to the war effort, but at the cost of suppressing dissent. Voluntary efforts also worked wonders in organizing industry, producing food, and financing the war. Labor, including women, made substantial wartime gains. The beginnings of black migration to northern cities led to racial tensions and riots.

America's soldiers took nearly a year to arrive in Europe, and they fought in only two major battles at the end of the war. America's main contribution to the Allied victory was to provide supplies, personnel, and improved morale. Wilson's immense prestige created high expectations for an idealistic peace, but his own political blunders and the stubborn opposition of European statesmen forced him to compromise his lofty aims.

As Lodge stalled the treaty, Wilson tried to rouse the country on behalf of his cherished League, but his own physical collapse and refusal to compromise killed the treaty and the League. Republican isolationists effectively turned Harding's victory in 1920 into a death sentence for the League.

DEVELOPING THE CHAPTER: SUGGESTED LECTURE OR DISCUSSION TOPICS

*   Explain the importance of Wilson's definition of war aims. Show why his sweeping declaration of the Fourteen Points stirred tremendous enthusiasm in both America and Europe, where seemingly meaningless slaughter had dragged on for years.

    REFERENCE: Thomas Knock, *To End All Wars: Woodrow Wilson and the Quest for a New World Order* (1992).

*   Analyze America's voluntary method of organizing for war (as opposed to the governmental coercion of European wartime regimes). Show how the feverish propaganda necessary for this approach caused war opponents to be treated as traitors.

    REFERENCE: David M. Kennedy, *Over Here: The First World War and American Society* (1980).

- Examine Wilson's negotiations at Paris. Point out how his own high idealism forced him onto the defensive, since every practical compromise appeared to be a betrayal, and how he came to focus all his hopes on the League.

  REFERENCE: Arthur Link, *Woodrow Wilson: War, Revolution, and Peace* (1979).

- Explain the defeat of the League and the treaty. Consider the way Lodge effectively exploited Wilson's weaknesses, especially his unwillingness to compromise what he saw as absolute principles.

  REFERENCES: Thomas Bailey, *Woodrow Wilson and the Lost Peace* (1944); Robert H. Ferrell, *Woodrow Wilson and World War I* (1985).

- Explore the causes and major events of World War I from the European perspective.

  REFERENCE: Samuel R. Williamson Jr. and Russell Van Wyk, *July 1914: Soldiers, Statesmen, and the Coming of the Great War—A Brief Documentary History* (2003).

FOR FURTHER INTEREST: ADDITIONAL CLASS TOPICS

- Use samples of wartime propaganda to show how the war was presented to the public and how patriotic commitment was aroused.

- Analyze the treatment of war opponents, especially socialists and German-Americans. Discuss whether stifling them was necessary for the war effort or whether it corrupted the war to "make the world safe for democracy."

- Analyze the impact of the war on the labor movement and the rights of workers.

- Analyze the impact of the war on women and African Americans. Consider the significance of passing the Nineteenth Amendment.

- Emphasize the Wilson-Lodge feud. Consider how their great political controversies were deepened by personal hatred and pride.

- Conduct a class debate over the following topics: for example, America Should Enter World War I, World War I Protesters Should Be Guaranteed Freedom of Speech, and The United States Should Join the League of Nations. Primary source readings will come from the following book: *Opposing Viewpoints in American History—Volume II: From Reconstruction to the Present*, San Diego, CA: Greenhaven Press, 1996. Another good source of debate topics is Larry Madaras and James M. SoRelle, *Taking Sides—Clashing Views on Controversial Issues in American History, Volume II: Reconstruction to the Present*, Connecticut: McGraw-Hill, 2000.

- Show students the following video: *The Century—America's Time* (ABC Video in association with The History Channel), *Volume I: 1914–1919: Shell Shock*. "World War I erupts, and with it, America suffers its greatest physical and emotional losses since The Civil War."

CHARACTER SKETCHES

George Creel (1876–1953)

Creel was the progressive journalist who became the energetic head of the American propaganda effort in World War I.

Creel quit high school after one year to become an ardent progressive journalist. He founded a newspaper, the *Kansas City Independent,* which crusaded against the Pendergast machine, prostitution, and child labor. Creel was a flamboyant figure who married a vaudeville actress and liked to associate with boxers and other athletes.

Besides war propaganda, Creel organized a massive effort to spread a wholesome view of the American way of life throughout the world via films, magazines, and books. Creel remained a liberal California journalist through the New Deal, but during and after World War II, he became an extreme right-winger who called for harsh vengeance against Germany and Japan.

Quote: "[I decided that] the desired results could be obtained without paying the price that formal law would have demanded.... Better to have the desired compulsions proceed from within than to apply them from without." (1920)

REFERENCE: Stephen L. Vaughn, *Holding Fast the Inner Line: Democracy, Nationalism, and the Committee on Public Information* (1980).

John J. Pershing (1860–1948)

Pershing was the commander of the Pershing expedition into Mexico and of the American Expeditionary Force in World War I.

He attended a normal school before winning a competition to enter the U.S. Military Academy. His first service was among the Indians, and for a time, he led a company of Sioux scouts. His nickname, "Black Jack," came from his having commanded a black cavalry unit but was also a reference to his tough drillmaster methods.

In the Mexican campaign, he applied new devices such as radios, airplanes, and machine guns to military uses. His ability to stay within the strict political guidelines given him in Mexico won him Wilson's favor and command of forces in World War I. Pershing was a model soldier—square-jawed, of rigid bearing, calm, forceful, discreet. Many of his junior officers later became the great American commanders in World War II.

Quote: "The most important question that confronted us in the preparation of our forces of citizen soldiery for efficient service was training.... Few people can realize what a stupendous undertaking it was to teach these vast numbers their various duties when most of them were ignorant of practically everything pertaining to the business of the soldier in war." (Memoirs, 1931)

REFERENCE: Gene Smith, *Until the Last Trumpet Sounds: The Life of General of the Armies John J. Pershing* (1998).

Henry Cabot Lodge (1850–1924)

Lodge was the aristocratic New England scholar and senator who successfully battled against Wilson's League of Nations.

A descendant of the ancient Lodge and Cabot lines of Massachusetts, Lodge married his cousin Ann Cabot Davis. He studied history under Henry Adams and wrote scholarly but strongly pro-Federalist biographies of Washington, Hamilton, Webster, and his grandfather George Cabot.

He was a close friend of Theodore Roosevelt and was also a friend of Wilson's antagonist at Princeton, Dean West.

Although highly intelligent, Lodge was narrow in outlook and comfortable only with those of his own background and class. He was rigid and opinionated and, like Wilson, tended to turn political disagreements into personal animosities.

Quote: "We have twice succeeded in creating a situation where Wilson either had to take the Treaty with strong reservations…or else was obliged to defeat it. He has twice taken the latter alternative. His personal selfishness goes beyond what I have seen in any human being. It is so extreme that it is entirely unenlightened and stupid.…" (Letter, 1920)

REFERENCE: William C. Widenor, *Henry Cabot Lodge and the Search for an American Foreign Policy* (1980).

GREAT DEBATES IN AMERICAN HISTORY

Great Debate (1919–1920):

Versailles Treaty and League of Nations. Should the United States ratify the Versailles Treaty and join the League of Nations?

Yes: Pro-League forces, led by President Wilson and his administration; most Democrats, led by Senators Pittman and Williams; many eastern business interests and international law advocates, led by former President Taft.

No: Anti-League forces, including strong reservationists, led by Lodge, Elihu Root, and Senator Cummins; irreconcilables, led by Senators Borah and Johnson; many midwesterners, Irish-Americans, and other ethnic groups.

ISSUE #1: The treaty. Would the Versailles Treaty ensure a just and workable peace?

Yes: Pro-League President Wilson: "The Treaty is a readjustment of all those great injustices that underlie the whole structure of European and Asian society.… The heart of the Treaty is that it undoes the injustice that Germany did…[and] organizes the world to see that such injustice will in the future be impossible.… [I]t has very, very few compromises in it, and is, most of it, laid down in straight lines according to American specifications."

No: Anti-League British economist John Maynard Keynes: "In the first place, this treaty ignores the economic solidarity of Europe, and by aiming at the destruction of the economic life of Germany it threatens the health and prosperity of the Allies themselves. In the second place, by making demands the execution of which is in the literal sense impossible, it stultifies itself and leaves Europe more unsettled than it found it. The treaty, by overstepping the limits of the possible, has in practice settled nothing."

ISSUE #2: Warmaking power. Would joining the League of Nations amount to a surrender of the sovereign power of the United States to decide matters of war and peace?

No: Pro-League President Wilson: "Article Ten has no operative force unless we vote

Yes: Anti-League Sen. Charles Townshend: "We are to be linked up in a league of more that it shall operate. The member of the Council representing the United States has to vote 'aye' before the United States or any other country can be advised to go to war under that agreement.... There is no compulsion upon us...except the compulsion of our good conscience and judgment. So it is perfectly evident that if, in the judgment of the people of the United States the Council adjudged wrong and that this is not a case of the use of force, there would be no necessity on the part of the Congress of the United States to vote the use of force."

than thirty nations.... If trouble occurs in Europe, which under the League and the Treaty the United States is bound to enter, our government must settle the trouble and pay the bills, even though a majority of its men are sacrificed and its whole treasure is exhausted, for morally we cannot turn our back or surrender when we enter the contract. In a partnership each partner is responsible for all the obligations of the firm.... American boys from American homes will have to serve in both Europe and Asia for many years."

ISSUE #3: Monroe Doctrine. Would the League permit international interference with American privileges under the Monroe Doctrine?

No: Pro-League President Wilson: "I spoke to the conference in Paris, and they at once inserted the provision which is now there that nothing in that Covenant shall be construed as affecting the validity of the Monroe Doctrine. ... At last, in the Covenant of the League of Nations, the Monroe Doctrine has become the doctrine of the world."

No: Anti-League Senator Henry Cabot Lodge: "In the first draft of the treaty that was presented to us the Monroe Doctrine was left somewhere among the voices heard in the air and the visions that are seen by capable visionaries, and we were told that the doctrine was safe because it had been extended to the whole world.... Now, however, there comes back a second draft with a direct statement in regard to the Monroe Doctrine putting it in a far worse position, in my judgment, than it was under the first draft, and that was bad enough."

ISSUE #4: Would the League violate America's long tradition of "no entangling alliances"?

No: Pro-League President Wilson: "When men tell you that we are, by going into the League of Nations, reversing the policy of the United States, they have not thought the thing out. The statement is not true.... The

Yes: Anti-League Senator William Borah: "If I have had a conviction throughout my life, it has been the conviction that we should stay out of European and Asiatic affairs. I do not think we can have here a great, powerful, point is that the United States is the only nation in the world that has sufficient moral force with the rest of the world.... What Washington had in mind was exactly what these gentlemen want to lead us back to. The day we have left behind us was a day of alliances.... This project of the League of Nations is a great policy of disentanglement."

independent, self-governing Republic and do anything else; I do not think it is possible for us to continue to be the leading intellectual and moral power in the world and do anything else.... Let the people of this country who are opposed to entering into an alliance with Europe, who are opposed to surrendering the policy of Washington and the doctrine of Monroe, understand that reservations...are made to get votes...."

REFERENCES: Thomas A. Bailey, *Woodrow Wilson and the Lost Peace* (1944); Bailey, *Woodrow Wilson and the Great Betrayal* (1945); Ralph Stone, *The Irreconcilables: The Fight Against the League of Nations* (1970); William Widenor, *Henry Cabot Lodge and the Search for an American Foreign Policy* (1980).

QUESTIONS FOR CLASS DISCUSSION

1. What were the ideological results of Wilson's proclamation of World War I as a "war to end all wars" and "a war to make the world safe for democracy"?

2. Was it necessary to suppress dissent in order to win the war?

3. Was the Treaty of Versailles a violation of Wilson's high wartime ideals or the best that could have been achieved under the circumstances?

4. What was the fundamental reason America failed to join the League of Nations?

EXPANDING THE "VARYING VIEWPOINTS"

- George Kennan, *American Diplomacy* (1950).

  A view of Wilson's diplomacy as naïve idealism:

  "Under the protecting shadow of this theory [Wilsonian idealism], the guns continued their terrible work for a final year and a half after our entry. Under the shadow of this theory Wilson went to Versailles unprepared to face the sordid but all-important details of the day of reckoning. Under this theory he suffered his tragic and historic failure. Under this theory things advanced with a deadly logic and precision to a peace which was indeed 'forced upon the loser, a victor's terms imposed upon the vanquished, accepted in humiliation, in duress'—a peace that did indeed leave a sting, a resentment, a bitter memory, and upon which its own terms came later to rest 'as upon quicksand.'"

- Arthur Link, *Wilson the Diplomatist* (1957).

  A view of Wilsonian diplomacy as a noble effort:

  "For Woodrow Wilson the Paris Peace Conference was more a time of heroic striving and impressive achievement than of failure. By fighting against odds that would have caused weaker men to surrender, he was able to prevent the Carthaginian kind of peace that we have seen to our regret in our own time; and he was able to create the machinery for the gradual attainment of the kind of effort that he would have liked to impose at once. The Paris settlement, therefore, was not inevitably a 'lost peace.' It could have been, rather, the foundation of a viable and secure world order and therefore a lasting memorial to its chief architect, if only the victors had maintained the will to enforce what Wilson had signed."

CHAPTER 31

American Life in the "Roaring Twenties," 1919–1929

AP FOCUS

- Concerned about the success of the Bolshevik Revolution, the United States, Britain, and other nations send troops to participate in the Russian Civil War in the hope of toppling Lenin's communist government. Domestically, a systematic effort to suppress Bolsheviks, or reds, is launched. A political cartoon in *The American Pageant* (14th ed., p. 771/15th ed., p. 703) makes it abundantly clear that leftists have no place in American life.

- Intolerance grows in the nation after World War I. A new and more virulent nativist strain emerges in the reborn Ku Klux Klan, which has expanded its influence across the nation.

- To shrink immigration from certain areas of the world, a quota system is put in place. That and the Immigration Act of 1924 dramatically reduce eastern and southern European immigration.

- To control social and moral behavior, the prohibition movement addresses alcohol consumption. In 1919, the Eighteenth Amendment is ratified, eliminating forever, or so supporters believe, the "manufacture, sale, or transportation of intoxicating liquors."

- Automotive production becomes an integral part of the economy, as it stimulates demand in other businesses, among them the gas and oil industry, and gives Americans relatively easy access to shopping (which itself is transformed by the auto), schools, and the workplace.

- The decade known as the roaring twenties witnesses cultural, social, and economic challenges to Victorian values. Women begin to defy gender stereotypes through, for example, fashion, smoking cigarettes in public, and jazz dancing.

AP teachers should take note of the following:

1. Henry Ford paid his workers handsomely (approximately $5 a day) and shortened their workday, but he expected their loyalty and established a paternalistic relationship with them that went even beyond the workplace—their personal lives were monitored by the company. Other companies followed suit, hoping to prevent labor strikes and other interferences in the production process.

2. Charles Lindbergh, known as "Lucky Lindy" because of his unprecedented feat of flying nonstop from New York to Paris, initiated a new age of air travel. The airplane fundamentally changed the nation and the world, allowing personal air travel and revolutionizing the military.

Focus on Historical Thinking:

Have students characterize the political, social, economic, and cultural climate of the 1920s in one clear, concise sentence for each.

FOCUS QUESTIONS

1. How did the Red Scare translate into the Ku Klux Klan and the anti-immigrant movements in American society?

2.   What were the arguments both for and against Prohibition and what were its consequences? How did the Eighteenth Amendment come about?

3.   What was it about the 1920s that made it Roaring?

4.   Who were some of the major literary figures and how did the literature reflect the mood of the 1920s?

CHAPTER THEMES

Theme: A disillusioned America turned away from idealism and reform after World War I and toward isolationism in foreign affairs, domestic social conservatism, and the pleasures of prosperity.

Theme: New technologies, mass-marketing techniques, and new forms of entertainment fostered rapid cultural change along with a focus on consumer goods. But the accompanying changes in moral values and uncertainty about the future produced cultural anxiety, as well as sharp intellectual critiques of American life.

CHAPTER SUMMARY

After the crusading idealism of World War I, America turned inward and became hostile to anything foreign or different. Radicals were targeted in the red scare and the Sacco-Vanzetti case, while the resurgent Ku Klux Klan joined other forces in bringing about pronounced restrictions on further immigration. Sharp cultural conflicts occurred over the Prohibition experiment and evolution.

A new mass-consumption economy fueled the spectacular prosperity of the 1920s. The automobile industry, led by Henry Ford, transformed the economy and altered American lifestyles.

The pervasive media of radio and film altered popular culture and values. Birth control and Freudian psychology overturned traditional sexual standards, especially for women. The stock-market boom symbolized the free-wheeling spirit of the decade.

American literary and artistic vision flourished during the 1920s. The emergence of modernism, first highlighted at the Armory Show in 1913, led writers, artists, and architects to question realism, social conventions, and traditional authority.

DEVELOPING THE CHAPTER: SUGGESTED LECTURE OR DISCUSSION TOPICS

*   Analyze the social turning inward of the 1920s as a disillusioned reaction to World War I. Show how the rise of the Klan and immigration restriction especially reflected a desire to preserve America against alien influences.

    REFERENCE: Nancy MacLean, *Behind the Mask of Chivalry: The Making of the Second KKK* (1993).

*   Discuss the Scopes trial as a focal point of the deep conflicts over religion and culture in the 1920s.

    REFERENCES: George Marsden, *Fundamentalism and American Culture* (1980); Jeffrey P. Morgan, *The Scopes Trial—A Brief History with Documents* (2002).

*   Examine the economic and cultural consequences of the new mass-consumption economy. Show how innovations such as credit buying, advertising, and automobile travel weakened the old Protestant ethic with a new emphasis on pleasure and excitement.

    REFERENCE: Ronald Marchand, *Advertising the American Dream: Making Way for Modernity* (1985).

- Consider the radical cultural transformations in moral and sexual values brought about by such developments as movies, birth control, Freudian psychology, jazz, and advanced literature, especially as they affected women. Examine the rise of the consumer culture and its impact on traditional moral and social values (for example, the impact of credit buying on the Puritan ethic).

  REFERENCE: Stanley Coben, *Rebellion Against Victorianism: The Impetus for Cultural Change in 1920s America* (1991).

FOR FURTHER INTEREST: ADDITIONAL CLASS TOPICS

- Explore the ideology and actions of the 1920s Klan. Consider similarities and differences in relation to the Klan of Reconstruction.

- Discuss the role of prohibition during the 1920s and its close relation to the rise of organized crime.

- Explore the complex and sometimes contradictory cultural values of the decade as symbolically represented by Charles Lindbergh's flight. Discuss how he symbolized technological innovation but also individual heroism in an increasingly mass society.

- Consider the role of both black and white artists in changing American culture in the 1920s. Consider where writers such as Fitzgerald and Hughes were reflecting similar concerns, and where their outlook was different.

- Have the students read Randolph Bourne's "Trans-National America" (1916) and "Twilight of Idols" (1917) in David A. Hollinger and Charles Capper's (Editors), *The American Intellectual Tradition: Volume II—1865 to the Present*, New York: Oxford University Press, 2001.

- Conduct a class debate over the following topics: for example, The Department of Justice Is Defending America from Communist Subversion, H.L. Mencken Critiques America, and Prohibition Is a Success. Primary source readings will come from the following book: *Opposing Viewpoints in American History—Volume II: From Reconstruction to the Present*, San Diego, CA: Greenhaven Press, 1996. Another good source of debate topics is Larry Madaras and James M. SoRelle, *Taking Sides—Clashing Views on Controversial Issues in American History, Volume II: Reconstruction to the Present*, Connecticut: McGraw-Hill, 2000.

- Have the students read Jerome Lawrence and Robert E. Lee's *Inherit the Wind* (1955)—a play based on the events of the Scopes trial and made into an award-winning movie in 1960.

- Have the students read selections from H.L. Mencken's *A Mencken Chrestomathy* (1949) and *A Second Mencken Chrestomathy* (1995); two volumes collected and edited from the vast writings of H.L. Mencken, the "American Voltaire."

CHARACTER SKETCHES

Henry Ford (1863–1947)

Ford was the automobile genius and industrialist who epitomized the new age of mass consumer production.

Although he hated farm work as a boy, Ford was always nostalgic about rural life and later re-created an idealized version of it in his Greenfield Village.

He was widely praised for paying his workers $5 a day—although not all of them earned that. In 1915, Ford paid for a Peace Ship full of American antiwar activists who sailed to Norway in a futile effort to end World War I. In the 1920s, he published a viciously anti-Semitic paper, *The Dearborn Independent*, which was distributed through Ford dealerships.

Ford enjoyed his own reputation as the voice of the uneducated common person and often sounded off on subjects about which he knew nothing. For example, he asserted that earlier civilizations had had airplanes and cars, that cows should be eliminated and milk produced artificially, and that all the art in the world was not worth five cents.

Quote: "I don't like to read books. They mess up my mind." (1919)

REFERENCE: David L. Lewis, *The Public Image of Henry Ford* (1976).

Alphonse Capone (1899–1947)

Capone was the brutal gangster who dominated Chicago organized crime in the late 1920s and early 1930s.

Capone's parents were Italian immigrants from Sicily who came to New York in 1893. Capone quit school after the fourth grade and soon linked up with other gang members, including Johnny Torrio. In one early gang fight, Capone was slashed across the face with a knife, giving him his nickname of "Scarface."

When Torrio moved from New York to Chicago, Capone followed him to help run the giant prostitution operation and other rackets in the city. In 1925, Torrio retired, and Capone seized control of all of Chicago's prohibition-era organized crime by gunning down his rivals. Capone's worth was estimated at over $100 million and for a time in the late 1920s, he had extensive power within Chicago's political, journalistic, and law-enforcement communities.

After his conviction for income-tax evasion and imprisonment on Alcatraz Island, he was discovered to be suffering from syphilis. He was released on parole in 1939.

Quote: "What's your racket?" (1927)

REFERENCES: John Kobler, *The Life and World of Al Capone* (1992); Laurence Bergreen, *Capone: The Man and the Era* (1994).

Charles A. Lindbergh (1902–1974)

Lindbergh was the pilot whose solo flight made him the greatest hero of the 1920s and who later became a leading isolationist spokesman before World War II.

A group of St. Louis businessmen put up the money for Lindbergh's plane, which had never been fully tested before he headed across the Atlantic. He dozed off several times during the flight but was awakened each time by the erratic movements of the plane. Vast crowds greeted him in Paris, although he landed in the dark.

Lindbergh was stunned by the unrelenting publicity and tried unsuccessfully to withdraw from the public eye. He married the daughter of diplomat Dwight Morrow. Anne Morrow Lindbergh later became a popular author. The kidnapping and murder of their two-year-old son in 1932 horrified America and caused the Lindberghs to move to Europe. Lindbergh's association with Nazism and isolationism in the 1930s cost him some popularity, but he sometimes advised the government on aviation matters even into the 1950s and 1960s.

Quote: "These wars in Europe are not wars in which our civilization is defending itself against some Asiatic intruder.... This is not a question of banding together to defend our white race against foreign invasions. This is simply one more of those age-old quarrels among our family of nations." (Radio address, 1939)

REFERENCE: Scott Berg, *Lindbergh* (1998).

H.L. (Henry Louis) Mencken (1880 – 1956)

Mencken (aka, the "Sage of Baltimore") was one of the leading cultural critics of American society throughout most of the early part of the twentieth century. Mencken was a journalist, editor, essayist, and satirist who spent most of his life in Baltimore, Maryland. He was known for his humor and wit and never missed an opportunity to criticize ignorance, intolerance, fraud, and organized religion (mostly fundamentalist Christianity).

Mencken was well read and popular throughout the 1920s, however, during the depression and World War II Mencken lost favor with many Americans.

Quote: "Such obscenities as the forthcoming trial of the Tennessee evolutionist, if they serve no other purpose, at least call attention dramatically to the fact that enlightenment, among mankind, is very narrowly dispersed. It is common to assume that human progress affects everyone—that even the dullest man, in these bright days, knows more than any man of, say, the Eighteenth Century, and is far more civilized. This assumption is quite erroneous. The men of the educated minority, no doubt, know more than their predecessors, and of some of them, perhaps, it may be said that they are more civilized ... but the great masses of men, even in this inspired republic, are precisely where the mob was at the dawn of history. They are ignorant, they are dishonest, they are cowardly, they are ignoble. They know little if anything that is worth knowing, and there is not the slightest sign of a natural desire among them to increase their knowledge." (*Homo Neanderthalensis*, 1925)

REFERENCE: Marion Elizabeth Rodgers, *Mencken: The American Iconoclast* (2005).

Marcus Garvey (1887–1940)

Garvey was the black nationalist leader whose Back to Africa movement had a major influence on African American culture in the 1920s.

Garvey was born in Jamaica and worked as a printer and union organizer. During travels to South America and Britain, he learned a great deal about the history and culture of African peoples, which led him to emphasize black racial pride and to formulate his plans for a return of all blacks to Africa.

His Universal Negro Improvement Association attracted tremendous support from American blacks in the early 1920s, but the government of Liberia (where Garvey hoped to migrate) thought him a revolutionary plotter and withdrew support from his Black Star steamship lines. His conviction for fraud and his deportation to Jamaica effectively ended his political career, but he remained a hero among many blacks for his emphasis on African culture and self-determination.

Quote: "Never allow anyone to convince you of your inferiority as a man. Rise in your dignity to justify all that is noble in your race.

My race is mine and I belong to it.

It climbs with me and I climb with it.

My pride is mine and I shall honor it.

It is the height on which I daily sit."

(*The Negro World*, 1923)

REFERENCE: J. Stein, *The World of Marcus Garvey* (1986).

F. Scott Fitzgerald (1896–1940)

Fitzgerald was the novelist whose literature and life symbolized and promoted the values of the jazz age in the 1920s.

His father was from an old aristocratic Maryland family whose ancestors included the author of "The Star-Spangled Banner." His mother was from a poor Irish background, and Fitzgerald claimed his dual ancestry gave him a unique view of American life.

At Princeton, Fitzgerald worked harder for social than academic success and was distressed when academic probation forced him to give up his campus literary activities. Fitzgerald's glamorous postwar life in Europe fell victim to lavish spending, alcoholism, and the mental illness of his wife Zelda.

In the 1930s, he returned to America and wrote *Tender Is the Night* (1934) and a brilliant story, "The Crack-Up," about his own mental distress and feared loss of talent. When he was sober, Fitzgerald was charming, elegant, and a fine conversationalist.

Quote: "America was going on the greatest, gaudiest spree in history. … The whole golden boom was in the air—its splendid generosities, its outrageous corruptions, and the death struggle of the old America in prohibition." (1935)

REFERENCE: William A. Fahey, *F. Scott Fitzgerald and the American Dream* (1973).

MAKERS OF AMERICA: THE POLES

Questions for Class Discussion

1.   How did both economic and religious factors contribute to Polish immigration?

2.   How was the Polish influence in America similar to that of other New Immigrants such as the Italians (see Chapter 25)? How was it different?

Suggested Student Exercises

- The text lists five cities that were centers of Polish immigration to America: Chicago, Buffalo, Pittsburgh, Detroit, and Milwaukee. Examine the impact of Polish-Americans in one of these cities over several generations.

- Critically analyze negative cultural stereotypes of Polish immigrants in the press and elsewhere in the 1920s and after. Consider what biases may underlie these stereotypes, and how some of the social and cultural changes in recent decades, in both the United States and Poland (for example, the Polish Pope John Paul II and the fall of communism), may work to undercut such stereotyping.

QUESTIONS FOR CLASS DISCUSSION

1.   Why did the United States, which had welcomed so many millions of immigrants for nearly a century, suddenly become so fearful of immigration in the 1920s that it virtually ended mass immigration for two decades?

2.   To what extent was the Scopes Trial only about competing theories of human origins, and to what extent was it a focal point for deeper concerns regarding the role of religion and traditional moral authorities in American life and the new cultural power of science?

3.   Was the new mass culture, as reflected in Hollywood films and radio, a source of moral and social change, or did it really reinforce the essentially conservative business and social values of the time? Consider the role of commercial advertising in particular.

4.   Were the intellectual critics of the 1920s really disillusioned with the fundamental character of American life, or were they actually loyal to a vision of a better America and only hiding their idealism behind a veneer of disillusionment and irony?

CHAPTER 32

The Politics of Boom and Bust, 1920–1932

AP FOCUS

- Harding is incorruptible, but some friends and appointees lack his honesty and tarnish Harding's administration. See the political cartoon in *The American Pageant* (14th ed., p. 800/15th ed., p. 729).

- Shocked by the enormous devastation that the war brought to Europe, the victorious world powers hold disarmament talks (Washington Naval Conference) and agree to reduce the size of their navies. As part of the agreement, Japan is not permitted to have a higher tonnage amount than Britain and the United States, but is granted hegemonic power in the Far East.

- Congress raises the protective tariff to augment the already big profits many businesses are amassing. European countries retaliate with their own high tariffs, which stymie international trade and debilitate Germany, already financially pressed by its obligation to pay war reparations.

- Determined to be repaid its war loans, the United States creates the Dawes Plan, a complicated method of financial payments that fails to get repayment but places considerable strain on European finances. See the chart (14th ed., p. 808/15th ed., p. 737), describing the plan as a "financial merry-go-round."

- The stock-market collapse (see the chart in the 14th ed., p. 813/15th ed., p. 741) starts a deep depression from which the nation will not fully recover until World War II. The rest of the world shares in this calamity.

- Near the end of Hoover's term in office, the Japanese invade China. The U.S. response is tepid and does little to deter the Japanese from taking future aggressive action.

AP teachers should take note of the following:

1. Farmers who purchased labor-saving technology, such as mechanized harvesters and reapers, dramatically increased production, but at a considerable cost; the price of their crops plummeted.

2. Aggravating the problem of underconsumption was the Mellon tax plan, which had lowered taxes on the rich, thereby concentrating even more wealth in a small percentage of the population.

3. Hoover's solution to the economic collapse reflected his faith in the resiliency of American capitalism. While he adopted drastic measures inconsistent with his own monetary philosophy, he still relied on volunteerism, local-government assistance to the unemployed, and rugged individualism to see the nation through, methods that were inadequate for this depression.

4. Hoover's brutal response to the Bonus Marchers eroded even further his rapidly declining popularity, a trend that did not bode well for the president's reelection prospects.

Focus on Historical Thinking:

Reproduce without captions the political cartoons on pp. 729 and 733 and the painting on p. 742 (15th ed.). Have students construct a single sentence for each figure that clearly expresses its main purpose.

FOCUS QUESTIONS

1. What was the economic philosophy of the Republican presidents of the 1920s? Did this environment help create the Great Depression?

2. What were the first tasks of the Harding administration?

3. What was the foreign policy philosophy of Coolidge and was he consistent?

4. Describe the political environment of the election of 1928? How did Hoover win the election?

5. What were the causes of the Great Depression?

6. What were the major foreign policy issues faced by the Hoover administration?

CHAPTER THEMES

Theme: The Republican administrations of the prosperous 1920s pursued conservative, probusiness policies at home, and economic unilateralism abroad.

Theme: The great crash of 1929 led to a severe, prolonged depression that devastated the American economy and spirit and resisted Hoover's limited efforts to correct it.

CHAPTER SUMMARY

The Republican governments of the 1920s carried out active, probusiness policies, while undermining much of the progressive legacy by neglect. The Washington Naval Conference indicated America's desire to withdraw from international involvements. Sky-high tariffs protected America's booming industry but caused severe economic troubles elsewhere in the world.

As the Harding scandals broke, the puritanical Calvin Coolidge replaced his morally easygoing predecessor. Feuding Democrats and La Follette progressives fell easy victims to Republican prosperity.

American demands for strict repayment of war debts created international economic difficulties. The Dawes plan provided temporary relief, but the Hawley-Smoot Tariff proved devastating to international trade.

The stock-market crash of 1929 brought a sudden end to prosperity and plunged America into a horrible depression. Herbert Hoover's reputation collapsed as he failed to relieve national suffering, although he did make unprecedented but limited efforts to revive the economy through federal assistance.

DEVELOPING THE CHAPTER: SUGGESTED LECTURE OR DISCUSSION TOPICS

*   Explain the central features of Republican economic and political conservatism in the 1920s: probusiness government, hostility to progressive social and economic regulation, and high tariffs to isolate the American economy from the troubled world economy.

    REFERENCE: Burl Noggle, *Into the Twenties* (1974).

*   Contrast Warren Harding and his corrupt cronies with the upright Coolidge and Hoover. Perhaps show how each of the three presidents represented a different emphasis within the general political consensus of the probusiness 1920s.

    REFERENCES: John D. Hicks, *Republican Ascendancy, 1921–1933* (1960); Joan Hoff Wilson, *Herbert Hoover, Forgotten Progressive* (1975).

*   Describe the stock-market crash and the depression. Examine various causes of the depression and indicate its paralyzing effect on ordinary citizens, as well as on the business and political leadership.

REFERENCE: Robert McElvaine, *The Great Depression* (1984).

- Consider the changing role of American workers in both the probusiness 1920s and during the early years of the Great Depression.

  REFERENCE: Robert Zieger, *American Workers, American Unions, 1920–1985* (1986).

FOR FURTHER INTEREST: ADDITIONAL CLASS TOPICS

- Focus on Harding's cronies and the Teapot Dome scandals.

- Discuss the futile Democratic and progressive efforts of the 1920s. The focus might be on the deep cultural divisions within the Democratic Party between urban immigrants and the rural South, epitomized in the 103-ballot Democratic convention of 1924.

- Examine Hoover's career, from humane administrator to business organizer to hapless president. Discuss why someone so successful proved so helpless in the face of the depression.

- Analyze the human consequences of the depression for both the unemployed and the many others who feared unemployment and found their living standard severely reduced.

- Show students the following video: *The Century—America's Time* (ABC Video in association with The History Channel), *Volume I: 1920–1929: Boom to Bust*. "An energetic postwar mentality emerges and old traditions are challenged during The Roaring 20's. Women take bold steps toward equality, threatening to upset the 'domestic balance' of the country."

CHARACTER SKETCHES

Warren G. Harding (1865–1923)

This simple, genial president was deeply mourned when he died in 1923, just before the news broke of the thoroughgoing corruption in his administration.

Rumors throughout Harding's career that he was part black were based only on hometown gossip and the fact that one of his great-grandparents had lived in a black neighborhood. There is no historical evidence that he had any black ancestors.

Harding was happy as a small-town editor and poker-playing U.S. senator, although his ambitious wife, "The Duchess," constantly pushed him to do greater things. Harding maintained several mistresses, and one of them—Nan Britton of Marion, Ohio—bore a child by him in 1919. As president, he would frequently sneak away to play poker with the "Ohio gang" at "the little green house on K street."

Harding was deeply distressed as he learned of his cronies' corrupt dealings. He seemed near collapse during his presidential trip to Alaska, on which he died, and frequently asked Secretary of Commerce Herbert Hoover what a president should do if there was dishonesty around him.

Quote: "My God, this is a hell of a job. I have no troubles with my enemies…but my God-damn friends!…" (1923)

REFERENCES: Robert K. Murray, *The Harding Era* (1969); Eugene P. Trani, *The Presidency of Warren G. Harding* (1977).

Calvin Coolidge (1872–1933)

Coolidge's rectitude and old-fashioned virtues provided welcome relief from the Harding scandals, while also offering the public a reassuring counterpoint to the wild cultural changes of the 1920s.

At Amherst College, Coolidge astounded classmates by constantly seeking ways to live more cheaply. He was personally kind and generous, but he was frequently moody and had few close friends. Even after he became a successful attorney, he used a party-line phone and refused to buy a car because it was too expensive.

Coolidge was generally ignorant of history and political theory, but he loved classical languages and sometimes translated Latin literary works into English. He had a malicious sense of humor and loved to play practical jokes like ringing for White House servants and then hiding from them. His poker-faced silence was the subject of much commentary and humor. When writer Dorothy Parker was told that Coolidge had died, she said, "How could they tell?"

Quote: "There are two ways to be self-respecting: to spend less than you make, and to make more than you spend." (1925)

REFERENCES: Hendrik Booraem, *The Provincial: Calvin Coolidge and His World* (1994); Robert Ferrell, *The Presidency of Calvin Coolidge* (1998).

Herbert Hoover (1874–1964)

Hoover was an international hero as food relief administrator during World War I and a popular secretary of commerce, but his single term as president made him a permanent symbol of economic and political disaster.

Hoover was the product of a strong Iowa Quaker background. His parents died before he was ten, and he was then raised by an uncle in Oregon. After graduating from Stanford, he lived outside the United States for nearly twenty years while working as an engineer and businessman. One of his interests was the history of mining, and he collected and had translated Renaissance classics on the subject.

As a public official, Hoover developed a large staff of deferential subordinates who called him "The Chief" and generated favorable publicity on his behalf. He was stiff, formal, humorless, and unyielding in his opinions once he had taken a stand. Those who worked intimately with him always liked him, but he was comfortable only in the company of people who he knew were on his side.

Quote: "We in America today are nearer to the final triumph over poverty than ever before in the history of any land.… We have not yet reached the goal, but given a chance to go forward with the policies of the last eight years, we shall soon with the help of God be in sight of the day when poverty will be banished from this nation." (Convention acceptance speech, 1928)

REFERENCE: Joan Hoff Wilson, *Herbert Hoover: Forgotten Progressive* (1975).

QUESTIONS FOR CLASS DISCUSSION

1. In what ways were the 1920s a reaction against the progressive era?

2. Was the American isolationism of the 1920s linked to the rise of movements such as the Ku Klux Klan? In what ways did movements such as fundamentalism reflect similar antimodern outlooks, and in what ways did they reflect more basic religious disagreements?

3. To what extent did the policies of the booming 1920s contribute to the depression? Was the depression inevitable, or could it have been avoided. Why or why not?

4. How did the depression challenge the traditional belief of Hoover and other Americans in rugged individualism?

CHAPTER 33

The Great Depression and the New Deal, 1933–1939

AP FOCUS

- The first hundred days of Roosevelt's presidency witness a torrent of executive and legislative programs, acts, and policies that attempt to deal with the Great Depression and to reform the economic system, so that the nation will never again experience such a devastating economic collapse.

- To jumpstart the economy, Roosevelt institutes an inflationary policy in which deficit spending is used to create jobs. It is hoped that this will reduce the number of people needing government aid and increase consumer spending, further stimulating demand and, consequently, higher employment. Income would be taxed to help defray the cost of federally funded jobs.

- The Tennessee Valley Authority creates thousands of jobs and brings electricity to rural areas along the Tennessee River. Critics claim that the TVA eliminates competition and is akin to government control of utilities similar to that found in socialist economies.

- One of the longest-lasting legacies of the New Deal is Social Security, which provides economic assistance to some of the nation's most vulnerable citizens, such as retired senior citizens.

- When the conservative Supreme Court begins ruling New Deal programs, such as the National Recovery Act, unconstitutional, FDR devises a plan to "pack" the court, an undertaking that is met with a storm of criticism. He withdraws the plan.

- Uncomfortable with deficit spending, FDR tries to balance the budget during the depression. Unemployment again rises, and capacity utilization declines significantly before he returns to his original economic plan.

AP teachers should take note of the following:

1. Francis Perkins, the secretary of labor, was the first female cabinet member in U.S. History.

2. Eleanor Roosevelt, one of the most active and energetic First Ladies in American history, actively campaigned for the rights of women, blacks, and labor. Remember that Reform is an AP theme.

3. At a time when many were out of work and going hungry, the government paid hard-pressed farmers not to grow food in order to boost the value, and therefore the price, of their crops.

4. Most historians agree that unemployment was fixed only when the nation entered World War II.

Focus on Historical Thinking:

Have students rank in order what they consider to be the five most positive effects and the five most negative effects of the New Deal.

FOCUS QUESTIONS

1. What were the differences between Hoover and Roosevelt, both personally and politically?

2.   What were Roosevelt's goals of relief, recovery, and reform to help America get out of the Great Depression?

3.   What were the main criticism, from both the left and the right, of Roosevelt's New Deal program?

4.   How did Roosevelt deal with the business community and what gains did labor make under his administration?

5.   What were the long- and short-term benefits to Roosevelt's New Deal?

CHAPTER THEMES

Theme: Roosevelt's New Deal tackled the Great Depression with massive federal programs designed to bring about relief, recovery, and reform.

CHAPTER SUMMARY

Confident, aristocratic Roosevelt swept into office with an urgent mandate to cope with the depression emergency. His bank holiday and frantic Hundred Days lifted spirits and created a host of new agencies to provide for relief to the unemployed, economic recovery, and permanent reform of the system.

Roosevelt's programs put millions of the unemployed back on the job through federal action. As popular demagogues such as Huey Long and Father Charles Coughlin increased their appeal to the suffering population, Roosevelt developed sweeping programs to reorganize and reform American history, labor, and agriculture. The TVA, Social Security, and the Wagner Act brought far-reaching changes that especially benefited the economically disadvantaged.

Conservatives furiously denounced the New Deal, but Roosevelt formed a powerful coalition of urbanites, labor, new immigrants, blacks, and the South that swept him to victory in 1936.

A decade after the ratification of the Nineteenth Amendment, women began to exercise their rights, both politically and intellectually.

Roosevelt's Court-packing plan failed, but the Court finally began approving New Deal legislation. The later New Deal encountered mounting conservative opposition and the stubborn persistence of unemployment. Although the New Deal was highly controversial, it saved America from extreme right-wing or left-wing dictatorship.

DEVELOPING THE CHAPTER: SUGGESTED LECTURE OR DISCUSSION TOPICS

•   Describe the impact of Roosevelt and the New Deal on deeply depressed ordinary Americans, perhaps focusing on how Roosevelt revived spirits and restored faith in the system, even for those who did not agree with all his programs. Include the experiences of ordinary men and women in the 1930s.

    REFERENCES: Studs Terkel, *Hard Times* (1970); Ann Banks, *First Person America.*

•   Examine the goals and activities of the major New Deal programs. The relief-recovery-reform distinction is useful for sorting out the alphabet agencies, as is the distinction between the early NRA-AAA approach and the later TVA–Social Security–Wagner Act reforms. A unifying theme for the whole New Deal is the search to provide greater security against the storms and uncertainties of unregulated capitalism.

    REFERENCE: David M. Kennedy, *Freedom from Fear* (1999).

- Explain the various challenges to Roosevelt from both the popular demagogues and the conservatives. Show how he skillfully "stole the thunder" from the former and used the latter as political whipping boys.

  REFERENCES: Alan Brinkley, *Voices of Protest: Huey Long, Father Coughlin, and the Great Depression* (1982); Richard Polenberg, *The Era of Franklin D. Roosevelt: 1933–1945 A Brief History with Documents* (2000).

- Consider the experience of women in the depression and in the making of the New Deal. Look at ordinary women in urban and rural areas, as well as more prominent reformers and government figures.

  REFERENCES: Lois Scharf, *To Work and to Wed: Female Employment, Feminism, and the Great Depression* (1980); Susan Ware, *Beyond Suffrage: Women in the New Deal* (1981).

FOR FURTHER INTEREST: ADDITIONAL CLASS TOPICS

- Compare and contrast the images and activities of FDR and Eleanor Roosevelt. Show how he pursued realistic political goals, while she took up the cause of the most disadvantaged citizens.

- Discuss the particular impact of the depression on women, families, and children.

- Use Steinbeck's *The Grapes of Wrath* (and perhaps the film) to discuss the plight of Dust Bowl farmers in the depression. Point out that, for most, the problem was not dust but impossibly low prices.

- Discuss the long-term, continuing impact of the New Deal today. Consider the controversies in the 1980s and after over the legacy of big government programs started by the New Deal.

- Conduct a class debate over the following topics: for example, Self-Help Is the Best Response to Unemployment, America Needs a New Deal, The New Deal Is a Momentous Achievement, and Social Security Will Harm America. Primary source readings will come from the following book: *Opposing Viewpoints in American History—Volume II: From Reconstruction to the Present*, San Diego, CA: Greenhaven Press, 1996. Another good source of debate topics is Larry Madaras and James M. SoRelle, *Taking Sides—Clashing Views on Controversial Issues in American History, Volume II: Reconstruction to the Present*, Connecticut: McGraw-Hill, 2000.

- Show students the following video: *The Century—America's Time* (ABC Video in association with The History Channel), *Volume II: 1929–1936: Stormy Weather*. "The stock market crashes, plunging the nation into the economic depths of The Great Depression. For the first time, the country reflects on a sobering question: Is there a limit to 'The American Dream'?"

- Have the students read Robert Penn Warren's *All the King's Men* (1947). A story about the rise and fall of Willie Talos, a Southern politician;, the story was based on the life of Huey Long, made into a movie in 1949.

- Show the students Charlie Chaplin's *Modern Times* (1936). Discuss the imagery and symbolism in the movie—what was Chaplin's purpose of satirizing the Great Depression. Was it effective? Why was the movie so popular?

- Have the students read Sidney Hook's "Communism Without Dogmas" (1934) in David A. Hollinger and Charles Capper's (Editors), *The American Intellectual Tradition: Volume II—1865 to the Present*, New York: Oxford University Press, 2001.

- Have the students read Clement Greenberg's "Avant-Garde and Kitsch" (1939) in David A. Hollinger and Charles Capper's (Editors), *The American Intellectual Tradition: Volume II—1865 to the Present*, New York: Oxford University Press, 2001.

- Have the students read FDR's fireside chats. The complete fireside chats, along with other documents from FDR (and all the presidents), can be read at The American Presidency Project, *Franklin D. Roosevelt's Fireside Chat*, (http://www.presidency.ucsb.edu/fireside.php) last accessed August 2008.

CHARACTER SKETCHES

Franklin Roosevelt (1882–1945)

Roosevelt came from a wealthy patrician family, and his advocacy on behalf of the common person in the depression led him to be called a "traitor to his class."

Thoroughly indulged as an only child, Roosevelt was taught primarily by private tutors. His mother, Sara Delano, was a strong-willed woman who exercised a dominant influence on him even during his adult life.

Roosevelt had been very athletic before being struck with polio in 1921. It took him several years of constant effort to regain his strength; after he discovered the therapeutic waters at Warm Springs, Georgia, he again participated in swimming, fishing, and sailing. Roosevelt was almost never photographed in a wheelchair, so many Americans did not know that the wheelchair was his normal means of getting around.

Roosevelt enjoyed political maneuvering and often pitted his advisers against one another. He once told two officials with contradictory proposals to "go in a room and weave them together."

Quote: "In every dark hour of our national life a leadership of frankness and vigor has met with that support and understanding of the people themselves which is essential to victory.... The money changers have fled from their high seats in the temple of our civilization.... This nation asks for action, and action now." (Inaugural address, 1933)

REFERENCE: Frank Freidel, *Franklin D. Roosevelt: Rendezvous with Destiny* (1990).

Eleanor Roosevelt (1884–1962)

Besides her role as Franklin Roosevelt's wife and adviser, Eleanor Roosevelt became an influential reformer and political leader in her own right, both before and after FDR's death.

Eleanor Roosevelt did not change names when she married her distant cousin. Her father, Elliott Roosevelt, was Theodore Roosevelt's younger brother and a troubled alcoholic who separated from his family when Eleanor was young. Her mother died when Eleanor was eight, and she was raised by a grandmother who made her feel unattractive and unwanted.

Her discovery of her husband's unfaithfulness led to a crisis in their marriage and her determination to create a political identity and career on her own. Her newspaper column, "My Day," became a highly popular feature in the 1930s and 1940s. She grew to be a skilled political operator and helped to engineer the nomination of Adlai Stevenson for president in 1952 and 1956.

Quote: "As time went by, I found that people no longer considered me a mouthpiece for my husband but realized that I had a point of view of my own with which he might not at all agree. Then I felt freer to state my views." (Autobiography, 1949)

REFERENCE: Blanche Wiesen Cook, *Eleanor Roosevelt: A Life* (1992).

Huey Long (1893–1935)

Long was the colorful "Kingfish" whose populist politics dominated Louisiana and who eventually challenged Roosevelt's leadership during the depression.

Originally from rural north Louisiana, Long always had a strong following among poor farmers. He was elected state railroad commissioner at age twenty-five, and used the office flamboyantly to attack monopolistic utilities. As governor and senator he ruled Louisiana with near-absolute control; every police officer, firefighter, and teacher in the state owed his or her job directly to Long.

Long spent lavishly for public works, roads, and schools, especially for the redneck areas. He also built up Louisiana State University, with particular emphasis on the football team and the band, and was known for leading the band on the sidelines during games.

Long would often hold court in hotel rooms in his pajamas, with reporters and advisers and citizens listening to his clever, humorous, obscene monologues. Long's plan was to run as an independent presidential candidate in 1936, building a base of support so he could win the White House in 1940.

Quote: "Why weep or slumber, America,

Land of brave and true?

With castles, and clothing, and food for all

All belongs to you.

Every Man a King! Every Man a King!" (Radio address, 1935)

REFERENCE: William Hair, *The Kingfish and His Realm: The Life and Times of Huey P. Long* (1991).

QUESTIONS FOR CLASS DISCUSSION

1. Which of Roosevelt's measures were most effective in fighting the depression? Why?

2. How did Roosevelt alter the role of the federal government in American life? Was this necessary for American survival?

3. How did ordinary workers and farmers effect social change in the 1930s?

4. What were the positive and negative effects of the New Deal's use of the federal government as an agency of social reform?

EXPANDING THE "VARYING VIEWPOINTS"

*   Arthur M. Schlesinger Jr., *The Age of Roosevelt: The Coming of the New Deal* (1959).

    A view of the New Deal as a radical transformation:

    "By bringing to Washington a government determined to govern, Roosevelt unlocked new energies in a people who had lost faith, not just in government's ability to meet the economic crisis, but almost in the ability of anyone to do anything. The feeling of movement was irresistible.... A despairing land had a vision of America as it might some day be.... 'It's more than a New Deal,' said Harold Ickes. 'It's a new world. People feel free again. They can breathe naturally. It's like quitting a morgue for the open woods.' 'We have had our revolution,' said Collier's, 'and we like it.'"

*   William E. Leuchtenberg, *Franklin D. Roosevelt and the New Deal* (1963).

    A view of the New Deal as a halfway revolution:

    "The New Deal achieved a more just society by recognizing groups which had been largely unrepresented—staple farmers, industrial workers, particular ethnic groups, and the new intellectual-administrative class. Yet this was still a halfway revolution. It swelled the ranks of the bourgeoisie but left many Americans—sharecroppers, slum dwellers, most Negroes—outside the new equilibrium.... The New Dealers perceived that they had done more in those years than had been done in any comparable period of American history, but they also saw that there was much still to be done, much, too, that continued to baffle them."

QUESTIONS ABOUT THE "VARYING VIEWPOINTS"

1. What does each of these historians regard as the fundamental achievement of the New Deal?

2. What weaknesses does Leuchtenberg see in the New Deal?

3. How might each of these historians interpret such programs as the AAA, Social Security, and the Wagner Act?

CHAPTER 34

Franklin D. Roosevelt and the Shadow of War, 1933–1941

AP FOCUS

- The U.S. withdrawal from the London Economic Conference illustrates FDR's determination not to associate his New Deal (inflationary) agenda with an international attempt to combat the effects of global depression by stabilizing international currencies.

- The Spanish Civil War is a prelude to World War II in that the two major fascist powers, Germany and Italy, provide economic and military aid to help General Franco defeat Spain's Loyalists. The Loyalists get assistance from the Soviet Union and volunteers from many countries. Western governments, however, remain aloof to the plight of the antifascist forces.

- To forestall another bloodbath like World War I, Britain and France adopt a policy of appeasement in dealing with German, Italian, and Japanese aggression and territorial expansion. In the summer of 1939, the world is stunned to learn that ideological archenemies Germany and the Soviet Union have signed a nonaggression pact. Consider the AP theme War and Diplomacy.

- To assist Britain, which stood alone against Germany after the fall of France in 1940, FDR circumvents the neutrality acts, giving the British destroyers in return for British military bases. The next step in providing much needed aid to Britain is the Lend-Lease Act. The map in *The American Pageant* (14th ed., p. 869/15th ed., p. 792) shows the flow of Lend-Lease aid.

- Six months after the German invasion of the Soviet Union, Japan launches a surprise attack on the American naval base at Pearl Harbor in Hawaii, catapulting the United States into the war.

AP teachers should take note of the following:

1. Many historians maintain that the United States adopted an isolationist policy or, at the very least, a policy of neutrality in the interwar years, pointing to the refusal to join the League of Nations and to support the Loyalist forces in the Spanish Civil War. Other historians challenge this interpretation and cite the numerous cases of U.S. intervention in the post–World War I era, as well as the economic and political agreements and treaties made with foreign nations.

2. In 1940, FDR sought an unprecedented third term as president. The Constitution placed no limits on how many terms one could serve, but George Washington had set a tradition that had been followed ever since.

Focus on Historical Thinking:

Have students compare and contrast the attitudes of Woodrow Wilson and Franklin Roosevelt toward U.S. involvement in World War I and World War II, respectively.

FOCUS QUESTIONS

1. What were the main characteristics of Roosevelt's foreign policy and why was the American public bent on isolationism during the 1930s?

2.   What were the steps that America took to try and remain neutral as Europe headed into World War II?

3.   What steps did Germany and Japan take to lead America into the European conflict?

CHAPTER THEMES

Theme: In the early and mid-1930s, the United States attempted to isolate itself from foreign involvements and wars. But by the end of the decade, the spread of totalitarianism and war in Europe forced Roosevelt to provide more and more assistance to desperate Britain, despite strong isolationist opposition.

CHAPTER SUMMARY

Roosevelt's early foreign policies, such as wrecking the London economic conference and establishing the Good Neighbor policy in Latin America, were governed by concern for domestic recovery and reflected America's desire for a less active role in the world. America virtually withdrew from all European affairs, and promised independence to the Philippines as an attempt to avoid Asian commitments.

Depression-spawned chaos in Europe and Asia strengthened the isolationist impulse, as Congress passed a series of Neutrality Acts designed to prevent America from being drawn into foreign wars. The United States adhered to the policy for a time, despite the aggression of Italy, Germany, and Japan. But after the outbreak of World War II in Europe, Roosevelt began to provide some aid to the Allies.

After the fall of France, Roosevelt gave greater assistance to desperate Britain in the destroyers-for-bases deal and in lend-lease. Still-powerful isolationists protested these measures, but Wendell Willkie refrained from attacking Roosevelt's foreign policy in the 1940 campaign.

Roosevelt and Winston Churchill issued the Atlantic Charter, and by the summer of 1941, the United States was fighting an undeclared naval war with Germany in the North Atlantic. After negotiations with Japan failed, the surprise attack on Pearl Harbor plunged the United States into World War II.

DEVELOPING THE CHAPTER: SUGGESTED LECTURE OR DISCUSSION TOPICS

- Explain the causes of American isolationism in the 1930s: domestic depression, disillusion with World War I, hostility to arms dealers, and other merchants of death.

    REFERENCE: Manfred Jonas, *Isolationism in America, 1935–1941* (1966).

- Examine the erosion of isolationism in response to the aggressions of Benito Mussolini, Adolf Hitler, and the Japanese warlords. Show the transition in American thinking from indifference to fear for democracy, as appeasement only fed the dictators' appetites.

    REFERENCE: David M. Kennedy, *Freedom from Fear* (1999).

- Describe the fierce debates between internationalists and isolationists, especially from 1939 to 1941. The emphasis might be on Roosevelt's carefully calibrated strategy of increasing aid at each stage, but never so rapidly as to hand the isolationists a political victory.

    REFERENCE: Kenneth S. Davis, *Franklin D. Roosevelt: Into the Storm, 1937–1941* (1993).

- Discuss the Japanese-American negotiations and the conflicts that set the stage for Pearl Harbor.

    REFERENCE: Donald Cameron Watt, *How the War Came: The Immediate Origins of the Second World War, 1938–1939* (1989).

FOR FURTHER INTEREST: ADDITIONAL CLASS TOPICS

- Focus on the merchants of death Nye hearings. Discuss how 1930s isolationism was strongly aimed at the factors that had supposedly led the United States into World War I.

- Examine the rise of Mussolini, Hitler, and the Japanese militarists. Consider why Americans were appalled by their doctrines, even if they did not want to fight them.

- Analyze the isolationist-internationalist debate, especially over lend-lease. Point out the isolationists' argument that such aid would inevitably lead to war and the internationalists' argument that helping Britain was the way to stay out of war. Consider whether FDR acted wisely in moving the United States closer to involvement.

- Discuss the causes of the Pacific war from the Japanese point of view. Consider whether the war was inevitable.

- Conduct a class debate over the following topic: for example, The United States Should Give Lend-Lease Aid to Great Britain. Primary source readings will come from the following book: *Opposing Viewpoints in American History—Volume II: From Reconstruction to the Present*, San Diego, CA: Greenhaven Press, 1996. Another good source of debate topics is Larry Madaras and James M. SoRelle, *Taking Sides—Clashing Views on Controversial Issues in American History, Volume II: Reconstruction to the Present*, Connecticut: McGraw-Hill, 2000.

- Show students the following video: *The Century—America's Time* (ABC Video in association with The History Channel), *Volume II: 1936–1941: Over the Edge*. "As Adolph Hitler's feared Third Reich cuts a deadly path through Europe, Americans must weigh the option of becoming involved in another bloody, global conflict."

- Show the students Charlie Chaplin's *The Great Dictator* (1940). Discuss the imagery and symbolism in the movie—what was Chaplin's purpose of satirizing Adolph Hitler? Was it effective? Why do you think the movie was so controversial?

- Use various aids (photographs, films, documents) to illustrate the Holocaust. Consider why many of the refugees felt grateful to America for providing a haven, but frustrated at their inability to do more for their fellow Jews.

- Use some examples of the work of Jewish refugee artists, composers, scientists, or writers (for example, Marc Chagall, Kurt Weill, Albert Einstein, Hannah Arendt, and Erich Fromm) to illustrate the refugee immigrants' cultural contribution to America. Consider how such contributions may have differed from the second- and third-generation cultural achievements of some other immigrant groups.

CHARACTER SKETCHES

Adolf Hitler (1889–1945)

Hitler was regarded as a vulgar laughingstock in Germany in the 1920s, but he eventually ruled more of Europe than anyone since Napoleon.

The son of a minor Austrian bureaucrat who was over fifty years old when Adolf was born, Hitler constantly envisioned himself as a great artist, but his grades and talent were so poor that he failed to get into a Vienna art school. He later painted pictures and baked them so he could sell them for high prices as valuable works by old masters.

Hitler was a total failure until he joined the German army during World War I and became completely caught up in the German cause. Through long years of speaking in beer halls, Hitler became adept at reading audiences. His emotional, ranting speeches had great hypnotic power. Except on matters of war and politics, Hitler was totally ignorant and had banal or vicious views that he nevertheless considered the thoughts of genius.

Quote: "Man has become great through struggle.... Whatever goal man has reached is due to his originality plus his brutality.... Through all the centuries force and power are the determining factors...." (*Mein Kampf,* 1924)

REFERENCE: Alan Bullock, *Hitler: A Study in Tyranny* (1962).

Winston Churchill (1874–1965)

Churchill was a powerful British politician and statesman, long before his heroic leadership against the Nazis in World War II.

Churchill's father was Lord Randolph Churchill, a descendant of the seventeenth-century duke of Marlborough. Churchill later wrote a biography of his distinguished ancestor, Marlborough. His mother was an American, and he always cherished his half-American ancestry.

The brash young Churchill dashed around the remote spots of the British Empire at its height in the 1890s, seeking adventure and glory. He found it during the Boer War and wrote dramatic accounts of how he escaped from Boers by hiding under floorboards.

Churchill became the powerful first lord of the admiralty during World War I at age thirty-nine, but the daring Gallipoli campaign in Turkey that he organized proved a disaster. Churchill then lost influence and spent much of the 1920s and 1930s as a political outcast, until the rise of Nazism gave him a new opportunity. He was stubborn and self-willed and almost childish in his vanity and outbursts of temper. Yet he was warm-hearted, generous, courageous, and capable of strong sympathy with others. During the London blitz, he insisted on sharing the hardships of the people and often wept when he saw bombed-out houses and churches.

Quote: "We shall fight on the beaches, we shall fight in the fields and streets, we shall fight in the hills, we shall never surrender." (Speech, 1940)

REFERENCE: William Manchester, *The Last Lion: Winston Spencer Churchill*, 2 vols. (1983, 1988).

Joseph Stalin (1879–1953)

Stalin's name and picture were everywhere in Russia during his brutal rule, but after de-Stalinization, his name and image were completely erased from the Soviet Union.

Stalin's real name was Joseph Dzhugashvili. He later chose Stalin (steel) as his revolutionary name. Stalin's parents sent him to a seminary to become a priest, but he joined revolutionary movements and was expelled.

At the height of his tyranny in the 1930s, Stalin exiled or killed millions of people, including even his closest associates and one of his own family members. His second wife committed suicide in 1932, leaving a letter accusing him of numerous crimes. For many years, all Soviet artists, writers, musicians, scientists, and others had to sing Stalin's praises and have their work approved by him. He was suspicious, cruel, and paranoid but could exude great charm on occasion.

Quote: "It may be asked how could the Soviet government have consented to conclude a non-aggression pact with such perfidious...fiends as Hitler and Ribbentrop? Was this not an error on the part of the Soviet government? No.... We secured to our country peace for a year and a half and the opportunity of preparing our forces." (1941)

REFERENCE: Adam Ulam, *Stalin: The Man and His Era* (1973).

GREAT DEBATES IN AMERICAN HISTORY

Great Debate (1939–1941)

Isolationism versus internationalism. Should the United States move away from isolationist neutrality and toward aiding the Allies in the fight against Hitler?

Yes: The internationalists, led by President Roosevelt and the administration; most big-business leaders and cosmopolitan city-dwellers; the Committee to Defend America by Aiding the Allies, led by William Allen White.

No: The isolationists, led by the America First Committee and Charles A. Lindbergh; some senators and representatives, led by William Borah, Robert Taft, and Hamilton Fish; some writers, like Charles Beard and Harry Elmer Barnes; some small-business and ethnic groups, especially in the Midwest; some leftists and socialists, led by Norman Thomas.

ISSUE #1: Isolation. Should the United States have any interest in events overseas?

Yes: Internationalist Roosevelt: "It becomes clearer and clearer that the world will be a shabby and dangerous place to live in—yes, even for Americans to live in—if it is ruled by force in the hands of a few…. I hope that we shall have fewer American ostriches in our midst. It is not good for the ultimate health of ostriches to bury their heads in the sand."

No: Isolationist poet Oliver Allstrom:
"Over there," there's mud and shedding of blood
And tongues confusing and strange.
So why lend a hand to an alien band
Whose dreams we can never change?

"No, no," comes the cry from the U.S. sky,
"We'll never be Allied tools.
Nor again parade in a foreign brigade
Like saps in a squad of fools."

"And Europe may strut through its bloody rut
And scheme with her Babel-snares.
But we'll stay home, this side of the foam
And mind our own affairs!"

ISSUE #2: Democracy. Are the Allies fighting for the democratic principles America believes in?

Yes: Internationalist Congressman Jerry Voorhis: "I have an interest in the way of life wherein free men can freely struggle to better their conditions, freely worship and believe according to their own conscience…. I know that this is not possible in a Nazi- or Communist-dominated nation. So…to aid Great Britain and the other nations attempting to resist the totalitarians has become part of American policy."

No: Isolationist Congressman Hamilton Fish: "The cause for which Hitler has thrown the German masses into war is damnably unholy. But the war of Chamberlain and Reynaud is not thereby rendered holy. The fact that Hitler is the opponent does not make the Allied war a fight for democracy…. The Allied governments have no idealism in the conflict, no war aims worthy of the sacrifice…of their peoples…."

ISSUE #3: War. Will aiding the Allies inevitably lead the United States into war?

No: Internationalist Roosevelt: "There is a far less chance of the United States getting into war if we do all we can now to support the

Yes: Isolationist Senator Arthur Vandenberg: "When H.R. 1776 [lend-lease] passed the Senate…we did vastly more than 'aid Britain.'

nations defending themselves against attack by the Axis than if we acquiesce in their defeat, submit tamely to an Axis victory, and wait our turn to be the object of attack in another war later on…. There is no demand for sending an American Expeditionary Force outside our own borders. There is no intention by any member of your government to send such a force. You can, therefore, nail any talk about sending armies to Europe as deliberate untruth."

We have thrown ourselves squarely into the power politics and the power wars of Europe, Asia, and Africa…. We have said to Britain, 'We will see you through to victory.' And it would be unbelievably dishonorable for us to stop short of full participation in the war if that be necessary to a victory…. But I fear this means we must actively engage in the war ourselves."

ISSUE #4: War and democracy. Would another war require dictatorial methods and destroy democracy within the United States?

No: Internationalist Roosevelt: "I reject the idea that only by abandoning our freedom, our ideals, our way of life, can we build our defenses adequately, can we match the strength of the aggressors…. I do not share these fears."

Yes: Isolationist socialist Norman Thomas: "The method of modern totalitarian warfare is self-defeating in terms of ideal ends. War itself is the only victor. Each particular war begets its more deadly successors. Intolerance, dictatorship, brutality, are its inevitable accompaniments…."

REFERENCES: William Langer and S. Everett Gleason, *The Challenge to Isolation, 1937–1940* (1952); Kenneth Davis, *FDR: Into the Storm, 1937–1940* (1993); Wayne Cole, *Charles Lindbergh and the Battle Against American Intervention in World War II* (1974).

QUESTIONS FOR CLASS DISCUSSION

1. Why did the neutrality laws fail to prevent America's growing involvement with the military conflicts in Europe and Asia?

2. How did the process of American entry into World War II compare with the entry into World War I?

3. Would it have been more straightforward of Roosevelt to have openly called for a declaration of war against Hitler rather than increasing involvement gradually while claiming that he did not want war?

4. Would the United States have entered World War II even if the Japanese had not attacked Pearl Harbor?

CHAPTER 35

America in World War II, 1941–1945

AP FOCUS

- Early in the war, Germany, Japan, and Italy have considerable military success. The Allies, except for France, which had surrendered in 1940, are fortunate not to be overwhelmed completely.

- Fearing that they will be disloyal, President Roosevelt orders the detention of Japanese Americans, a serious violation of basic American civil rights. See the photograph and the passage by a young Japanese-American woman in *The American Pageant* (14th ed., pp. 876, 877/15th ed., pp. 799, 802).

- Millions die in the Holocaust, a systematic attempt by the Nazis to destroy those they consider to be inferior—Slavs, the mentally ill, homosexuals, political prisoners, and, especially, Jews.

- The war occasions extensive demographic changes (one of the AP themes). Urban areas expand to meet the demand for labor in war-related industries. Rural and less-developed areas in the West and Southwest grow as well, a result of receiving government military contracts.

- As in every American war, blacks contribute significantly in World War II, despite the obstacles placed before them. But the military will not be desegregated until 1948.

- The considerable financial resources needed to wage war drive up the national debt. In fact, New Deal spending pales in comparison with wartime military expenditures—see the chart on the national debt (14th ed., p. 885/15th ed., p. 808).

- The success of the D-Day landing in the summer of 1944 affords the Allies a bridgehead in France from which they can move inland and ultimately invade Germany itself. With the Soviets counterattacking from the east and the British and Americans closing in from the west, Hitler's Third Reich is doomed. In April 1945, shortly after Hitler killed himself, Germany surrenders, a victory President Roosevelt does not see, having died suddenly the month before.

- With the war in Europe over, the Allies turn all of their attention to defeating Japan. After bloody battles in the Pacific, President Truman orders atomic bombs dropped on Hiroshima and Nagasaki, inflicting enormous civilian casualties. Japan soon surrenders.

AP teachers should take note of the following:

1. See the photograph and poster (14th ed., p. 881/15th ed., p. 804), depicting the important role women played in the war effort; they replaced male workers who were in the military.

2. In 1944, FDR successfully won reelection for a fourth term, in large part, because of the military successes and grassroots support from such groups as organized labor.

Focus on Historical Thinking:

Have students state what they consider to be the most important political, economic, and social changes World War II caused domestically, using one clear, concise sentence for each type of change.

FOCUS QUESTIONS

1. How was America transformed from a peacetime to a wartime economy? What were the steps that America took to mobilize for their war with the Axis powers?

2. What was the impact of the war on domestic America?

3. What was America's strategy for winning the war against the Axis powers?

4. What turned the tide of the war in the Pacific for American troops?

5. How did World War II end and what were the terms of settlement?

CHAPTER THEMES

Theme: Unified by Pearl Harbor, America effectively carried out a war mobilization effort that produced vast social and economic changes within American society.

Theme: Following its "get Hitler first" strategy, the United States and its Allies invaded and liberated conquered Europe from Fascist rule. The slower strategy of island-hopping against Japan also proceeded successfully until the atomic bomb brought a sudden end to World War II.

CHAPTER SUMMARY

America was wounded but roused to national unity by Pearl Harbor. Roosevelt settled on a fundamental strategy of dealing with Hitler first, while doing just enough in the Pacific to block the Japanese advance.

With the ugly exception of the Japanese-American concentration camps, World War II proceeded in the United States without the fanaticism and violations of civil liberties that occurred in World War I. The economy was effectively mobilized, using new sources of labor such as women and Mexican *braceros*. Numerous African Americans and Indians also left their traditional rural homelands and migrated to war-industry jobs in the cities of the North and West. The war brought full employment and prosperity, as well as enduring social changes, as millions of Americans were uprooted and thrown together in the military and in new communities across the country. Unlike European and Asian nations, however, the United States experienced relatively little economic and social devastation from the war.

The tide of Japanese conquest was stemmed at the Battles of Midway and the Coral Sea, and American forces then began a slow strategy of island hopping toward Tokyo. Allied troops first invaded North Africa and Italy in 1942–1943, providing a small, compromise second front that attempted to appease the badly weakened Soviet Union as well as the anxious British. The real second front came in June 1944 with the D-Day invasion of France. The Allies moved rapidly across France, but faced a setback in the Battle of the Bulge in the Low Countries.

Meanwhile, American capture of the Marianas Islands established the basis for extensive bombing of the Japanese home islands. Roosevelt won a fourth term as Allied troops entered Germany and finally met the Russians, bringing an end to Hitler's rule in May 1945. After a last round of brutal warfare on Okinawa and Iwo Jima, the dropping of two atomic bombs ended the war against Japan in August 1945.

DEVELOPING THE CHAPTER: SUGGESTED LECTURE OR DISCUSSION TOPICS

*   Explain the basic strategic military decisions of the war. The emphasis might be on the fact that there were, in a sense, two separate wars that had to be conducted simultaneously and that the European war required delicate political and military coordination with Britain and Russia.

    REFERENCE: H.P. Willmott, *The Great Crusade: A New Complete History of the Second World War* (1990).

- Describe the social and economic changes brought by the war. Particular attention could be given to war-spawned prosperity after the depression and to the beginnings of the Sunbelt migrations that continued in the postwar era, including the African American exodus to the North and West.

  REFERENCE: John W. Jeffries, *Wartime America: The World War II Homefront* (1996).

- Examine the major military battles in Europe, Asia, and the Middle East, and their relation to the political tensions among the United States, Britain, and the Soviet Union.

  REFERENCES: Gerhard Weinberg, *A World at Arms* (1990); David M. Kennedy, *Freedom from Fear* (1999).

- Analyze the events of the war against Japan, including the development and use of the atomic bomb. The emphasis might be on the controversy over why the bomb was used.

  REFERENCES: Martin J. Sherwin, *A World Destroyed: The Atomic Bomb and the Grand Alliance* (1975); Ronald Spector, *Eagle Against the Sun: The American War with Japan* (1985).

FOR FURTHER INTEREST: ADDITIONAL CLASS TOPICS

- Examine the role of women during the war. Discuss the text's point that American women's lives were not altered as much as were the lives of women in other belligerent nations.

- Discuss the varieties of warfare conducted by American forces during the conflict, ranging from the savage island fighting in the Pacific to the strategic bombing of German and Japanese military and civilian targets.

- Focus on Roosevelt, Churchill, and Stalin as the Big Three wartime leaders. Perhaps use their major decision-making meetings—Casablanca, Teheran, Yalta—to define the stages of the war.

- Analyze the immediate and long-term consequences of the war. Show how the basic international structure of the postwar world was determined by World War II, including the rivalry between the United States and the Soviet Union.

- Conduct a class debate over the following topics: for example, The Internment of Japanese-Americans Was Justified and The United States Should Not Drop the Atomic Bomb on Japan. Primary source readings will come from the following book: *Opposing Viewpoints in American History—Volume II: From Reconstruction to the Present*, San Diego, CA: Greenhaven Press, 1996. Another good source of debate topics is Larry Madaras and James M. SoRelle, *Taking Sides—Clashing Views on Controversial Issues in American History, Volume II: Reconstruction to the Present*, Connecticut: McGraw-Hill, 2000.

- Show students the following videos: *The Century—America's Time* (ABC Video in association with The History Channel), *Volume III: Civilians at War*: "For the first time in history, more civilians than soldiers are killed during wartime. From Nazi concentration camps, to the blitz of London, to the atomic bombings of Japan, ordinary citizens come face-to-face with the horrors of war." **Warning:** this is a very graphic episode—some students may find the images very disturbing. *Volume III: 1941–1945: Homefront*: "The Japanese attack Pearl Harbor and force American industries to retool for the Allies' war effort. As a result, The Great Depression lifts, making way for Southern blacks and women to enter the work force in record numbers."

CHARACTER SKETCHES

A. Philip Randolph (1889–1979)

Randolph was the longtime head of the Brotherhood of Sleeping Car Porters and an early black civil rights advocate.

A black minister's son, Randolph became converted to socialism. In 1917, he and Chandler Owen started a radical black magazine, *The Messenger,* which called World War I a "white man's war" and urged blacks to refuse to fight—in contrast to W.E.B. Du Bois's support for the war effort and black soldiers.

In the 1920s, Randolph was considered a political spokesman for the racially conscious "new negro," who emerged especially in Harlem and other northern ghettos. In 1925, Pullman porters, who were the lowest-paid rail workers and were all patronizingly called "George," approached Randolph and asked him to head their union. In 1937, the brotherhood finally won a contract.

Randolph's proposed March on Washington in 1941 never occurred, but the idea remained alive in the black community, and Randolph was one of the speakers at the 1963 March on Washington where Martin Luther King Jr. delivered his "I Have a Dream" speech.

Quote: "This is an hour of crisis.… To American Negroes, it is the denial of jobs in government defense projects. It is racial discrimination in government departments. It is widespread Jim-Crowism in the armed forces of the Nation.… What a runaround! What a disgrace! What a blow below the belt!" (Call for March on Washington, 1941)

REFERENCES: Paula Pfeffer, *A. Philip Randolph: Pioneer of the Civil Rights Movement* (2001); William Harris, *Keeping the Faith: A. Philip Randolph, Milton Webster, and the Brotherhood of Sleeping Car Porters* (1977).

Douglas MacArthur (1880–1964)

MacArthur was the American army commander in the Pacific in World War II, the governor of occupied Japan, and the UN commander who was fired by President Truman during the Korean War.

His father, Arthur MacArthur, was a famous American officer in the Civil War, Spanish-American War, and Philippine War. Douglas MacArthur's strong-arm tactics in ousting the Bonus Army from Washington in 1932 made him a controversial figure, and he remained surrounded by controversy for much of his career.

Although he is best known for saying "I shall return" to the Philippines, MacArthur's greatest military accomplishment in World War II was actually his difficult battles in New Guinea and Los Negros.

MacArthur was virtually the absolute ruler of Japan from 1945 to 1947, and many Japanese looked on him as a kind of "white emperor." Republicans several times approached MacArthur about running for president, but he always refused. In public, MacArthur was arrogant, egotistical, and self-promoting, but in private he was more genial and easygoing.

Quote: "When I joined the Army, even before the turn of the century, it was the fulfillment of all my boyish hopes and dreams.… I still remember the refrain of one of the most popular barrack ballads of that day, which proclaimed, most proudly, that 'Old soldiers never die. They just fade away.' And like the old soldier of that ballad, I now close my military career and just fade away." (Speech to Congress, 1951)

REFERENCES: William Manchester, *American Caesar* (1978); Geoffrey Parrett. *Old Soldiers Never Die: The Life of Douglas MacArthur* (1996).

George Patton (1885–1945)

Patton was the American tank commander of World War II whose belligerent behavior and ideas made him a focus of controversy.

Descended from Revolutionary and Confederate officers, Patton grew up captivated by tales of his ancestors' heroic military exploits. He was raised on his wealthy grandfather's California estate and did not attend school until he was twelve years old.

Patton's tactical skill, especially in the conquest of Sicily, earned great praise, but he was nearly fired from his command when he slapped and browbeat two shell-shocked GIs in an army hospital. Eisenhower reprimanded Patton but permitted him to remain at his post, deciding that his military ability was necessary to the war.

After his spectacular tank breakthrough across France, he entered Germany but became embroiled in further controversy when he advocated that American forces continue on and fight the Russians and that they use Nazi officials and soldiers to do so. Patton was an extreme personality, known for his hysterical outbursts, his constant profanity, and his sentimentality.

Quote: "Americans love to fight, traditionally. All real Americans love the sting and clash of battle. America loves a winner. America will not tolerate a loser." (Speech to his troops before D-Day, 1944)

REFERENCE: Martin Bluminson, *Patton: The Man Behind the Legend, 1888–1945* (1985).

QUESTIONS FOR CLASS DISCUSSION

1. How did America's domestic response to World War II differ from its reaction to World War I?

2. What was the wisest strategic decision in World War II, and what was the most questionable?

3. How were the European and Pacific wars similar and how were they different?

4. What was the significance of the dropping of the atomic bomb, then and now?

MAKERS OF AMERICA: THE JAPANESE

Questions for Class Discussion

1. How were the Japanese immigrants similar to other immigrants from East Asia, such as the Chinese and Filipinos? How were they different?

2. Should the World War II internment experience be seen as the most significant event in the Japanese-American experience? How did it affect those who lived through it and their descendants?

Suggested Student Exercises

- Use photographs or documents from early Japanese immigrants to glean their views of the United States.

- Consider the lives and careers of some prominent Japanese-Americans (such as Senator Daniel Inouye of Hawaii) in relation to the general Japanese-American experience.

EXPANDING THE "VARYING VIEWPOINTS"

- Gar Alperovitz, *Atomic Diplomacy* (rev. ed., 1985).

  A view of the atomic bomb as aimed at Russia rather than Japan:

"The decision to use the weapon did not derive from overriding military considerations.... *Before the atomic bomb was dropped each of the Joint Chiefs of Staff advised that it was highly likely that Japan could be forced to surrender 'unconditionally,' without use of the bomb and without an invasion....* Unquestionably, political considerations related to Russia played a major role in the decision; from at least mid-May American policy makers hoped to end the hostilities before the Red Army entered Manchuria.... A combat demonstration was needed to convince the Russians to accept the American plan for a stable peace."

- Martin Sherwin, *A World Destroyed* (1975).

A view of the atomic bomb as primarily aimed at Japan:

"Caught between the remnants of war and the uncertainties of peace, policymakers and scientists were trapped by their own unquestioned assumptions.... The secret development of this terrible weapon, during a war fought for a total victory, created a logic of its own: a quest for a total solution of a set of related problems that appeared incapable of being resolved incrementally.... As Szilard first suggested in January 1944, the bomb might provide its own solution.... The decision to use the bomb to end the war could no longer be distinguished from the desire to use it to stabilize the peace."

QUESTIONS ABOUT THE "VARYING VIEWPOINTS"

1. Assess the validity of the claim that the dropping of the bombs on Japan was not so much an attempt to end the war against the Japanese, as it was "the first salvos in the emerging Cold War."

2. What does each of these historians see as American officials' thinking about the relationship between the bomb and the ending of the war against Japan? What does each regard as the primary reason for the use of the bomb?

3. What conclusions might be drawn from each of these views about the political and moral justifications for dropping the bomb? Could the use of the atomic bombs have been avoided?

CHAPTER 36

The Cold War Begins, 1945–1952

AP FOCUS

- At the end of World War II, the U.S. economy suffers from a variety of maladies, but once the economy rebounds, the nation experiences an economic boom that will last until the early 1970s.

- Between 1945 and 1960, the nation witnesses a huge "baby boom."

- A major housing shortage is eased, as suburban communities are developed. The fastest growing region is the Sunbelt, stretching from Florida to California. Drawn by jobs, a temperate climate, and lower taxes, many Americans relocate from the industrial Northeast. (See the map in *The American Pageant,* 14th ed., p. 916/15th ed., p. 835) Demographic Changes is an AP theme.

- Tensions between the United States and the Soviet Union intensify after the war, as the former allies now eye each other with growing (and dangerous) mistrust, which turns into the Cold War.

- The Marshall Plan and the Truman Doctrine are put in place to contain communism in Eastern Europe. The map in the textbook (14th ed., p. 930/15th ed., p. 848), shows the flow of U.S. foreign aid.

- When the Soviets test their first nuclear weapon in 1949, the United States loses its atomic monopoly. The Cold War spreads to China, Korea, and other areas in Asia.

- Believing that communist sympathizers are imbedded in American public and private institutions, the House Un-American Activities Committee launches an investigation designed to find them.

- Thinking Globally (14th ed., pp. 924–925/15th ed., pp. 842-843) highlights the role of the United States in shaping the political and economic world order following World War II.

AP teachers should take note of the following:

1. Historians debate the causes and responsibility for starting the Cold War. Some claim that hostility and tension were prevalent even before World War II was over.

2. Historians also debate the use of atomic weapons in Japan. Some contend that President Truman's decision, in the long run, saved both American and Japanese lives. Critics contend that dropping the bombs was the first act of the Cold War, one designed to intimidate the Soviets, and that given Japan's willingness to surrender, using the bombs was not necessary.

3. In 1948, the Soviets blocked access roads into West Berlin in an effort to absorb it into communist East Berlin, and therefore, the Soviet sphere of influence. President Truman thwarted the move by ordering that supplies be airlifted to the city. The Berlin airlift lasted for a year.

4. Suburban development meant that middle- and lower-middle–class Americans could have the American Dream of owning a home, removed from the congestion and problems associated with urban life. Critics complained that suburban communities were off limits to blacks, bred conformity, and exacted a high ecological toll in the form of lost farms and undeveloped land.

Focus on Historical Thinking:

> Have students create a timeline of what they consider to be the fifty most important bits of specific factual information from 1607 to 1945.

FOCUS QUESTIONS

1. What were some of the reasons for the postwar anxieties and prosperity brought about after World War II?

2. What were the reasons for the standoff between the United States and the Soviet Union?

3. What major issues needed to be resolved in the postwar years in Europe and Japan?

4. What role did each of the following play with regard to the Cold War; Berlin airlift, containment policy, Marshall Plan, Truman Doctrine, NATO, and the Korean War?

5. What domestic concerns were brought about as a result of the Cold War?

CHAPTER THEMES

Theme: America emerged from World War II as the world's strongest economic power and commenced a postwar economic boom that lasted for two decades. A bulging population migrated to the suburbs and Sunbelt, leaving the cities increasingly to minorities and the poor.

Theme: The end of World War II left the United States and the Soviet Union as the two dominant world powers, and they soon became locked in a Cold War confrontation. The Cold War spread from Europe to become a global ideological conflict between democracy and communism. Among its effects were a nasty hot war in Korea and a domestic crusade against disloyalty.

CHAPTER SUMMARY

In the immediate postwar years, there were widespread fears of a return to depression. But fueled by cheap energy, increased worker productivity, and government programs such as the GI Bill of Rights, the economy began a spectacular expansion that lasted from 1950 to 1970. This burst of affluence transformed American industry and society, and particularly drew more women into the workforce.

Footloose Americans migrated to the Sunbelts of the South and West, and to the growing suburbs, leaving the northeastern cities with poorer populations. Families grew rapidly, as the baby boom created a population bulge that would last for decades.

The Yalta agreement, near the end of World War II, left major issues undecided and created controversy over postwar relations with the Soviet Union. With feisty Truman in the White House, the two new superpowers soon found themselves at odds over Eastern Europe, Germany, and the Middle East.

The Truman Doctrine announced military aid and an ideological crusade against international communism. The Marshall Plan provided economic assistance to starving and communist-threatened Europe, which soon joined the United States in the NATO military alliance.

The Cold War and revelations of spying aroused deep fears of communist subversion at home that culminated in McCarthy's witch-hunting. Fear of communist advances abroad and social change at home generated national and local assaults on many people perceived to be different. Issues of the Cold War and civil rights fractured the Democratic Party three ways in 1948, but a gutsy Truman campaign overcame the divisions to win a triumphant underdog victory.

The Communist Chinese won a civil war against the Nationalists. North Korea invaded South Korea, and the Americans and Chinese joined in fighting the seesaw war to a bloody stalemate. MacArthur's insubordination and threats to expand the war to China led Truman to fire him.

DEVELOPING THE CHAPTER: SUGGESTED LECTURE OR DISCUSSION TOPICS

- Explain the changes in American economic development since World War II. The emphasis might be on America's uncontested postwar economic domination and on the eventual weakening of the heavy-industrial base and the turn to other economic activities.

  REFERENCE: John Patrick Diggins, *The Proud Decades: America in War and Peace, 1941–1960* (1988).

- Explain the complex causes of the Cold War. The emphasis might be on the vacuum of power created by the destruction of Europe and the decline of Britain, as well as on the specific ideological and political battles over Poland, Germany, and Greece.

  REFERENCES: Daniel Yergin, *Shattered Peace* (1977); Melvyn P. Leffler, *A Preponderance of Power: National Security, the Truman Administration, and the Cold War* (1992).

- Examine the rise of suburbs in relation to the changes in postwar economic, social, and racial life. Consider suburbia as an expression of both rising affluence and geographic mobility (especially in the South and West). Perhaps consider some of the critics and defenders of the suburbs in the 1950s.

  REFERENCE: Kenneth Jackson, *Crabgrass Frontier* (1986).

- Analyze the connection between the Cold War abroad and the hunt for subversion at home, perhaps focusing on the difference between the attacks on actual Soviet spies and the broader attack on all American Communists and the use of the Communist charge as a way to smear and suppress all sorts of people with unconventional views and lifestyles.

  REFERENCES: Richard Fried, *Nightmare in Red* (1990); Ellen Schrecker, *Many Are the Crimes* (1998).

FOR FURTHER INTEREST: ADDITIONAL CLASS TOPICS

- Contrast the economic, social, and cultural life of a typical family of the 1940s and 1950s and a similar family of the 1990s.

- Examine the significance of divided Germany and the captive nations of Eastern Europe in the Cold War.

- Analyze one or more of the key subversion cases—for example, the Hiss or Rosenberg cases. Consider how they became decades-long symbols of Cold War divisiveness.

- Discuss the frustrations of Korea as a limited and stalemated war. Special emphasis could be placed on the firing of MacArthur.

- Conduct a class debate over the following topics: for example, America Should Seek Peace with the Soviet Union and Communist Subversives Threaten America. Primary source readings will come from the following book: *Opposing Viewpoints in American History—Volume II: From Reconstruction to the Present*, San Diego, CA: Greenhaven Press, 1996. Another good source of debate topics is Larry Madaras and James M. SoRelle, *Taking Sides—Clashing Views on Controversial Issues in American History, Volume II: Reconstruction to the Present*, Connecticut: McGraw-Hill, 2000.

- Show students the following video: *The Century—America's Time* (ABC Video in association with The History Channel), *Volume III: 1946–1952: Best Years*. "Exhausted but victorious, American GIs return home to a changed nation. The enormous task of rebuilding Europe falls to the only capable country—the U.S. But after four grueling years of battle, would we be up to the job? "

- Have the students read Hannah Arendt's "Ideology and Terror" (1953) in David A. Hollinger and Charles Capper's (Editors), *The American Intellectual Tradition: Volume II—1865 to the Present*, New York: Oxford University Press, 2001.

- Have the students read selections from Erik H. Erikson's *Childhood and Society* (1950) in David A. Hollinger and Charles Capper's (Editors), *The American Intellectual Tradition: Volume II—1865 to the Present*, New York: Oxford University Press, 2001.

- Have the students examine America's involvement during the cold war by reading selections from Ernest R. May, *American Cold War Strategy—Interpreting NSC 68* (1993).

- Have the students explore the issues surrounding McCarthyism by reading selections from Ellen W. Schrecker, *The Age of McCarthyism—A Brief History with Documents* (2002).

CHARACTER SKETCHES

Benjamin Spock (1903–1998)

Spock is the pediatrician whose child-rearing guide, *Baby and Child Care*, has been used by millions of American parents.

A 1929 graduate of Columbia Medical School, Spock became a well-known New York pediatrician for such people as Margaret Mead. He wrote *Baby and Child Care* while serving in the navy during World War II. The book has sold over 25 million copies—the best-selling original title ever published in the United States.

Although the book was criticized as permissive, it was actually a moderate reaction against the rigid feeding schedules and strict discipline imposed by child-care experts of the 1920s and 1930s.

Spock became an active opponent of the Vietnam War in the 1960s. He was indicted and convicted for encouraging draft resistance, but the conviction was overturned on appeal in 1969. In 1972, he ran as the presidential candidate of the small People's Party. Even in his radical political activities, his image was that of a kindly, grandfatherly gentleman.

Quote: "I may as well let the cat out of the bag as far as my opinion goes and say that strictness or permissiveness is not the real issue. Good-hearted parents who aren't afraid to be firm when necessary can get good results with either strictness or moderate permissiveness." (*Baby and Child Care*, 1946)

REFERENCE: Thomas Maier, *Dr. Spock: An American Life* (1998).

Harry S Truman (1884–1972)

Truman was the Missouri haberdasher and machine politician who came to be regarded as one of the great American presidents.

The *S* in the middle of Truman's name did not stand for anything. Both of his grandfathers had *S* names, so his parents just gave Harry the letter rather than choose either one.

Being very nearsighted, even as a boy, Truman spent much time playing the piano and reading history. His hero in American history was Andrew Jackson.

Truman worked on the family farm and at many odd jobs before becoming a popular artillery officer in World War I—an experience that remained one of the highlights of his life. The men's clothing store he started in 1919 failed two years later, and he then began his career in machine politics. Judge Truman controlled a large patronage army but was never involved in corruption.

His quick temper and blunt-spoken ways were legendary. He often wrote angry letters to critics but only occasionally mailed them.

Quote: "The Republicans work for the benefit of the few bloodsuckers who have offices in Wall Street. This is a crusade of the people against the special interests, a crusade to keep the country from going to the dogs. You back me up and we'll win that crusade." (Campaign speech, 1948)

REFERENCE: David McCulloch, *Truman* (1992).

George Kennan (1904–2005)

Kennan was the American diplomat and ambassador to Russia who is credited with formulating the containment policy but later became a critic of many American Cold War policies, including Vietnam.

There was a distantly related nineteenth-century George Kennan whose career eerily paralleled that of the twentieth-century Kennan. Both were born on the same day, and both became leading American Russia scholars and diplomats of their time.

Kennan served as a U.S. diplomat in Germany and Riga, Latvia, before World War II. He became a scholarly expert on Russia, and his telegrams to Washington, based partly on his close observations of Stalin and the Russians, set out the basic principles of containment even before he wrote his "X" article in *Foreign Affairs.*

Kennan's brief term as ambassador to the Soviet Union in 1952 was cut short when the Soviet government expelled him, supposedly for critical remarks he had made about the communist rulers. Kennan later objected to the militarization of American foreign policy and ironically became, in the 1960s and 1970s, probably the most influential critic of the American Cold War policies he is credited with initiating.

Quote: "There is nothing—I repeat nothing—in the history of the Soviet regime which could justify us in assuming that the men who are now in power in Russia, or even those who have chances of assuming power within the foreseeable future, would hesitate for a moment to apply this power against us if by so doing they thought it would materially improve their power position in the world." (Telegram to Washington, 1945)

REFERENCES: George F. Kennan, *Memoirs, 1925–1950* (1967); David Meyers, *George Kennan and the Dilemmas of U.S. Foreign Policy* (1998); a collection of all of Kennan's published articles in Foreign Affairs, < http://www.foreignaffairs.org/background/kennan>, last accessed August 2008.

Thomas Dewey (1902–1971)

Dewey was the losing Republican presidential candidate in 1944 and 1948.

Originally a student of music, Dewey tried for an opera-singing career in Chicago. In 1931, he became the youngest ever U.S. attorney, and in 1935, he became a special prosecutor for racketeering, going after such notorious gangsters as Dutch Schultz and Lucky Luciano. His career as a relentless prosecutor formed the basis for several Hollywood movies.

Dewey grew his mustache to please his wife, who liked it, but his advisers constantly urged him to shave it off, saying it made him look sinister. Although he was lively and pungent in private, Dewey was obsessed with maintaining a proper public image. He never allowed himself to be photographed except in a tie and vest.

He long remained a power in Republican politics and helped engineer the nominations of Dwight Eisenhower and Richard Nixon.

Quote: "I do not know about the accommodations at the White House for the family…. There is of course no rush about it." (Letter, fall 1948)

REFERENCE: Richard Norton Smith, *Thomas E. Dewey and His Times* (1982).

QUESTIONS FOR CLASS DISCUSSION

1. Which development caused the greatest change in American society in the immediate postwar years: increased affluence, the migration to the suburbs, the entry of women into the workforce, or the baby boom?

2. Was the primary threat from the Soviet Union military or ideological—that is, was the danger that the Soviet army would invade Western Europe or that more and more people in Europe and elsewhere would be attracted to communist ideas?

3. Were there any legitimate concerns behind the red-hunting anticommunism of the late 1940s and early 1950s? How were McCarthy and others able to turn the search for spies and subversives into an assault on freethinkers, adulterers, homosexuals, and others deemed different in some way?

4. Was Truman right to fire MacArthur when and how he did? What would have happened if MacArthur had gotten his way and expanded the conflict with the Chinese?

MAKERS OF AMERICA: THE SUBURBANITES

Questions for Class Discussion

1. To what extent was the migration to suburbia a flight from the city and its problems, and to what extent was it a flight to a vision of a new pastoral way of life?

2. Were the new problems that accompanied the early growth of suburbia, for example, traffic congestion, pollution, racial segregation, and the confinement of women to domestic roles, a result of the suburban migration itself, or would they have come to the fore even if most postwar Americans had continued to live in central cities?

Suggested Student Exercises

*   Examine the maps of four or five major metropolitan areas of the United States to discover the geographic relations of central cities to suburbs. Looking at maps over the course of several decades (for example, from 1950, 1965, 1980, and 1995), examine the growth of suburban settlement patterns, and consider their relation to patterns of railroads, highways, and mass transit in areas where it has a prominent role (for example, Washington, D.C., Chicago, Atlanta, San Francisco).

*   Select a dozen or more major American corporations, and determine the location of their corporate headquarters in relation to central cities and suburbs. Consider the extent to which the traditional pattern of "live in the suburbs, work in the city" has been altered in some metropolitan areas, and to what extent it remains in place.

EXPANDING THE "VARYING VIEWPOINTS"

*   Walter LaFeber, *America, Russia, and the Cold War, 1945–1984* (1985).

    A view of the United States as primarily responsible for the Cold War:

    "Having failed to budge the Russians in face-to-face negotiations, even when backed by atomic bombs, the State Department next tried to buckle Stalin's iron fence with economic pressures.... More important, it made American officials ponder the awful possibility that Stalin's ambitions included not only strategic positions in Eastern Europe, but the imposition of Communist regimes upon Asia and the Middle East. Stating the Soviet dictator's alternatives in this way no doubt badly distorts his true policies.... Stalin's thrusts after 1944 were rooted more in the Soviets' desire to secure certain specific strategic bases, raw materials, and above all, to break up what Stalin considered to be the growing Western encirclement of Russia.... However, American officials saw little reason to worry about such distinctions."

- John Lewis Gaddis, *The United States and the Origins of the Cold War* (1972).

A view of the Cold War as caused primarily by Soviet aggression:

"If one must assign responsibility for the Cold War, the most meaningful way to proceed is to ask which side had the greater opportunity to accommodate itself, at least in part, to the other's position, given the range of alternatives as they appeared at the time. Revisionists have argued that American policy-makers possessed greater freedom of action, but their view ignores the constraints imposed by domestic policies.... The Russian dictator was immune from pressures of Congress, public opinion, or the press.... This is not to say that Stalin wanted a Cold War.... But his absolute powers did give him more chances to surmount the internal restraints on his policy than were available to his democratic counterparts in the West."

QUESTIONS ABOUT THE "VARYING VIEWPOINTS"

1. How does each of these historians see American and Soviet motives in the Cold War?

2. On what basis does each assign primary responsibility for initiating Cold War conflicts?

3. How would each of these historians likely interpret the confrontation over Greece and the Truman Doctrine?

CHAPTER 37

The Eisenhower Era, 1952–1960

AP FOCUS

- The economic boom is further stimulated by advances in science and technology. More Americans than ever become white-collar workers. Opportunities for women gradually open up, as the chart in *The American Pageant* (14th ed., p. 945/15th ed., p. 862) shows. But as older smokestack industries, the foundation of union membership, begin to contract, so too do unions themselves. Remember the AP theme of Economic Transformations.

- Television and TV advertising fundamentally transform the social, political, and cultural landscape of the nation in ways that few could predict in the early 1950s.

- Fearful of communist sympathizers, the public is susceptible to the rhetoric and accusations of Senator Joseph McCarthy of Wisconsin, and the second Red Scare grips the nation for years.

- The *Brown* v. *Board of Education* decision by the Supreme Court in 1954 requires white Americans to accept black citizens as their equals in regard to education. In the process of negating the *Plessy* v. *Ferguson* (1896) "separate but equal" decision, the court overturns (legally, at least) years of racial segregation. When the governor of Arkansas blocks integration in Little Rock, the president sends in the U.S. Army to enforce the law of the land.

- The inability of the United States to assist the Hungarian revolutionaries to break free from Soviet hegemony in 1956 illustrates the limits of brinksmanship.

- With the creation of NATO and the Soviet's response, the Warsaw Pact, two armed camps stare each other down. However, some steps are taken to ease the Cold War. Eisenhower even warns Americans of the dangers of a rapidly developing military-industrial complex.

- The successful Cuban revolution, led by Fidel Castro in 1959, shows the limits of the containment policy even in the Western Hemisphere, as Castro soon aligns himself with the Soviet Union.

AP teachers should take note of the following:

1. Rosa Parks's refusal to give up a seat on a bus to a white person sparked a successful local boycott and showed Americans the demeaning status of blacks. The boycott brought into the national spotlight Dr. Martin Luther King, Jr. Slavery and its legacies in North America is an AP theme.

2. The Eisenhower Doctrine, which can be seen as an extension of the Truman Doctrine, was spurred by the Suez Crisis and growing Arab nationalism.

3. In 1954, the United States backed a coup against the democratically elected leftist government of Guatemala as part of the American effort to keep communism out of the Western Hemisphere. Another motive was to protect the financial investments of American companies in Guatemala.

4. Religion was an issue in the 1961 election as John Kennedy, a Catholic, ran for president; the country had never elected a Catholic president. Religion is an AP theme.

Focus on Historical Thinking:

> Have students compare and contrast (either in chart or essay form) the 1920s and the 1950s with regard to the political, social, and economic changes associated with each decade.

FOCUS QUESTIONS

1. What was the driving force behind the affluence and the consumer culture of the 1950s?

2. How did the Brown decision and the confrontation in Little Rock set the stage for the civil rights movement of the 1950s?

3. What were the differences between Eisenhower's foreign policy and those of his predecessors in the battle of the Cold War?

4. What were the major issues facing Eisenhower in Europe and Asia?

5. How did the literature reflect the attitudes and feelings during the 1950s?

CHAPTER THEMES

Theme: The Eisenhower years were characterized by prosperity and moderate conservatism at home and by the tensions of the Cold War abroad.

Theme: The 1950s witnessed a huge expansion of the middle class and the blossoming of a consumer culture. Crucial to the development of a new lifestyle of leisure and affluence was the rise of the new technology of television.

Theme: While Dwight Eisenhower and the majority of Americans held to a cautious, family-oriented perspective on domestic social questions, an emerging civil rights movement and the influence of television and popular music presented challenges to the spirit of national consensus.

CHAPTER SUMMARY

Using the new medium of television to enhance his great popularity, grandfatherly "Ike" was ideally suited to soothe an America badly shaken by the Cold War and Korea. Eisenhower was slow to go after Joseph McCarthy, but the demagogue's bubble finally burst. Eisenhower also reacted cautiously to the beginnings of the civil rights movement but sent troops to Little Rock to enforce court orders. While his domestic policies were moderately conservative, they left most of the New Deal in place.

Despite John Dulles's tough talk, Eisenhower's foreign policies were also generally cautious. He avoided military involvement in Vietnam, although aiding Diem, and pressured Britain, France, and Israel to resolve the Suez crisis.

He also refused to intervene in the Hungarian revolt and sought negotiations to thaw the frigid Cold War. Dealing with Nikita Khrushchev proved difficult, as Sputnik, the Berlin Crisis, the U-2 incident, and Fidel Castro's Cuban revolution all kept Cold War tensions high. In a tight election, Senator John Kennedy defeated Eisenhower's vice president, Richard Nixon, by calling for the country to "get moving again" by more vigorously countering the Soviets.

American society grew ever more prosperous in the Eisenhower era, as science, technology, and the Cold War fueled burgeoning new industries such as electronics and aviation. Women joined the movement into the increasingly white-collar workforce, and chafed at widespread restrictions they faced.

A new consumer culture, centered on television, fostered a new ethic of leisure and enjoyment, including more open expressions of sexuality in popular entertainment. Intellectuals and artists criticized the focus on private affluence rather than the public good. The abstract expressionism of Jackson Pollock and the "Pop" Art of Andy Warhol challenged traditional views of painting. Many mainstream writers focused on the dilemmas of modern post-war society, particularly on the problems of middle-class suburbanites. Formerly under-represented groups such as Jewish, African American, and southern writers had a striking new impact on American culture.

DEVELOPING THE CHAPTER: SUGGESTED LECTURE OR DISCUSSION TOPICS

- Describe the general domestic atmosphere of the Eisenhower years: broad economic prosperity (with occasional recessions) and broad social consensus based on the New Deal and anticommunism. The emphasis might be on seeing this harmony as a reaction to the turbulent 1930s and 1940s and also noting some of the hidden anxieties of the time.

  REFERENCE: David Halberstam, *The Fifties* (1993).

- Explain the up-and-down atmosphere of the Cold War in the 1950s. Note the general improvement in relations from Stalin's day, but also the numerous conflicts and the arms race that constantly threatened nuclear annihilation.

  REFERENCE: Thomas J. McCormick, *America's Half Century: U.S. Foreign Policy in the Cold War* (1989).

- Examine the growing importance of civil rights issues in the 1950s, as illustrated by *Brown* v. *Board of Education* and King's Montgomery bus boycott. The slow pace of court-ordered desegregation might be contrasted with the increasing determination of blacks to attack the still pervasive Jim Crow system.

  REFERENCE: Taylor Branch, *Parting the Waters: America in the King Years, 1954–1963* (1988).

- Consider the initial impact of television on all areas of American life in the 1950s, including politics, consumption (advertising), family life, religion, and popular culture.

  REFERENCE: Lynn Spiegel, *Make Room for TV: Television and the Family Ideal in Postwar America* (1992).

FOR FURTHER INTEREST: ADDITIONAL CLASS TOPICS

- Focus on the Army-McCarthy hearings and the decline, at last, of "low-blow Joe." Perhaps discuss Eisenhower's reluctance to take on McCarthy when he was popular.

- Consider America's relation to the French war in Vietnam or the installation of the shah in Iran. Discuss how American policies, while avoiding immediate conflicts, sowed the seeds of later, more serious difficulties.

- Examine the Kennedy-Nixon campaign of 1960 for the specific light it shed on wider themes of the time, including anticommunism, the new importance of television, and tensions that accompanied the movement of previously marginal groups like Catholics into the center of American life.

- Consider the relation between economic transformations and the role of women in the 1950s. Show both the new emphasis on domesticity and childrearing, and the beginnings of rebellion by suburban women.

- Conduct a class debate over the following topics: for example, Racial Segregation in Public Schools Is Unconstitutional, The Suburbs: The New American Dream, and America Should Send a Man to the Moon. Primary source readings will come from the following book: *Opposing Viewpoints in American History—Volume II: From Reconstruction to the Present*, San Diego, CA: Greenhaven Press, 1996. Another good source of debate topics is Larry Madaras and James M. SoRelle, *Taking*

Sides—Clashing Views on Controversial Issues in American History, Volume II: Reconstruction to the Present, Connecticut: McGraw-Hill, 2000.

- Show students the following video: *The Century—America's Time* (ABC Video in association with The History Channel), *Volume IV: 1953–1960: Happy Daze.* "Despite America's renewed identity and prosperity, paranoia about Communism gives rise to the 'witch-hunts' of McCarthyism. The sound of a new generation emerges as rock 'n' roll fills the airwaves, while African Americans, angered at their second-class citizenship, let their discontent be known. "

- Have the students read Sloan Wilson's *The Man in the Gray Flannel Suit* (1955). Use this novel to discuss the tensions faced by average Americans during the height of the 1950s. This was made into an award-winning movie in 1956.

- Have the students watch the movie *Edward Scissorhands* (1990). What is the symbolism of this movie—how does it portray life of the 1950s? Does it do so in a positive or negative light? The movie is rated PG-13.

- Have the students read selections from C. Wright Mills's *White Collar: The American Middle Classes* (1951), *The Sociological Imagination* (1959), and *The Power Elite* (1956). Important works in American Intellectual Thought of the 1950s.

- Have the students read C. Wright Mills's "Letter to the New Left" (1960) in David A. Hollinger and Charles Capper's (Editors), *The American Intellectual Tradition: Volume II—1865 to the Present*, New York: Oxford University Press, 2001.

- Have the students watch the movie *Invasion of the Body Snatchers* (1956). In what ways can this be seen as a critique of McCarthyism and the notion of Big Brother? The movie is unrated.

- Have the students read Jack Kerouac's *On the Road* (1957). Why is this novel known as the Bible of the Beat Generation?

- Have the students watch political campaign commercials from the Living Room Candidate website, especially the elections of 1952 and 1960; have the students discuss the role of TV on politics (http://www.livingroomcandidate.org/index.php), last accessed August 2008.

CHARACTER SKETCHES

Joseph McCarthy (1908–1957)

McCarthy was the demagogic Wisconsin senator whose name has entered the dictionary as a synonym for exaggerated and irresponsible attacks on others' reputations.

He began his career as a small-time Wisconsin judge before serving as an intelligence officer in World War II. McCarthy never saw military action and resigned before the war was over, but he later fabricated the story that, as "tail-gunner Joe," he had been wounded in air battles.

Before he launched his anticommunist crusade, McCarthy was primarily known in the Senate for his personal rudeness and for backing the soft-drink industry. McCarthy's speeches attacking alleged communists in government were nothing new, but his constant claim to have evidence (which somehow never appeared) kept him always on the offensive. McCarthy was loud, vulgar, boisterous, and self-promoting. He lied so constantly and grandly that no one knew when he was telling the truth, perhaps not even himself.

Quote: "[General Marshall] is part of a conspiracy so immense and in infamy so black as to dwarf any previous such venture in the history of man.... [There is] a pattern which finds his decisions maintained with great stubbornness and skill, always and invariably serving the world policy of the Kremlin." (1951)

REFERENCES: Arthur Herman, *Joseph McCarthy* (1999); Richard Rovere, *Senator Joe McCarthy* (1959).

John Foster Dulles (1888–1959)

Dulles was Eisenhower's secretary of state and a leading architect of American strategy in the Cold War.

The son of a New York Presbyterian minister, Dulles grew up under strong religious influences, which stayed with him all his life. His maternal grandfather, John Watson Foster, had been secretary of state under Benjamin Harrison, and Dulles met such men as William Taft, Andrew Carnegie, and Bernard Baruch when they visited his father.

Dulles served in the American delegation at Versailles but in the 1930s, he became the leading Republican expert on foreign policy. In 1936, he made a controversial speech that expressed sympathy for Germany and appeared to welcome Nazism. Dulles's brother Allen was a top American intelligence officer in World War II and later head of the CIA.

Always a controversial personality, Dulles expressed firm opinions and engaged in moral posturing that grated on many people, including Churchill and Eisenhower, but he often won them over by the force of his character and intelligence.

Quote: "Some say we were brought to the verge of war. Of course we were brought to the verge of war.... If you try to run away from it, if you are scared to go to the brink, you are lost." (1956)

REFERENCE: Leonard Mosely, *Dulles* (1978).

Dwight David Eisenhower (1890–1969)

Eisenhower's rise from obscure colonel to supreme Allied commander in World War II was spectacular, but Marshall and others had long taken note of his talents and marked him for future advancement.

His parents were basically of middle-class background, but at the time of Eisenhower's birth, his father had been laid off, and the family had temporarily moved from Abilene, Kansas, to Denison, Texas, where "Ike" was born.

Eisenhower and George Patton were both reprimanded for urging the use of tanks in World War I. During his World War II years in Europe, "Ike" spent much time with his driver, Kay Summersby, leading to rumors that he and Mamie planned to divorce.

His excellent personal relations with Soviet Marshal Zhukov gave Eisenhower a different view of the Russians and led him to seek personal contacts with them.

Before the 1952 campaign he tried to teach Nixon how to fish and was disappointed when his running mate proved unwilling or unable to learn the sport.

Quote: "My first day at the President's desk. Plenty of worries and difficult problems. But such has been my portion for a long time. The result is that this seems (today) like a continuation of all I've been doing since July 1941—even before that." (Diary entry, January 1953)

REFERENCE: Stephen Ambrose, *Eisenhower* [2 vols.] (1983, 1984).

Rosa Parks (1913–2005)

Parks is the black seamstress whose refusal to move to the back of a bus in Montgomery, Alabama, on December 5, 1955, set off a bus boycott and the beginning of the civil rights movement.

Even though she took her action on her own, Parks had previous acquaintance with black protest ideas and leaders. As a young woman, she had tried to organize an NAACP youth chapter in Montgomery, though without success. She had met A. Philip Randolph and Roy Wilkins and knew black leaders in Montgomery. She was also a leader in her local church, St. Paul AME Church.

She had planned ahead that she was going to sit in the front of the bus that day and refuse to move. After her arrest, she went to E.D. Nixon, head of the local Brotherhood of Sleeping Car Porters, who circulated leaflets calling for the wider protest.

Parks worked with the civil rights movement for years. She moved to Detroit in 1967 and remained active in black causes.

Quote: "I just decided I was not going to be moved out of that seat." (Interview, 1978)

REFERENCE: Douglas Brinkley, *Rosa Parks* (2000).

Elvis Aron Presley (1935–1977)

Presley was the rock-and-roll star who helped transform American popular musical styles in the 1950s and after.

Presley grew up in Memphis, Tennessee, where he learned both gospel music and black blues music. His first recordings were done for Sam Phillips, a producer who had been looking for a white singer who sounded like a black man. After signing a contract with RCA Victor in 1955, his career came under the control of Colonel Tom Parker, who promoted him into a national phenomenon.

Presley's sexually suggestive style led to many protests from parents and conservative groups, as a result of which he was shown only from the waist up in his first television appearance in 1956. Presley's thirty-three movies were nearly as popular as his records and his drafting into the army in 1960 was treated as a major event. After his death, his home in Memphis became a virtual pilgrimage shrine for his fans.

Quote: "Please, Mr. Sholes, don't make me stand still. If I can't move I can't sing." (To a record producer, 1954)

REFERENCE: Albert Harry Goldman, *Elvis* (1981).

MAKERS OF AMERICA: THE GREAT AFRICAN AMERICAN MIGRATION

Questions for Class Discussion

1. Why did World War II finally provide the historic impetus to cause African Americans to leave their ancient conditions of oppression in the rural South?

2. What benefits did African Americans gain from their migration north and west, and what problems did they still have?

Suggested Student Exercises

*   Use photographs or other documents of the African American migration to northern cities in the World War II era. Examine what evidence the photographs provide about the economic conditions of the migrants.

*   Read passages from one of the novels of the era, for example, Richard Wright's *Native Son* or Ralph Ellison's *Invisible Man,* to illustrate the feelings and perceptions of African Americans as they entered life in the large northern cities. Wright's autobiography, *Black Boy,* also explains the conditions and aspirations that led many young blacks to leave the rural South and move north.

QUESTIONS FOR CLASS DISCUSSION

1. How does Eisenhower's political leadership compare with that of other general-presidents: Washington, Jackson, Taylor, and Grant?

2. Was Eisenhower's seeming caution and inactivity a lack of vigorous leadership or a wise prudence in the exercise of power?

3. Was the 1950s a time of American triumph abroad and affluence at home, or was it a period that actually suppressed many problems of race, women's roles, and cultural conformity?

4. Which writers and artists best expressed the concerns of American culture in the 1950s? Was there a connection between the rise of pop-culture figures such as Elvis Presley and Marilyn Monroe and the changes in art and writing (such as the Beats and the new southern writers)?

5. Compare and contrast the literary outpouring of World War I with that of World War II. What caused the shift from a realism in literature to a more fantasized and psychedelic prose?

CHAPTER 38

The Stormy Sixties, 1960–1968

AP FOCUS

- President Kennedy launches his New Frontier. His domestic program addresses education, health care, and equal employment opportunities. He also calls for a more vigorous space program.

- The Soviet decision to stem the tide of refugees from East Berlin to the West by constructing the Berlin Wall exacerbates Cold War tensions and exposes the nature of Soviet hegemony.

- Inheriting a CIA-backed scheme, developed during the Eisenhower administration, JFK approves the plan to help Cuban exiles bring down Castro's regime. The attempted coup fails miserably.

- In a standoff that brings the superpowers close to a military confrontation, the Cuban missile crisis is, to the relief of the world, resolved after considerable maneuvering by both sides.

- The struggle for racial equality continues, despite interference and obstructionism by assorted local and state governments. The Kennedy administration works to confront these obstacles, but it is often grassroots movements that propel the crusade. See the quote from Kennedy's 1963 civil rights address in *The American Pageant* (14th ed., p. 982/15th ed., p. 898).

- Kennedy's assassination in 1963 stuns the nation. Lyndon Johnson finishes out JFK's term and wins election in his own right in a landslide victory in 1964, over his conservative Republican opponent, Barry Goldwater. Johnson launches an ambitious program, the Great Society, designed to address poverty and a multitude of other societal problems and promote racial justice. Two key civil rights bills pass despite efforts by southern congressmen to block them: the 1964 Civil Rights Act and the 1965 Voting Rights Act. The Great Society brought dramatic reform (an AP theme).

- As a growing insurgency, supported by communist North Vietnam, threatens to topple the U.S.-backed government of South Vietnam, Johnson escalates U.S. involvement in Southeast Asia. With the 1968 Tet offensive, the tide of the Vietnam War turns against the United States.

- The 1960s is a turning point in the civil rights movement (for blacks, women, Native Americans, and gays). Concurrently, people begin to challenge what they view as oppressive cultural, social, and moral norms of American society; some even identify with the "counterculture." Seeing the direction the nation is taking as secular and valueless, many turn to Christian fundamentalism. Religion—an AP theme—will increasingly become enmeshed in politics.

AP teachers should take note of the following:

1. In a trend that started after World War II, a Republican, Barry Goldwater, carried most of the Deep South in the 1964 presidential race. He lost the election, but the next Republican candidate, Richard Nixon, benefited handsomely from white southerners' exodus from the Democratic Party.

2. The black civil rights movement was not cohesive. Radical black leaders held that nonviolence was too passive in the face of outrageous attacks on black citizens and their white supporters. Militant, even violent black groups and leaders, such as the Black Panthers and the charismatic Malcolm X, emerged. Compare Martin Luther King's and Malcolm X's messages (14th ed., p. 990/15th ed., p. 905).

Focus on Historical Thinking:

> Have students complete a Main Idea Log for each section in the text narrative. Students should write out each section heading, turn it into a question, and answer that question in one clear, concise sentence.

FOCUS QUESTIONS

1. What was Kennedy's New Frontier? How was that philosophy played out, both domestically and internationally, within the first few years of Kennedy's administration?

2. What was flexible response and how was that different from the foreign policy philosophy of the previous administrations?

3. How did Kennedy and Johnson deal with the civil rights issue? What were their goals and were these goals actualized by the end of the decade?

4. What role did each of the presidents have within the Vietnam conflict?

5. What were the major goals of Johnson's Great Society? How successful were they?

CHAPTER THEMES

Theme: The Kennedy administration's flexible response doctrine to combat Third World communism bore ill fruit in Cuba and especially Vietnam. Johnson's massive escalation of the war failed to defeat the Communist Vietnamese forces, while growing domestic opposition finally forced him from power.

Theme: The Kennedy administration's domestic stalemate ended in the mid-1960s, as Johnson's Great Society and the black civil rights movement brought a tide of liberal social reform. But the diversion of resources and the social upheavals caused by the Vietnam War wrecked the Great Society.

CHAPTER SUMMARY

Kennedy's New Frontier initiatives bogged down in congressional stalemate. Cold War confrontations over Berlin and Russian missiles in Cuba created threats of war. Countering Third World communism through flexible response led the administration into dangerous involvement in Vietnam and elsewhere.

Johnson succeeded Kennedy and overwhelmingly defeated Goldwater. The black movement for integration and voting rights won great victories. Johnson used his huge congressional majorities to push through a mass of liberal Great Society legislation. Northern black ghettos erupted in violence amid calls for black power.

Johnson escalated military involvement in the Dominican Republic and Vietnam. As the number of troops and casualties grew without producing military success, dovish protests against the war gained strength. Political opposition forced Johnson not to seek reelection, and the deep Democratic divisions over the war allowed Nixon to win the White House.

DEVELOPING THE CHAPTER: SUGGESTED LECTURE OR DISCUSSION TOPICS

*   Explain the Kennedy administration's vigorous activism in the Cold War, both against the Russians and against Third World communists. The emphasis might be on the contrast between relative success dealing with the Russians (for example, the Cuban missile crisis) versus frustration in the Third World (for example, the Bay of Pigs and Vietnam).

    REFERENCE: James N. Giglio, *The Presidency of John F. Kennedy* (1991).

- Examine the black movements of the sixties, from civil rights to black power, perhaps focusing on the fact that the nonviolent movement's great successes in integration and voting rights were not considered adequate by those trapped in northern black ghettos.

  REFERENCE: Harvard Sitkoff, *The Struggle for Black Equality, 1954–1980* (1981).

- Describe the escalation of the Vietnam War. Explain the political as well as the military side of the war (for example, the constant fear that the Saigon government would collapse if the United States did not provide greater support).

  REFERENCES: Stanley Karnow, *Vietnam: A History* (1983); Marilyn B. Young, *The Vietnam Wars, 1945–1990* (1991).

- Consider the domestic political and social turmoil of the sixties, brought on by social and cultural upheavals as well as Vietnam. Point out the deep polarization of American society, as evidenced by the turbulent events of 1968.

  REFERENCES: Allen Matusow, *The Unraveling of America* (1984); Maurice Isserman and Michael Kazin, *America Divided: The Civil War of the 1960s* (2000).

FOR FURTHER INTEREST: ADDITIONAL CLASS TOPICS

- Focus on the Kennedy image. Compare the vision of Camelot with the historical realities of Kennedy's performance as president and controversies over his private behavior and character.

- Use Martin Luther King Jr.'s life and work to explain the principles of the nonviolent civil rights movement. Perhaps show how King came under assault from some whites and blacks during his lifetime for being either too militant or not militant enough.

- Discuss the causes and consequences of the Vietnam War. Consider why it so divided American society.

- Examine the cultural rebellions of the 1960s in relation to traditional American values such as distrust of authority and individualism. Examine the sexual revolution and the changes in the family as they impacted broader issues of public authority and the role of institutions like the school and church.

- Conduct a class debate over the following topics: for example, U.S. Actions in Vietnam Are Justified and America's Youth Must Lead a New Revolution. Primary source readings will come from the following book: *Opposing Viewpoints in American History—Volume II: From Reconstruction to the Present*, San Diego, CA: Greenhaven Press, 1996. Another good source of debate topics is Larry Madaras and James M. SoRelle, *Taking Sides—Clashing Views on Controversial Issues in American History, Volume II: Reconstruction to the Present*, Connecticut: McGraw-Hill, 2000.

- Show students the following videos: *The Century—America's Time* (ABC Video in association with The History Channel), *Volume IV: 1960–1964: Poisoned Dreams*: "President John Kennedy balances the explosive Cuban missile crisis while suppressing clashes between the races over equal rights at home. Kennedy emerges as the preeminent global power broker, but his assassination leaves an indelible wound on the American psyche." *Volume IV: 1965–1970: Unpinned*: "With no end in sight to the Vietnam War, the radical 'counterculture' erupts in violent protest. Political and cultural norms are challenged through music, literature and style, reflecting the country's most turbulent era during the century's second half."

- Have the students read Daniel Bell's "The End of Ideology in the West" (1960) in David A. Hollinger and Charles Capper's (Editors), *The American Intellectual Tradition: Volume II—1865 to the Present*, New York: Oxford University Press, 2001.

- Have the students read Martin Luther King Jr. "Letter from a Birmingham Jail" (1963) and Malcolm X's "The Ballot or the Bullet" (1964) in David A. Hollinger and Charles Capper's (Editors) *The American Intellectual Tradition: Volume II—1865 to the Present*, New York: Oxford University Press, 2001.

- Have the students read Betty Friedan's "Selection from *The Feminine Mystique*" (1963) in David A. Hollinger and Charles Capper's (Editors), *The American Intellectual Tradition: Volume II—1865 to the Present*, New York: Oxford University Press, 2001.

- Have the students watch the following movies *Malcolm X, JFK, Nixon, Thirteen Days*, and *All the President's Men*.

- Have the students explore the speeches and writings of Kennedy. Robert Dallek and Terry Golway, *Let Every Nation Know: John F. Kennedy in His Own Words* (2006), a book with a listening CD of excerpts of Kennedy's most famous speeches along with background information on each speech; Theodore C. Sorensen (Editor), *"Let the Word go Forth"—The Speeches, Statements, and Writings of John F. Kennedy* (1988); The American Presidency Project, (http://www.presidency.ucsb.edu/), last accessed August 2008.

- Have the students explore the programs of Johnson. James MacGregor Burns (Editor), *To Heal and to Build—The Programs of President Lyndon B. Johnson* (1968).

- Have the students watch the presidential campaign commercials, The Living Room Candidate, (http://www.livingroomcandidate.org/index.php), last accessed August 2008.

CHARACTER SKETCHES

Lyndon Baines Johnson (1908–1973)

Johnson was a highly skilled Senate majority leader in the 1950s and was frustrated by his powerlessness as Kennedy's vice president.

The son of a flamboyant Texas state senator, Lyndon often joined him amid the colorful, corrupt atmosphere of Austin. Johnson's first venture into politics came at San Marcos Teachers' College, where he formed a student political group, the White Stars, to take control of campus activities and jobs from a rival group, the Black Stars.

Johnson briefly taught high school in Houston and organized successful student debate teams that traveled all over the state. He became a congressional assistant in Washington and learned to imitate the congressman's voice on the phone well enough to carry on extensive conversations with callers.

Roosevelt treated Johnson as a special young protégé and invited him to go sailing as a particular favor. Johnson lost his first Senate race in 1941 but won his next try in 1948 by eighty-seven votes—a result that earned him the nickname "Landslide Lyndon."

Quote: "I knew from the start that I was bound to be crucified either way I moved. If I left the woman I loved—the Great Society—in order to get involved with that bitch of a war on the other side of the world, then I would lose everything at home. All my programs, all my dreams. But if I left that war and let the communists take over South Vietnam, then I would be seen as a coward and my nation would be seen as an appeaser and we would find it impossible to accomplish anything for anyone anywhere on the entire globe." (Conversation, 1970)

REFERENCE: Robert Dallek, *Lone Star Rising: Lyndon Johnson and His Times, 1908–1960* (1991).

Martin Luther King Jr. (1928–1968)

King was much criticized in his lifetime, but in 1986, his birthday began to be celebrated as a national holiday—the first such honor given to a black American.

He came from a long line of Baptist preachers. His father, Martin Luther King Sr. was pastor at Ebenezer Baptist Church in Atlanta, and Martin Jr. was for a time copastor with him.

King and his wife, Coretta Scott, both came from the middle-class Atlanta black community. He experienced sharper discrimination when he went north to study theology. King earned his doctorate from Boston University with a dissertation on the doctrine of God and also studied the nonviolent teachings of Gandhi. Later, he and his wife visited India to learn more about Gandhian techniques.

During King's civil rights campaign in Chicago in 1966, he lived in a ghetto slum on the West Side. His outspoken attacks on the Vietnam War caused considerable criticism that he was not sticking to civil rights issues. At the time of his assassination, he was conducting a campaign for black garbage workers in Memphis.

Quote: "When we let freedom ring, when we let it ring from every village and every hamlet, from every state and every city, we will be able to speed up that day when all of God's children, black men and white men, Jews and Gentiles, Protestants and Catholics, will be able to join hands and sing in the words of that old Negro spiritual, 'Free at last! Free at last! Thank God almighty, we are free at last!'" ("I Have a Dream" speech, 1963)

REFERENCE: David L. Garrow, *Bearing the Cross*: *Martin Luther King and the Southern Christian Leadership Conference* (1986).

John Fitzgerald Kennedy (1917–1963)

Kennedy achieved a narrow victory in 1960 and, for most of his time in office, had to battle for political support, but after his assassination he entered the pantheon of national heroes.

Through much of his youth, Kennedy struggled to compete with his more athletic and glamorous older brother, Joseph Kennedy Jr. After Joe's combat death in World War II, John took his place as the focus of his father's ambitions for the presidency.

Kennedy's Harvard senior thesis was published as a book, *Why England Slept,* with the aid of his father. During his youth, Kennedy was often seriously ill with back troubles compounded by Addison's disease, which was thought to be life-threatening. In 1954, he underwent major back surgery and missed the Senate vote censuring Joseph McCarthy.

Kennedy was cool, skeptical, sardonic, and well read. He had a reputation as a playboy but was also a sober, well-disciplined, determined politician who used his abilities to the fullest.

Quote: "Let the word go forth from this time and place, to friend and foe alike, that the torch has been passed to a new generation of Americans, born in this century, tempered by war, disciplined by a hard and bitter peace, proud of our ancient heritage, and unwilling to witness or permit the slow undoing of those human rights to which this nation has always been committed, and to which we are committed today at home and throughout the world." (Inaugural address, 1961)

REFERENCES: Herbert Parmet, *Jack: The Struggles of John F. Kennedy* (1980); Herbert Parmet, *JFK: The Presidency of John F. Kennedy* (1983); Thomas Reeves, *A Question of Character: A Life of John Kennedy* (1991).

Robert Francis Kennedy (1925–1968)

Kennedy was the younger brother of President John Kennedy who became a leader of the anti–Vietnam War movement before his assassination during the presidential campaign of 1968.

The third of the Kennedy brothers, Robert had great difficulty keeping up with his older, favored brothers Josep, Jr. and John. For much of his political career he operated in the background as John Kennedy's political manager and adviser.

Kennedy was long distrusted by liberals because of his association with Senator Joseph McCarthy and by labor because of his involvement with Senate committees investigating union racketeering. During his years as attorney general (1961–1964), he carried on a fierce prosecution of Teamster boss James Hoffa and eventually saw him convicted.

Kennedy became deeply depressed after his brother's assassination, but revived once he resigned as attorney general and won election as U.S. senator from New York in 1964. He disliked Johnson intensely, but at first hesitated to break with him because he thought Johnson would regard Kennedy's antiwar position as a purely personal vendetta.

Quote: "Few will have the greatness to bend history itself, but each of us can work to change a small portion of events, and in the total of all those acts will be written the history of this generation." (*To Seek a Newer World,* 1967)

REFERENCE: Arthur M. Schlesinger Jr., *Robert F. Kennedy and His Times* (1978).

GREAT DEBATES IN AMERICAN HISTORY

Great Debate (1961–1973):

Vietnam. Should the United States fight a major war in Vietnam in order to save the anticommunist government of South Vietnam from falling to the Communist Vietnamese?

Yes: Vietnam "hawks," led by President Johnson and his administration; the Cold War foreign-policy establishment; many political conservatives, led by Barry Goldwater and Richard Nixon; many labor groups, led by George Meany.

No: Vietnam "doves," led by Senators Morse, Fulbright, and McCarthy; some foreign-policy experts, led by George Kennan, Walter Lippmann, and Hans Morgenthau; many students and other young people.

ISSUE #1: Should the United States fight a war to preserve freedom and independence for the South Vietnamese anticommunists?

Yes: "Hawk" President Johnson: "The first reality is that North Vietnam has attacked the independent nation of South Vietnam. Its object is total conquest.... Women and children are strangled in the night because their men are loyal to their government. And helpless villages are ravaged by sneak attack.... Our objective is

No: "Dove" journalist Neil Sheehan: "The regimes [of South Vietnam] were and are composed of men...who are allied with mandarin families.... Most of the men who rule Saigon have, like the Bourbons, learned nothing and forgotten nothing. They seek to retain what privileges they have and to regain those they have lost....

the independence of South Vietnam and its freedom from attack. We want nothing for ourselves—only that the people of South Vietnam be allowed to guide their country in their own way."

The Communist party is the one truly national organization that permeates both North and South Vietnam. The men who lead the party today…directed the struggle for independence from France and in the process captured much of the deeply felt nationalism of the Vietnamese people."

ISSUE #2: Should the United States fight a war in Vietnam to prevent the spread of communism to the rest of Asia and beyond?

Yes: "Hawk" President Johnson: "Let no one suppose that a retreat from Vietnam would bring an end to conflict. The battle would be renewed in one country and then another. The central lesson of our time is that the appetite of aggression is never satisfied.… There are those who say that all our effort there will be futile—that China's power is such that it is bound to dominate all Southeast Asia. But there is no end to that argument until all of the nations of Asia are swallowed up."

No: "Dove" Senator J. William Fulbright: "The war is described as an exemplary war, a war, that is, that will prove to the communists once and for all that so-called 'wars of national liberation' cannot succeed. In fact, we are not proving that. It is said that if we were not fighting in Vietnam we would have to be fighting much closer to home, in Hawaii or even California. I regard this contention as a slander on the U.S. Navy and Air Force.… I do not accept your [Secretary Rusk's] version as to why there may be an intrusion of communist forces into Thailand.… As long as the war is going on, isn't this fact an incitement to intrusion by the other side?"

ISSUE #3: Should the United States fight a war in Vietnam to fulfill the commitments it has made and preserve its national credibility as a great power?

Yes: "Hawk" President Johnson: "Our power, therefore, is a very vital shield. If we are driven from the field in Vietnam, then no nation can ever again have the same confidence in American promise or American protection.… Three Presidents—President Eisenhower, President Kennedy, and your present President— over 11 years have committed

No: "Dove" Senator Stuart Symington: "I believe what is going on now in Vietnam has hurt the concept of our capability in the minds of our friends and allies as well as our enemies. It has hurt the national will in this country because of increasing dissension and I am afraid it has made the people who are opposed to us reduce their belief in our capacity."

themselves and have promised to defend this small and valiant nation.… We just cannot now dishonor our word, or abandon our commitment, or leave those who believed us and trusted us to the terror and repression and murder that would follow."

ISSUE #4: Are the goals in Vietnam worth the cost to the United States of fighting the war?

Yes: "Hawk" President Johnson: "Peace will come also because America sent her sons to help secure it. It has not been easy—far from it.… I have lived daily and nightly with the cost of this war. I know the pain it has inflicted.… Throughout this entire long period, I have been sustained by a single principle: that what we are doing now, in Vietnam, is vital not only to the security of Southeast Asia, but it is vital to the security of every American.… I believe the men who endure the dangers of battle…are helping the entire world avoid far greater conflicts, far wider wars, far more destructive than this one."

No: "Dove" Senator Joseph Clark: "Vietnam is a cancer which is devouring our youth, our morals, our national wealth, and the energies of our leadership. The casualty list from this war only begins on the battlefield. As victims we must count the programs of the Great Society, the balance of payments, a sound budget, a stable dollar, the world's good will, détente with the Soviet Union, and hopes for a durable world peace. The toll of this war can never be measured in terms of lives lost and dollars spent—they are only the tip of a vast iceberg whose bulk can never be accurately measured."

REFERENCES: Marilyn B. Young, *The Vietnam Wars, 1945–1990* (1991); Jeffrey P. Kimball, ed., *To Reason Why: The Debate About the Causes of U.S. Involvement in the Vietnam War* (1990).

QUESTIONS FOR CLASS DISCUSSION

1. Did Kennedy fulfill his promise to "get America moving again"? Why or why not?

2. Was the nonviolent civil rights movement of the 1960s a success? Why or why not? Can it be argued that the violent protests of the civil rights movement were more successful than the nonviolent protests?

3. What were the causes of the Vietnam War?

4. Was America justified going into Vietnam? What if the Communist countries invaded a country to "contain the spread of Democracy," would this be justified? What is the difference between the two situations?

5. Were the cultural upheavals of the 1960s a result of the political crisis, or were developments like the sexual revolution and the student revolts inevitable results of affluence and the baby boom?

EXPANDING THE "VARYING VIEWPOINTS"

- Todd Gitlin, *The Sixties: Years of Hope, Days of Rage* (1987).

A view of the sixties as fundamentally constructive:

"Say what we will about the Sixties' failures, limits, disasters, America's political and cultural space would probably not have opened up as much as it did without the movement's divine delirium…. This side of an ever-receding millennium, the changes wrought by the Sixties, however beleaguered, averted some of the worst abuses of power, and made life more decent for millions. The movement in its best moments and broadest definition made philosophical breakthroughs which are still working themselves out."

- William O'Neill, *Coming Apart* (1971).

A view of the sixties as fundamentally destructive:

"Though much in the counter-culture was attractive and valuable, it was dangerous in three ways. First, self-indulgence frequently led to self-destruction. Second, the counter-culture increased social hostility. The generation gap was one example, but the class gap another. Working-class youngsters resented the counter-culture. The counter-culture flourished in cities and on campuses. Elsewhere, in Middle America, it was hated and feared. The result was a national division between the counter-culture and those adults who admired or tolerated it, and the silent majority of workers and Middle Americans who didn't. The tensions between these groups made solving social and political problems all the more difficult and were, indeed, part of the problem. Finally, the counter-culture was hell on standards."

CHAPTER 39

The Stalemated Seventies, 1968–1980

AP FOCUS

- In the 1970s, the U.S. economy slumps, although economists still do not agree on the causes. Note the chart and political cartoon in *The American Pageant* (14th ed., p. 1003/15th ed., pp. 916, 917).

- Responding to antiwar protests, Nixon puts forth a plan, called Vietnamization, to gradually withdraw U.S. forces while preparing the South Vietnamese to carry on the fight. With U.S. involvement in Vietnam seemingly coming to an end, Nixon wins reelection handily against Senator George McGovern. In 1974, Nixon is the first president ever to resign—he faced impeachment for covering up a burglary by his campaign committee.

- Nixon visits China, a surprise to many. He later visits the Soviet Union and is able to work out, with the Soviet leadership, agreements to reduce nuclear arms.

- Economic opportunities for minorities are a major national concern. The environment—an AP theme—also dominates as research indicates that pollution is affecting longevity and health.

- It is revealed that while Nixon claimed to be winding down the Vietnam War, he had secretly expanded it by ordering the bombing of neutral Cambodia to assail North Vietnamese troops that had taken refuge there. Even after the 1973 cease-fire with North Vietnam, Nixon continued attacks on communist positions, despite Congressional calls for a cessation of the bombings.

- Outraged by U.S. support for Israel, Arab nations retaliate by imposing an oil embargo on the U.S.

- An attempt to add an Equal Rights Amendment to the Constitution is defeated.

- Looking for a fresh political face, an outsider untainted by Washington politics, the Democrats nominate Georgia Governor Jimmy Carter, who wins the presidency in 1976. The crowning achievement of Carter's administration is the Camp David Agreement, which offers hope for peace in the Mideast. But economic problems, energy concerns, huge federal and trade deficits, and what critics see as an amateurish foreign policy sap support for the administration.

AP teachers should take note of the following:

1. In 1971, the Supreme Court handed down one of its most controversial decisions in the case *Roe* v. *Wade*, which legalized abortion.

2. The War Powers Act of 1973 became a congressional imperative, given the undeclared war in Vietnam and President Nixon's decision to bomb Cambodia, a neutral nation.

Focus on Historical Thinking:

> Create a list of 80 key terms from 1607 through 1980. Give students the opportunity to study those terms, then assign one or two twenty-five question matching quizzes on those terms to jog their memory.

FOCUS QUESTIONS

1. What were the causes of the economic stagnation during the 1970s?

2. How did Nixon's foreign policy of détente differ from the previous administrations? How did détente help or hurt relations with China and the Soviet Union?

3. How did the Vietnam conflict escalate under the Nixon administration?

4. What was Watergate and how did the episode tarnish the office of the presidency?

5. What were the major challenges faced by the Carter administration, both foreign and domestic?

CHAPTER THEMES

Theme: As the war in Vietnam finally came to a disastrous conclusion, the United States struggled to create a more stable international climate. Détente with the two communist powers temporarily reduced Cold War tensions, but trouble in the Middle East threatened America's energy supplies and economic stability.

Theme: Weakened by political difficulties of their own and others' making, the administrations of the 1970s had trouble coping with America's growing economic problems. The public also had trouble facing up to a sharp sense of limits and a general disillusionment with society. With the notable exception of the highly successful feminist movement, the social reform efforts of the 1960s fractured and stalled, as the country settled into a frustrating and politically divisive stalemate.

CHAPTER SUMMARY

Nixon's Vietnamization policy reduced American ground participation in the war, but his Cambodia invasion sparked massive protest. Nixon's journeys to Communist Moscow and Beijing (Peking) established a new rapprochement with these powers. In domestic policy, Nixon and the Supreme Court promoted affirmative action and environmental protection.

The 1972 election victory and the cease-fire in Vietnam were negated when Nixon became bogged down in the Watergate scandal and congressional protest over the secret bombing of Cambodia, which led to the War Powers Act. The Middle East War of 1973 and the Arab oil embargo created energy and economic difficulties that lasted through the decade. Americans gradually awoke to their costly and dangerous dependence on Middle Eastern oil and began to take tentative steps toward conservation and alternative energy sources.

Nonelected Gerald Ford took over after Watergate forced Nixon to resign. The Communist Vietnamese finally overran the South Vietnamese government in 1975. The defeat in Vietnam added to a general sense of disillusionment with society and a new sense of limits on American power. The civil rights movement fractured, and divisive issues of busing and affirmative action enhanced racial tensions. The most successful social movement was feminism, which achieved widespread social breakthroughs though failing to pass the Equal Rights Amendment.

Campaigning against Washington and Watergate, outsider Jimmy Carter proved unable to master Congress or the economy once he took office. The Camp David agreement brought peace between Egypt and Israel, but the Iranian revolution led to new energy troubles. The invasion of Afghanistan and the holding of American hostages in Iran added to Carter's woes.

DEVELOPING THE CHAPTER: SUGGESTED LECTURE OR DISCUSSION TOPICS

- Examine Nixon's domestic policies, including his corruption and resignation after Watergate. Explain the connection between the immediate Watergate scandal and the wider attacks on the imperial presidency as reflected in, for example, the War Powers Act.

  REFERENCES: Stephen Ambrose, *Nixon* (1989); Stanley Kutler, *The Wars of Watergate* (1990).

- Analyze the ebb and flow of American foreign policy in the seventies, from Nixon's Moscow-Beijing (Peking) visits to Afghanistan. Particular attention might be paid to the difficulties in implementing Kissinger's plans for a stabilizing agreement among the three great powers in a still-volatile world, and to Jimmy Carter's attempt to bring a stronger moral dimension to American foreign relations.

  REFERENCES: Robert D. Schulzinger, *Henry Kissinger: Doctor of Diplomacy* (1989); Gaddis Smith, *Morality, Reason, and Power* (1986).

- Explain the closely interrelated problems of the Middle East, energy, and economics in the seventies, perhaps focusing on the way America's growing economic difficulties made it more vulnerable to Middle East events, which in turn added to economic trouble. Consider the U.S. crisis with Iran in relation to the general political tensions of the region.

  REFERENCES: Michael B. Stoff, *Oil, War and American Security* (1980); James Bill, *The Eagle and the Lion: The Tragedy of American-Iranian Relations* (1987).

- Examine the reasons for the successes of American feminism at a time when most social movements spawned in the 1960s had fragmented and lost broader public appeal. Consider the relationship between more liberal or radical feminist activists who actively promoted social and culture changes and the large numbers of American women who entered the workforce and altered family roles even if they were not politically engaged.

  REFERENCE: Susan M. Hartmann, *The Other Feminists: Activists in the Liberal Establishment* (1998).

FOR FURTHER INTEREST: ADDITIONAL CLASS TOPICS

- Focus on Nixon and Watergate. Consider whether Watergate was in the end a victory for democracy or whether it created national cynicism about leaders and weakened Americans' faith in democracy and the presidency.

- Examine the rise of the environmental movement. Consider the relations of environmental concerns to economic issues in the 1970s, including oil and other energy sources.

- Consider the origins of the conflicts over busing and affirmative action. Explain how the broad American consensus in favor of civil rights, voting rights, integration, and economic opportunity fell apart on the questions of positive government action to advance African Americans' economic and political standing.

- Discuss the Iranian revolution in relation to the rise of militant Islam in the Middle East. Consider why Americans (including government officials) had such difficulty comprehending Islamic fundamentalism.

- Conduct a class debate over the following topics: for example, America Needs an Equal Rights Amendment and a Defense of the Nixon Presidency. Primary source readings will come from the following book: *Opposing Viewpoints in American History—Volume II: From Reconstruction to the Present*, San Diego, CA: Greenhaven Press, 1996. Another good source of debate topics is Larry Madaras and James M. SoRelle, *Taking Sides—Clashing Views on Controversial Issues in American History, Volume II: Reconstruction to the Present*, Connecticut: McGraw-Hill, 2000.

- Show students the following videos: *The Century—America's Time* (ABC Video in association with The History Channel), *Volume V: 1971–1975: Approaching the Apocalypse*: "The public's faith in their government shatters with the disclosure of Watergate. Nixon becomes the first President in U.S. history to resign, as corruption and politics truly become synonymous. Can America's trust in its leaders ever be restored?" *Volume V: 1976–1980: Starting Over*: "The upheavals of the 60's and

70's now leave many confronting the emotional fallout, including forced interracial busing and women torn between their roles as housewives and breadwinners. Meanwhile, the sounds and style of Disco dominate the decade."

- Have the students read selections from John Rawls's *A Theory of Justice* (1971) and Robert Nozick's *Anarchy, State, and Utopia* (1974). Both books are considered classics of American political thought—both arrive at very different conclusions.

- Have the students read Ira Levin's *The Stepford Wives* (1972). Use the novel to explore issues about the dangers of forced conformity, made into a movie in 1975 and again in 2004.

- Have the students read Carter's "Crisis of Confidence" speech to the American people; *Opposing Viewpoints in American History—Volume II: From Reconstruction to the Present* (1996).

CHARACTER SKETCHES

Richard Nixon (1913–1994)

Nixon was the most controversial politician of his generation and has remained a source of intrigue and puzzlement for scholars and the public.

The second of five sons of a devout Quaker family, Nixon was third in his class of twenty-five at Duke Law School. He wanted to be an FBI agent but instead became a local California attorney and later joined the Office of Price Administration and the navy.

He defeated Jerry Voorhis, a prominent New Deal Democratic congressman, in 1946 and won national fame for his work on the Hiss case. His 1950 campaign against Helen Gahagan Douglas was dominated by his red-baiting charges against her.

Thomas Dewey promoted Nixon for the vice presidency in 1952. His 1962 defeat for the California governorship was generally considered to have marked the end of his political career, so his recovery to win the 1968 GOP nomination was nearly miraculous.

Quote: "You won't have Nixon to kick around anymore, because gentlemen, this is my last press conference." (Press conference after election loss, 1962)

REFERENCES: Joan Hoff Wilson, *Nixon Reconsidered* (1994); Rachel Barron, *Richard Nixon* (1999).

Henry Kissinger (1923–   )

At the height of his power in the 1970s, Kissinger exercised more influence over American foreign policy than any secretary of state since George Marshall, and perhaps since William Seward.

Born in southern Germany, the son of a high school teacher, Heinz Kissinger (his original name) was frequently beaten up by anti-Semitic gangs. His father lost his job, and the family was forced to flee to the United States in 1938. Many writers have seen a connection between the instability of Kissinger's youth and his strong pursuit of order and stability in international relations.

His family never fully assimilated to America, and Kissinger retained his thick German accent throughout his life. In the U.S. Army, he became a translator and eventually administered a small district in occupied Germany.

His book *Nuclear Weapons and Foreign Policy* (1957), which advocated the use of limited nuclear weapons, brought him to the attention of Nelson Rockefeller and began his career as an influential foreign-policy and defense theorist.

Quote: "The deepest international conflict in the world today is not between us and the Soviet Union, but between the Soviet Union and Communist China.... Therefore, one of the positive prospects in the current situation is that, whatever the basic intentions of Soviet leaders, confronted with the prospect of a China growing in strength...they may want a period of détente in the West."

REFERENCE: Walter Isaacson, *Kissinger: A Biography* (1993).

Sam Ervin (1896–1985)

Ervin was the North Carolina senator who gained fame for heading the Senate Watergate investigations.

After growing up in rural North Carolina, Ervin was wounded and decorated for valor in World War I and earned a Harvard law degree in 1922. He helped defeat a North Carolina law banning the teaching of evolution. He was also a longtime judge and U.S. congressman.

Ervin was considered the Senate's most noted authority on the U.S. Constitution and was a strong advocate of civil liberties and legal rights for the indigent.

His bobbing eyebrows, thick jowls, and down-home sense of humor made him a popular hero during the Watergate hearings. He had a vast fund of quotations from the Bible, Shakespeare, English history, and American constitutional history at his command and often used them to enliven the proceedings. Although he always called himself a "simple country lawyer," he was in fact a highly learned and skilled jurist.

Quote: "As long as I have a mind to think, a tongue to speak, and a heart to love my country, I shall deny that the Constitution confers any autocratic power on the President, or authorizes him to convert George Washington's America into Caesar's Rome.... When all is said, the only sure antidote for future Watergates is understanding of fundamental principles and intellectual and moral integrity in the men and women who achieve or are entrusted with governmental or political power." (*Report of Senate Watergate Committee,* 1974)

REFERENCE: Dick Dabney, *A Good Man: The Life of Sam Ervin* (1976).

QUESTIONS FOR CLASS DISCUSSION

1. Could any of Nixon's achievements in office compensate for his Watergate crimes? What should history say about the Nixon presidency?

2. What were the short- and long-term consequences of the communists' victory in Vietnam? How do these affect an assessment of the war? What could America have done differently to win the war in Vietnam?

3. How was the civil rights movement affected by federal policies in the 1970s, especially affirmative action?

4. What were the consequences of America's new economic vulnerability? How did it affect politics at home and abroad during the 1970s?

MAKERS OF AMERICA: THE VIETNAMESE

Questions for Class Discussion

1. How do the Vietnamese immigrants fit into the long tradition of immigration to America? How did the particular conditions of their initial migration—the loss of an unpopular war—affect their entry into American society?

2. In what ways do the Vietnamese-Americans appear to be preserving their traditions? In what ways might they likely adapt their traditions to American conditions, as previous immigrant groups have done?

Suggested Student Exercises

- Compare the experience of the Vietnamese with other immigrants from Asia, for example, the Chinese (see Chapter 24), the Filipinos (see Chapter 30), and the Japanese (see Chapter 38). Consider whether the term *Asian-American* is too broad to describe all these groups.

- Given the history of earlier immigrant groups, consider what issues will likely face the Vietnamese-American communities in the near future. Examine whether there is a natural generational transition that can be expected to affect the children and grandchildren of those who have immigrated.

MAKERS OF AMERICA: THE FEMINISTS

Questions for Class Discussion

1. In what ways is the feminist movement similar to other movements for equality and social justice in American history (for example, the abolitionist movement, the labor movement, and the civil rights movement), and in what ways is it different? How is feminism affected by the fact that most women have intense personal relationships with men?

2. What are the roots of the disagreements between equal rights feminism and those feminists who advocate attention to gender difference? What are the implications of each position for government policy (for example, regarding workplace protections, regulation of pornography, or separate-sex education)?

Suggested Student Exercises

- Select one nineteenth-century or early twentieth-century women's leader (for example, Lucretia Mott, Frances Willard, Jane Addams, or Charlotte Perkins Gilman), and compare and contrast their ideas about women's issues and roles in society with that of a prominent second wave feminist leader (for example, Betty Friedan, Gloria Steinem, Bella Abzug, or Catherine Mackinnon). Consider which differences are due to the different times in which they lived, and which reflect underlying philosophical disagreeements about gender and society.

- Trace the changing numbers and roles of women in the U.S. Congress from the 1950s to the present. Examine a few female representatives' and senators' careers and voting records to uncover their relationship to the visible feminist movement. (Perhaps compare two female officials from different party affiliations or different regions of the country.)

CHAPTER 40

The Resurgence of Conservatism, 1980–1992

AP FOCUS

- The 1980s see the rise of neoconservatives in American politics and government. This group challenges most liberal domestic and foreign policies and favors laissez-faire capitalism.

- By 1980, the Republicans have recovered from Nixon's resignation and Ford's loss to Carter in 1976. Their candidate, former actor and governor of California Ronald Reagan, easily defeats Carter. The map of the electoral vote in *The American Pageant* (14th ed., p. 1033/15th ed., p. 944), shows just how easily.

- Reagan promises to reduce the federal budget and bureaucracy and give more authority to the states. He slashes social programs that he sees as relics of a "welfare state" and seeks deep tax cuts. His supply-side economics has uneven results and does not dent unemployment. The military buildup is costly, as is the Savings and Loan bailout. See the chart (14th ed., p. 1042/15th ed. p. 952), showing the increase in the national debt since 1930. Use Reagan's economics to take up the AP theme Economic Transformations.

- A staunch anti-communist, Reagan uses U.S. troops for operations against leftist groups and governments in the Western Hemisphere—in some cases, critics contend, a violation of the law.

- Reagan is reelected in a landslide, trouncing Democrat Senator Walter Mondale and Congresswoman Geraldine Ferraro (the first female to run as a candidate for vice president).

- In his one term as president, George H. W. Bush's most significant accomplishment is his organization of Operation Desert Storm, which drives the invading Iraqi army from Kuwait. Bush is unable to address the nation's economic problems; his 1988 campaign promise not to raise new taxes is embarrassingly reversed. He loses the 1992 presidential race.

AP teachers should take note of the following:

1. Critics of Reagan's supply-side economics contend that it merely allowed the rich to get richer. The nation was woefully in debt by the end of his presidency. Supporters, however, contend that Reagan's policies reduced citizens' dependence on the government, shrank the bureaucracy, and built an impressive military that persuaded the Soviet leadership to end the Cold War.

2. Due in part to the ability of its leaders (some of whom were televangelists) to organize successfully at the grassroots level, the religious right began to play an increasingly important role in elections across the nation. Religion is an AP theme.

Focus on Historical Thinking:

> Have students construct a chart listing specific key pieces of domestic and foreign policy for the presidencies of Kennedy, Johnson, Nixon, Ford, Carter, and Reagan.

FOCUS QUESTIONS

1. What were the causes for the rise of the New Right and how did that movement differ from the Old Right?

2. What were the domestic goals of the Reagan administration, and was he successful in achieving those goals in his two terms as president?

3. What is going to be Reagan's legacy, both in terms of domestic and foreign policy?

4. How was the New Right influential in both religion and the Supreme Court?

5. What were the major issues faced by George H.W. Bush in his administration?

CHAPTER THEMES

Theme: Leading a conservative movement to power in Washington, Ronald Reagan vigorously pursued new right economic and social policies. Under Reagan and his successor George Bush, these policies brought both economic growth and massive budget deficits that put severe constraints on the federal government.

Theme: Religion pervaded American politics in the 1980s; especially conspicuous was a coalition of conservative, evangelical Christians known as the religious right – led by Jerry Falwell, an evangelical from Virginia. An organization called the Moral Majority rose to oppose what they viewed as the moral deterioration of American values.

Theme: The 1980s saw a revival of Cold War confrontation, but the decade ended with the collapse of Communism, first in Eastern Europe and then in the Soviet Union itself. With the end of the Cold War and the U.S.-led victory over Iraq in the Persian Gulf War, America remained the world's only superpower. A series of relatively small military interventions in the Caribbean, Africa, and the Balkans raised questions about the proper use of American force in the underdeveloped world.

CHAPTER SUMMARY

Reagan led Republicans to sweeping victories in 1980 and 1984 over divided and demoralized Democrats. Riding a conservative national tide, Reagan pushed both his supply-side economic program of lower taxes and the new-right social policies, especially opposition to affirmative action, abortion, and drugs. These policies brought economic recovery and lower inflation, as well as record budget deficits that severely restricted big government.

The Supreme Court under Reagan and his successor, George Bush, became increasingly conservative, while the confirmation hearings of Justice Clarence Thomas highlighted issues of sexual harassment.

Reagan revived the Cold War confrontation with the Soviet Union and engaged the United States in assertive military support for antileftist forces in Latin America and elsewhere. The ratcheting up of military spending, along with the attempted reforms led by Mikhail Gorbachev, contributed to the unraveling of Communism in Eastern Europe and the Soviet Union in 1989–1991. With America as the only remaining superpower, George Bush led an international coalition to victory in the Persian Gulf War, but the Middle East remained a dangerous tinderbox despite new efforts to resolve the Israel-Arab conflict.

DEVELOPING THE CHAPTER: SUGGESTED LECTURE OR DISCUSSION TOPICS

*   Describe the rise of conservatism in the 1980s. Explain Reagan's unique ability to link economic, social-policy, and foreign-policy conservative principles into a potent political coalition. Discuss the successes and failures of Reagan's supply-side economics, as well as the ideological polarization of America's culture wars.

    REFERENCE: William C. Berman, *America's Right Turn: From Nixon to Bush* (1994).

- Explain the revival of the Cold War in the 1980s. Examine the relation between American policies and the internal changes within the Soviet bloc, culminating in the collapse of Communism, the reunification of Germany, and the dissolution of the Soviet Union. Include consideration of the new problems for the United States created by the breakup of Communism in places such as the former Soviet Union and the former Yugoslavia.

   REFERENCE: Theodore Draper, *The Devil We Knew: Americans and the Cold War* (1993).

- Examine the increasing importance of religion in American politics and culture in the 1980s and 1990s. Include consideration of the religious right and evangelical movements, as well as other religious voices such as those of the Catholic Church, the black churches, and rapidly growing religious groups such as American Muslims and Buddhists affiliated with the immigration boom of the period.

   REFERENCES: Garry Wills, *Under God: Religion and American Politics* (1990); James Davidson Hunger, *Culture Wars: The Struggle to Define America* (1991).

- Explore the rise of the Conservative right, how it seized political power and maintained it throughout the 1980s and the consequences that followed it.

   REFERENCE: Sean Wilentz, *The Age of Reagan: A History, 1974–2008* (2008).

FOR FURTHER INTEREST: ADDITIONAL CLASS TOPICS

- Focus on Reagan as personality and political leader. Discuss why his personal popularity seemed to transcend his politically controversial policies, and what legacy he left to the Republican Party and American politics generally.

- Examine the growing role of women and women's issues in the politics of the 1980s and 1990s. Consider the increasing impact of women in public and political life, perhaps by examining the careers of prominent figures such as Sandra Day O'Connor, Dianne Feinstein, Hillary Rodham Clinton, and Ruth Bader Ginsburg.

- Discuss the new importance of the Third World in American foreign policy of the 1980s and 1990s. The involvement of the United States in the underdeveloped world can be considered in relation to both military issues (for example, the Latin American civil wars of the 1980s and the Persian Gulf War), as well as economic issues involving NAFTA and trade with countries such as Mexico and China.

- Conduct a class debate over the following topics: for example, America Is Facing a Crisis of Confidence and The End of the Cold War Marked a Great Triumph for the U.S. Primary source readings will come from the following book: *Opposing Viewpoints in American History—Volume II: From Reconstruction to the Present*, San Diego, CA: Greenhaven Press, 1996. Another good source of debate topics is Larry Madaras and James M. SoRelle, *Taking Sides—Clashing Views on Controversial Issues in American History, Volume II: Reconstruction to the Present*, Connecticut: McGraw-Hill, 2000.

- Show students the following video: *The Century—America's Time* (ABC Video in association with The History Channel), *Volume VI: 1981–1989: A New World*. "Cold War tensions escalate until a new Soviet leader suddenly dissolves the long-standing Communist rule in Eastern Bloc countries, and the word 'glastnost' is the international mantra of the era. At home, another G-word changes lives and fortunes when the Guru of Greek, Ivan Boesky, preaches the gospel of guiltless profitmaking."

- Have students listen to Billy Joel's "We Didn't Start the Fire." Have students compete to try and see who knows the most references to the words in the song. A great website with a PowerPoint presentation of the song, complete with images: (http://yeli.us/Flash/Fire.html), last accessed August 2008.

- Have the students read Richard Rorty's "Science as Solidarity" (1986) in David A. Hollinger and Charles Capper's (Editors), *The American Intellectual Tradition: Volume II—1865 to the Present*, New York: Oxford University Press, 2001.

- Have the students investigate the rise of the Conservative movement; Ronald Story and Bruce Laurie, *The Rise of Conservatism in America, 1945–2000: A Brief History with Documents* (2008).

- Have the students read the speeches and writings of Reagan. The American Presidency Project, (http://www.presidency.ucsb.edu/), last accessed August 2008.

CHARACTER SKETCHES

Edward Kennedy (1932–2009)

Kennedy was a Massachusetts senator and heir to the Kennedy legacy in American politics.

The ninth child and fourth son of the family, Kennedy was indulged by his father and not pushed into competitive activities as the older children had been.

In his freshman year at Harvard, Kennedy was expelled for having someone else take a Spanish exam for him. He later returned to graduate from Harvard and the University of Virginia Law School.

His first run for the Senate came in 1962, only a few days after his thirtieth birthday, and provoked much criticism. But he conducted a successful campaign with the slogan "He can do more for Massachusetts."

The 1969 accident at Chappaquiddick Island in which a young woman drowned has remained Kennedy's greatest political liability. He was most sharply criticized not for the accident, but for his failure to report it until the next morning and for his unconvincing explanations of the events surrounding it.

Quote: "I understand that people feel strongly about me, as they felt about my brothers before me…. [Some] people have been enthusiastic supporters, and others have been harsh critics. I would expect that to be the case as long as I'm in public life." (1974)

REFERENCE: James MacGregor Burns, *Edward Kennedy and the Camelot Legacy* (1976).

Ronald Reagan (1911–2004)

The oldest president before Reagan was Eisenhower, who was about seventy when he left office; Reagan was that age when he first took office.

Reagan's unemployed father worked for a time for Roosevelt's WPA program. As a youthful lifeguard, Reagan saved over seventy people from drowning, and he was amazed that many of them later criticized him and claimed that they had not been in danger.

His break into movies came in 1937, when Warner Brothers signed him to a seven-year contract for $200 a week. In the movie *King's Row* (1941), he played an amputee who said, "Where's the rest of me?" Reagan used this line as the title of his 1965 autobiography.

His involvement with many liberal causes continued until the late 1940s, when he took the lead in driving communists from the Screen Actors Guild. His second marriage, to the daughter of a politically conservative doctor, also helped turn him into a staunch conservative.

Reagan first won national political attention for a speech on behalf of Barry Goldwater in 1964. His first try for the presidency came in 1968, when he lost the nomination to Nixon.

Quote: "Either we accept the responsibility for our own destiny, or we abandon the American Revolution and confess that an intellectual belief in a far-distant capital can plan our lives for us better than we can plan them for ourselves. You and I have a rendezvous with destiny. We can preserve for our children this last best hope of man on earth or we can sentence them to take the first step into a thousand years of darkness." (1964)

REFERENCE: Lou Cannon, *President Reagan: The Role of a Lifetime* (1992).

Sandra Day O'Connor (1930–   )

O'Connor is the Arizona judge who became the first woman U.S. Supreme Court justice.

Her childhood was spent on a ranch in Arizona. At Stanford Law School, Chief Justice William Rehnquist was first in her law class, and she was third.

She served as an assistant attorney general and was elected to two terms in the Arizona state senate, where she became majority leader. A Democratic governor appointed her to the state appeals court in 1979.

In her early days on the Supreme Court, O'Connor was considered a conservative who almost always followed the lead of Justices Rehnquist and Powell. She showed an independent streak, however, in breaking with them on some civil rights and civil liberties issues. She also began as a strong critic of the *Roe* v. *Wade* abortion decision and was widely expected to join other Reagan-Bush appointees in a new majority to overturn it. But in *Casey* v. *Planned Parenthood* and recent decisions, O'Connor sided with two other justices (David Souter and Anthony Kennedy) in upholding *Roe*, while accepting various state restrictions on abortion. In the 1990s, O'Connor was usually the key swing vote on the Court, especially on issues of affirmative action and abortion.

Quote: "Our decisions…establish that the party seeking to uphold a statute that classifies individuals on the basis of their gender must carry the burden of showing an 'exceedingly persuasive justification' for the classification.… That this statute discriminates against males rather than females does not exempt it from scrutiny or reduce the standard of review." (Opinion in *Mississippi University for Women* v. *Hogan*, 1982)

REFERENCE: Vincent Blasi, ed., *The Burger Court* (1983).

George Herbert Walker Bush (1924–   )

George Bush is the longtime Republican politician who won the presidency as Ronald Reagan's successor in 1988 but lost his bid for reelection in 1992.

Bush is the son of wealthy Connecticut senator Prescott Bush. His private-school and Ivy League education at Yale were long seen as political handicaps, but he counteracted them by emphasizing his World War II service in the navy and such down-home pursuits as eating pork rinds and pitching horseshoes.

During Bush's youthful oil-business career, and his two terms in Congress as a representative from the Houston area, he formed strong alliances with the Texas business community. An associate from those days, James Baker, became his closest political ally and later served as his secretary of state.

Bush held a long series of appointed positions—chairman of the Republican Party, head of the CIA, ambassador to China—before becoming Reagan's vice president. Bush's extensive foreign-policy experience led him to focus his administration on international rather than domestic affairs, at considerable political cost. In the 1988 election and afterward, Bush denied any knowledge or involvement in the Iran-Contra affair, although other Reagan officials, among them George Schulz and Caspar Weinberger, maintained that Bush was not "out of the loop."

After his defeat in 1992, Bush retired to Texas. His son, George Bush Jr., was elected governor of Texas in 1994 and president in 2000.

Quote: "We are not the sum of our possessions. They are not the measure of our lives. In our hearts we know what matters. We must give [our children] a sense of what it means to be a loyal friend, a loving parent, a citizen who leaves his home, neighborhood, and town better than he found it." (Inaugural address, 1989)

REFERENCES: Peter Golman and Tom Matthew, *The Quest for the Presidency, 1988* (1989); Bill Minutaglio, *First Son: George W. Bush and the Bush Family Dynasty* (1999).

QUESTIONS FOR CLASS DISCUSSION

1.   To what extent was the election of Reagan an endorsement of his conservative ideology, and to what extent was it a repudiation of the perceived failures of federal government policies in the stalemated 1970s?

2.   In what ways might the 1980s and 1990s be compared with the 1920s in economic, social, and foreign policies? Did the economic boom of each period represent a genuine revival of American innovation, or was it fundamentally marred by the growing gap between rich and poor?

3.   What were the successes and failures of American foreign policy in the post–Cold War era? Was the use of American military power in the Persian Gulf War and the Balkans a model for how American power could be effectively brought to bear, or did it demonstrate the limits of even the sole superpower's ability to resolve regional conflicts?

4.   What was the real cause of the end of the Cold War? Did America win the Cold War, or did the Soviets lose the Cold War? Is there a difference?

5.   Compare and contrast the rise of the Moral Majority in the 1980s with that of the Beats of the 1950s and the Hippies of the 1960s and 1970s. What commonalities do they have with each other?

6.   How should history view the presidency of Ronald Reagan? Was he a great, good, fair, or bad president and why?

EXPANDING THE "VARYING VIEWPOINTS"

• Daniel Bell, ed., *The Radical Right* (1963).

A view of modern conservatism as an extremist and paranoid fringe movement:

"Anti-elitism oriented toward groups that cannot be regarded as oppressed minorities or victims of bigotry, or anti-Communism directed against the agents or dupes of an evil foreign power, can serve as palatable outlets for those who require a scapegoat…. Intolerant movements, while often powerful, have never been able seriously to endanger the normal processes of American democracy…. But if such movements can not come to power, they can damage the democratic process for short periods of time, and they can and have injured innocent people."

• Kevin Phillips, *Post-Conservative America* (1982).

A view of modern conservatism as more deeply rooted in American history:

"I submit that the New Right combines three powerful trend patterns that recur in American history and politics. First, to some measure it is an extension of the Wallace movement, and as such represents a current expression of the ongoing populism of the white lower middle classes, principally in the South and West…. Second, the New Right is closely allied with the sometimes potent right-to-life or antiabortion movement, the current version, perhaps, of the great one-issue moral crusades of the American past…. And this one-issue element, in turn, folds into the third phenomenon—the possible fourth occurrence of the religious revivals or 'Great Awakenings' that have swept across the land since the middle of the eighteenth century. If so, the religious wing of the New Right may be the political wing of a major national awakening."

CHAPTER 41

America Confronts the Post-Cold War Era, 1992–2011

AP FOCUS

- Bill Clinton becomes president after defeating two other candidates, President George H. W. Bush and businessman Ross Perot. Clinton claims to represent a new type of Democrat, a centrist.

- Deficit reduction is a key element of Clinton's economic plan; the deficit does contract, and he uses his political capital to get passage for NAFTA and the establishment of the World Trade Organization, both important for Globalization, an AP theme. He also gets an anticrime bill with limitations on certain assault weapons.

- In 1994, Republicans run on the Contract with America and capture Congress.

- In 1995, antigovernment extremists blow up a federal building in Oklahoma, killing scores of workers and children. It is the worst act of domestic terrorism the nation has yet experienced.

- In 1998, Clinton is embroiled in a scandal stemming from a sexual affair with a White House intern that leads to his impeachment. In a bipartisan vote, the Senate does not have enough votes to remove the president from office.

- The 2000 election, one of the most controversial in American history, ultimately involves the U.S. Supreme Court. Republican George W. Bush, Governor of Texas, is declared the winner.

- On September 11, 2001, the United States suffers a devastating attack by Al Qaeda, a terrorist organization led by Osama bin Laden. The United States invades Afghanistan in search of bin Laden. In 2003, Bush uses Iraq's defiance of U.N. inspections to topple its president, Saddam Hussein. But Bush has little support from other countries, and Iraq proves hard to control.

- Despite apprehensions about the war in Iraq, the economy, and the skyrocketing deficit, Bush defeats his Democratic challenger, Senator John Kerry, in the 2004 presidential election.

- The government's bungled response to the havoc wrecked on New Orleans by Hurricane Katrina in August 2005 significantly tarnishes the Bush administration's reputation and provides fodder for the Democrats' efforts to regain control of Congress in the 2006 midterm elections.

- In 2008, the economy slips into recession. The collapse of the housing market precipitates a financial crisis. Worried about the economy and convinced that Republican John McCain is too intimately connected to the failed policies of the Bush administration, Americans elect Democrat Barack Obama, the nation's first African American president.

- Thinking Globally (*The American Pageant*, 14th ed., pp. 1074–1075/15th ed., pp. 980-981) notes that American political, military, and economic domination, unquestioned before 9/11, is now being challenged in many quarters.

AP teachers should take note of the following:

1. Removing Saddam Hussein from power was made a U.S. policy objective during Clinton's term.

2.   An essential ingredient of Bush's economic program is tax cuts, which have had mixed results.

Focus on Historical Thinking:

> Choose twenty important terms from Chapters 1 through 41. Give students ample time to prepare to write composite sentences (see "Focus on Historical Thinking" activity for Chapter 5) for each of the terms. Quiz students on five of the terms, giving no more than two minutes for each term.

FOCUS QUESTIONS

1.   What were the main issues facing Bill Clinton when he entered office? How did he reconcile the traditional liberal values of the past Democrats and his vision for a different America?

2.   What were the main causes of the economic prosperity of the 1990s under Clinton's administration?

3.   How did the attack of 9/11 affect the country, both politically and spiritually?

4.   What effect did the election of 2000 have on the American political scene? Was the rift that was driven between America healed under the Bush administration?

5.   What were the successes and failures of George W. Bush's administration? How did these affect the outcome of the election of 2008?

CHAPTER THEMES

Theme: Elected as the first baby-boom president, Bill Clinton tried to turn the Democratic Party in a more centrist direction. Ideological conflicts and sharp partisan battles in the 1990s were partly overshadowed by a booming economy, a balanced federal budget, and America's search to define its role in the increasingly global economy and system of international relations.

Theme: The 2000 election, between Bush and Gore, and the subsequent events that followed it would deeply divide the nation and alienate the United States from traditional allies in the world community.

Theme: The reelection of George W. Bush to a second term in 2004 brought about additional issues and concerns across the country; most notably, the war in Iraq continued to plague America and its reputation around the world. Bush saw his reelection as a mandate to continue his conservative agenda and focused his second term on addressing issues such as attacking many of the New Deal programs, adding conservative elements to the Supreme Court, and standing up for his position on the War on Terror.

CHAPTER SUMMARY

The dynamic young baby-boomer Bill Clinton defeated Bush in 1992, and promoted an ambitious reform agenda within the context of his centrist new Democrat ideology. Clinton's stumbles over health care reform and foreign policy opened the door to aggressive conservative Republicans, who gained control of Congress in 1994 for the first time in fifty years advocating a "contract with America." But the Newt Gingrich–led Republicans' overreaching enabled Clinton to revive and win a second term in 1996.

In his second term, Clinton downplayed reform and successfully claimed the political middle ground on issues such as welfare reform, affirmative action, smoking, and gun control. A booming economy created budget surpluses and encouraged Clinton's efforts toward ending international trade barriers. Conflicts in the Middle East and the Balkans led to American diplomatic and military involvements, with mixed results. A series of scandals, culminating in the Monica Lewinsky affair, led to Clinton's impeachment and acquittal in 1999.

Texas Governor George Walker Bush defeated Clinton's vice president, Al Gore, in a contested cliffhanging election in 2000 that was finally decided by a Supreme Court decision. As the fourth president elected in American history to lose the popular vote, George W. Bush entered the oval office promising to bring to Washington the conciliatory skills he had fine tuned as Republican governor of

Texas, where he had worked well with the Democratic majority in the state's legislature. But as president, Bush proved to be more of a divider than a uniter, focusing on social issues such as abortion, a constitutional amendment to ban same-sex marriages, embryonic stem cell research, the environment, and add to that an increasing budget deficit—these polarizing policies both reflected and deepened the cultural chasm that divided American society.

On September 11, 2001, suicidal terrorists slammed two hijacked airliners into the twin towers of New York City's World Trade Center, a third plane crashed into the Pentagon, and a fourth plane was forced down by its heroic passengers in rural Pennsylvania. Osama bin Laden had been identified as the mastermind behind the World Trade Center attack, and when the Taliban refused to turn over bin Laden to American officials, Bush ordered a massive military campaign against Afghanistan. Within three months, American and Afghani rebel forces had overthrown the Taliban but failed to find bin Laden.

The fear of future threats lead American officials to take aggressive and controversial actions following the events of September 11: congressional passage of the USA-Patriot Act, creation of the Department of Homeland Security, rounding up and trying suspected terrorists in military tribunals (where the usual rules and procedures do not apply), and the controversial invasion and occupation of Iraq.

With the reelection of George W. Bush in 2004, the war in Iraq continued to be a critical issue with the American public. But more important, Bush saw his reelection as a Conservative mandate, to which he continued many of the same policies he began in 2000. However, Bush overplayed his hand with this and in the midterm elections of 2006, Democrats regained control of both houses of Congress for the first time since 1994.

DEVELOPING THE CHAPTER: SUGGESTED LECTURE OR DISCUSSION TOPICS

- Examine the ideas and politics of Bill Clinton in relation to the changed ideological climate of the 1990s. Consider how Clinton attempted to steer a middle course between the more aggressively conservative Republicans and his own party's traditional liberal base on issues such as welfare, social security, civil rights, and the environment.

    REFERENCE: James MacGregor Burns and Georgia Sorenson, *Dead Center: Clinton-Gore Leadership and the Politics of Moderation* (1999).

- Compare and contrast the foreign policy of distinct eras in American history: first, that of the beginning of the twentieth century (for example, under the presidencies of McKinley, Roosevelt, and Wilson); second, that of the end of the twentieth century (for example, under the presidencies of George H. Bush and Bill Clinton); and third, that of the beginning of the twenty-first century (for example, under the presidency of George W. Bush).

    REFERENCES: John B. Judis, *The Folly of Empire* (2004); Walter Nugent, *Habits of Empire: A History of American Expansion* (2008).

FOR FURTHER INTEREST: ADDITIONAL CLASS TOPICS

- Compare Clinton's impeachment and trial to that of Andrew Johnson in the 1860s. Focus on the parallel claims that the impeachment was fundamentally motivated by partisan spite and personal disdain for the president, as well as on the substantial differences in the political circumstances and in the charges themselves.

- Compare and contrast the elections of the four people in American history to lose the election for presidency but win the popular vote: Andrew Jackson (1824), Samuel J. Tilden (1876), Grover Cleveland (1888), and Albert Gore (2000). Discuss the pluses and minuses of the electoral college.

Is the electoral college outdated? Is it democratic to have an election where the will of the majority does not prevail? What would have to happen to change the way America selects a president?

CHARACTER SKETCHES

William "Bill" Jefferson Clinton (1946–   )

Bill Clinton served many terms as Arkansas governor before being elected the nation's forty-second president in 1992.

Clinton was born William Blythe in Arkansas. His father died in an automobile accident before Bill was born, and after his mother remarried, Bill took her new husband's last name. Perhaps the most decisive event in Clinton's early life was winning a scholarship to Georgetown University, a Catholic university in Washington, D.C. He so impressed some of his teachers that they suggested that he might consider becoming a priest, until he told them that he was a Southern Baptist.

After graduation from Georgetown in 1968, Clinton won a Rhodes scholarship to study politics at Britain's Oxford University. After graduation from Yale University Law School, Clinton returned to Arkansas in 1973 to teach at the University of Arkansas Law School. In 1975, he married Hillary Rodham, a fellow Yale Law school graduate and Arkansas law professor. Clinton ran for Congress in 1974 but lost to a popular Republican. In 1976, he won election as attorney general of Arkansas.

At the time of his election as chief executive of Arkansas in 1978, Clinton was the nation's youngest governor. He lost a race for reelection but regained the office in 1982 and every two years thereafter until his election as president.

Quote: "We are on the verge of a new way of doing things, grounded in our most enduring values, a philosophy that says America owes all of us an opportunity if we will assume responsibility for ourselves, our community, and our country. No more something for nothing. We're all in this together." (Speech, July 1993)

REFERENCE: David Maraniss, *First in His Class* (1994).

George Walker Bush (1946–   )

The presidency of the United States is only the second public office to which George W. Bush was elected, after the governorship of Texas.

George W. Bush was born in New Haven, Connecticut, and moved with his family to Texas at the age of two. He is the oldest of five living children (four boys and one girl) of George H.W. Bush and Barbara Bush (another girl died of leukemia in 1953 at age three). While his father was a rising star in Republican politics, George W. attended Philips Andover Academy in Massachusetts and Yale University, graduating in 1968. After several years of dissolution, drifting, unemployment, and occasional political work in Texas, Alabama, and Florida, he entered Harvard University, earning a Master of Business Administration degree in 1975.

He then moved to the west Texas town of Midland and married a school librarian, Laura Welch. His younger brother Jeb, now governor of Florida, was considered the future politician of the family, while George W.'s talents were widely disregarded. This judgment seemed confirmed when he ran for Congress from Midland in 1978, but lost to a Democrat.

The several oil business ventures he attempted, the Arbusto and Spectrum Companies, were not very successful either, but earned enough, along with family support, for him to become the lead investor in buying the Texas Rangers baseball team for $600,000 in 1988 (he eventually sold his share a decade later for $15 million).

In 1986, he underwent a born again religious conversion, and moved from his family's traditional Episcopal faith into the Methodist Church. In 1994, Bush was nominated by the Republicans to run against the popular Democratic Texas governor Ann Richards, and his victory was considered a great upset. His reelection victory with 65 percent of the vote propelled him into the leading position for the Republican presidential nomination in 2000.

Quote: "Our country has been through a long and trying period, with the outcome of the presidential election not finalized for longer than any of us could imagine... I believe things happen for a reason, and I hope the wait of the last five weeks will heighten a desire to move beyond the bitterness and partisanship of the recent past." (Victory speech, December 13, 2000).

QUESTIONS FOR CLASS DISCUSSION

1. What is likely to be the enduring legacy of Bill Clinton in American politics? Did the focus on his personality and the scandals leading to impeachment drastically alter the way he is likely to be viewed by future historians, or will his economic policies and his political success in steering the Democratic Party toward the political center be viewed as substantive achievements outweighing the weaknesses?

2. Compare and contrast American foreign policy at the beginning of the twentieth century to that of the beginning of the twenty-first century. What differences are there? Are there any similarities?

3. What similarities are there to the spread of Communism during the post–World War II era to the spread of Democracy in the post–Cold War era? If America was justified in intervening in halting the spread of communism in Asia, would Iraqi insurgents be justified in intervening in halting the spread of democracy in Iraq? Why or why not?

4. How successful was America in punishing the attackers of 9/11? Was America's "war on terror" a success or failure? Why or why not?

5. What is likely to be the enduring legacy of George W. Bush in American politics? How will American history view his presidency; great, good, fair, or poor? Justify and support your answers.

CHAPTER 42

The American People Face a New Century

AP FOCUS

- Science and technology have an enormous impact on nearly every aspect of American life. In addition, they open up new employment fields while eliminating outmoded means of production.

- The gap between wealth and poverty widens. See the photographs and the table on income inequality in *The American Pageant* (14th ed., pp. 1086, 1087/15th ed., p. 992).

- Women continue to make significant strides in entering every aspect of American life, including what were once male professional and educational bastions.

- With older baby boomers retiring, an enormous burden is being placed on the institutions and agencies designed to assist senior citizens. See the graph (14th ed., p. 1094/15th ed., p. 999), showing the considerable cost of maintaining New Deal, Great Society, and other reform programs. Reform is an AP theme.

- A new wave of immigrants, some illegal, has reshaped the American demographic landscape. Many of today's immigrants hail from Latin America and the Caribbean, Asia, and Africa.

- Minorities have made significant strides, but still lag behind in most economic indicators of financial success.

- The election of Barack Obama as the first African American president signifies that racism in the United States is waning.

- Historically, the nation has had the resources to address its domestic and international concerns. The challenges posed in the twenty-first century will test how effectively we continue to use those resources.

AP teachers should take note of the following:

1. Slightly more than one in three Americans live at or below the poverty line.

2. Given their numbers, need for social services, and traditionally low-paying jobs, illegal immigrants have become a hot-button issue. Debate rages over whether illegal immigrants contribute more to the economy in taxes and consumer spending than they extract.

Focus on Historical Thinking:

Have students express in one clear, concise sentence the major change over time in each of the units (chronological periods) you have covered this year. Additionally, you may wish to have them list 10 pieces of specific factual information that support that change over time.

FOCUS QUESTIONS

1. How has the new technology, as well as developments in science and medicine, altered the landscape of American society?

2. What are the major issues that American's will have to face as they move into the twenty-first century?

3.   What changes have taken place for groups such as feminists, Hispanics, and other minorities to alter the American scene and will take America into the twenty-first century?

4.   How has immigration influenced policies and practices of America? What possible changes might take place?

5.   How has art, literature, and the media reflected the American character?

CHAPTER THEMES

Theme: The United States underwent drastic economic and social change in the final decades of the twentieth century. The economic transformation from an industrial age to an information age produced new economic advances, as well as a rapidly increasing income gap between the wealthy and the poor. Changes in women's roles, the family, and the arrival of new immigrant groups substantially altered the ways Americans live and work.

Theme: Despite the weaknesses of television and problems in U.S. education, American culture, literature, and art remained the most dynamic and influential in the world. The new types of media, diversity of gender, ethnic, and racial voices contributed to the vital energy that made American democracy not simply a political system but an ever-changing source of fresh ideas and popular images.

CHAPTER SUMMARY

In the 1980s and 1990s, the American culture and economy underwent dynamic changes from an age of heavy industry to an age of computerized information and mass culture. Science and education increasingly drove the new forms of wealth, and growth of new media and the Internet helped fuel a new economy linked with the rest of the world. The benefits of the new wealth did not reach everyone, however, as the gaps between those with education and those without contributed to an increasingly severe inequality in Americans' wealth and income.

The decades-long movement into the workforce of women, including mothers of young children, opened ever-wider doors of opportunity, and contributed to changes in men's roles, as well as in family life. Women's concern for issues of health and child care created a persistent political gender gap between Democrats and Republicans in national elections. With fewer families being formed, and fewer children being born to native-born Americans, the population began to age and the elderly became both a potent lobbying force and an economic threat to the viability of social welfare programs like Social Security and Medicare.

A vast new wave of immigration, especially from Asia and Latin America, brought newcomers seeking economic opportunity and liberties unavailable in their homelands. Hispanics, Asians, and Indians all asserted their own identity and pride, and made areas like the American Southwest a bicultural zone. Political efforts to deal with the rising tide of immigration have been divisive and unsuccessful.

The problems of poverty, increasingly concentrated in inner cities ringed by affluent suburbs, remained stubborn and frustrating to millions of Americans, including many minorities. The African American community made great strides in education, politics, and other areas, but there was a growing gap between the upwardly mobile and those left behind. America's cities were plagued by problems of drugs and crime, but the soaring crime rates of the 1980s were reversed and turned downward in the 1990s. In the same decade many cities began to show signs of renewal.

American culture remained incredibly dynamic and inventive, both in high culture and pop culture. The new voices of westerners, women, African Americans, Asians, and others were increasingly influential and popular, contributing to the pluralism and cultural diversity of U.S. society. Post-modernist thought emphasizing skepticism, relativity, and multiplicity has resulted in a mixing of styles in architecture, literature, music, and dance.

America was born a revolutionary force in the world. In the twentieth century, it became more conservative in a world swept by global change. Yet the powerful values of American democracy presented persistent challenges to Americans to live up to their high ideals as "the last, best hope on earth."

DEVELOPING THE CHAPTER: SUGGESTED LECTURE OR DISCUSSION TOPICS

- Explain the broad changes in American economic and social development since 1975. The emphasis might be on the severe difficulties caused by the new vulnerability of the United States in the world economy, as well as innovations in technology and business management. Consider the way economic change has altered American society, including family transformations and population migrations.

  REFERENCE: Paul Boyer, *Promises to Keep: The United States Since World War II* (1995).

- Analyze the impact of the feminist movement on women, men, and U.S. culture and society as a whole. Examine not only the structural changes in women's economic and political roles, but also the transformation in values, images, and perceptions in the last two decades. Consider the real gains women have made, as well as the issues and concerns that remain.

  REFERENCES: Rosalind Rosenberg, *Divided Lives* (1992); William Chafe, *The Paradox of Change: American Women in the Twentieth Century* (1991).

- Examine the new immigration to America in the 1980s and 1990s, including its impact on the American economy and society. Perhaps compare late twentieth-century immigration to earlier waves of immigration—including some of the reactions of native-born Americans.

  REFERENCE: David Reimers, *Still the Golden Door: The Third World Comes to America* (1986).

- Look at the transformations of American culture and literature, especially the challenges to traditional views of proper culture and education. Consider whether the culture wars of the 1990s represented a real change from the American past, or whether the influence of new female and minority writers and artists was actually a revitalization of traditional American values of individualism, democracy, and equality.

  REFERENCE: Henry Louis Gates Jr., *Loose Canons: Notes on the Culture Wars* (1993).

FOR FURTHER INTEREST: ADDITIONAL CLASS TOPICS

- Contrast the economic, social, and cultural life of a typical family of the 1970s with a similar family of the 1990s.

- Select one of the less-well-known new immigrant groups, for example, Asian Indians or West Indians. Look at their reasons for immigration, their patterns of occupation and settlement, and the opportunities and obstacles they have experienced.

- Examine the new patterns of population movement, urbanization, and suburbanization as represented in the 2000 census. Consider particularly the population explosion in states such as California, Texas, and Florida, and the corresponding growth in political strength of groups such as Hispanics and the elderly.

- Select one novel and one painting as exemplary of the new forces in postwar American art. Perhaps consider why a once-neglected work like Hurston's *Their Eyes Were Watching God* has been rediscovered and celebrated in the 1990s.

CHARACTER SKETCHES

Betty Friedan (1921–2006)

Friedan is the author of *The Feminine Mystique* (1963) and the founder of the National Organization for Women (NOW), which became the principal arm of the postwar feminist movement.

Born Betty Naomi Goldstein in Peoria, Illinois, Friedan graduated from Smith College in 1942 and studied psychology at the University of California. While raising her family, she worked as a writer for women's magazines such as *Redbook* and *Ladies' Home Journal.* A 1957 article for *Ladies' Home Journal* about her Smith classmates gave her the idea for *The Feminine Mystique,* which she wrote during five years of work at the New York Public Library. The book was an instant success and eventually sold millions of copies.

NOW was founded in her Washington hotel room after a 1964 federal government-sponsored conference in which women's concerns were ignored. Friedan created the name "National Organization *for* Women" in order to include men. She later came under sharp attack from more militant feminists for not supporting their more radical ideas.

Quote: "Who knows what women can be when they are finally free to become themselves?… The time is at hand when the voices of the feminine mystique can no longer drown out the inner voice that is driving women to become more complete." (*The Feminine Mystique,* 1963)

REFERENCES: Justine Blau, *Betty Friedan* (1990); Daniel Horowitz, *Betty Friedan and the Making of 'The Feminine Mystique'* (1998).

James Baldwin (1924–1987)

James Baldwin was the black writer whose powerful fiction and nonfiction works expressed his personal vision of the world and helped awaken white America to the depths of the racial crisis.

Baldwin was born in Harlem and spent most of his early life there. His father was an authoritarian, often cruel, Fundamentalist preacher. Many of Baldwin's more autobiographical works, including *Go Tell It on the Mountain* (1953), the work that first gained him literary fame, reveal the difficulties of his childhood and relations with his father.

Baldwin spent much time abroad, especially in Paris, where he felt he could escape the racial restrictions of the United States. However, he always returned to what he felt was his home in America. His book *The Fire Next Time* (1963) caused great controversy when it was published because of its predictions of racial violence but was later considered prophetic of the crises of the 1960s.

Quote: "The nation, the entire nation, has spent a hundred years avoiding the question of the place of the black man in it…. Any honest examination of the national life proves how far we are from the standard of human freedom with which we began. The recovery of this standard demands of everyone who loves this country a hard look at himself." (*Nobody Knows My Name,* 1961)

REFERENCE: David Leeming, *James Baldwin: A Biography* (1994).

Jackson Pollock (1912–1956)

Pollock was the most influential American artist of the immediate postwar era and is considered one of the great modern masters of painting.

The son of an unsuccessful Wyoming rancher, Pollock developed a deep love of nature while working summer jobs at the Grand Canyon.

In school, Pollock was interested only in art and frequently got into academic and disciplinary difficulty. He studied with Thomas Hart Benton, the great American regionalist painter. Pollock's early nature paintings show Benton's influence but also reflect a tendency toward the abstraction that he later developed.

From 1935 to 1943, Pollock worked for the federal WPA Art Project. In the early 1940s, he was influenced by Jungian therapy and the work of Picasso and André Breton. He made his breakthrough to abstract expressionism and later developed his techniques of dripping and splattering paint on the canvas to create complex special effects. Some of his works that originally sold for $600 were later bought for over $2 million.

Pollock seldom appeared in public and cultivated an image as a somewhat rough and mysterious character. He died in an auto accident in 1956.

Quote: "When I am *in* my painting I'm not aware of what I'm doing.… I have no fears of making changes, destroying the image, etc., because the painting has a life of its own. I try to let it come through."

REFERENCE: Steven Naifeh and Gregory White Smith, *Jackson Pollock* (1990).

QUESTIONS FOR CLASS DISCUSSION

1. Was the growing inequality in American wealth and incomes the result of natural economic market forces, or was it encouraged by deliberate political policies, especially the tax cuts and trade policies of the 1980s?

2. Has the American family been in decline, or has it simply changed forms while developing different kinds of strengths? What causes the fears of a generational war between the expanding numbers of elderly and younger Americans?

3. Has the nature of American race relations been substantially altered since the 1960s civil rights movement, or are relations between whites and African Americans fundamentally the same? Has African American society itself undergone substantial changes?

4. Why has culture become the focus of a series of wars between different intellectuals and social groups in the past ten years? Why are many of these wars over issues fought in American colleges and universities?

5. What lies in America's future? What kinds of cultural, economic, and foreign dilemmas will future American politicians face? What will be the defining moment in the twenty-first century?

MAKERS OF AMERICA: THE LATINOS

Questions for Class Discussion

1. What distinctive conditions have shaped the experience of Latin American immigrants, especially Mexican-Americans, in the United States?

2. How has the proximity of Mexico to the United States affected the relations of Mexican-Americans with both their old and their new countries?

Suggested Student Exercises

*   Examine those areas of the United States that have been most affected by Hispanic or Mexican immigration. Consider the likely impact of a large Hispanic presence on the politics, economics, religion, and culture of those areas.

*   Examine the changing image of Hispanic-Americans in films, television, music, and other forms of popular culture. Perhaps use some samples of earlier stereotypes from the 1940s or 1950s to demonstrate the changes.